Zwingliana 40 (2013)

Zwingliana

Beiträge zur Geschichte des Protestantismus
in der Schweiz und seiner Ausstrahlung

Band 40
2013

Jahrbuch des Zwinglivereins

TVZ

Theologischer Verlag Zürich

Zwingliana erscheint unter Mitwirkung des Instituts für Schweizerische Reformationsgeschichte an der Theologischen Fakultät der Universität Zürich

Gedruckt mit Unterstützung der Schweizerischen Akademie der Geistes- und Sozialwissenschaften

Frühere Jahrgänge der Zwingliana, weitere Informationen zum Jahrbuch sowie Richtlinien für Autorinnen und Autoren sind elektronisch abrufbar unter www.zwingliana.ch

Satz: Christian Moser
Druck und Bindung: Freiburger Graphische Betriebe

ISSN 0254-4407
ISBN 978-3-290-17724-9

Inhalt

ISSN 0254-4407 – Zwingliana 40 (2013), 1–35

Biblical and Theological Themes in Heinrich Bullinger's »De Testamento« (1534)

Joe Mock

Bullinger's treatise on the covenant, *De testamento* (1534)[1], is surprisingly rich in biblical and theological themes. Most studies on the theology of Heinrich Bullinger have focussed, naturally enough, on the *Decades* and *The Second Helvetic Confession.*[2] Many of Bullinger's works are either historical or biblical theological in their emphasis. Moser has identified that Bullinger's historical works can be classified as salvation history and history of the covenant.[3] Moreover, Walser affirms that Bullinger was primarily a biblical theologian and that, therefore, his theology reflects the non-systematic character of the Bible itself.[4] In this connection, *De testamento* has primarily been viewed as Bullinger's

[1] Heinrich *Bullinger*, De testamento seu foedere Dei unico et aeterno, Zurich: Christoph Froschauer the Elder, 1534 (Manfred Vischer, Bibliographie der Zürcher Druckschriften des 15. und 16. Jahrhunderts, Baden-Baden 1991 [BZD], no C 226).

[2] See, for example, Peter *Opitz,* Heinrich Bullinger als Theologe: Eine Studie zu den »Dekaden«, Zurich 2004, for a comprehensive examination of Bullinger's theology in the *Decades* and Edward A. *Dowey*, Heinrich Bullinger as Theologian: Thematic, Comprehensive, and Systematic, in: Architect of Reformation, ed. Bruce Gordon and Emidio Campi, Grand Rapids, MI 2004, 39, for an argument that »The Second Helvetic Confession is his crowning theological masterpiece.«

[3] Christian *Moser*, Die Dignität des Ereignisses: Studien zu Heinrich Bullingers Reformationsgeschichtsschreibung, Leiden 2012 (Studies in the History of Christian Traditions 163), 20–25.

[4] Peter *Walser*, Die Prädestination bei Heinrich Bullinger, Zurich 1957, 244.

extended exposition of Genesis 17 and the outlining of the nature of the covenant, the parties of the covenant, the conditions of the covenant, that the covenant is the subject of all Scripture as well as his understanding of the sacrament of the covenant.[5] This article seeks to demonstrate that close investigation of *De testamento* reveals a raft of biblical and theological themes in addition to that of the covenant. The fact that, from 1537 onwards, *De testamento* was appended to *In omnes apostolicas epistolas* (1537)[6] together with *Utriusque in Christo naturae divinae quam humanae* (1534)[7] indicates Bullinger's desire for his readers to see the intimate link between the incarnation and the plan of salvation that was expressed in the Scriptures through the theme of the covenant.

For too long Bullinger has been considered a theological lightweight in comparison with other reformers. However, with careful study of Bullinger's meticulous use of terminology and the high number of quotations and allusions to the Scriptures, this article shows that *De testamento* was not just a work hastily put together to address the ongoing challenges of Anabaptism or the charge that the reformed faith was heretical as it was adjudged to have deviated from the true faith. *De testamento* expresses Bullinger's understanding of the message of the canon which Bullinger began to work on and develop during his productive period at Kappel am Albis. Hence there is a plethora of biblical and theological themes in a work written in the shadow of the defeat at the *Zweiter Kappelerkrieg* and Bullinger's own stirring *Karlstag* sermon of 1532.[8] Bullinger's *De testamento* deserves a more prominent place in the Reformation corpus.

[5] A summary of this may be found in Antonius J. van 't *Hooft*, De Theologie van Heinrich Bullinger in betrekking tot de Nederlandsche Reformatie, Amsterdam 1888, 44–51 and Willem van 't *Spijker*, Bullinger als Bundestheologe, in: Heinrich Bullinger: Life – Thought – Influence, ed. Emido Campi and Peter Opitz, Zurich 2007 (Zürcher Beiträge zur Reformationsgeschichte 24), 579–581.

[6] Heinrich *Bullinger*, In omnes apostolicas epistolas commentarii, Zurich: Christoph Froschauer the Elder, 1537 (BZD C 261).

[7] Heinrich *Bullinger*, Utriusque in Christo naturae tam divinae quam humanae assertio, Zurich: Christoph Froschauer the Elder, 1534 (BZD C 229).

[8] Heinrich *Bullinger*, De prophetae officio et quomodo digne administrari possit oratio, Zurich: Christoph Froschauer the Elder, 1532 (BZD C 209).

1. The title page

As was his usual practice, on the title page of *De testamento* Bullinger cited Matthew 17:5 in the following manner:

IESUS
HIC est filius dilectus in quo
placata est anima mea, ipsum audite.
Matthaei 17.

The particular significance of Matthew 17:5 for *De testamento*, in particular, indicates that Bullinger believed Jesus to be the goal or focus of the covenant and, thereby, the goal of the whole canon. Hence his name is printed in upper case. Opitz also sees in this passage a reference to both the priestly and rabbinic role of Christ who, as Redeemer, fulfills the covenant.[9]

The transfiguration of Christ together with Moses and Elijah reaffirmed for Bullinger that the Law and the Prophets find their climax in and were fulfilled in Christ. To hear Christ only was equivalent to hearing only what Scripture says. Bullinger had in the back of his mind the prophet to come referred to in Deuteronomy 18:15. Certainly Bullinger emphasized the significance of Acts 3:22 in *De testamento*.[10] Moreover, it is apparent that Bullinger is indicating that Christ came to bring the new Torah (His Word which would be written on the hearts of men and women in fulfillment of Jeremiah 31) which would replace the Torah of the Old Testament. In *De testamento* Bullinger emphasizes that the Torah had already been inscribed on the hearts of the patriarchs before it was inscripturated at the time of Moses and that it was written more fully by the Spirit with the coming of Christ and the new covenant. In an earlier work, *Antwort an Burchard*,[11] Bullinger was insistent that one should listen to Christ alone, which means to obey only him.[12] In his commentary on Matthew (1542) Bullinger directly

[9] *Opitz*, Heinrich Bullinger als Theologe, 333.

[10] *Bullinger*, De testamento, 3r. Deuteronomy 18:15 is cited by Peter at Acts 3:22.

[11] Heinrich Bullinger: Theologische Schriften, vol. 2, Zurich 1991 [HBTS 2], 134–172. Cf. Heinrich *Bullinger*, In d. Petri apostoli epistolam utranque commentarius, Zurich: Christoph Froschauer the Elder, 1534 (BZD C 227), 94r–v.

[12] Cf. Joseph *Ratzinger*, Many Religions – One Covenant, San Francisco 1999, 70: »The Torah of the Messiah is the Messiah, Jesus himself. It is to him that the command, ›Listen to him,‹ refers.«

referred to Deuteronomy 18 and Peter's sermon of Acts 3 as well as Stephen's sermon of Acts 7.[13]

2. Justification by faith

The fact that Bullinger prefers *placata* to *placita* on the title page of his books underscores the fact that the central theme in Bullinger is that of reconciliation with God through justification by faith, despite Baker's insistence that the covenant is the centre of Bullinger's thought.[14] The covenant is indeed central to Bullinger without being the actual centre of his works. Significantly, one of the main themes of *The Old Faith* (1537) is that the patriarchs of the Old Testament were justified by faith in Christ in the same way as saints in the new covenant. Justification by faith alone in Christ alone is clearly expressed in *De testamento* as is evident from the following quote:

> »Abraham was assuredly justified by faith alone, prior to circumcision and prior to the law, without the ceremonies, without the law. He also saw the day of the Lord Jesus and he rejoiced.«[15]

Each of these phrases was carefully chosen, *viz.* »by faith alone«, »without ceremonies«, »prior to the circumcision«, »prior to the law« and »without the law«. Indeed, these phrases need to be borne in mind when reading *De testamento*, especially whenever Bullinger refers to the »conditions« of the covenant. The direct citation of John 8:56 was Bullinger's tacit manner of stating that Abraham was justified by faith alone in Christ alone. The fact that

[13] Heinrich *Bullinger*, In sacrosanctum Iesu Christi domini nostri Evangelium secundum Matthaeum commentariorum libri XII, Zurich: Christoph Froschauer the Elder, 1542 (BZD C 304), 166r.

[14] J. Wayne *Baker*, Heinrich Bullinger and the Covenant: The Other Reformed Tradition, Athens, OH 1980; J. Wayne *Baker*, Heinrich Bullinger, the Covenant, and the Reformed Tradition in Retrospect, in: The Sixteenth Century Journal 29/2 (1998), 359–376.

[15] »Abraham certe ante circuncisionem et legem, sine ceremoniis, fide duntaxat, iustificatus est, idem vidit diem domini Iesu et gavisus est.« *Bullinger*, De testamento, 25r. Unless otherwise indicated, the English translations of *De testamento* are taken from Charles S. *McCoy* and J. Wayne *Baker*, Fountainhead of Federalism: Heinrich Bullinger and the Covenant Tradition, Louisville, KY 1991, 101–138.

Abraham was justified before he was circumcised was repeated by Bullinger in the Epilogue.[16] In clearly alluding to the catch-cry of the Reformation of *sola fide*, Bullinger was underscoring the fact that the faith taught and practised by the reformers was indeed faithful to a true understanding of Scripture. This is further unpacked by Bullinger in the Epilogue of *De testamento* where he writes: »... in order that I might indicate in passing the clarity, simplicity, and antiquity of Scripture and of our religion, which today is ill-spoken of by many people, as if it were heretical.«[17]

Because of the extended discussion in *De testamento* of the »conditions« of the covenant many have incorrectly deduced that Bullinger was synergic in his understanding of justification because his emphasis on the covenant was adduced to be »bilateral«. In point of fact, Bullinger viewed the covenant in a monopleuric manner for his discussion of the covenant must be seen in the context of God's accommodation to the customs of mankind.[18] There is no doubt that, for Bullinger, salvation is all of God's grace. Thus Bullinger points out that: »This certainly is the origin of our religion and it is its principal point: we are saved only through the goodness and mercy of God.«[19]

3. God's accommodation to mankind

One unmistakeable and overarching theme in *De testamento* is the accommodation of God. As is widely known, this also is emphasized in Calvin's works. Garcia Archilla notes that Bullinger underscores the covenant as the accommodation of God: »Bullinger has established, on a Biblical basis, his understanding of the covenant. He is most conscious that this is not a deal between equal partners, but once more underlines that it is an accommodation by God to our imbecillitas, our incapacity to stand at the same level

[16] *Bullinger*, De testamento, 47v.

[17] *Bullinger*, De testamento, 47r.

[18] Aurelio *Garcia Archilla*, Bullinger's De testamento: The Amply Biblical Basis of Reformed Origins, in: Heinrich Bullinger: Life – Thought – Influence, ed. Emido Campi and Peter Opitz, Zurich 2007 (Zürcher Beiträge zur Reformationsgeschichte 24), 674f.

[19] »Haec nimirum religionis nostrae origo et illud caput primarium est, sola Dei bonitate et misercordiae nos salvari.« *Bullinger*, De testamento, 6v.

with God on account of our creatureness.«[20] Bullinger explains that God was pleased to use a human expression (*humana appellatione*) and follow human custom (*humanum morem*) on account of the weakness (*imbecillitatem*) of human nature when he initiated the covenant.[21] Indeed, Bullinger makes a point to state that »God has acted according to human custom at every point.«[22] Bullinger understands God's accommodation to mankind through the covenant as a condescension to the finiteness and frailty of humanity. He expresses this in terms of »... sets forth the divine nature, *as much as he wishes to show himself to us.*«[23]

There is no doubt whatsoever that Bullinger upheld the Reformation formula of *sola gratia*.[24] Because of his repeated emphasis on faithful obedience to the covenant and because he was cited by the Remonstrants at the Council of Dordt, Bullinger came to be suspected of being semi-Pelagian. However, careful study of *De testamento* reveals this not to be the case at all. Bullinger always upheld justification by faith alone. Several times in *De testamento* Bullinger emphasizes that it is God who initiated the covenant. It was »not in any way because of the merits of humans but rather out of ... the sheer goodness and mercy of God.«[25] Then in a reference to the Anabaptists, who over focused on the »conditions« of the covenant taken out of their biblical context, Bullinger argues that »those people who consider only the conditions of the covenant and in fact disregard the grace and promise of God exclude infants from the covenant.«[26]

A correct understanding of God's accommodation means that *El Shaddai* employed human customs and human language to express and explain his gracious relationship with mankind. Following scholars such as Mendenhall and others, it might appear natural to refer to Hittite suzerain treaties to explain the Biblical covenant with their measure of mutuality between the two parties. However, a more accurate parallel, albeit limited, is that of the covenant of

[20] *Garcia Archilla*, Bullinger's De testamento, 674.
[21] *Bullinger*, De testamento, 4v.
[22] »Deum omni modo morem retulisse humanum«, *Bullinger*, De testamento, 5v.
[23] *Bullinger*, De testamento, 11v. Italics added.
[24] *Garcia Archilla*, Bullinger's De testamento, 674–676.
[25] *Bullinger*, De testamento, 6v.
[26] *Bullinger*, De testamento, 7v–8r.

royal grant.[27] The manner that Bullinger unpacks the biblical witness of the covenant is closest to the covenant of royal grant. This can be illustrated by the fact that Bullinger cites Micah 6:8 in *De testamento* which he employs to explain what it means to respond to God in faith for »It is our duty to adhere firmly by faith to the one God, inasmuch as he is the one and only author of all good things, and to walk in innocence of life for his pleasure.«[28]

One related aspect of Bullinger's understanding of God's accommodation is his fondness for explaining that God gives *himself* and that God *pours himself* into the believer. In doing so, Bullinger is re-echoing the testimony of Scripture that the covenant is not so much the means of giving blessings to the covenant people but the very giving of *El Shaddai* himself for the good of his elect. Thus Bullinger explains that »The God of heaven, that highest and eternal power and majesty ... offers himself for their benefit.«[29] He further adds that God »poured out his entire self for us.«[30] Bullinger's emphasis on God giving himself through the covenant and of pouring himself into the believer (hence union with the believer) is further developed by him in the *Decades*.[31] Bullinger thus acknowledges God's accommodation to mankind is expressed in the Scriptures through anthropomorphic language. Although Bullinger may refer to »binding« and »conditions« and the like in terms of God's covenant relationship with mankind these terms must not be viewed through the lens of mutual, human pacts. There is no doubt whatsoever that Bullinger believed unreservedly in *sola gratia* as is illustrated by his comment that »circumcision was given to those to whom the grace and the covenant of God was first offered, through the assistance and the institution of God who did not scorn being the God of little children and who also first offered

[27] Moshe *Weinfield*, The Covenant of Grant in the Old Testament and in the Ancient Near East, in: Journal of the American Oriental Society 90 (1970), 184–203; Moshe *Weinfield*, Covenant Terminology in the Ancient East and its Influence on the West, in: Journal of the American Oriental Society 93 (1973), 190–199. Especially characteristic of the covenant of grant are the following: »he kept my charge,« »walked before me in truth,« »his heart was whole to his master,« »walked in perfection.«

[28] *Bullinger*, De testamento, 16r.

[29] *Bullinger*, De testamento, 14r.

[30] *Bullinger*, De testamento, 22r.

[31] Sermon III.6, cf. John V. *Fesko*, Heinrich Bullinger on Union with Christ and Justification, in: The Confessional Presbyterian 6 (2010), 3–10.

himself to us out of sheer grace (*mera gratia*) and said, ›I will be your God.‹«[32]

Furthermore, akin to the Apostle Paul's doxology at the end of Romans 11, Bullinger is aware that, because of the finiteness of mankind, it is beyond human ability to fully understand the significance of God's accommodation through the covenant. Hence, he observes: »I do not know whether humans are capable either of conceiving this mystery fully or conveying how praiseworthy it is.«[33]

4. The covenant is the subject of all Scripture

Bullinger contends that the covenant is »the subject of all Scripture«. He refers to the covenant as a »target at which all Scripture aims«.[34] The following lengthy quote demonstrates how Bullinger understands the covenant to be central to the message of the canon:

> »For whatever things have been said in the Holy Scripture about the unity, power, majesty, goodness and glory of God are included in this one expression of the covenant: ›I am the all-sufficient Lord‹. Whatever promises have been written about bodily blessings, glory, the kingdom, victories, labors, and the basic needs of life, are included in this one expression of the covenant: ›I will give to you and to your descendants the land of Canaan; I will be their God‹. In the same way, those things which have been handed down afterwards at various times about Christ the Lord, both in figure and in truth, whatever has been said about his justice, about the sanctification and redemption of the faithful, about the sacrifice, the priesthood, and the satisfaction of Christ, about the kingdom and eternal life, and, further, about the calling of all peoples, about spiritual blessings, about the abrogation of the law, about the glory of the church gathered from the Gentiles and Jews, are foretold in this single promise: ›And all the nations will be blessed in you and you will be the father of many peoples.‹«[35]

[32] *Bullinger*, De testamento, 44r.

[33] *Bullinger*, De testamento, 6r.

[34] The marginal comment on folio 16r reads: »Omnis Scriptura ad foedus ceu scopum refertur«.

[35] *Bullinger*, De testamento, 16v–17r.

Key theological themes are referred to by Bullinger in this extended quote which are directly related to the overarching theme of covenant in Scripture. In particular, the theme of the covenant is linked with the theme of the kingdom in the context of promise and fulfillment. Indeed, the King, Christ, is Kyrios in whom is fulfilled the priesthood and sacrificial system of the Old Testament, whose fully satisfactory sacrifice demonstrates the justice of God for the redemption and sanctification of mankind (both Jew and Gentile) who are gathered as members of His church. It is thus abundantly evident that, for Bullinger, the covenant is the backbone and basis to all biblical themes.

In his study of the *Decades*, Opitz correctly concludes that, for Bullinger, the message of the whole canon is first and foremost theological and then christological. This is evident from the chapter headings in his book.[36] Bullinger views the main message of the Bible as reconciliation with God through being justified by faith in Christ alone. The covenant, for Bullinger, is the way that God unfolds his plan for the salvation of the elect. His emphasis on God as *cornucopia* or »the all-sufficient Lord« points to the theological focus of Scripture. On the other hand, his frequent reference, in his writings, to Christ as the seed of the second Eve who fulfils the *protoevangelium* of Genesis 3:15 points to the Christological focus of Scripture. A consideration of all the works of Bullinger may lead to the conclusion that he views Genesis 1,2 and Revelation 21,22 as an *inclusio* to the whole canon which is, therefore, theological in focus while Genesis 3 to Revelation 20 constitutes the »theology of history«[37] which is clearly christological in focus with the covenant as its *scopus*. Like Irenaeus, Bullinger regards that one of the main purposes of Scripture was to prepare the people of God in each generation for the *parousia*.

[36] »Gemeinschaft mit Gott im Hören auf Gottes Wort«; »Gemeinschaft mit dem dreieinigen Gott«; »Gemeinschaft mit Gott als pneumatische Christusgemeinschaft«; »Gemeinschaft als Leben im Bund«; »Gemeinschaft mit Gott als Leben mit dem Gesetz« and »Gemeinschaft mit Gott als Gemeinschaft der Heiligen«.

[37] To use the title of *Garcia Archilla's* book: The Theology of History and Apologetic Historiography in Heinrich Bullinger, San Fransisco 1992.

4.1 De testamento and the covenant with Adam

Although Bullinger refers to Adam several times in *De testamento*[38] it is not well known that he did, in fact, refer to the *protoevangelium* of Genesis 3:15 in *De testamento* in one of its textual versions. There appear to be two major textual versions of *De testamento, viz.* the text of 1534[39] and the text appended to *In omnes apostolicas epistolas* (1537).[40] As might be expected, there are several minor orthographical differences between the two texts. The major differences concern a revision of dates cited by Bullinger and the insertion of some extra words.[41] The most significant change, however, is the insertion of three sentences that make a specific reference to the covenant with Adam. Inserted between the sentence on folio 29v which reads, »Semen mulieris calcabit caput serpentis …« and the sentence which reads »Ergon inquis legem citra consilium rationemque …« the 1537 text has the following additional sentences:

> »Non enim hoc primum omnium foedus est quod pepigit cum Abraham, sed illud primum est quod pepigit cum Adam. Unde disertis verbis in consequentibus pactionibus dicitur, Erigam vel confirmabo vel statuam pactum meum tecum, id est foedus semel initum firmiter servabo. Saepe enim renovatum est, idque certas ob caussas, ut cum Noe post diluvium nunc cum Abraham, postea cum Mose. Unum tamen atque idem foedus est quod confirmatur et stratuitur cum illis omnibus.«[42]

[38] *Bullinger*, De testamento, 7r, 48r, 50r.

[39] This is the text used for the translation by *McCoy* and *Baker* and that of Detlef *Roth* in Heinrich Bullinger Schriften, ed. Emidio Campi et al., vol. 1, Zurich 2004, 47–101.

[40] See Joe *Mock*, Bullinger and the Covenant with Adam, in: Reformed Theological Review 70/3 (2011), 185–205 where some of the following discussion has been published.

[41] »6733« is replaced by »5508« and the following words inserted after »5199«: »quibus si addas 1534 habebis ab initio mundi 6733 sed nos sequi maluimus sacra Biblia quam Graecorum Commentaria« (*Bullinger*, De testamento, 50r).

[42] *Bullinger*, In omnes apostolicas epistolas, 162. The text of the 1537 version is used for the translation of Peter A. *Lillback*, The Binding of God: Calvin's Role in the Development of Covenant Theology, Dissertation Westminster Theological Seminary, 1985.

This may be translated as follows:

> Indeed, the covenant which he made with Abraham is not the first of all the covenants. Rather, the first covenant is the one which he made with Adam. From which covenant with explicit words in the covenants that followed he may say, »I will erect« or »I will confirm« or »I will establish my covenant with you«, that is »I will keep firmly the covenant made at the beginning«. In fact, the covenant was often renewed. This was because of certain causes, as with Noah after the flood, then with Abraham, and afterwards with Moses. Nevertheless, it is the one and the same covenant which is confirmed and established with all of these.

Although Bullinger does refer to »covenants« in the plural, he clearly considers them the one and the same covenant that God made with Adam. Thus, Bullinger emphasized that Christ came to renew and fulfill the covenant both as the son of Adam and as the seed of Eve. As with Zwingli in his *In catabaptisarum strophas elenchus*,[43] Bullinger interprets the *protoevangelium* of Genesis 3:15 as referring to a covenant with Adam and his seed, which would subsequently be renewed through the covenant with Abraham and his seed.[44]

Bullinger first referred to the covenant with Adam in *Vom dem Touff*[45] and *Antwort an Burchard*.[46] The clearest expression of Bullinger's understanding of the theological significance of Genesis 3:15, however, is found in *The Old Faith* (1537)[47]. It may be reasonably assumed, therefore, that since *The Old Faith* makes such a significant and pointed reference to a covenant with Adam that Bullinger decided to revise *De testamento* in 1537 with the insertion of the three sentences referred to above. Subsequent writings of Bullinger certainly referred to the covenant with Adam.[48] A stu-

[43] Huldreich Zwinglis sämtliche Werke [Z], vol. 6/1, Zurich 1961 (Corpus Reformatorum 93/1), 157.

[44] *Opitz*, Heinrich Bullinger als Theologe, 80f.

[45] HBTS 2, 66–85.

[46] HBTS 2, 134–172.

[47] Heinrich *Bullinger*, Das der Christen gloub von anfang der wålt gewåret habe der recht und ungezwyflet glouben sye, Basel: Wolfgang Fries, 1537 (Heinrich Bullinger Bibliographie, vol. 1, ed. Joachim Staedtke, Zurich 1972 [HBBibl], no 99).

[48] Apart from key sections in the *Decades*, Bullinger referred to the covenant with Adam in the following works: The Evangelical Churches are neither Heretical nor Schismatic (1552); Von dem heiligen Nachtmal unsers Herrenn Jesu Christi (1553); Von dem Heil der Gloeubigen (1555), Summa christenlicher Religion (1556), Sermons for the

dy of all the letters that Bullinger wrote in the period 1534–1537, however, reveals no reference to any change in *De testamento*.

Zwingli had referred to a covenant with Adam in *In catabaptisarum strophas elenchus* (1527). Although there is ongoing debate about the dating of *Vom dem Touff* and *Antwort an Burchard* a case can be made for Bullinger's reference to the covenant with Adam prior to that of Zwingli.[49] It is clear, nonetheless, that for both Zwingli and Bullinger the covenant with Adam was an infralapsarian covenant of grace. The fact that some have misread Bullinger's understanding of the covenant with Adam is illustrated by Dowey who pointed out that no less than a scholar such as Koch[50] has misunderstood Bullinger in reaching his conclusion that Bullinger spoke of an »Adamic« covenant which laid the groundwork for a »supralapsarian covenant of creation.«[51]

What is significant is that Bullinger refers to Adam twice in the Epilogue of *De testamento*. On the first occasion it is in the context of noting that the patriarchs before Abraham pleased God through faith without circumcision.[52] While on the other occasion Bullinger asserts: »We have proven that the faith of Abraham, Adam, and Christ was the same.«[53]

4.2 The unity of the Old and New Testaments

In explaining the meaning of the title *De testamento*, Bullinger underlines the fact that the testament or covenant is both one and everlasting. Bullinger argues that God established one single covenant and that both old and new covenants had the same essence and the same basic requirements of faith and obedience leading to love of God and neighbour. The people of the new covenant are

Feast Days of Our Lord and Savior Jesus Christ (1558), the 1569 version of Compendium Christianae Religionis; Bullinger's commentary on Daniel (1565), Epitome temporum et rerum ab orbe condito ad primum usque annum Iothan Regis Iudae (1565), and Von der schweren langwirigen vervolgung der Heiligen Christlichen Kirchen (1573).

[49] Cf. *Mock*, Covenant with Adam.

[50] Ernst *Koch*, Die Theologie der Confessio Helvetica Posterior, Neukirchen-Vluyn 1968, 397.

[51] *Dowey*, Bullinger as Theologian, 39.

[52] *Bullinger*, De testamento, 47v–48r.

[53] *Bullinger*, De testamento, 50r.

co-continuous with the people of the old covenant. Bullinger's point is that the patriarchs had the same *religio vera* as that of the new covenant because the *substantia* was the same.[54] In almost a parallel to John 14:6 Bullinger further declares: »There is therefore one covenant and one church of all the saints before and after Christ, one way to heaven, and one unchanging religion of all the saints.«[55] In citing 1 Corinthians 10:1–4 Bullinger points out that the saints of both the old and new testaments had the same spiritual food and drink. He further cites Augustine extensively from his *Commentary on the Gospel of John* to justify his assertion that both the old covenant patriarchs and the new covenant church believe in Christ having the same faith: »The times are different, but not the faith. Although the times did indeed differ, we see that those of both times entered through the one doorway of faith, that is, through Christ.«[56] Moreover, Bullinger put in upper case the declaration that *there is one faith.*[57] Bullinger also cites Augustine from his *De Baptismo contra Donatistas* to further substantiate his point.[58] Hence, Bullinger sums up as follows: »From all of this I think it is truly evident that there is only one church and one covenant, the same for the patriarchs and for us.«[59]

Bullinger does acknowledge that Scripture refers to the terms »old« and »new« covenants as he cites Jeremiah 31:31–34,[60] Eze-

[54] »Praeterea multis hactenus approbavimus nihil apud posteros de religione vera, quantum scilicet substantiam attinet, dictum fuisse, quod non audierint priores.« *Bullinger*, De testamento, 25r.

[55] »Unicum ergo testamentum est et una omnium ante et post Christum sanctorum ecclesia, unica ad coelos via, unica item constansque omnium sanctorum religio.« *Bullinger*, De testamento, 25r.

[56] »Tempora variata sunt non fides. Diversis quidem temporibus, sed utrosque per unum fidei ostium, hoc est per Christum videmus ingressos.« *Bullinger*, De testamento, 27r.

[57] »Apostolos dicit: Et nos credimus propter quod et loquimur. Ut scias autem quod una sit fides, audi dicentem. Habentes eundem spiritum fidei et nos credimus.« *Bullinger*, De testamento, 27v.

[58] *Bullinger*, De testamento, 27v.

[59] »Ex his vero omnibus liquere puto unam esse duntaxat ecclesiam, Testamentum unum veterum et nostrum.« *Bullinger*, De testamento, 28r.

[60] See Joshua *Moon*, Restitutio ad Integrum: An »Augustinian« Reading of Jeremiah 31:31–34 in Dialogue with the Christian Tradition, Dissertation St. Andrews University, 2007, 86–93 for a helpful discussion of Bullinger's understanding of the old and new covenant vis-à-vis Jeremiah 31:31–34.

kiel 36:26, and Galatians 4:24 which says: »These are two covenants (*testamenta*).« Significantly, Bullinger uses *testamentum* twice in his citation of the Jeremiah 31 passage whereas the Vulgate has *foedus* and *pactum*. Bullinger's argument is that the terms »old« and »new« did not arise from the essence (*substantia*) of the covenant but because of »certain foreign and unessential things« (*accidentibus*) which were not »perpetual and particularly necessary things for salvation«.[61] Bullinger thus uses the Aristotelian concepts of »substance« and »accidents« to explain the continuity and discontinuity between the old covenant and the new covenant.[62] The »accidents« are clearly explained by Bullinger to be the Aaronic priesthood, the sacrificial system of the old covenant, the rites of purification, food and dietary laws, instructions for the construction of the tabernacle and the like.[63]

Bullinger points out that the most important aspect of what transpired through the Mosaic covenant was that the main points of the covenant were reinstated but »unfolded more fully.« Subsequently, the ceremonies (which the patriarchs did not have) were added to restrain Israel from idolatry as well as to serve as types of Christ who was to come as promised. Thus, apart from the ceremonies, Bullinger declares: »Now, therefore, in respect to the Decalogue and civil laws, no difference at all has arisen regarding the covenant and the people of God. For everywhere the love of God and the neighbor, faith, and love maintain the mastery.«[64]

Bullinger further asserts that under the old covenant there was indeed forgiveness of sins (through Christ) and that there was an emphasis on faith and love. Because of this, the new covenant cannot be called »new« entirely on account of these facts, »since it teaches nothing new.«[65] The new covenant is called »new« because all the ceremonies were fulfilled in Christ. Thus the »ancient religion« was »renewed (*innovata*) and restored more fully (*plenius*)

[61] *Bullinger*, De testamento, 28v.

[62] Cf. David *Steinmetz*, Reformers in the Wings, Oxford 2001, 138: »the distinction between the Old and New Testaments does not touch the substance of the covenant, but only its accidents.« Cf. Calvin's use of *substantia* and *administratio* in the Institutes II.10.2.

[63] *Bullinger*, De testamento, 28v–29r.

[64] *Bullinger*, De testamento, 31r.

[65] *Bullinger*, De testamento, 31v.

and more clearly (*dilucidius*) by Christ and made perfect (*absolutaque*) with a new people, namely the Gentiles.«[66] In addition, Bullinger refers to the »enduring, spiritual terms of the covenant or the promise of God.«[67] To further underscore the continuity between the Testaments Bullinger declares that, »Even the Spirit is the same in both Testaments.«[68] He illustrates this through citing Stephen's sermon in Acts 7 that Stephen »proved with almost countless examples from the ancients that faith in God *before the law, under the law, and after the law* was pleasing to God, not ceremonies.«[69]

While Bullinger clearly emphasizes the unity of the Old and New Testaments, he acknowledges, at the same time, that there is both *continuity* and *discontinuity* between the Testaments. For example, Bullinger refers in a marginal comment to the reality that »we surpass the ancients.«[70] On the one hand, Bullinger cites the close connection we have with the patriarchs whose religion »rested upon faith and innocence without ceremonies, that is, *on the basic terms of the covenant* ...«[71] Furthermore, Bullinger alludes to the fact that »the typological foreshadowings have been fulfilled.«[72] But, on the other hand, Bullinger also points out that with the coming of Christ, as promised, »God has made our church superior to the church of our dead fathers ... He has given his Spirit most abundantly.«[73]

Bullinger anticipates objections to his view by considering, in turn, Matthew 5, 2 Corinthians 3 and Deuteronomy 5. With respect to Matthew 5, Bullinger argues that, »Christ attacked the Pharisees, not the spirit of the law itself or of the prophets.«[74] Similarly, Bullinger concludes of 2 Corinthians that, »Indeed, in that passage he does not speak of the entire law but only that part

[66] *Bullinger*, De testamento, 31v.

[67] *Bullinger*, De testamento, 32r: »solidis et spiritualibus testamenti seu promissioni Dei.«

[68] *Bullinger*, De testamento, 34v: »Spiritus quoque idem est utrisque.«

[69] *Bullinger*, De testamento, 34r. Italics added.

[70] *Bullinger*, De testamento, 34v: »Quibus rebus praecelamus veteres.«

[71] *Bullinger*, De testamento, 35r. Italics added.

[72] *Bullinger*, De testamento, 35r.

[73] *Bullinger*, De testamento, 35r.

[74] *Bullinger*, De testamento, 36r.

of the law which is abolished.«[75] In referring to Deuteronomy 5 Bullinger cites both Augustine and Oecolampadius.[76]

A consideration of Bullinger's references to the unity of the Old and New Testaments in *De testamento* thus amplifies the significance of the »one« in the title of the treatise: *The One and Eternal Testament or Covenant of God.*

4.3 The seed of Abraham

Since Bullinger based his treatise on the covenant as an exposition of Genesis 17 there is constant reference in *De testamento* to the theme of the seed of Abraham. Folio 6r commences a paragraph with the marginal heading »Deus iniit foedus cum semine Abraham«. The immediate following paragraph has the marginal heading »Qui sint semen Abrahae«.[77] Bullinger underscores that Christ is the seed of Adam through his incarnation, that he is the seed of Eve[78] and the true seed of Abraham (*de vero semine Abrahae*).[79] Bullinger further points out that the seed of Abraham who inherit the covenant promises given to him and his seed are the spiritual seed of Abraham who, in turn, have received true circumcision as referred to by Jeremiah in chapter 4 and Paul in Romans 2.[80] In citing Galatians 3:29 Bullinger affirms that »Those who are Christ's are the seed of Abraham.«[81] Bullinger's explanation of the true seed of Abraham must be seen in the context of the unity of the Old and New Testaments. Hence Bullinger affirms that: »Abraham was clearly justified by faith alone, without ceremonies, prior to circumcision and the law (Romans 4:1–13). He saw the day of the Lord Jesus and rejoiced (John 8:56).«[82]

[75] *Bullinger*, De testamento, 36v–37r.

[76] *Bullinger*, De testamento, 38r–v. Bullinger, however, deletes several lines from Oecolampadius to suit his purposes.

[77] *Bullinger*, De testamento, 7v.

[78] *Bullinger*, De testamento, 29v.

[79] *Bullinger*, De testamento, 9v.

[80] *Bullinger*, De testamento, 9r.

[81] *Bullinger*, De testamento, 10r.

[82] *Bullinger*, De testamento, 25r.

Since *De testamento* was written by Bullinger[83] *inter alia* to grapple with issues raised by the Anabaptists, Bullinger emphasizes that the children of believers are the seed of Abraham and, therefore, should receive baptism, the sign of the new covenant.[84] Furthermore, since texts of *De testamento* which were appended to *In omnes apostolicas epistolas* clearly referred to the *protoevangelium* of Genesis 3:15, Bullinger also emphasized that Christ was the seed of Eve. As the seed of Eve, Christ came as the blessed Seed of God. Indeed the linking of Genesis 3:15, Genesis 17:7 and Galatians 3:16 is a constant theme in *The Old Faith* as can be attested by the number of times »seed«, »blessed Seed« and »promised Seed« are referred to.[85]

4.4 The covenant and right living

The well-known opening thematic statement of Calvin's *Institutes* appears to reflect what is clearly in Bullinger's mind when he explains in *De testamento* concerning the covenant: »The entire sum of piety consists in these very brief main points of the covenant. Indeed, it is evident that nothing else was handed down to the saints of all ages, throughout the entire Scripture, other than what is included in these main points of the covenant, although each point is set forth more profusely and more clearly in the succession of times.«[86] Just as *religio* in Calvin's *Institutio Christianae Religionis* referred primarily to Christian »living« rather than »doctrine« so Bullinger's *De testamento* focusses on right living in a right relationship with *El Shaddai*. This fact must surely be underscored by the only Swiss German sentence in the whole treatise: »Schickt dich wohl und råcht zewandeln und zelåbenn« – prepare yourself to walk and live uprightly.[87]

[83] J. Wayne *Baker*, Church, State, and Dissent: The Crisis of the Swiss Reformation, 1531–1536, in: Church History 57 (1988), 135–152.

[84] *Bullinger*, De testamento, 9v–10r.

[85] »seed« is referred to 67 times in Miles Coverdale's translation of The Old Faith (1547, HBBibl no 105).

[86] *Bullinger*, De testamento, 16r–v.

[87] *Bullinger*, De testamento, 15r. Bullinger used a fuller version in the German version of *De testamento* (Heinrich *Bullinger*, Von dem einigen unnd ewigen Testament oder Pundt Gottes kurtzer bericht, [Zurich]: [Christoph Froschauer the Elder], [1534]

There is no doubt that Bullinger was concerned not only for the right interpretation of Scripture but also for right living. Indeed, most of his works are highly pastoral in emphasis. As Garcia Archilla rightly observes: »*De testamento* does not constitute a systematic and exhaustive treatment of all theological loci ... The function of *De testamento* is not to provide a full systematic doctrine, but to show the consistency, coherence and integrity of the Biblical testimony about God's plan of salvation by means of the promise/foedus/testament cluster of concepts.«[88] *De testamento* concludes with a word of encouragement citing Psalm 25:10 that reflects Bullinger's pastoral heart: »All the paths of the Lord are grace and faith to those who keep his testament and covenant.«[89]

4.5 The Holy Spirit and the covenant

Garcia Archilla has argued that there is insufficient reference to the role of the Holy Spirit in *De testamento*.[90] However, in point of fact, there is a catena of references to the Spirit in *De testamento*. The very first sentence of *De testamento* is an affirmation of the fact that the Scriptures were inspired by the Spirit and that with the assistance of that same Spirit Bullinger is seeking to give an exposition of the testament or covenant of God.[91] He further points out that it is the same Spirit who continues to speak through of the Old Testament and the New Testament.[92] On several occasions Bullinger refers to spiritual Israel vis-à-vis Israel that is only concerned for the ceremonies for it is the spirit that counts and not the flesh.[93] While acknowledging the role of the Holy Spirit in the old covenant, Bullinger does assert that God »has given his Spirit most abundantly« (i.e. to the church post-Christ).[94]

[HBBibl no 60], B3r): »Schick dich vor mir zewandlen. Das ist also vil geredt: flyß dich wohl und recht vor mir zelåben.«

[88] *Garcia Archilla*, Bullinger's De testamento, 691.

[89] *Bullinger*, De testamento,52r.

[90] *Garcia Archilla*, Bullinger's De testamento, 690.

[91] *Bullinger*, De testamento 2r.

[92] *Bullinger*, De testamento, 9v, cf. 34v: »Spiritus quoque idem est utrisque.«

[93] *Bullinger*, De testamento, 32r–v, cf. 33r: »Spiritum ergo non carnem vel in Israëlitis probavit and populum ex Israëlitis spiritualem habuit.«

[94] *Bullinger*, De testamento, 35r.

Bullinger thus views the Spirit as the author of Scripture as well as the Enabler amongst the elect (whom he terms »spiritual Israel« in the Old Testament era) so that they might live *integer* before *El Shaddai*. It is through the Spirit that the covenant is inscribed on the hearts of the Patriarchs before its inscripturation at the time of Moses. It is through the Spirit that the Torah of Christ is inscribed on the heart of believers in the new covenant.

5. The Law and the covenant

The Law summarizes for Bullinger the »conditions« of the covenant for »the Law truly teaches, with the Lord himself as witness, partly the love of God and partly the love of neighbour.«[95] Bullinger understands Torah as »instruction« rather than in a forensic sense. Bullinger thus declares: »the Decalogue itself seems to be almost a paraphrase of the conditions of the covenant.«[96] Since the Decalogue was inscribed on tablets of stone by the very finger of God when given to the Israelites at the time of Moses,[97] Bullinger seeks to declare that God is not only the giver of the Law but He is also the witness (*testis*) so that the Law achieves its purpose of instructing the seed of Abraham.

Bullinger is thus insistent that nothing »new« was introduced at the time of Moses with the inscripturation of the Law. His point is that the Law was already written on the heart.[98] For, as a written record of the covenant, the Law set forth how to love God and to love one's neighbour and, at the same time, looked forward to Christ who is the goal of the covenant. Indeed, Bullinger points out that Christ himself also »taught partly faith in God and partly love of the neighbour. The former explains the first aim of the covenant, the latter the second.«[99] In the context of salvation history

[95] *Bullinger*, De testamento, 17v: »Nam lex (ut de hac primum dicamus) etiam ipso domino teste partim amorem Dei, partim amnorem proximi tradit.«

[96] *Bullinger*, De testamento, 17v.

[97] *Bullinger*, De testamento, 30r.

[98] *Bullinger*, De testamento, 45r: »Quanquam vero Dominus priscis illis patribus nullas conscribi curarit tabulas. Nam illi foedus digito dei cordibus inscriptum gerebant.«

[99] *Bullinger*, De testamento, 23v.

(prior to Sinai, post Sinai and post Christ) Bullinger states that the Decalogue and the civil laws continue to apply to the seed of Abraham in the new covenant for »everywhere the love of God and the neighbour, faith, and love maintain the mastery.«[100] Bullinger's basis for this is his assertion that, prior to Sinai, Abraham was already keeping the civil laws.[101] It is clear that Bullinger does not intend that the *minutiae* of the civil or judicial laws of the Old Testament still apply to Christians. What is apparent is that Bullinger's exposition of the covenant provides a basis for the role of the Magistrate in Zurich alongside that of the ministers whose ministry parallels that of the Old Testament prophets. The Magistrate is directly referred to on folio 19v.

Bullinger makes a point, through a mini excursus, to examine some key Scriptures to deal with possible objections to his understanding of Law in the context of covenant. It is precisely in this context that Bullinger cites Romans 10:4 to the effect that Christ »is the fulfillment of the law for the justification for all who believe.« What has been abolished are the ceremonial aspects of the law. He specifically cites Deuteronomy 5 to make the point that the »circumstantial legalities« or the Torah in its details were given because of the threat of idolatry and apostasy but that they, nonetheless, »return to those ten words of the tablet of the covenant.«[102] Bullinger also addresses the charge that he is guilty of espousing a view of the Law similar to the Ebionites, i.e. that *sola fide* was insufficient and that, therefore, the Law must be kept. He thus underlines his doctrine »of the single and eternal covenant of God, and of the abrogation of legalities (*abrogatione legalium*).«[103] Bullinger chooses his terminology carefully. What has been abrogated is not the Law but the »legalities«.[104]

In the final section of *De testamento*, immediately prior to the Epilogue, Bullinger has a section on »The documents of the covenant« (*Tabulae testamenti conscribuntur*) in which Bullinger reiterates that the whole canon is the record of the covenant. In par-

[100] *Bullinger*, De testamento, 31r.
[101] *Bullinger*, De testamento, 18v–19r.
[102] *Bullinger*, De testamento, 38v.
[103] *Bullinger*, De testamento, 37v.
[104] »Gesetzesvorschriften«, Heinrich Bullinger Schriften, vol. 1, 88.

ticular, he draws the reader's attention to Psalm 19 and 2 Timothy 3.[105] Significantly, the second part of Psalm 19 is a focus on Torah in the context of God's revelation while 2 Timothy 3 emphasizes Scripture in the context of instruction and right living.

5.1 The conditions of the covenant

Most scholars, in our opinion, wrongly interpret Bullinger's reference to the »conditions« of the covenant. This is because they regard the covenant in Bullinger as a mutual pact where the two parties, the omnipotent God and horn of plenty on the one hand and mankind on the other, have conditions to fulfill for the covenant to be operating.[106] Others regard the fulfilling of the conditions as necessary for receiving the blessings of the covenant. For example, Lee contends that: »In short, testaments or covenants are legal documents that set forth a series of conditions and promised blessings. These conditions and blessings are the content of both testaments, the *substantia*, which remains unchanged despite the fact that the covenantal records, and the manner in which the substance is communicated, changes.«[107] However, as Bullinger makes it abundantly clear in *De testamento*, the covenant purely arises from God's initiative and is based purely on grace.

The »condition« of God is merely the affirmation of who God is: »I am the abundantly all-sufficient God, the horn of plenty«[108] which is encapsulated in His name, *El Shaddai*, revealed to Abraham. Although the term »condition« is used, the marginal comment clearly refers to God's promise of giving Himself.[109] The »conditions« of mankind are delineated in the section which has

[105] *Bullinger*, De testamento, 46v.

[106] For example, Scott A. *Gillies*, Origin of the Reformed Covenant 1524–7, in: Scottish Journal of Theology 54 (2001), 29f.: »As Baker has demonstrated, covenant thought, as it developed in Zurich, was in fact a bilateral conditional covenant stressing both God's and man's obligations towards one another in a pact.«

[107] Brian J. *Lee*, Johannes Cocceius and the Exegetical Roots of Federal Theology: Reformation Developments in the Interpretation of Hebrews 7–10, Göttingen 2009 (Reformed Historical Theology 7), 83.

[108] *Bullinger*, De testamento, 11v–12r: »Ego sum Deus omnisufficientia plenitudo et copiae cornu.«

[109] *Bullinger*, De testamento, 11v: »Promissionem Dei, et qualem se nobis hoc foedere offerat.«

the marginal heading »The offices of man and what is fitting for him.«[110] It is to be noted that in this context that Bullinger cites Deuteronomy 10:12 and Micah 6:8. In doing so, it is evident that Bullinger understands that what is required of men and women in covenant relationship with God is that they arrange their lives in every aspect according to his will. Significantly, both these passages cited by Bullinger focus on the importance of love as an act of the will as Israel's response or »condition« of the covenant. The Deuteronomy passage calls on Israel, who were about to enter the Promised Land, to love the God of the covenant while the Micah passage reminds Israel in the period of the monarchy that God desires love (*hesed*) from them. Bullinger goes on to state in a later section of the treatise that »love is the fountainhead of innocence and uprightness of life.«[111]

Furthermore, what is paramount for Israel in covenant relationship with *El Shaddai* is the heart. They are to rely utterly on God. This follows from Bullinger's understanding of *El Shaddai.* The reference to Deuteronomy 13:4 in folio 15v confirms the conclusion that Deuteronomy 18:15 underlies the inscription on title page of *De testamento*. Deuteronomy 18 commences with warnings of a »false« prophet. The coming of the true prophet referred to in Deuteronomy 18:15 was fulfilled with the coming of Christ. Since the apostles testify to this prophet, he thus continues to speak to men and women through the Scriptures. Hence men and women are called to »hear Him!« In a later section, Bullinger points out that »in the life of Christ, which the Gospels have described rather diligently as in a mirror so to speak, we see what we ought to follow or avoid, what pleases or displeases God.«[112] The message of Christ which descendants of Abraham through the ages must pay particular attention to is to live in a way to please God. As a man, Christ gave the example of how to live in a way pleasing to God, trusting in the provision of *El Shaddai*. This underlies Bullin-

[110] *Bullinger*, De testamento, 14v: »Officia hominis et quae ipsum deceant.«

[111] *Bullinger*, De testamento, 23v–24r. Cf. Oecolampadius who espoused the view that the eternal covenant with God with man was the law of love in his commentary of Isaiah. Diane M. *Poythress*, Johannes Oecolampadius' Exposition of Isaiah Chapters 36–37, Dissertation Westminster Theological Seminary, 1992, 546.

[112] *Bullinger*, De testamento, 23r.

ger's use of *placatus* rather than *placitus* on the title page, for the goal of the covenant is restored relationship between *El Shaddai* and His people which was achieved through Christ. In the context of this restored relationship the people of God are called to live to please him. Hence, in the Epilogue, Bullinger cites Noah, Enoch, Seth, Abel and Adam who (without Law) »pleased God through faith without circumcision.«[113]

The clearest reference to the Anabaptists in *De testamento* occurs when Bullinger points out: »For those people who consider only the conditions of the covenant and in fact disregard the grace and promise of God exclude infants from the covenant.«[114] In juxtaposing the »conditions« of the covenant with the grace and promise of God, it is evident that for Bullinger the *conditiones* of the *testamentum* and *foedus* with God cannot be equated with the conditions of human pacts, covenants, alliances, treaties or agreements. Indeed, Bullinger points out that the people of God in all ages are called »to walk in innocence of life *for his pleasure.*«[115] Bullinger also asserts that the »conditions« of the covenant were inscribed on the hearts of the patriarchs: »The Lord did not bother to have any records written for the ancient patriarchs, for they bore the covenant in their hearts, inscribed by the finger of God.«[116]

5.2 The ceremonies and the covenant

In contrast to the other reformers, what appears to be expressed only by Bullinger is to view a sort of hiatus between the patriarchal period and that ushered in by the coming of Christ with respect to the Law. For Bullinger, it appears not to be a case of progressive revelation *simpliciter* but, rather, »back to the future.« That is to say, the Law (understanding Torah as »instruction« rather than in a forensic sense) was already given in the time of Adam when it was written on the heart. But at the time of Moses the Law was

[113] *Bullinger*, De testamento, 48r: »qui sine circumcisione per fidem Deo placuerunt.«

[114] *Bullinger*, De testamento, 7v–8r: »Qui enim conditiones duntaxat foederis expendunt, gratiam vero et promissionem Dei negligunt, infantes foedere excludunt.«

[115] *Bullinger*, De testamento, 16r. Italics added.

[116] *Bullinger*, De testamento, 45r.

inscripturated (on tablets of stone) and given together with the ceremonies. With the coming of Christ the Law was once again written on the heart through the Holy Spirit. This time more clearly and the ceremonies were abolished. The Law that is written on the heart with the coming of Christ is the Torah of Christ and underlies *ipsum audite*.

What is abundantly clear is that Bullinger concludes that the »holy patriarchs« (Enoch, Noah, Abraham, Isaac, Jacob, Joseph) were pleasing to God without the »ceremonies«.[117] In citing Galatians 3:16–17 he affirms, »Hence the patriarchs were saved by the blessing of the covenant, not of the law or of the ceremonies.«[118] Significantly, Bullinger emphasizes at this point that the law which »originated 430 years later does not make void this covenant *established earlier by God in Christ.*«[119] In this sentence Bullinger is affirming the role of Christ in the covenant in the Old Testament era prior to his incarnation. Just as, for Bullinger, the New Testament can be viewed as case of 'back to the future' so the covenant in Old Testament times is rightly termed a »testament« because of its future fulfillment in the death, resurrection and ascension of Christ.

At the bottom of folio 28v Bullinger commences an explanation for the giving of the »ceremonies« (the Aaronic priesthood, laws for sacrifices and purification, food laws, instructions for the tabernacle etc). Precisely on folio 29v immediately after the insertion of the extra three sentences (*vide supra*) that refer to the covenant with Adam, Bullinger has an extended section on the institution of the Law[120] and the »ceremonies«. Bullinger's point is that because the Israelites had become corrupted by their time in Egypt with the result that they forgot the covenant with God and were falling more and more into idolatry that God came to »the aid of the collapsing covenant with certain supports.« The first »support« was the inscripturating of the original covenant by having its main points inscribed on tablets of stone by his own finger. The second »support« was the ceremonies which included *inter alia* guidelines

[117] *Bullinger*, De testamento, 29r.
[118] *Bullinger*, De testamento, 29r.
[119] *Bullinger*, De testamento, 29r. Italics added.
[120] The marginal comment is »Lex instituta«.

for worshipping God. Bullinger emphasizes that the patriarchs did not have these ceremonies. The ceremonies were added to the in-scripturation of the covenant to counteract the incipient danger of idolatry when Israel »continued to be unfaithful and wicked.«[121] Bullinger continues to explain that the giving of the Law and the ceremonies confirmed the covenant and, at the same time, God »enveloped the mystery of Christ in these ceremonies as types.«[122] The point being made by Bullinger is that when the »anti-type« has come to fulfill the types then the types are dispensed with. Thus Bullinger explains: »... all the ceremonies were fulfilled by Christ, whom alone it (i.e. the new covenant) proclaims. Since they were types and shadows of eternal things, they became obsolete.«[123] Bullinger further points out concerning the ceremonies that, in the sovereignty of God, they functioned as types and shadows of eternal things and they were »spiritual« in their own right. This is highlighted by Bullinger on folio 32r. Bullinger's point is that there were spiritual men and women in the Old Testament for whom the ceremonies had a spiritual significance. The carnal person, on the other hand, was the person »who depends on legalities without knowledge and without the spirit and who firmly believes that he can be saved through these legalities.«[124]

In perhaps one of the most enigmatic sentences of the treatise, Bullinger makes this following observation on the instructions for worship given together with the ceremonies: »Therefore, God instituted his own worship, and he declared that it was pleasing to him (Psalm 50), which he actually despised, so that, with this plan, he confirmed the covenant, and in addition to that he enveloped the mystery of Christ in these ceremonies as types.«[125] The point being made by Bullinger is that, to counteract the danger of falling into idolatry, God gave to Israel, through Moses, instructions for worship. The patriarchs had worshipped God without such instructions. Although this was not the worship God truly desired

[121] *Bullinger*, De testamento, 30r: »Verum dum isti infidels et perfidi esse pergerent.«

[122] *Bullinger*, De testamento, 30r.

[123] *Bullinger*, De testamento, 31v.

[124] *Bullinger*, De testamento, 32r.

[125] *Bullinger*, De testamento, 30r: »propria ergo instituit, eaque sibi placere pronunciavit, quae revera negligebat, ut vel ista ratione testamentum confirmaret, praeterea et Christi mysterium hisce velut typis involuret.«

from His people, nonetheless, he was able to use it to confirm the covenant and, at thc same time, employ them as types to be fulfilled and abolished in Christ.

One concrete example that illustrates Bullinger's understanding of Law and the ceremonies for the Christian is his understanding of the Sabbath. On the one hand, he affirms that the Decalogue still applies to believers in the new covenant as it was already written on the heart of the saints well before they were given to Moses. But on the other hand, in comparing believers in the new covenant with the Old Testament patriarchs he points out that »corporal circumcision did not exist with them, nor did the observance of the Sabbath (just as we do not observe it).«[126] Clearly Bullinger is referring to spiritual circumcision as opposed to physical circumcision and a spiritual observance of the Sabbath as opposed to a ceremonial observance of the Sabbath.

6. The sacrament of the covenant

In yet another example of God's accommodation to mankind in the covenant, Bullinger commences a section concerning circumcision as the sacrament of the covenant by stating »Deus sanguine foedus hoc dedicat«. Bullinger regards the blood shed through circumcision as finding its fulfillment in the death of Christ, the true seed of Abraham. Thus the blood that is shed in circumcision that sealed the old covenant, for Bullinger, foreshadows the blood of the cross. Bullinger states that, in giving circumcision as a proleptic sign of Christ, God »willed that the seed of Abraham itself be circumcised, signifying that the true seed of Abraham itself be circumcised, signifying that the true seed of Abraham, Christ the Lord, would confirm that covenant (*testamentum*) by his death and blood.«[127]

Bullinger cites the words of Jesus from Matthew 26:28 »Hic est sanguis meus, qui est novi testamenti« and, in doing so, states that »those signs which prefigured the future death of Christ had to be

[126] *Bullinger*, De testamento, 50v.
[127] *Bullinger*, De testamento, 43r.

changed and, in their place, signs substituted that, with their meaning, signify the completion of the most perfect justification.«[128] He further explains that Baptism and the Eucharist replaced circumcision and the Passover as sacraments of the new covenant.[129] Circumcision, therefore, was not only a sign of the covenant and a sign of God's grace for it also signified the binding of the faithful to God. It is because of this understanding that Bullinger is able to state: »... the entire covenant was contained in the sacrament of the covenant; in the same manner, the entire essence of the renewed covenant is contained in our sacraments, Baptism and the Eucharist.«[130]

On the basis of Jeremiah 4 and Romans 2 Bullinger points out that, from the beginning, with reference to »the true circumcision« there was reference to the spiritual seed of Abraham as opposed to the carnal seed who trusted »in their birth and circumcision, or, if you prefer, trusting in the flesh and in the ceremony of initiation and taking pride in external things.«[131] Bullinger, therefore, sees a »spiritual Israel« in Old Testament times who have been circumcised spiritually as opposed to »carnal Israel« whose circumcision was merely external. Although true spiritual circumcision was to be fulfilled in the age of the new covenant, Bullinger, nonetheless, viewed spiritual circumcision proleptically operating on the hearts of »spiritual Israel« in Old Testament times. He further outlines the folly of the carnal Jew as neglecting the basic conditions of the covenant while, at the same time glorifying in their election as the people of God because they are the physical descendants of Abraham.[132]

Significantly, Bullinger did not link circumcision with the Law. Circumcision was first and foremost a sign and seal of the covenant. In the old covenant God »offers himself« to Israel »out of sheer grace« and through circumcision binds the faithful to himself. Bullinger views that the whole extent of the old covenant was

[128] *Bullinger*, De testamento, 43v. We note here the link between circumcision and justification, clearly in the context of God's grace.

[129] *Bullinger*, De testamento, 43v.

[130] *Bullinger*, De testamento, 44r.

[131] *Bullinger*, De testamento, 9v.

[132] *Bullinger*, De testamento, 9r.

encapsulated in the sacrament of circumcision and that »entire essence of the renewed covenant« in contained in Baptism and the Eucharist.[133]

7. Bullinger's covenant terminology in »De testamento«

Because of the continued use of the Latin Bible in the early part of the 16th century Bullinger was careful with respect to his use of the terms for »covenant«. The terms *foedus*, *testamentum* and *pactum* were used interchangeably by Bullinger in *De testamento* though, at times, particular nuances may be intended.[134] Only a couple of years prior to *De testamento*, at a critical point of his ministry, Bullinger linked the terms *testamentum*, *pactum* and *foedus* in his *Karlstag* sermon (1532).[135] Moreover, in his commentary on Hebrews (1532) he writes: »Testamentum hoc, foedus et illud dei pactum est.«[136] It is not surprising, therefore, that on several occasions in *De testamento* Bullinger juxtaposes these Latin terms.[137]

An analysis of the use of the words that Bullinger used for »covenant« in *De testamento* and the *Decades* yielded the following results:

	De testamento	*Decades*
foedus	109	85
testamentum	59	57

[133] *Bullinger*, De testamento, 44r: »Ex quibus patet etiam sacramento foederis totum contineri foedus: quemadmodum et sacramentis nostris baptismo et eucharistia continetur innovati foederis ratio.«

[134] *Spijker*, Bullinger als Bundestheologe, 576; Joe *Mock*, The One and Eternal Covenant of God, in: John A. *Davies* / Allan M. *Harman* (eds.), An Everlasting Covenant: Biblical and Theological Essays in Honour of William J. Dumbrell, Doncaster 2010, 201–233.

[135] *Bullinger*, De prophetae officio, ivv–vr: »Testamenti enim voce pactum intelligimus foedus et conventionem, eam videlicet, qua Deus convenit cum universo mortalium genere.«

[136] Heinrich *Bullinger*, In piam et eruditam Pauli ad Hebraeos epistolam commentarius, Zurich: Christoph Froschauer the Elder, 1532 (BZD C 211), 82.

[137] *Bullinger*, De testamento, 4v: »in feriendo foedere vel testament institutione«; 24v: »testamentum sive foedus«; 37v: »foedus … pactum«; 45r: »foederis sive testamenti, de testamento seu foedere, foedus vel testamentum, foederis tabulas et testamentum«; 46v: »de testamento sive foedere«.

pactum	19	12
pactio	1	3
contractum	–	2
confoederatio	1	1
confoederatum	–	1
amicitia	1	1
compactio	–	1
pollicitatio	1	–
coniunctio	1	–

The weak disjunctive *seu* in *De testamento seu foedere Dei* indicates that Bullinger intended these terms to be interchangeable.[138] *De testamento* commences with Bullinger's understanding of the philological derivation and meaning of the terms *testamentum* and *foedus* in that order. Significantly, Bullinger has no discussion on *pactum*. Cocceius, on the other hand, clearly differentiated between *foedus* and *testamentum* as is evident from his *Summa doctrinae de foedere et testamento Dei* (Leiden, 1648).

An examination of Bullinger's use of *pactum* in *De testamento* reveals that Bullinger did use *pactum* on occasions to refer to the covenant between God and mankind.[139] However, in the majority of the cases when *pactum* was used in *De testamento*, Bullinger was quoting from the Latin Bible. On folio 38r Bullinger does have a sentence which reads: »Verbis pactus est cum Abraham dominus.«[140] But this is the perfect participle active of *paciscor* and is a (modified) quote from Oecolampadius' commentary on Jeremiah. In Bullinger's own translations of Scripture he often replaced *pactum* in the Vulgate with *foedus*.[141] Hence Strehle's comment that »the word pactum pervades both Bullinger's and the Franciscan's (i.e. Bonaventura) treatment of the covenant«[142] is manifestly off

[138] Furthermore, *testamentum* occurs before *foedus* in the title of the treatise.

[139] *Bullinger*, De testamento, 7v: »pacto«; 20r: »pactis«; 21v: »pactum«.

[140] Which *McCoy* and *Baker*, Fountainhead, 128 translate as: »The Lord made a pact with Abraham with words.« *Roth's* translation (Heinrich Bullinger Schriften, vol. 1, 88) has: »Mit Worten hat der Herr mit Abraham einen Bund geschlossen.«

[141] This can be illustrated from his translations of Isaiah 33:8; 55:3; Jeremiah 31:32; 31:33; 32:40; 33:20 (twice); 33:21; 33;25; 34:10 and 34:15.

[142] Stephen *Strehle*, Calvinism, Federalism, and Scholasticism: A Study of the Reformed Doctrine of Covenant, Bern et al. 1988, 147.

the mark. Bullinger chose to use *pactum* sparingly to minimize any reading of nominalist *pactum* theology into his works.

These references cited indicate the careful and deliberate way Bullinger used *testamentum*. Sometimes it was the word of choice for Bullinger while at other times it was interchangeable with *foedus*. Contrary to Lee, Bullinger was consistent in the use of the terms for covenant.[143] What is apparently striking in the use of the terms for »covenant« from the above word analysis of *De testamento* is Bullinger's preference for the term *foedus*, his relative frequent use of *testamentum* and the deliberately sparing use of *pactum*. This is clearly reflected in the title of the treatise – *De testamento seu foedere dei* – where the order is *testamentum* before *foedus*. Furthermore, a similar use of the terms for covenant by Bullinger is evident in the *Decades*. Indeed, Bullinger is consistent with his use of these terms in the *Studiorum ratio* (1527).[144]

A study of Bullinger's Swiss German version of *De testamento* – *Von dem einigen unnd ewigen testament oder pundt gottes* (1537) – reveals that Bullinger used *pundt* 158 times,[145] *testament* 73 times and *pact* one time. Significantly each time *pactum* is used in *De testamento* it is replaced by *pundt* in this work aimed at the wider audience rather than the academy. Another striking feature is that fact that Bullinger juxtaposed *pundt* with *testament* as many as 21 times.

Bullinger's use of the terms is somewhat distinct from that of Calvin's whose special focus on the covenant in the *Institutes* can be found in Book II, sections 10 and 11. A study of these sections reveals that Calvin used *foedus* 21 times,[146] *testamentum* 8 times[147] and *pactum* 3 times.[148] Despite Lillback's assertion that, for Cal-

[143] *Lee*, Johannes Cocceius, 31–37.

[144] Heinrich Bullinger Studiorum Ratio – Studienanleitung, ed. Peter Stotz, Zurich 1987, §20: »Deus caeli, Deus ille omnipotens pepigit cum humano genere testamentum, pactum seu foedus sempiternum.«

[145] This count includes *pundt* in compound nouns.

[146] The participle *foederatos* was used once at II.10.1.

[147] Not counting the occasions when the reference was directly to either the Old Testament or the New Testament. In Calvin's French edition of the Institutes (Geneva: Philbert Hamelin, 1554) *l'alliance* was used to translate both *foedus* and *testamentum* in II.10 and II.11.

[148] These three times occur in Calvin's citation of Jer 31:31–34 in the Vulgate. Bullinger, on the other hand, replaced *pactum* with *foedus* in his translation of Jer 31:31–34.

vin, *testamentum* is a true synonym for *foedus* and *pactum*, there appears to be no evidence for this in the *Institutes* II.10,11.[149]

The conclusions reached here, therefore, are at variance with those proposed by Hagen who sought to examine the use of *testamentum* by the early Luther.[150] Hagen's thesis is that there was a development from testament to covenant theology in the first quarter of the sixteenth century.[151] Some have suggested that Bullinger was influenced by Luther's use of the terms for »covenant« in his *De captivitate Babylonica ecclessiae praeludium (*1520).[152] Although Luther did juxtapose the terms *pactum*, *foedus* and *testamentum* on one occasion in this work,[153] it is apparent that, in the section that deals with »testament« or »covenant«, *foedus* is used only very sparingly.[154] Clearly, Luther did not view the terms *foedus* and *testamentum* as interchangeable. Bullinger's use of *testamentum*, however, reflects the usage by both Irenaeus[155] and Augustine[156] linked to his conviction that the saints in the old covenant had faith in Christ, in particular, proleptically in his death and resurrection.

8. Bullinger and Zwingli on the covenant

The vast majority of scholarly opinion is clearly of the view that Zwingli wrote about the covenant *before* Bullinger who subsequently followed Zwingli's lead and further developed the theme

149 *Lillback*, The Binding of God, has been influenced by Battles' footnote (n. 6) at II.11.4: »In this section and elsewhere Calvin uses the words *testamentum* and *foedus* interchangeably, as they are used in the Vulgate.« Institutes of the Christian religion, ed. John T. McNeill, transl. and indexed by Ford Lewis Battles, 2 vols, London/Philadelphia, PA 1960 (Library of Christian Classics 20–21).

150 Kenneth *Hagen*, A Theology of Testament in the Young Luther: The Lectures on Hebrews, Leiden 1974 (Studies in Medieval and Reformation Thought 12).

151 Kenneth *Hagen*, From Testament to Covenant in the Early Sixteenth Century, in: Sixteenth Century Journal 3/1 (1972), 1–24.

152 *Garcia Archilla*, The Theology of History, 11f.

153 D. Martin Luthers Werke: Kritische Gesammtausgabe [WA], vol. 6, Weimar 1888, 514.

154 *Testamentum* 23 times; *foedus* 3 times (WA 6, 513–518).

155 *Garcia Archilla*, De testamento, 69f., n. 53, cf. Joe *Mock*, Bullinger and the Covenant: New Insights, Dissertation Australian College of Theology, 2012, 167–179.

156 *Lillback*, The Binding of God, 38.

of the covenant.[157] The main hinge of this view is the contention of Cottrell that Bullinger himself in *Von warer und falscher leer* (1527) stated that, as a Josiah figure, Zwingli rediscovered the covenant.[158] However, in light of Bullinger's *Diarium* entry of 12 September 1524, it is abundantly clear that Bullinger was willing to be deliberately self-effacing in order to accentuate the positive contributions of Zwingli while seeking to downplay Zwingli's negative contributions. Indeed, it is apparent that Bullinger did not just follow Zwingli's lead and then develop the ideas that are presented in *De testamento*. As several scholars have noted, Bullinger did not refer to election in connection with the covenant as Zwingli had clearly done in his *In catabaptistarum strophas elenchus*.[159] Election appears to be only hinted at in *De testamento* through Bullinger's several references to »spiritual« Israel as the true seed of Abraham vis-à-vis »carnal« Israel. Lillback[160] has also contended that in *De testamento* Bullinger amplified Zwingli's outline based on Genesis 17 which is found in his *Antwort über Balthasar Hubmaiers Taufbüchlein*.[161] However, the outline that Lillback has constructed from Zwingli is so general that any comparison would be of limited value. As indicated above, Bullinger made a point of emphasizing the covenant with Adam in the 1537 version of *De testamento*. Examination of the covenant with Adam in both Zwingli and Bullinger suggests that Bullinger was prior to Zwingli with respect to the covenant and influenced Zwingli rather than *vice versa*.[162]

With respect to the terms for »covenant«, Zwingli states in an earlier work, *Auslegen und Gründe der Schlußreden* (1523), that

[157] *Garcia Archilla*, De testamento, 676; *Opitz*, Heinrich Bullinger als Theologe, 317, 320f.; Gottlob *Schrenk*, Gottesreich und Bund in älteren Protestantismus vornehmlich bei Johannes Coccejus, Gütersloh 1923, 40.

[158] Jack Warren *Cottrell*, Is Bullinger the source for Zwingli's doctrine of the covenant? in: Heinrich Bullinger 1504–1575: Gesammelte Aufsätze zum 400. Todestag, eds. Ulrich Gäbler and Erland Herkenrath, Zurich 1975, 75–83, 338f.

[159] Z 6/1, 172–184.

[160] *Lillback*, The Binding of God, 113; Peter A. *Lillback*, The Early Reformed Covenant Paradigm, in: Peter Martyr Vermigli and the European Reformations: Semper Reformanda, ed. Frank A. James III, Leiden 2004 (Studies in the History of Christian Traditions 115), 72f.

[161] Z 4, 638.

[162] *Mock*, Covenant with Adam, 185–205.

»*Testamentum, pactum* and *foedus* are often used interchangeably in scripture. But *testamentum* is used most often. We therefore refer to it here. It means ›legacy‹, but it is also used to mean ›agreement‹ or ›covenant‹ ...«[163] A few lines later on Zwingli juxtaposed several German terms for »covenant«.[164] Locher assumed that Zwingli was influenced by Budaeus for his developing an understanding of the covenant.[165] Nonetheless, although Zwingli may have been influenced by Budaeus philologically with respect to the use of the Latin words for »covenant« as the use of these terms were in a state of flux at the beginning of the 16th century, it is proposed here that Zwingli was influenced by Bullinger for the theological understanding of both Latin and German terms for »covenant«.

An examination of Zwingli's works reveals that in *Von der Taufe* (May 1525) he juxtaposes *pact* and *pflicht*.[166] *In subsidium sive coronis de eucharistia* (August 1525) *pactum* and *foedus* are juxtaposed,[167] *foedus* and *testamentum* are juxtaposed (four times)[168] while *testamentum*, *foedus* and *pactum* occur together on one occasion.[169] In *Antwort über Balthasar Hubmaiers Taufbüchlein* (November 1525) *pundt* and *testament* are juxtaposed (four times)[170] while *pundt* and *pflicht* are juxtaposed (two times).[171] In *De peccato originali declaratio ad Urbanum Rhegium* (August 1526) *foedus* and *testamentum* are interchangeable.[172] In *Amica*

[163] Huldrych Zwingli Writings Volume One: In Search of True Religion. Reformation, Pastoral and Eucharistic Writings, eds. Edward J. *Furcha* and H. Wayne *Pipkin*, Allison Park, PA 1984, 107. This is part of a commentary on the eighteenth article. The text reads (Z 2, 131): »Testamentum, pactum und foedus wirdt in der geschrifft offt für einandren gebrucht, doch würt testamentum aller meist gebruchet, der maß es uns hie dienet, und heißt ein erbgmächt; wirt aber ouch gebrucht für ein pundt oder verstand, so man pfligt mit einandren ze machen umb frydens willen.«

[164] »Pundt«, »testament« and »verpüntnus«.

[165] Gottfried. W. *Locher*, Zwingli's Thought: New Perspectives, Leiden 1981 (Studies in the History of Christian Thought 25), 219.

[166] Z 4, 227.

[167] Z 4, 499.

[168] Z 4, 500f.

[169] Z 4, 501: »Hoc autem testamentum, foedus aut pactum morte ac sanguine Christi partum esse.«

[170] Z 4, 604, 621, 637.

[171] Z 4, 630, 631.

[172] Z 5, 386.

Exegesis, id est: expositio eucharistiae negocii ad Martinum Lutherum (February 1527) Zwingli juxtaposes *testamentum* and *foedus*[173] as well as *testamentum* and *pactum*.[174] *Testamentum* is by far the term of choice for Zwingli in this work.[175] In the Third Part of *In catabaptistarum strophas elenchus* (July 1527) which focuses on the covenant and election, Zwingli uses *foedus* 36 times, *testamentum* 36 times while *pactum* does not even occur once. Furthermore, *foedus* and *testamentum* are juxtaposed five times.[176] What is somewhat intriguing is that in the first part of this section[177] *foedus* is predominantly used while *testamentum* occurs more often in the second section.[178] In both the *Fidei ratio* (July 1530)[179] and *De convitiis Eckii* (August 1530)[180] *foedus* was the word of choice for Zwingli.

These data reveal some subtle differences between Zwingli and Bullinger. Firstly, through his continued use of *pflicht*, Zwingli emphasizes the response of the believer to the covenant. This goes in tandem with his understanding of *sacramentum*. Secondly, notwithstanding his declaration in the *Auslegen* with respect to the terms for »covenant«, Zwingli does not really use the terms *foedus* and *testamentum* as interchangeable in his works, although he does juxtapose them on occasions. Bullinger, on the other hand, places more emphasis on the sacraments as signs and seals of God's grace and his initiative. Indeed, he points out that circumcision points to God binding the elect to himself. Furthermore, throughout his works from the *Studiorum ratio* (1527) onwards, Bullinger was consistent with the use of *foedus* and *testamentum* which he viewed as interchangeable.

173 Z 5, 746.
174 Z 5, 746.
175 In Z 5, 745f. *Testamentum* is used 26 times, *foedus* two times and *pactum* one time.
176 Z 6/1, 155, 161, 164f.
177 Z 6/1, 155–163.
178 Z 6/1, 164–172.
179 Z 6/2, 803.
180 Z 6/3, 254.

9. Conclusion

De testamento is a biblical theological and a biblical historical treatise in which Bullinger cites many biblical and theological themes. Far from being a work that only focuses on the covenant, on the contrary, *De testamento* reveals Bullinger as a biblical theologian who is committed to challenge the elect to live *integer* before the sovereign *El Shaddai*. Bullinger is consistent in his use for the terms for »covenant« which differentiates him from Zwingli. This indicates a measure of independence from Zwingli in his understanding of the covenant.

Joe Mock, Rev. Dr., Sydney

Abstract: De testamento is a both theological and a historically biblical treatise in which Bullinger discusses themes such as, for example, justification by faith, God's accommodation to mankind, the covenant as the subject or focus of all Scripture, the covenant with Adam, the unity of the Old and New Testaments, the seed of Abraham, the covenant and right living, the Holy Spirit and covenant, the Law and covenant, the conditions of covenant, the ceremonies of covenant and the sacrament of the covenant. Far from being a work that only focuses on the covenant *De testamento* reveals Bullinger as a biblical theologian who is committed to challenge the elect to live *integer* before the sovereign El Shaddai. An examination of the Latin terms for »covenant« (*foedus*, *testamentum* and *pactum*) reveals that, for Bullinger, the terms are interchangeable. However, he avoids using *pactum* lest pactum theology be read into his work. His use of the terms are more consistent than that of Zwingli which indicates a measure of independence from Zwingli in his understanding of the covenant.

Keywords: Heinrich Bullinger, Covenant, Biblical Theology, Salvation History

ISSN 0254-4407 – Zwingliana 40 (2013), 37–71

Briefe an Heinrich Bullinger im Blick auf Entstehung, Abfassung und Rezeption der »Confessio Raetica« (1552/53)

Jan-Andrea Bernhard

1. Einleitung

Als ich im Rahmen der Abfassung eines Beitrages über die Bündner Reformation wieder einmal die älteste Handschrift der *Confessio Raetica* (1552/53) im Synodal- und Kirchenratsarchiv in Chur konsultierte,[1] bin ich auf einen Brief gestoßen, der mir bislang unbekannt war. Philipp Gallicius, der Verfasser der *Confessio Raetica*, legte nämlich im Juli 1555 der Synode eine Abschrift der *Con-*

[1] Vgl. Fides ac Placita synodi Evangelium Christi in Tribus Rhetiae foederibus praedicantium [...], Chur Synodal- und Kirchenratsarchiv [Chur SKA], B 1, 1–84, ediert in: Eberhard *Busch*, Confessio Raetica von 1552/1553, in: Reformierte Bekenntnisschriften, hg. von Heiner Faulenbach et al., Bd. 1/3: 1550–1558, Neukirchen-Vluyn 2007, 256–275; vgl. Emil *Camenisch*, Die Confessio Raetica: Ein Beitrag zur bündnerischen Reformationsgeschichte, in: Jahrbuch der Historischen Gesellschaft von Graubünden 43 (1914), 223–259; Die Lehrartikel der Confessio raetica von 1552, in: Die Bekenntnisschriften der reformierten Kirchen, hg. von Ernst Friedrich Karl Müller, Leipzig 1903, 163–170; vgl. Ulrich *Pfister*, Konfessionskirchen, Glaubenspraxis und Konflikt in Graubünden, 16.–18. Jahrhundert, Würzburg 2012 (Religion und Politik 1), 122f. 129f.; Werner *Graf*, Die Ordnung der Evangelischen Kirche in Graubünden von der Reformation bis 1980, in: Jahrbuch der Historischen Gesellschaft von Graubünden 112 (1982), 21–25, 29f.; Wilhelm *Jenny*, Johannes Comander: Lebensgeschichte des Reformators der Stadt Chur, 2 Bde., Chur 1969–1970, hier Bd. 2, 392–398; Jakob Rudolf *Truog*, Aus der Geschichte der evangelisch-rätischen Synode 1537–1937, Chur 1937, 14–23.

fessio Raetica vor, eingetragen in einem in Leder gefassten Band in Quartformat, dem ältesten im Synodal- und Kirchenratsarchiv erhaltenen Band.[2] Der Niederschrift der *Confessio*, umfassend die *Fides synodi* und die *Placita synodi*, ordnete Gallicius allerdings den die Hintergründe der Abfassung der *Confessio* schildernden Brief Comanders und Gallicius' an Bullinger vom 22. April 1553 vor;[3] dem Text der *Confessio* folgt schließlich der mir bislang unbekannte Brief Gallicius' an Bullinger vom 2. September 1553.[4] Daran fügte Gallicius weiter eine, wohl erst 1555 verfasste, mit dem Synodalgelübde endende *Epitome necessarissimorum articulorum*, d.h. eine Zusammenfassung der zentralen Artikel aus der *Confessio Raetica* bei, auf die sich die Kandidaten zu verpflichten hatten.[5] Dann folgen die einzelnen handschriftlichen Einträge sämtlicher Geistlichen, die in die Synode aufgenommen worden sind, beginnend mit Comander und Gallicius.[6]

Eine Kontrolle in der Kartei der Heinrich Bullinger-Briefwechseledition ergab ein interessantes Bild. Kurt Jakob Rüetschi, ehemaliger Mitarbeiter an der Heinrich Bullinger-Briefwechseledition, hielt auf der Verweiskarte fest, dass Emil Camenisch in seinem Beitrag zur *Confessio Raetica* diesen Brief vom 2. September 1553 erwähne und dabei auf das Matrikelbuch der Synode (1555–1761) verweise; gemäß Camenisch hat Gallicius diesem Brief an Bullinger auch die definitive Fassung der *Confessio* beigelegt.[7] Rüetschi schreibt aber weiter: »Ein Brief vom 2. September 1553 würde zwar gut passen in der Abfolge der Briefe an Bullinger von Gallicius (z.T. mit Comander) über die rätische Konfession und Synodal-/Kirchenordnung vom 22. April, 6. Juni, 4. Juli, 19. August

[2] »Descriptus est hic liber Capitulo nostro mense Iulio annj. 1555.« (Notiz von Philipp Gallicius, Chur SKA, B 1, 88).

[3] Vgl. Johannes Comander und Philipp Gallicius an Heinrich Bullinger, 22. April 1553, Chur SKA, B 1, 2r–5r.

[4] Vgl. Philipp Gallicius an Heinrich Bullinger, 2. September 1553, Chur SKA, B 1, 86–87.

[5] Vgl. Epitome necessarissimorum articulorum quos pro catholicis tenemus exigimusque ab omnibus Dominum Jesum praedicare volentibus, Chur SKA, B 1, 93–96 (= *Camenisch*, Confessio Raetica, 259f.).

[6] Vgl. Matricula synodalis, Chur SKA, B 1, 96. Diese Praxis wird bis auf den heutigen Tag fortgesetzt, so dass die lückenlose Synodalmatrikel seit 1555 erhalten ist.

[7] Vgl. *Camenisch*, Confessio Raetica, 228f.

1553 [...]; aber vielleicht[8] doch Irrtum für: Comander und Gallicius an Bullinger, Chur, 22. April 1553. [...] Hat sich Camenisch verlesen und damit einen Phantom-Brief erfunden? (Vermutlich ja).«[9]

Die Vermutung von Rüetschi kann nun allerdings, nach dem Fund des Briefes vom 2. September 1553, nicht mehr als richtig erkannt werden, zumal Camenisch selbst bereits in seinem Aufsatz eine Rohübersetzung des Briefes von Gallicius angefertigt hat.[10] Der Vergleich des Briefes aus dem Matrikelbuch und der Übersetzung von Camenisch belegt einwandfrei, dass es sich um denselben Brief handelt. Freilich hatten die derzeitigen und früheren Mitarbeiter der Heinrich Bullinger-Briefwechseledition bislang keine gesicherte Kenntnis von der Existenz dieses Briefes, geschweige denn war der Text des Briefes bekannt. Haben ihn doch, gewissermaßen als Anhang der ungleich wichtigeren *Confessio Raetica*, auch andere Forscher übersehen, so dass er in Vergessenheit geraten ist.[11] Gar der bedeutende Kirchenhistoriker Petrus Domenicus Rosius à Porta, der als erster die *Confessio* auf der Grundlage der Handschrift aus dem Matrikelbuch in seiner *Historia Reformationis Raeticarum Ecclesiarum* (Chur/Lindau 1771) gedruckt hat,[12] hat diesen Brief übersehen, währenddem er Dutzende andere Briefe – darunter auch denjenigen vom 22. April 1553 – in seinem monumentalen Werk *in extenso*, andere immerhin auszugsweise gedruckt hat.[13]

Diese Umstände haben mich bewogen, nachdem ich mit dem Leiter der Heinrich Bullinger-Briefwechseledition, Herrn Dr. Rein-

[8] Darüber geschrieben: »wahrscheinlich«.

[9] Notizen von Kurt Jakob Rüetschi auf Verweiskarte zum Brief vom 2. September 1553, Zürich: Heinrich Bullinger-Briefwechseledition, Briefwechselkartei.

[10] Vgl. Philipp Gallicius an Heinrich Bullinger, 2. September 1553, in: *Camenisch*, Confessio Raetica, 257 (deutsche, paraphrasierende Übersetzung).

[11] Eine löbliche Ausnahme bildet dabei Eberhard Busch, der in seiner vor einigen Jahren erschienen kritischen Edition der *Confessio Raetica* auf den Brief gestoßen ist und gleichfalls daraus zitiert (vgl. *Busch*, Confessio Raetica, 249, 253).

[12] Vgl. Petrus Dominicus Rosius *de Porta*, Historia Reformationis Ecclesiarum Raeticarum ex genuinis fontibus et adhuc maximam partem numquam impressis sine partium studio deducta, Bd. I/2, Chur/Lindau 1771, 197–224.

[13] Vgl. Jan-Andrea *Bernhard*, Rosius à Porta (1734–1806): Ein Leben im Spannungsfeld von Orthodoxie, Aufklärung und Pietismus, Zürich 2005 (Zürcher Beiträge zur Reformationsgeschichte 22), 512f.

hard Bodenmann, Rücksprache gehalten habe, diesen bislang unbekannten Brief in dem größeren Zusammenhang der Entstehung der *Confessio Raetica* zu publizieren. In Anbetracht dessen, dass in den jüngsten Studien, in denen die *Confessio Raetica* thematisiert wird,[14] verschiedene Angaben vorliegen, die die Informationen aus den Briefen im Vorfeld bzw. im Zusammenhang mit der Abfassung der *Confessio Raetica* nicht berücksichtigen, ja teilweise denselben geradezu widersprechen, ist es sinnvoll, auch fünf andere Briefe an Bullinger zu edieren. Die der Edition vorangestellte Einführung thematisiert freilich nur die einzelnen Entwicklungsschritte der Entstehung, Abfassung und Rezeption der *Confessio Raetica* und nicht alle in den Briefen angesprochenen Themenbereiche.[15]

2. Entstehung, Abfassung und Rezeption der »Confessio Raetica«

Es ist in der Forschung seit langem bekannt, dass aus Anlass der Wiedereinführung der heiligen Inquisition (1542)[16] eine große Anzahl italienischer Humanisten und reformatorisch Gesinnter, wollten sie nicht widerrufen oder fortan als Nikodemit leben, Italien verlassen hat und in die Südtäler der Drei Bünde, wozu auch die Untertanenlanden (Veltlin, Grafschaften Chiavenna und Bormio) gehörten, geflohen ist und daselbst gewirkt hat.[17] Abgesehen von sogenannten Konformisten wie Agostino Mainardo, Pier Paolo

[14] Vgl. *Pfister*, Konfessionskirchen, 121–131; *Busch*, Confessio Raetica, 252f.

[15] Letztere werden im Anmerkungsapparat zu den einzelnen Briefen in aller gebotenen Kürze thematisiert.

[16] Die heilige Inquisition, die *Sacra Congregatio Romanae et universalis Inquisitionis*, wurde am 4. Juli 1542 von Papst Paul III. mit der Bulle *Liceat ab initio* wieder eingeführt (vgl. Gerd *Schwerhoff*, Die Inquisition: Ketzerverfolgung in Mittelalter und Neuzeit, München 2004, 98).

[17] Vgl. Conradin *Bonorand*, Reformatorische Emigration aus Italien in die Drei Bünde: Ihre Auswirkungen auf die kirchlichen Verhältnisse – ein Literaturbericht, Chur 2000 (Beiheft zum Bündner Monatsblatt 9), 39–105, 136–188; Antonio *Rotondò*, Studi di storia ereticale del Cinquecento, Bd. 2, Florenz 2008 (Studi e testi per la storia religiosa del Cinquecento 15), 403–442; George Hunston *Williams*, The Radical Reformation, Kirksville, MO ³2000 (Sixteenth Century Essays and Studies Series 15), 835–896; Manfred E. *Welti*, Kleine Geschichte der italienischen Reformation, Gütersloh 1985 (Schriften des Vereins für Reformationsgeschichte 193), 91–95.

Vergerio, Girolamo Zanchi oder Scipione Lentolo ist dabei auch an zahlreiche sogenannte Nonkonformisten – oft waren sie dies gar nicht, doch ihr Bibelhumanismus und ihre tolerante Haltung machte sie des Nonkonformismus verdächtig – zu denken, die in die Drei Bünde geflohen sind und ein vorübergehendes oder längeres Exil gefunden haben: Francesco Negri, Francesco Calabrese, Camillo Renato, Lelio Sozzini, Ludovico Fieri, Bernardino Ochino, Pietro Leonie, Giambattista Bovio, Marcello Squarcialupi, Mino Celsi und andere. Gemeinsam ist allen diesen reformatorischen Emigranten, dass sie einen nicht unwesentlichen Beitrag zur Annahme der Reformation in verschiedenen Gemeinden der bündnerischen Südtäler geleistet haben.[18] Hintergrund der Möglichkeit ihres Wirkens war vor allem die »demokratisch-föderalistische« Staatsform im Dreibündestaat, deren Ursprung in den Ilanzer Artikelbriefen (1524/1526) begründet lagen, die den Gemeinden unter anderem das Recht einräumten, ihre Geistlichen zu wählen und zu entlassen.[19] Mit diesem komunalen Recht waren die Kompetenzen des Bischofs bzw. des Landesherrn empfindlich beschnitten. Faktisch hieß dies nämlich, dass nicht mehr der Landesherr oder die Bundeshäupter, sondern die Gemeinden über die Religion frei bestimmten. Die Artikelbriefe waren einer der wesentlichen Gründe, warum die Drei Bünde seit dem 16. Jahrhundert konfessionell paritätisch waren.[20]

Die »demokratisch-föderalistische« Staatsform wurde von den italienischen Emigranten ganz besonders geschätzt, wie Pier Paolo Vergerio, der ehemalige Bischof von Capodistria,[21] der unter dem

[18] Vgl. Peter *Dalbert*, Die Reformation in den italienischen Talschaften Graubündens nach dem Briefwechsel Bullingers: Ein Beitrag zur Geschichte der Reformation in der Schweiz, Zürich 1948; Jan-Andrea *Bernhard*, Zwischen Gewissensfreiheit und Inquisition: Der Beitrag italienischer Nonkonformisten zur Konfessionsbildung in den Drei Bünden (Graubünden mit Untertanenlanden), erscheint in: Reformed Majorities and Minorities in Early Modern Europe, hg. von Herman J. Selderhuis, Göttingen 2013.

[19] Vgl. Martin *Bundi*, Gewissensfreiheit und Inquisition im rätischen Alpenraum: Demokratischer Staat und Gewissensfreiheit. Von der Proklamation der »Religionsfreiheit« zu den Glaubens- und Hexenverfolgungen im Freistaat der Drei Bünde (16. Jahrhundert), Bern 2003, 27–34, 259f.

[20] Vgl. Immaculata *Saulle Hippenmeyer*, Nachbarschaft, Pfarrei und Gemeinde in Graubünden 1400–1600, Chur 1997 (Quellen und Forschungen zur Bündner Geschichte 7), 176–181.

[21] Zu Pier Paolo Vergerio: *Bonorand*, Emigration, 96–98; Pier Paolo Vergerio il Gio-

Eindruck des Todes von Francesco Spiera (gest. 1548) dem alten Glauben absagte und 1549 in die italienischen Talschaften Bündens zog,[22] in seiner Schrift *Del battesimo e de fiumi che nascono ne paesi de signori Grisoni* ([Poschiavo] 1550) betont. Die Gewissensfreiheit sei ein Rettungsanker für die nach Freiheit dürstenden Italiener: Während die erwachende Botschaft in Italien behindert und verfolgt werde, könne sie sich hier in den hohen Bergen sicher und ruhig entfalten, frei von allen Inquisitoren und Verwaltern von Aberglauben und Finsternis.[23] Gleichzeitig provozierten mehrere italienische Flüchtlinge wegen ihres libertinischen Gedankengutes zahlreiche Auseinandersetzungen, so dass die im Jahre 1537 gegründete Synode, der der Bundstag das Recht übertragen hatte, denjenigen Geistlichen, der in seinem Amte in der Lehre oder in seinem Leben als »ergerlich und unerber erfunden« würde, zu ermahnen, zu verweisen, allenfalls zu suspendieren oder gar auszuschließen,[24] vor außerordentlich großen Herausforderungen stand.

vane, un polemista attraverso l'Europa del Cinquecento, hg. von Ugo Rozzo, Udine 2000; Salvatore *Caponetto*, La Riforma protestante nell' Italia del Cinquecento, Turin 1997, 173–187; Silvano *Cavazza*, Pier Paolo Vergerio nei Grigioni e in Valtellina (1549–1553), in: Riforma e società nei Grigioni: Valtellina e Valchiavenna tra '500 e '600, hg. von Alessandro Pastore, Mailand 1991, 33–62; Angelika *Hauser*, Pietro Paolo Vergerios protestantische Zeit, Tübingen 1980; Anne *Jacobson Schutte*, Pier Paolo Vergerio: The Making of an Italian Reformer, Genf 1977 (Travaux d'Humanisme et Renaissance 160); *Dalbert*, Reformation, 87–107. Für das Curriculum von Vergerio sind immer noch Schiess' Ausführungen, basierend auf Bullingers Korrespondenz mit den Bündnern, richtungsweisend (vgl. Traugott *Schiess*, Bullingers Korrespondenz mit den Graubündnern, 3 Bde., Basel 1904–1906 [Quellen zur Schweizer Geschichte 23–35], hier Bd. 1, LXXI–LXXXIII).

[22] Vgl. Daniele *Walker*, Pier Paolo Vergerio (1498–1565) e il »Caso Spiera« (1548), in: Studi di teologia: Rivista teologica semestrale 19/1 (1998), 7–56.

[23] Vgl. Pier Paolo *Vergerio*, Del battesimo e de fiumi che nascono ne paesi de signori Grisoni, [Poschiavo] 1550, A6v–A7r. Auch vom Kirchenhistoriker Rosius à Porta wurden diese freiheitlichen Strukturen – er gebraucht die Ausdrücke »libertatis conscientiae diploma« und »fundamentalem Democratiae legem« (vgl. *De Porta*, Historia, Bd. 1/1, 146; Bd. I/2, 37) – als wichtige Voraussetzung für die Immigration reformatorischer Flüchtlinge aus Italien gewürdigt und als für die Entwicklung der reformierten Kirche Bündens befruchtend gewertet (vgl. *Bernhard*, Rosius à Porta, 332–334, 348–350).

[24] Weiter wurde in der Gründungsurkunde der Synode vom 14. Januar 1537 festgehalten, dass die Synode berechtigt sei, fremde Prädikanten, die ins Land zögen und sich hier niederließen, zu verhören und zu prüfen, »ob sy gschickt gnugsam in der leer«. Der Bundstag hatte der Synode also das Recht der Rezeptions- und Zensurgewalt übertragen (vgl. Gründungsurkunde der Synode, 14. Januar 1537, in: *Truog*, Geschichte, 11).

In vielen Briefen Comanders, Gallicius' und anderer an Bullinger, Gwalther oder Simler wurde seit den 1540er Jahren die theologische Haltung italienischer Emigranten regelmäßig thematisiert.[25]

Aufgrund mehrerer Klagen und heftiger Auseinandersetzungen betreffend Tätigkeit der italienischen Emigranten in den Südtälern, die verschiedene Lehren vertraten (Spiritualisten, Antitrinitarier, Täufer, usw.), verfügte der Bundstag am 1. November 1552 in Davos nach dem Eingang der Gemeindemehren, dass Privaten im Veltlin die Beschäftigung von reformatorischen Lehrern und Prädikanten gestattet sei, sofern diese von der Synode rezipiert seien. Zudem hätten die Prädikanten und Lehrer zur jährlichen Zusammenkunft der Synode zu erscheinen, über ihr Leben und ihre Lehre Rechenschaft abzulegen und den Beschlüssen der Synode (Zensur, Suspension, usw.) nachzukommen.[26] Vergerio meldete noch gleichentags den Beschluss des Bundstages an Bullinger, sehr erfreut darüber, dass der Aufenthalt reformatorischer Prediger im Veltlin nun offiziell erlaubt sei.[27] Diese frohe Kunde und die bundstägliche Ermahung, dass alle Prädikanten und Lehrer an der Synode teilzunehmen hätten, mögen Vergerio auch bewogen haben, an der nach dem Bundstag einberufenen Synode teilzunehmen, obwohl er gegenüber Bullinger am 3. März desselben Jahres festgehalten hatte, dass er an der Synode nicht mehr teilnehmen wolle.[28] Bereits am 15. November meldete er an Bullinger, dass er zwar nach der Sy-

[25] Vgl. *Schiess*, Korrespondenz, Bd. 1, 40–150 et passim.

[26] Vgl. Abschied der zu Davos versammelten Ratsboten Gemeiner III Bünde, 1. November 1552, in: Materialien zur Standes- und Landesgeschichte Gem. III. Bünde (Graubünden) 1464–1803, hg. von Fritz Jecklin, Bd. 2: Texte, Basel 1909, 246f. (= *Bundi*, Gewissensfreiheit, 272f.).

[27] Vgl. Pier Paolo Vergerio an Heinrich Bullinger, 1. November 1552, in: *Schiess*, Korrespondenz, Bd. 1, Nr. 195.

[28] Vgl. Pier Paolo Vergerio an Heinrich Bullinger, 3. März 1552, in: *Schiess*, Korrespondenz, Bd. 1, Nr. 180. Hintergrund dessen war, dass Vergerios »eigenwillige Vorgehensweise« – unter anderem wollte er in den Südtälern eine eigenständige Synode gründen – bei den Churer Pfarrern zu etwelchem Ärgernis Anlass gab; im Laufe des Jahres 1552 fand also eine Entfremdung zwischen den Churer Pfarrern und Vergerio statt, welche sich in der Korrespondenz mit Bullinger reichhaltig niederschlug (vgl. Philipp Gallicius an Heinrich Bullinger, 23. und 29. Februar 1552, in: *Schiess*, Korrespondenz, Bd. 1, Nr. 177 und 179; Johannes Comander an Heinrich Bullinger, 5. April 1552, in: *Schiess*, Korrespondenz, Bd. 1, Nr. 181 et passim); vgl. *Pfister*, Konfessionskirchen, 122; *Dalbert*, Reformation, 92–94; *Schiess*, Korrespondenz, Bd. 1, XXVIf. LXXVIf.

node, welche in Chur stattfinde, zuerst noch nach Vicosoprano zurückkehren müsse, zwecks Erledigung dringender Geschäfte, schließlich aber bald nach Zürich kommen möchte. Die Synode habe viele Geschäfte zu erledigen, unter anderem gehe es auch darum, dass Camillo Renato aus den Drei Bünden ausgewiesen werden solle.[29] Weitere Details zu den Verhandlungen der Synode, die mindestens bis am 20. November gedauert hatte,[30] meldete Vergerio nicht. Allerdings wissen wir aus einem späteren Brief an Bullinger, welchen bedeutenden Beschluss die Synode gefällt und welchen Auftrag sie erteilt hatte. Der Münstertaler Philipp Gallicius (1504–1566), der spätestens seit 1526 dem reformatorischen Lager angehörte und seit 1551 in Chur an der Regulakirche wirkte,[31] wandte sich nämlich, auch im Namen von Johannes Comander, am 12. Dezember an Bullinger. Darin hielt er fest, dass den Velt-

[29] Vgl. Pier Paolo Vergerio an Heinrich Bullinger, 15. November 1552, unten S. 55, Brief 1. Camillo Renato, der 1542 in die Untertanenlande der Drei Bünde geflohen war und sich in Tirano, Caspano und andernorts als Hauslehrer betätigt hatte, forderte seit 1545 in Chiavenna, wegen seiner nonkonformistischen Haltung in der Sakramentsfrage und anderen Bereichen, Mainardo heraus, was zu einer offenen Auseinandersetzung führte, so dass Renato, nach einer Visitation von Johannes Blasius im Veltlin anfangs September 1547, auf die Umstände in Chiavenna aufmerksam geworden, 1548 vor die Synode zitiert worden war; schließlich wurde er von der reformierten Gemeinde in Chiavenna 1550 exkommuniziert, hielt sich aber, nach einer vorübergehenden Festnahme in Bergamo, weiterhin in den Untertanenlanden auf (vgl. Heinrich Bullinger Briefwechsel [HBBW], Bd. 12, Zürich 2006, 242; *Pfister*, Konfessionskirchen, 110, 120–122; Jan-Andrea *Bernhard*, Francesco Negri zwischen konfessionellen und geographischen Grenzen, in: Zwingliana 37 (2010), 109–111; George Hunston *Williams*, Camillo Renato, in: Italian Reformation: Studies in Honour of Laelius Socinus, hg. von John A. Tedeschi, Florenz 1965, 160–180; Delio *Cantimori*, Italienische Häretiker der Spätrenaissance, Basel 1949, 64–72; *Dalbert*, Reformation, 58–85). Dank des Briefwechsels von Mainardo, Renato, Negri und Vergerio mit Bullinger sind wir über die komplexen Beziehungen und Vorgänge relativ genau unterrichtet (vgl. *Schiess*, Korrespondenz, Bd. 1, 112–291; Camillo *Renato*, Opere: Documenti e testimonianze, hg. von Antonio Rotondò, Florenz 1968 (Corpus Reformatorum Italicorum), 159–163, 205–259).

[30] Vergerio schreibt nämlich am 20. November noch aus Chur an Bullinger, bevor er nach Vicosoprano zurückkehrt, woher er am 30. November erneut an Bullinger schreibt (vgl. *Schiess*, Korrespondenz, Bd. 1, Nr. 195/3–4).

[31] Zu Philipp Gallicius: HBBW, Bd. 7, Zürich 1998, 170f.; Conradin *Bonorand*, Die Engadiner Reformatoren Philipp Gallicius, Jachiam Tütschett Bifrun und Durich Chiampell: Voraussetzungen und Möglichkeiten ihres Wirkens aus der Perspektive der Reformation im allgemeinen, Chur 1987, 52–60; *Schiess*, Korrespondenz, Bd. 1, XIX–XXXVII; Traugott *Schiess*, Philipp Gallicius (1504–1566): Ein Lebensbild, Chur 1904. Bis heute ist eine umfassende Untersuchung zu Gallicius ein Desiderat der Forschung.

linern nun reformatorische Prediger und Lehrer anzustellen erlaubt worden sei. An der Synode sei weiter über Renato verhandelt worden, ja gar eine Schrift von ihm verlesen worden. Zudem hoffe er, dass er in acht Tagen die synodalen Ordnungen Bündens (»omnia instituta synodi nostrae in Foederibus«) zusenden könne, die zu prüfen sie alle Bullinger bitten würden.[32] Diese Bitte von Gallicius ist der erste Hinweis darauf, dass die Synode den Beschluss gefällt hatte, eine Synodalordnung zu verfassen, und den Auftrag an Gallicius, der dafür die geeignete Persönlichkeit war, übergeben hatte. Allerdings hat Gallicius zur Zeit der Abfassung des Briefes den Aufrag noch nicht vollendet, weswegen er Bullinger lediglich über die Bitte der Synodalen bereits in Kenntnis setzte. Der Beschluss zur Abfassung einer Synodalordnung – im Brief vom 12. Dezember steht noch nichts von einem Bekenntnis – ist zweifelsohne in Zusammenhang mit verschiedenen Problemen betreffend Aufenthalt italienischer Glaubensflüchtlinge zu setzen und eine Folge des Bundstagsbeschlusses vom 1. November, wie dies auch ein späterer Brief von Comander und Gallicius vom 22. April 1553 unmissverständlich ausdrückt. Damit ist unzweifelhaft belegt, dass nicht bereits eine Frühjahrssynode 1552, wie in verschiedener Forschungsliteratur festgehalten, den Beschluss gefasst hatte, ein Bekenntnis ausarbeiten zu lassen,[33] sondern erst die Herbstsynode nach Martini den Auftrag gab, eine Synodalordnung zu verfassen. Dies hat auch der Altmeister der Edition von Bullingerbriefen, Traugott Schiess, in seinem ersten Band von *Bullingers Korrespondenz mit den Graubündnern* (Basel 1904) festgehalten: »Es scheint, dass gerade durch den jüngsten Bundestagsbeschluss [...] das Bedürfnis nach einer für alle Synodalen verbindlichen Ordnung wieder geweckt worden war.«[34]

Aus den versprochenen acht Tagen sind allerdings ganze vier Monate geworden. Die Hintergründe dafür sollen hier knapp thematisiert werden: Einmal hat man bereits Anfang Januar Kenntnis

[32] Vgl. Johannes Comander und Philipp Gallicius an Heinrich Bullinger, 12. Dezember 1552, unten S. 57, Brief 2. Zur im Brief angesprochenen Schrift von Camillo Renato siehe unten S. 58, Anm. 6.

[33] Zuletzt: *Busch*, Confessio Raetica, 252. Diese Ansicht wurde allerdings, ohne eine Quelle zu nennen, bereits von Rosius à Porta vertreten (vgl. *De Porta*, Historia, Bd. I/2, 191f.).

[34] Vgl. *Schiess*, Korrespondenz, Bd. 1, LXXIX; *Schiess*, Gallicius, 19.

davon erhalten, dass Bullinger krank sei, und deswegen haben die Churer Pfarrer beschlossen, Bullinger nicht unnötig zu belasten.[35] Auch im Brief vom 6. März weisen Comander und Bullinger darauf hin, dass sie auf Bullingers Gesundheit Rücksicht nehmen möchten.[36] In demselben Brief wird aber auch ein anderer Grund für Gallicius' Zuwarten genannt: Vergerio und andere Italiener würden nämlich den von der Synode aufgestellten Ordnungen widerstreben. Dennoch würde aber die Mehrheit der Amtsbrüder Bullinger bitten, dieselbe zu lesen und allfällige notwendige Verbesserungen zu nennen. Das Büchlein sei von bescheidenem Umfang, und Bullinger werde es sicher in zwei Stunden gelesen haben.[37]

Gallicius' explizite Erwähnung von Vergerio und der Italiener ist nicht nur ein Hinweis auf die zunehmende Entfremdung zwischen den Churer Pfarrern und Vergerio – beide »Parteien« versuchten in den Jahren 1552/1553 mittels ihrer Briefe an Bullinger dessen Gunst zu erwirken –, sondern auch ein Hinweis auf die freiheitliche, dem italienischen Bibelhumanismus entsprungene Gesinnung vieler italienischer Emigranten, die sich zu einer verpflichtenden Ordnung, geschweige denn Bekenntnis kritisch stellten. Die ursprünglich so »freiheitliche« Gesinnung der Drei Bünde hatte ja Vergerio bereits im Jahre 1550 besungen, so dass ihm, aber auch mehreren anderen, vor allem nonkonformistisch gesinnten italienischen Emigranten, diese Freiheit mit der Annahme einer verpflichtenden Synodalordnung in Gefahr schien; zudem widerstrebte Vergerio derselben, weil er immer noch die Bildung einer italienischsprachigen Synode der Südtäler im Blick hatte, wozu er wohl auch die von ihm der Reformation zugeführten Oberengadiner

[35] »Magno cum dolore audivimus ex Tschernero te febri quadam aut dolore non parvo arreptum; ob id noluimus tibi molesti esse.« (Johannes Comander und Philipp Gallicius an Heinrich Bullinger, 2. Januar 1553, in: *Schiess*, Korrespondenz, Bd. 1, Nr. 198/2). Es ist bekannt, dass Bullinger am 13. Dezember erkrankte und erst am 17. Januar seine Amtsgeschäfte wieder aufnehmen konnte, vgl. Heinrich Bullingers Diarium (Annales vitae) der Jahre 1504–1574, hg. von Emil Egli, Basel 1904 (Quellen zur Schweizerischen Reformationsgeschichte 2), 43.

[36] Noch Ende April trägt Gallicius Sorge wegen Bullingers Schwäche (vgl. Philipp Gallicius an Heinrich Bullinger, Ende April 1553, in: *Schiess*, Korrespondenz, Bd. 1, Nr. 210).

[37] Vgl. Johannes Comander und Philipp Gallicius an Heinrich Bullinger, 6. März 1553, unten S. 59, Brief 3.

Gemeinden gezählt haben wollte. Der Vorwurf, dass Vergerio – er war mitnichten ein »Heterodoxer«, wie Pfister schreibt[38] – die Spaltung der Bündner Kirche provoziert hätte, ist dennoch vollkommen verfehlt, wenn man bedenkt, dass er aus Sorge darum, dass das Veltlin wieder in den Einflussbereich der Altgläubigen falle, gar – zumindest vorübergehend – einen Ruf an den Hof des Herzogs Christoph von Württemberg nicht annehmen wollte.[39]

Gallicius wollte die ersten Monate des Jahres 1553 insbesondere nutzen, um die Italiener für eine gemeinsame Synodalordnung zu gewinnen. So hielt er nämlich im Brief vom 6. Juni an Bullinger exlizit fest, dass nun alle Italiener die Ordnung angenommen hätten, wenn auch sie an drei Artikeln noch Kritik geübt hätten.[40] Für diesen Erfolg ist im Hintergrund viel Verhandlungsgeschick notwendig gewesen, was vor allem das Verdienst der Bemühungen von Gallicius war. Freilich mag auch Bullinger durch seine vermittelnde Tätigkeit einen Beitrag geleistet haben, doch leider sind fast alle Briefe Bullingers aus diesen beiden Jahren, von denen wir indirekt Kenntnis haben, verloren gegangen, so dass wir über Bullingers direkte Einflussnahme kaum Aussagen machen können.

Als dritter Aspekt, warum Gallicius mit der Übersendung der Synodalordnung noch zuwartete, ist zu nennen, dass Gallicius dieselbe noch nicht beendet hatte. Dies liegt nicht nur aufgrund der oben genannten Umstände nahe, sondern lässt sich auch sprachlich in den Briefen von Gallicius[41] an Bullinger festmachen. So teilt Gallicius im Brief vom 12. Dezember und 6. März mit, dass er die »instituta synodi nostrae« demnächst senden werde, er spricht also noch sehr allgemein von den synodalen Ordnungen, ohne zu definieren, welche Bereiche die »instituta« nun betreffen würden. Erstmals nennt Gallicius im Brief vom 10. April die Synodalord-

[38] Vgl. *Pfister*, Konfessionskirchen, 108, 537. Gallicius äußert zwar an Vergerios Orthodoxie – unter anderem, weil er Camillo Renato verschiedentlich in Schutz genommen habe – auch seine Bedenken, doch faktisch basiert sein Urteil nicht auf einer Prüfung von Schriften Vergerios, sondern auf seinem Unmut darüber, dass Vergerio in der Januarsynode sein Anliegen einer eigenen italienischsprachigen Synode geäußert hatte (vgl. Philipp Gallicius an Heinrich Bullinger, 29. Februar 1552, in: *Schiess*, Korrespondenz, Bd. 1, Nr. 179).

[39] Vgl. Pier Paolo Vergerio an Heinrich Bullinger, 23. Januar 1553, in: *Schiess*, Korrespondenz, Bd. 1, Nr. 201.

[40] Vgl. unten S. 67, Brief 5.

[41] Die Briefe wurden z.T. mit Comander gemeinsam an Bullinger gesandt.

nung, die er bald zu senden verspricht, »placita nostra«, so wie der zweite Teil des Textes tatsächlich beginnt.[42] Gallicius hatte offenbar Anfang April die Synodalordnung zu großen Teilen vollendet. Schießlich übersandte er dieselbe mit dem Brief vom 22. April an Bullinger, umfassend allerdings nicht nur die Synodalordnung, sondern auch das Bekenntnis der Synode. Zwar nennt Gallicius zu Beginn des Briefes dieselbe nur »placita illa nostra«, präzisiert aber im Laufe des Briefes mit dem Hinweis auf die »fides ac placita haec nostra«; infolge der verschiedenen Ansichten einzelner Italiener sei es notwendig gewesen, die »fidem et decreta nostra perscribere«, wenn dieselben in die Synode aufgenommen werden wollten.[43] Tatsächlich beginnt der Text der übersandten »Synodalordnung« mit den Worten »Fides ac placita synodi Evangelium Christi in tribus Rhetiae Foederibus praedicantium«, umfassend also ein Glaubensbekenntnis (*Fides*) und eine Synodalordnung (*Placita*), die gemeinhin unter dem Namen *Confessio Raetica* in die Geschichte eingegangen ist.[44]

Wir haben die Hintergründe für die Notwendigkeit zur Abfassung der *Fides ac placita synodi* bereits angesprochen. Facettenreich hat diese Hintergründe erstmals Emil Camenisch in seiner Studie über die *Confessio Raetica* dargelegt, begründend warum gewisse Artikel (*Loci*) in der *Confessio* ausführlicher, andere knapper beschrieben seien. Gerade die *Fides* sollte die Geistlichen der Südtäler auf ein reformiertes Bekenntnis verpflichten.[45] Bereits Gallicius selbst hat ja im Brief vom 22. April zahlreiche Angaben dazu gemacht, indem er betonte, mit welchen theologischen Richtungen und Ansichten die Synode sich auseinanderzusetzen habe. Außer Francesco Calabrese hat aber Gallicius in besagtem Brief keine Namen genannt.[46] Aufschluss über die verschiedenen theologi-

[42] Vgl. Philipp Gallicius an Heinrich Bullinger, 10. April 1553, in: *Schiess*, Korrespondenz, Bd. 1, Nr. 208.

[43] Vgl. Johannes Comander und Philipp Gallicius an Heinrich Bullinger, 22. April 1553, unten S. 62, Brief 4.

[44] Vgl. Fides ac placita synodi Evangelium Christi in tribus Rhetiae Foederibus praedicantium, Chur SKA, B 1, 1 (= *Busch*, Confessio Raetica, 256).

[45] Vgl. *Camenisch*, Confessio Raetica, 225–228.

[46] So schreiben Gallicius und Comander an Bullinger, dass beinahe jeder italienische Flüchtling der Synode eine eigene Bekenntnisschrift vorlege (vgl. Johannes Comander und Philipp Gallicius an Heinrich Bullinger, 22. April 1553, unten S. 62, Brief 4). Zu Francesco Calabrese siehe unten S. 64, Anm. 10.

schen Richtungen der reformatorischen Emigration aus Italien in die Drei Bünde gibt vor allem Conradin Bonorands letztes, posthum erschienenes Werk.[47] In der vorliegenden Studie wollen wir uns aber, die betreffenden Briefe an Bullinger aus der besagten Zeit auswertend, vor allem der Frage vom Anfang der Abfassung bis zur definitiven Rezeption der *Confessio Raetica* widmen. Im Brief vom 22. April baten also Comander und Gallicius, neben der detaillierten Schilderung der Entstehungshintergründe sowie des Zwecks der Abfassung der *Fides ac placita synodi*, nämlich der innerkirchlichen Willkür reformiert Bündens durch ein gemeinsames Bekenntnis und eine Synodalordnung Einhalt zu gebieten, Bullinger um Durchsicht, Prüfung und Korrektur des Textes; die Einhaltung der *Fides ac placita synodi* soll künftig nämlich Bedingung für die Aufnahme in die Synode sein.[48] Zudem sei es wichtig, dass Bullinger bedenke, dass die Drei Bünde paritätisch seien, welcher Tatsache man bei der Abfassung habe Rechnung tragen müssen. Bullinger möge das Büchlein (»libellus«) in acht bis vierzehn Tagen zurücksenden.[49]

Bullinger ist der Bitte nachgekommen und hat noch im Monat Mai Bekenntnis und Synodalordnung geprüft. Doch leider ist sein Antwortbrief nicht mehr erhalten. Wir wissen davon aber aus einem Brief vom 6. Juni. Darin dankt Gallicius namens aller Amts-

[47] Vgl. *Bonorand*, Emigration, 39–105, 129–188. Dalbert behandelt in seiner Dissertation die theologischen Richtungen der in den Briefen thematisierten Personen nur selektiv (vgl. *Dalbert*, Reformation).

[48] Die Aufnahme in die Synode war bekanntlich die Voraussetzung, auf dem Hoheitsgebiet der Drei Bünde als reformierter Prediger oder Lehrer wirken zu dürfen. Freilich stieß sich dieses Rezeptions- und Zensurrecht der Synode mit dem kommunalen Recht, die Geistlichen zu wählen und zu entlassen; durch die Gründung der Synode wurde also das »unbeschränkte« Pfarrwahlrecht der Gemeinden wesentlich eingeschränkt, doch manche Prediger und Lehrer, auch wenn sie nie in die Synode aufgenommen oder aus dieser ausgeschlossen worden sind, waren weiterhin in den Drei Bünden tätig. Neben dem populärsten Beispiel eines Camillo Renato ist insbesondere auch auf Girolamo Turriani oder Michelangelo Florio zu verweisen (vgl. *Bonorand*, Emigration, 141–144, 176–181; Jan-Andrea *Bernhard*, Reformation and Confessionalization in Grisons, erscheint in: A Companion to the Swiss Reformation, hg. von Amy Nelson Burnett und Emidio Campi, Leiden 2013). Entgegen Pfister ist festzuhalten, dass die zögernde Durchsetzung der Zensurgewalt der Synode weniger mit der mangelnden Insitutionalisierung der Synode zu tun hatte als vielmehr mit dem ausgeprägten Verständnis von Gemeindeautonomie (vgl. *Pfister*, Konfessionskirchen, 119–130).

[49] Vgl. Johannes Comander und Philipp Gallicius, 22. April 1553, unten S. 62, Brief 4.

brüder, die sich zur Synode in Chur versammelt hätten, Bullinger für die Prüfung der Synodalordnung. Er werde aber die definitive Fassung erst schicken, wenn sie »esset denuo receptum ab omnibus«. Gallicius erklärte dieses »denuo« auch sogleich: Zwar hätten alle Italiener die Ordnung angenommen, doch vor allem an drei Artikeln Kritik geübt, nämlich dass beim Abendmahl ungesäuertes Brot verwendet werden solle, bei der Taufe Taufzeugen notwendig seien und dass der Vater sein eigenes Kind nicht taufen dürfe. Die Synodalen, allen voran Gallicius, hätten die Italiener aber zu Eintracht und Frieden ermahnt, und so sei es gelungen eine Einigung zu erzielen. Abschließend hält Gallicus fest, dass auch die Taufformel, wie sie in Zürich zu gebrauchen gepflegt werde, in die Ordnung aufgenommen worden sei.[50]

Die Ausführungen von Gallicius machen deutlich, dass die Synodalordnung, nachdem sie Bullinger korrigiert zurückgesandt hat, in der Synode detailliert besprochen wurde und dabei noch einzelne Artikel geändert wurden. Weder haben wir also Kenntnis vom Text der ursprünglichen Fassung, die Gallicius am 22. April übersandte, noch von den Korrekturen, die Bullinger angebracht hat. Einzig die strittigen Punkte der Frühjahrssynode 1553 sind uns bekannt. Die definitive, in einzelnen Artikeln gegenüber der Urfassung veränderte *Fides ac placita synodi* wollte nun Gallicius an Bullinger übersenden. Dies versprach er in Briefen vom 4. Juli und 19. August erneut.[51] Tatsächlich übersandte hat er die »fidei confessionem et placita synodi« erst am 2. September an Bullinger. Gallicius betonte dabei, dass Bekenntnis und Ordnung sowohl von den Synodalen als auch von den Ratsboten, d.h. dem Bundstag,[52] angenommen worden seien. Aus dem Brief spürt man die sichtliche Erleichterung von Gallicius, dass die *Fides ac placita synodi* trotz des anfänglichen Widerstandes einiger Italiener zustandegekom-

[50] Vgl. Philipp Gallicius an Heinrich Bullinger, 6. Juni 1553, unten S. 67, Brief 5.

[51] »Placita synodi imaiam absolvo [...]« (Philipp Gallicius an Heinrich Bullinger, 4. Juli 1553, in: *Schiess*, Korrespondenz, Bd. 1, Nr. 213), sowie »Libellum confessionis illius nostrae tibi descriptum mittam, [...]« (Philipp Gallicius an Heinrich Bullinger, 19. August 1553, in: *Schiess*, Korrespondenz, Bd. 1, Nr. 218).

[52] Dies hält auch Ulrich Campell in seiner *Historia Raetica*, verfasst in den Jahren 1573–1576, also etwa zwanzig Jahre nach Annahme der *Confessio Raetica*, fest, vgl. Ulrich *Campell*, Historia Raetica, hg. von Placidus Plattner, Bd. 2, Basel 1890 (Quellen zur Schweizer Geschichte 9), 309.

men sei. Natürlich hätte sich Bullinger durch seine beratende Stellung darum auch wesentlich verdient gemacht.[53]

Der im Brief vom 2. September Bullinger zugesandte Text ist derjenige, der, obwohl die *Confessio Raetica* ausschließlich territoriale Bedeutung für die Drei Bünde hatte, bis ins 19. Jahrhundert – freilich neben der *Confessio Helvetica posterior* (1566) – verbindlichen Charakter behielt. Der erste Teil der *Confessio Raetica*, d.h. die *Fides synodi*, beginnt mit dem Bekenntnis zu den heiligen Schriften beider Testamente und zu den drei altkirchlichen Symbolen – daran messe sich die Wahrheit des Glaubens (§ 1–4). Anschließend werden, betonend, dass die folgenden Artikel insbesondere »propter haereticos« verfasst worden seien (§ 4), Fragen der Soteriologie (§ 5–6), der Gotteslehre (§ 7–10) und der Sakramentslehre (§ 11–19) thematisiert.[54] Aufs Ganze gesehen steht die *Fides* ohne Zweifel in reformierter Tradition, und insofern wird mit Recht am Ende derselben festgehalten, dass nur der in die Synode aufgenommen werde, der die Artikel kenne und beachte (§ 20).[55]

Der zweite, umfangreichere Teil der *Confessio Raetica*, d.h. die *Placita synodi*, ist hingegen, wie bereits Truog erkannt hat,[56] nicht nur Folge der Auseinandersetzungen mit italienischen Nonkonformisten, sondern auch ein Ertrag der in den 1540er Jahren gemachten Erfahrungen bei den Synodalverhandlungen, bei der Umsetzung reformierter Kirchlichkeit in den Gemeinden und bei der synodalen Inpflichtnahme der Geistlichen. Dementsprechend regelt die *Placita synodi* die Synodalverhandlungen (§ 22–29), die zu fei-

[53] Vgl. Philipp Gallicius an Heinrich Bullinger, 2. September 1553, unten S. 69, Brief 6.

[54] Vgl. *Busch*, Confessio Raetica, 256–265.

[55] In der Abschrift der *Confessio Raetica* von 1584, die von N[ikolaus] K[esel], Pfarrer in Castrisch, später in Sondrio Monte, angefertigt wurde und noch heute im Churer Stadtarchiv aufbewahrt wird, wird unmittelbar vor diesem letzten Abschnitt des 1. Teiles (§ 20) der Passus, dass schon die Frommen des alten Bundes durch Kraft und Verdienst Christi das Heil erlangt hätten, eingefügt (vgl. Fides ac placita synodi Evangelium Christi in tribus Rhetiae Foederibus praedicantium, 1584, Chur Stadtarchiv, AB III/S 01.01, 17). Dies ist ein Hinweis darauf, dass Bullingers Bundestheologie auch in den 1580er Jahren für die Synode als maßgebend erachtet wurde (vgl. Jan-Andrea *Bernhard*, »Vna cuorta et christiauna fuorma da intraguider la giuuentüna«: Der erste Katechismus Bündens als Zeugnis der Ausstrahlungen der Zürcher Reformation, in: Zwingliana 35 [2008], 67f.).

[56] Vgl. *Truog*, Geschichte, 13.

ernden Festtage (§ 30–32), den Gottesdienst und die religiöse Unterweisung der Kinder (§ 33–35), die Taufe (§ 44–47, 65), das Abendmahl und die Eheschließung (§ 43, 48–51) sowie die Amtsführung der Synodalen und ihre Kontrolle durch die Rezeption und die Zensur (§ 52–64). Anders als die *Fides* besaßen die *Placita* nicht den Anspruch auf »göttliche, unvergängliche Autorität«, sondern konnten angepasst werden.[57] Die Synodalordnung verfolgte das erklärte Ziel, die Kirchlichkeit in den reformierten Gemeinden zu vereinheitlichen, und gleichermaßen die Synodalversammlungen aufzuwerten, auf dass diese die Geistlichen gegenseitig anregen und erziehen mögen. Rechtlich bindend waren aber nur die bereits im Bundstagsbeschluss von 1537 festgehaltene Rezeption und Zensur, alle anderen Bestimmungen waren lediglich »Ermahnungen« an die Gemeinde und die Synodalen.

Leider ist die an Bullinger übersandte *Fides ac placita synodi* in Zürich nicht erhalten geblieben, gleichfalls fehlt Gallicius' Begleitbrief, der glücklicherweise, als Gallicius' eigenhändige Abschrift, im Synodal- und Kirchenratsarchiv in Chur aufbewahrt wird. Gallicius selbst schien also die von ihm angefertigten und erhaltenen Briefe aufbewahrt zu haben, so dass er auch zwei Jahre später, im Juli 1555, bei der Niederschrift der *Confessio Raetica* in den in Leder eingefassten Band die Briefe an Bullinger noch zur Hand

[57] Vgl. *Busch*, Confessio Raetica, 265 (vgl. *Camenisch*, Confessio Raetica, 258). Die *Placita synodi* wurden tatsächlich bereits 1584, als Nikolaus Kesel die Abschrift verfasste, den neuen Gegebenheiten angepasst: Einerseits wurden die Artikel der *Placita* in eine andere Reihenfolge gesetzt, andererseits mit mehreren neuen Artikeln ergänzt (vgl. Fides ac placita synodi [...], 1584, Chur Stadtarchiv, AB III/S 01.01, 18–49; die kleinere, weniger kunstvolle Schrift und die andere Tinte, die auf den S. 50–53 der *Placita* im erwähnten Folio-Band des Stadtarchivs verwendet wurden, sind Hinweis darauf, dass nach 1584 die Synodalordnung erneut mit weiteren Artikeln ergänzt wurde). Hintergrund der Ergänzungen waren unter anderem – wie eine Unterschrift Gantners belegt – die Ereignisse um Johannes Gantner im Jahre 1571, der wegen seiner Parteinahme für Jörg Frell aus der Synode ausgeschlossen wurde, in den 1580er Jahren aber wieder um Aufnahme in die Synode bat, so dass er schließlich ab 1586 in Maienfeld und ab 1595 in Chur, an der Martinskirche, wirkte (vgl. Christian *Scheidegger*, Zwischen den konfessionellen Fronten: Schriften des Buchhändlers und Schwenckfelders Jörg Frell [um 1530 – um 1597] von Chur, Chur 2013 [Quellen und Forschungen zur Bündner Geschichte 29]; Erich *Wenneker*, Heinrich Bullinger und der Gantnerhandel in Chur [1570–1574], in: Zwingliana 24 [1997], 102–114). Eine weitere Neufassung der Synodalordnungen lag in den gedruckten *Leges synodales ecclesiae Raeticae reformatae* (Chur 1645) vor.

hatte. Von welchem Glück könnten wir uns preisen, wenn sein Nachlass eines Tages noch gefunden werden könnte? Um so dankbarer sind wir – bedenkend, dass das erste Protokollbuch der Synode, umfassend die 40er bis 60er Jahre des 16. Jahrhunderts, verschollen ist – für die in Zürich erhaltenen Briefe, die uns einen reichen Einblick in Entstehung, Abfassung und Rezeption der *Confessio Raetica* geben.

3. Edition von sechs Briefen an Heinrich Bullinger[58]

Übersicht über die edierten sechs Briefe, die insbesondere die Entstehung, Abfassung und Rezeption der *Confessio Raetica* betreffen:

1 Pier Paolo Vergerio, Chur, 15. November 1552, an Heinrich Bullinger (Autograph: Zürich Staatsarchiv [StA], E II 356, 497f.).
2 Johannes Comander und Philipp Gallicius, Chur, 12. Dezember 1552, an Heinrich Bullinger (Autograph Gallicius: Zürich StA, E II 365, 104).
3 Johannes Comander und Philipp Gallicius, Chur, 6. März 1553, an Heinrich Bullinger (Autograph Gallicius: Zürich StA, E II 365, 123f.).
4 Johannes Comander und Philipp Gallicius, Chur, 22. April 1553, an Heinrich Bullinger (Autograph Gallicius: Zürich StA, E II 365, 127–129).
5 Philipp Gallicius, Chur, 6. Juni 1553, an Heinrich Bullinger (Autograph: Zürich StA, E II 365, 143f.).
6 Philipp Gallicius, Chur, 2. September 1553, an Heinrich Bullinger (Autographe Abschrift: Chur SKA, B 1, 86f.).

Vorbemerkungen zur Edition
Die Edition der sechs Briefe orientiert sich an den Gepflogenheiten der Heinrich Bullinger-Briefwechseledition. Den einzelnen Briefen liegt jeweils die älteste erhaltene Handschrift zugrunde, so dass der

[58] Ein besonderer Dank gebührt Dr. Reinhard Bodenmann, Leiter der Heinrich Bullinger-Briefwechseledition, für seine wertvollen Ratschläge und Hinweise bei der Vorbereitung und Kollationierung dieser Edition.

Text teilweise unterschiedlich zu Schiess' Edition im ersten Band von *Bullingers Korrespondenz mit den Graubündnern* (Basel 1904) ist. Sämtliche Abbreviaturen werden ausgeschrieben; eckige Klammern werden dann gesetzt, wenn Textverlust vorliegt. Die Groß-/Kleinschreibung der Vorlage wurde beibehalten.

Um der besseren Lesbarkeit willen sind die einzelnen Briefe inhaltlich in Abschnitte gegliedert. Die Interpunktion ist teilweise den heutigen Gegebenheiten angepasst worden. Textkritische Anmerkungen werden sehr zurückhaltend verwendet; Schreibvarianten in jüngeren Abschriften werden nicht explizit erwähnt. In den sachlichen Anmerkungen werden Angaben zu den erwähnten Namen und Ortschaften gemacht sowie weiterführende Hinweise zum besseren Verständnis der Briefe gegeben.

1 Pier Paolo Vergerio an Heinrich Bullinger
Chur, 15. November 1552
Autograph: Zürich StA, E II 356, 497f. (Siegelspur)
Gedruckt: *Schiess*, Korrespondenz, Bd. 1, 271, Nr. 195/2

Bullingers Brief vom 10. November hat Vergerio in Chur, wo er sich aus Anlass der Synode aufhält, erhalten. Nach Beendigung der Synode wird er noch allerhand in Vicosoprano und im Veltlin ordnen, dann aber nach Zürich kommen. Es ist bekannt, dass die Reise des Bischofs [Thomas Planta] von Chur nach Rom »Höflinge« ermuntert hat, über eine Rache in Bünden nachzudenken. Des weiteren haben zwei bedeutende Kardinäle [reißende Wölfe] mit acht Bischöfen sowie anderem Gefolge vor etwa zwei Monaten mit Messen und Lösegeld Leute verführt, auf dass sie Vergerio nachstellen. Er vertraut aber auf den Herrn und die Gebete der Zürcher. Anfangs Januar möchte er in Zürich sein. Er bittet, inzwischen ein Fass nach Chur zu senden. Francesco Bonetto lässt Bullinger grüßen. – Die Synode hat viel zu erledigen; Camillo Renato soll ausgewiesen werden. – Lebewohl.

Vir clarissime, hodie Curiam veni, et accepi tuas literas diei X. huiusce mensis,[1] quę sane iucundae mihi fuere multis nominibus. Nunc paucis rescribo. Peracta sinodo adhuc redeundum est mihi ad ministerium et componenda multa tum illic, tum in Valle Tellina. At facta cena cum meis tandem veniam ad te, mi Bullingeri; nam ea non modo Vicosoprani[2], sed in Valle illa nuper aquisita[3] celebranda erit, ut capiamus possessionem. At audi, frater in Christo: profectio Curiensis episcopi[4] Romam primum excitavit curtisanos ad cogitandum de Raetia et cogitandum de ultione; sed postea, quum duo ex summis Carpinalibus[5] fere duorum mensium spatio

[1] Nicht erhalten.

[2] Vergerio wirkte im Jahre 1552 in verschiedenen Gemeinden der Untertanenlande, des Bergells und des Oberengadins als Reformator, doch blieb Vicosoprano, wohin er 1550 berufen worden war (vgl. Pier Paolo Vergerio an Johannes Calvin, 3. Januar 1550, in: Ioannis Calvini opera quae supersunt omnia, Bd. 13, Braunschweig 1875, Nr. 1336), seine »Heimpfarrei«. Von hier aus fanden nicht nur seine »reformatorischen Missionen« statt, sondern zog er auch immer wieder in nördlich gelegene »reformierte« Städte wie Chur, St. Gallen, Zürich, Straßburg, Basel, Bern, Lausanne oder Genf (vgl. *Cavazza*, Vergerio, 37f.).

[3] Das Veltlin kam 1512 als Untertanenlande in den Besitz der Drei Bünde (vgl. 1512 – Die Bünder im Veltlin, in Bormio und in Chiavenna, hg. von Augusta Corbellini und Florian Hitz, Sondrio/Poschiavo 2012).

[4] 1549 wurde Thomas Planta (1520–1565), ein Verwandter von Johannes Travers, zum Bischof von Chur gewählt; geweiht wurde er allerdings erst 1551 in Rom, wo er unter anderem am Tridentinum teilnahm (vgl. Historisches Lexikon der Schweiz [HLS], Bd. 9, Basel 2009, 770; Otto P. *Clavdetscher* und Werner *Kundert*, Das Bistum Chur, in: Helvetia Sacra, Bd. I/1, Bern 1972, 495).

huc iter fecerint cum octo episcopis et alia turba, certo scias illos corrupisse prece et prętio nonnullos, qui me perdant. Res, inquam, certa es[t]; itaque humana prudentia atque ope vix evadam. Ita omnia sunt insidiis referta.[6] At confido in domino: vos me orationibus vestris iuvate. Circiter kalendas ianuarias vobiscum ero, si Deus voluerit. Interim mitte vasculum[7] huc Curiam, quod te rogo. D. Franciscus Bonetus[8] comunicavit mihi literas, quas ad eum nuper scripsisti. Te bonus ille frater amat ex animo et tibi salutem plurimam.

Multa sunt nobis hic in synodo[9] expedienda; inter cetera affirmo fore, ut uter ille venenatus (Camillum dico)[10] exterminetur è Raetia.

[5] Gemeint ist *cardinalibus*, wobei Vergerio ein Wortspiel mit *carpo* macht, um den Leser an Mt 7,15 (»lupi rapaces«) – *carpo* und *rapio* sind bedeutungsähnlich – erinnern zu lassen. Vergerio übernimmt damit eine allerdings bereits gängige Formulierung für Kardinäle; so heißt es in dem *Evangelium Pasquilli olim Romani jam peregrini* bereits zu Beginn: »[...] dixit papa rapax carpinalibus suis [...]« (Pasquillorum Tomi duo, Basel 1544, 302; vgl. Pier Paolo Vergerio an Heinrich Bullinger, 15. Oktober 1552 bzw. 5. April 1553, in: *Schiess*, Korrespondenz, Bd. 1, 267, 292). Schließlich wird der Ausdruck *carpinalis* bzw. *carpinalibus* auch in den *Decimateria centuria ecclesiasticae historiae [...]* (Basel 1574) immer wieder verwendet.

[6] Im Hintergrund steht wohl, dass Vergerio im Frühling und Sommer 1552 wegen seines »forschen« Predigens des Evangeliums im Veltlin das Missfallen der Katholiken erregte (vgl. *Cavazza*, Vergerio, 38, 56–59; *Dalbert*, Reformation, 94f.; *Schiess*, Korrespondenz, Bd. 1, LXXVII–LXXIX); Genaueres über diese von Vergerio erwähnte Tätigkeit der beiden Kardinäle und der Bischöfe ist uns aber nicht bekannt.

[7] Vergerio erwartete aus Basel ein Fass mit Büchern (vgl. Pier Paolo Vergerio an Heinrich Bullinger, 26. Februar 1553, in: *Schiess*, Korrespondenz, Bd. 1, Nr. 205). Über den Buchtransfer von Basel über Graubünden nach Italien vgl. *Bonorand*, Emigration, 109–120; Jan-Andrea *Bernhard*, Il cudisch en Grischun: Derivonza, diever, funcziun, rimnada ed effects da cudischs, collecziuns da cudischs e da bibliotecas ellas Treis Ligias (1500–1800), erscheint in: Annalas da la Societad Retorumantscha 2013.

[8] Francesco Bonetto ist ein Glaubensflüchtling aus Bergamo, der sich seit 1550 in Bünden aufhielt, später aber in die Hände der Inquisition gelangte, weswegen Friedrich von Salis-Samedan nach Venedig abgeordnet wurde. Bonetto, der später in Chur als Kaufmann wirkte, genoss bei Bullinger wie auch bei den reformierten Predigern Bündens, wie die Korrespondenz belegt, hohes Ansehen (vgl. *Schiess*, Korrespondenz, Bd. 3, XXV).

[9] Die Synode in Chur fand nach Martini statt und dauerte mindestens bis am 20. November (vgl. *Schiess*, Korrespondenz, Bd. 1, Nr. 195/3–4).

[10] Camillo Renato (vgl. oben S. 44, Anm. 29) wurde 1550 exkommuniziert und zog nach Bergamo, wo er festgenommen, auf Bitte der Bündner aber wieder freigelassen wurde und ins Veltlin zurückkehrte. Daselbst wurde er erneut zum Stein des Anstoßes, wie die Briefe Vergerios und Gallicius' belegen (vgl. *Renato*, Opere, 235–259; *Schiess*, Korrespondenz, Bd. 1, 259–291); vgl. *Bonorand*, Emigration, 142.

Vale et salve cum tota familia, scola atque ecclesia. Dominus benedicat vestris laboribus. Amen.

Curiae, XV. novembris 1552.

Vergerius tuus.

2 Johannes Comander und Philipp Gallicius an Heinrich Bullinger

Chur, 12. Dezember 1552

Autograph (Gallicius): Zürich StA, E II 365, 104 (Siegelspur)

Gedruckt:[1] *Schiess*, Korrespondenz, Bd. 1, 276f., Nr. 198/1

Gallicius – auch im Namen von Comander – will nicht lange Lobreden verlieren, da Bullinger sehr vielbeschäftigt sei, und verdankt den am heutigen Tag eingetroffenen Brief. Davos, das sich vor einigen Jahren der Reformation zugewandt hat und vier Predigtstätten umfasst, hat keinen Prediger, obwohl der jährliche Lohn bei 100 rheinischen Gulden liegt. Wenn Bullinger keinen Pfarrer für die Davoser nennen kann, wissen sie nicht, wohin sich wenden. Auch zahlreiche andere Gemeinden sind ohne Prediger. Die Bezahlung ist meist gering und schwankt zwischen 50 und 60 rheinischen Gulden; nur Comander erhält 120 Gulden. Zudem mangelt es auch an Lehrern. – Den Veltlinern sind Prediger und Lehrer erlaubt worden unter Bedingungen, die der Überbringer mitteilen kann. – Gallicius sendet Exzerpte aus einer Schrift von Camillo Renato, die auch an der Synode verlesen worden ist; er wird über diesen und anderes an die Potestaten im Veltlin schreiben. Er hofft, in acht Tagen ein ausführliches Schriftstück über die bündnerische Synodalordnung senden zu können, die Bullinger prüfen soll. – Lebwohl. Neuigkeiten aus Italien werden gemolden, wenn erwünscht.

S. Vir modis omnibus maxime, hoc enim vero elogio amputatas volo omnium exordiorum ambages; scio enim, quam aliis sis occupatus et quam brevibus mihi omnia absolvenda. Literas tuas[2] accepimus hodie. Davasenses pauculos ante annos quatuor alebant sacrificos missantes; mox totam suam regionem in unam parochiam coegerunt concionatori unico dantes quotannis centum aureos Renenses, qui praedicet quatuor in templis.[3] Apud nos nullus est,

[1] Teildruck: *De Porta*, Historia, Bd. 1/2, 313.

[2] Nicht erhalten.

[3] In Davos wurde am Platz die Reformation 1526 eingeführt (vgl. Paul *Gillardon*, Geschichte des Zehngerichtebundes, Davos 1936, 94f.; Emil *Camenisch*, Bündner Reformationsgeschichte, Chur 1920, 213–223), bald darauf zog aber auch die ganze Landschaft nach. Die angesprochenen vier Kirchen sind St. Johann (Davos Platz), St. Theodor (Sertig Dörfli), St. Maria (Frauenkirch) und St. Nikolaus (Glaris).

quem iudicemus nos aptum eis; sperabamus a vobis istinc gravem aliquem virum.[4] Nunc pulchra hac spe frustrati nescimus, quo nos convertamus; speramus ex improviso deum appariturum. Multae apud nos parochiae sunt carentes concionatoribus; offerunt Renenses aureos quinquaginta, quaedam sexaginta. Nosce volunt omnes, mercedem solvere nemo. Multi ecclesiastae in Foederibus, crede, famem paciuntur; maxima enim pars plus non habet quam 60 Renenses. Qui maxima salaria habent, ad Renenses perveniunt 120; solus tamen Comander noster totidem habet. Scholastici in Foederibus, de quibus speres aliquid hac in re praestatum iri, sunt nulli. Quo deventura res in Foederibus sit, deus novit.

Veltelinensibus nostris concessi sunt concionatores et magistri pacto eo, quo tibi dicet lator hic, homo apud nos magni nominis et senator nobis omnibus faventissimus.[5]

Camillum ut pernoscas, tibi mitto hic libellum,[6] imo syllogismos fere tantum ex eius libro Italice fusissime scripto collectos per me. Etiamsi mea haec omnia sint verba, credas tamen me fideliter omnia egisse; lectus enim est a fratribus synodi, in quo ipse praesens fuit. Hoc ipso tamen die scribo ad potestates Vallis Tellinae de eo et aliis ad rem facientibus. Camilli aristas istas lege, si videtur, et quum perlegeris, post aliquot dies remitte ad nos. Proximo octiduo prolixissimas meas, si deus voluerit, videbis literas de omnibus in-

[4] Gemäß Brief vom 6. Dezember 1552 ist der bisherige Amtsinhaber, Andreas Schmid (Fabricius), Pfarrer in Davos seit 1527, in hohem Alter verstorben; wegen des Mangels an Geistlichen haben sich Comander und Gallicius an Bullinger gewandt (vgl. Johannes Comander und Philipp Gallicius an Heinrich Bullinger, 6. Dezember 1552, in: *Schiess*, Korrespondenz, Bd. 1, Nr. 196).

[5] Comander und Gallicius sprechen hier den Abschied der zu Davos am 1. November versammelten Ratsboten der Drei Bünde an, in dem bestimmt wurde, dass von der Synode geprüfte Prädikanten und Schulmeister im Veltlin auf eigene Kosten und im Privathaushalt ohne Behinderungen angestellt werden dürfen. Zudem sollen die Prädikanten jährlich auf der Synode Rechenschaft abgeben und sich dem Urteil bzw. der Zensur derselben unterwerfen (vgl. Abschied der zu Davos versammelten Ratsboten Gemeiner III Bünde, 1. November 1552, in: Materialien zur Standes- und Landesgeschichte Gem. III. Bünde, 246f. [= *Bundi*, Gewissensfreiheit, 272f.]).

[6] Diese Angaben genügen nicht, um definitiv zu sagen, welcher »libellus« von Renato in der Synode verlesen worden ist. Es legt sich aber nahe, dass es sich um den *Trattato del battesimo e della santa cena* (1547) handelte (vgl. *Renato*, Opere, 93–108, 291–297).

stitutis synodi nostrae[7] in Foederibus, quas ut legere et cognoscere et iudicare velis, rogamus omnes.

Interim vale, virorum nobis observandissime. Nova de rebus bellicis ex Italia dicet tibi hic, si rogaris. Interim vale iterum. Ex Curia Rhetiarum, die 12. decembris anni 1552.

Tui Ioannes Comander[8] et Philippus Gallicius.

[Adresse:] Vere magno viro D. Heinricho Bullingero, domino ac fratri suo etc. Tiguri.

3 Johannes Comander und Philipp Gallicius
an Heinrich Bullinger
Chur, 6. März 1553
Autograph (Gallicius): Zürich StA, E II 365, 123f.
(Siegelspur)
Gedruckt:[1] *Schiess*, Korrespondenz, Bd. 1, 288f., Nr. 206

Comander und Gallicius haben den Brief erhalten, in welchem Bullinger Vergerio sowie die gefährliche Hartnäckigkeit der Synodalen thematisiert. Klage über den undankbaren Geiz der bündnerischen Gemeinden: Einst gaben sie freiwillig 100 goldene Kronen für Lügen, heute geben sie denen, die die Wahrheit predigen, schäbige 20 Kronen. Obwohl die Prädikanten betonen, dass sie davon nicht leben könnten, glaubt man ihnen nicht. Einige werden zwar in die Schule geschickt, doch es sind wenige, die die schönen Künste zu studieren begehren, obwohl man es nicht unterlässt, die Gemeinden zu ermahnen. Doch dies ist ja Bullinger bereits bekannt. – Vergerio und andere Italiener widerstreben einer Synodalordnung. Alle Amtsbrüder bitten aber, dass Bullinger dieselbe lese und, wenn Verbesserungen notwendig seien, Bullinger sie nennen möge. Die Ordnung schicken sie aber erst, wenn Bullinger sich erholt hat. Das Büchlein sei von bescheidenem Umfang, so dass Bullinger es in zwei Stunden lesen werde. – Den Brief an Vergerio, den Gallicius von Bullinger erhalten hat, hat er sogleich an Johannes Travers gesandt, der auch informiert darüber ist, wie sie Vergerio in seiner Arbeit gegen die Papisten beraten haben. Vergerio ist nun aus dem Veltlin ins Engadin gekommen; allerdings befürchten sie, dass er zu heftig vorgehe. Lebewohl. – Tod des französischen Gesandten Jean Jacques de Castion.

[7] Dies ist der erste Hinweis darauf, dass Gallicius damit beschäftigt ist, die Synodalordnungen zu verfassen, die dann Bullinger, nach der Zusendung, prüfen soll.

[8] Johannes Comander hat nicht selbst unterschrieben.

[1] Teildruck: *De Porta*, Historia, Bd. 1/1, 180; Bd. 1/2, 191f.

S. Literas tuas accepimus, vir humanissime, quibus Vergerio rescribis ac nobis conquerens de perniciosa nostrorum tenacitate.[2] Certe crudeliter in se ipsos sunt avari, dum bonis pastoribus carere malunt quam numerare, quibus illi possint vivere. Proh hominum ingratitudinem! quibus olim pro mendaciis centum aureorum coronatorum liberaliter dabant, iis nunc pro veritate, quam praedicant, maligne persolvunt viginti. Nos quidem hoc ipsum clamamus ubique et, quibuscumque possumus modis et quotiescunque datur, omnibus inculcamus: fore propediem, ut neque concionatores neque missatores sint habituri. Sed surdo, quod dicitur, narramus fabulam.[3] Mittunt quidem nonnulli liberos suos in scholas, sed ut discant legere possintque rationes suas scribere; paucissimi sunt, qui liberos in bonis artibus cupiant erudiri.[4] Nos tamen monere communitates nostras non desinemus. Haec et ante tibi dicta repetimus, quod nunc alia, quae scribamus, prorsus nulla habeamus, tu tamen velis tibi responderi aliquid.

Paravimus synodi nostrae instituta quaedam, quibus vehementer Vergerius et Itali apud nos refragantur. Fratres nostrates omnes rogant, ut legas et, si quid emendandum putes, moneas. Nos nunc temporis non mittimus illa ad te, parcentes nimirum valetudini tuae, quod plene fortassis nondum revalueris;[5] mittemus tamen, quam primum intellexerimus te robustiorem factum. Ne tamen deterrearis magnitudine libelli. Opellam diei unius vix sibi deposcunt; duabus enim horis poteris totum perlegere, imo minore spatio.

[2] Im Brief, der nicht erhalten ist, muss unter anderem thematisiert worden sein, dass Vergerio und einige Italiener keine verpflichtende Synodalordnung annehmen wollten, die Mehrheit der Synodalen hingegen eine solche beschlossen hatte; Gallicius versuchte nun zwischen den beiden Parteien zu vermitteln.

[3] Über die schlechte Bezahlung berichten Comander und Gallicius bereits im Brief vom 12. Dezember 1552, vgl. oben Brief 2.

[4] Tatsächlich ist es eine bescheidene Anzahl von Bündnern, die bis Mitte des 16. Jahrhunderts ihre Studien in Zürich oder Basel, geschweige denn an Universitäten des deutschen Reiches, absolvierten. Leider ist eine umfassende Untersuchung der Studentenbewegungen (»Peregrination«) aus den Drei Bünden noch ein Desiderat der Forschung; um so dankbarer sind wir über Studien von Janett Michel, Jakob Rudolf Truog, Fritz Jecklin, Oskar Vasella, Conradin Bonorand oder Felici Maissen (Literatur dazu in: *Bernhard*, Reformation and Confessionalization).

[5] Zur Erkrankung Bullingers vom 13. Dezember 1552 bis 17. Januar 1553 siehe oben S. 46, mit Anm. 35.

Vergerii literas statim, ut accepi abs te, misi ad Ioannem Traversium,[6] qui illi redderet una cum aliis, quas nos Vergerio in auxilium contra papistas scripsimus. Secesserat enim Vergerius in Ingadinam[7] ex Valle Tellina, homo certe plus satis vehemens nostro iudicio; ita enim timemus. Tu interim vale in domino Iesu, vir humanissime, nosque redamare perge. Datum Curiae, die 6. marcii anni 1553.

Tuae integritatis toti Iohannes Com[ander][8],[9] Philippus Gallicius.

Has cum scripsissemus literas, nuntiatur certo legatum regis Gallorum hic, D. Ioannem Iacobi Castilioneum,[10] mortuum esse, et certe mort[uus est][11]. Aiunt cras ductum iri ex urbe nostra in castrum suum sepultum.

[6] Der humanistisch gebildete Politiker Johannes Travers (1483–1563) stand mit vielen Gelehrten seiner Zeit in Korrespondenz und unterstützte indirekt die Reformideen in den Drei Bünden, obwohl er selbst erst im Laufe des Frühjahrs 1552 – nach der Lektüre einer Schrift Calvins (vgl. Heinrich Bullinger an Johannes Travers, 27. November 1551, in: *Schiess*, Korrespondenz, Bd. 1, Nr. 169; Johannes Travers an Heinrich Bullinger, 21. Juli 1553, in: *Schiess*, Korrespondenz, Bd. 1, Nr. 214) – die Messe nicht mehr besuchte, sich offen zur Reformation bekannte und die Durchführung derselben im Oberengadin aktiv unterstützte (vgl. HBBW, Bd. 9, Zürich 2002, 62; *Pfister*, Konfessionskirchen, 113; Conradin *Bonorand*, Vadian und Graubünden: Aspekte der Personen- und Kommunikationsgeschichte im Zeitalter des Humanismus und der Reformation, Chur 1991 [Quellen und Forschungen zur Bündner Geschichte 3], 121 f.; Constant *Wieser*, Johann Travers 1483–1563, in: Bedeutende Bündner aus fünf Jahrhunderten, hg. von der Graubündner Kantonalbank, Bd. 1, Chur 1970, 43–61).

[7] Vergerio verhalf der Reformation im Oberengadin seit 1551 zum Durchbruch, so unter anderem in Samedan, Bever, Pontresina, Silvaplana und Sils im Engadin (vgl. *Bonorand*, Emigration, 96–98, 104).

[8] Textverlust.

[9] Der ganze Brief, inklusive Nachtrag, ist von Gallicius geschrieben worden, der Name Comanders hat Gallicius allerdings mit anderer Tinte, wohl nach der Einsichtnahme des Briefes durch Comander, nachräglich eingesetzt; mit der gleichen Tinte ist auch der Nachtrag geschrieben worden.

[10] Der mailändische Diplomat Jean Jacques de Castion (gest. 6. März 1553) war zwischen 1536 und 1553 französischer Gesandter bei den Drei Bünden; 1541 erwarb er die Herrschaft Haldenstein, ließ 1544–48 ein neues Schloss errichten und stellte 1549 die Herrschaft unter Schutz und Schirm der sieben eidgenössischen Orte (vgl. HLS, Bd. 3, Basel 2004, 239).

[11] Textverlust.

[Adresse:] Vere magno viro D. Heinricho Bullingero, domino ac fratri suo colendissimo. Tiguri.

4 Johannes Comander und Philipp Gallicius an Heinrich Bullinger

Chur, 22. April 1553

Autograph (Gallicius):[1] Zürich StA, E II 365, 127–129 (Siegelspur)

Gedruckt:[2] *Schiess*, Korrespondenz, Bd. 1, 294–297, Nr. 209

Comander und Gallicius schicken endlich die Synodalordnung [Placita] und alle Amtsbrüder bitten um Prüfung bzw. Korrektur derselben. Die Ausführlichkeit gewisser Artikel liegt daran, dass manche Italiener – es gibt zwar solche, die rechtgläubig sind und sich ruhig verhalten – absonderliche Lehren vertreten. Sie glauben, dass alles in den heiligen Schriften enthalten sei und Bekenntnisse und Synodalordnungen darum nicht notwendig seien, gleichzeitig würden sie verdächtige, verkehrte und ketzerische Lehren vertreten. Gallicius (und Comander) weisen insbesondere auf solche hin, die die Trinität leugnen, die Jesus Christus die göttliche Natur absprechen, die das Opfer Christi als überflüssig betrachten, die Gott zum Urheber des Bösen machen sowie solche, die einen Libertinismus vertreten. Denen zufolge gebe es keine Hölle, und auch im Himmel sei niemand außer jener Verbrecher aus Lukas [23,43]. Explizit wird Francesco Calabrese erwähnt, dessentwegen [1544] eine Disputation [in Susch] stattgefunden hat. Einige Prediger ehren auch den Sonntag nicht, andere halten sich nicht an die anerkannte Taufliturgie, sondern benutzen eine eigene Formel. Schließlich wollen verschiedene Geistliche nicht an der Synode teilnehmen, um nicht den Anschein zu erwecken, die Synodalordnung [Fides ac placita synodi] angenommen zu haben. Einige haben keine Schulbildung, ja verstehen außer des Italienischen nichts. Letztere behaupten, dass ein guter Lehrer den Geist besitzen müsse, und nicht den Buchstaben, wie es auch in der Apostelgeschichte bezeugt sei. – Gallicius will abschließend einzig festhalten, dass jeder, der in die Drei Bünde komme, ein eigenes Bekenntnis mit zahlreichen zweifelhaften Ansichten habe. Darum war es notwendig, die Glaubensartikel und Verordnungen zusammenzustellen, deren Einhaltung Bedingung für die Aufnahme in die Synode sei. – Zudem soll Bullinger bedenken, dass die Drei Bünde paritätisch seien. Dem mussten sie bei der Abfassung des Bekenntnisses Rechnung tragen, indem sie der katholischen Kir-

[1] Eine autographe Abschrift aus dem Jahre 1555 findet sich als Beilage zur ältesten Handschrift der *Fides ac placita synodi*, der sogenannten *Confessio Raetica*, welche der Synodalmatrikel vorgeordnet ist (vgl. Chur SKA, B 1, 2r–5r); eine weitere Abschrift aus dem Jahre 1584, angefertigt von N[ikolaus] K[esel], Pfarrer in Castrisch und später in Sondrio Monte, findet sich in dem in der einleitenden Studie erwähnten Folio-Band des Stadtarchives Chur, enthaltend eine prachtvolle Abschrift *Fides ac placita synodi*, verschiedene die Synode betreffende Bundstagsbeschlüsse, sowie zwei Briefe (22. April und 2. September 1553) von Gallicius an Bullinger (vgl. Chur Stadtarchiv, AB III/S 01.01).

[2] Erstmals vollständig gedruckt wurde der Brief, gleichfalls der *Confessio Raetica* vorgeordnet, in: *De Porta*, Historia, Bd. 1/2, 193–196.

che keine Veranlassung geben durften, gegen das reformierte Bekenntnis vorzugehen. – Bullinger soll nun das Bekenntnis gewissenhaft lesen und korrigieren; in acht bis vierzehn Tagen möge er es zurücksenden, den Empfang der Sendung solle er aber direkt bestätigen. – Gallicius und Comander bitten zudem um Auskunft über Joachim Gachlinger, aus Kempten, der kürzlich in den Drei Bünden angekommen sei. – Lebewohl. – Bitte um Übermittlung eines Briefes an Nikolaus Baling in Bern.

S. Placita[3] illa nostra, de quibus et ante scripsimus ad te, nunc tandem mittimus. Fratres te rogant omnes, ut digneris legere, nec hoc tantum, verum etiam ut corrigas, mutes et in[4] his omnibus, quod patrem decet, agas. Te enim agnoscimus ac facile recipimus ut oculatiorem nobis et cui dominus longe maiorem prudentiam dederit quam multis aliis. Ne vero credas plura decreta nos sanxisse, quam sit necesse, aut enucleatius curiosiusve multa nobis posita, quam sit opus, scias super his omnibus, quae hic constituimus, nos iam saepe tentatos ab advenis, maxime omnium ab Italis quibusdam morosis[5], quibus nihil fere placet, nisi quod sit rarum aut quod saltem a communi usu variet aut certe ab ipsis primo profectum. Propiores enim nobis sunt quam vobis, et cum his quotidie nobis agendum, imo et saepius conflictandum, etiamsi de omnibus non loquamur. Nam novimus aliquot ex Italis etiam sanos in fide, quietos ac tranquillos; sed de perturbatis ingeniis hic conquerimur. Confitentur omnes se credere, quaecunque contineantur in scripturis sanctis, adeo ut his nullis decretis nec ullis aliis clarioribus verbis opus esse dixeris. Sed accuratius attentiusque examinati deprehenduntur aut prorsus importuni atque absurdi aut pestilentibus doctrinis infecti: subinde evomentes absona quaedam horrendaque paradoxa, ingenia redolentia corrupta distortaque. Alius sanctam illam trinitatem confiteri non vult; alius Christum esse

[3] Der Ausdruck *Placita* steht, wie auch später im Brief festgehalten, für *Fides et placita synodi*, umfassend das Bekenntnis (*Fides*) und die Synodalordnung (*Placita*).

[4] Wiederholt.

[5] Eigensinnig und unbequem (»morosi«) wurden die italienischen Emigranten genannt, weil manche von ihnen, wie im Brief ausgeführt, nicht orthodoxe, sondern sogenannte nonkonformistische Lehrmeinungen vertraten, und darum auch eine Unterschrift unter die Synodalordnungen ablehnten (vgl. Philipp Gallicius an Heinrich Bullinger, 6. März 1553, oben Brief 3); Vergerio wehrte sich gleichfalls gegen eine Unterschrift, weswegen es ihm schließlich leichter fiel, dem Ruf an den Hof des Herzogs Christoph von Württemberg schließlich doch noch Folge zu leisten (vgl. Briefwechsel zwischen Christoph, Herzog von Württemberg, und Petrus Paulus Vergerius, gesammelt und hg. von Eduard von Kausler und Theodor Schott, Tübingen 1875).

deum aequalem patri affirmare non audet.[6] Iste servatos nos gratia dei affirmat, non fuisse ergo opus Christi descensu in terras ad nos nec corpore eius sanguineque, cum soli gratiae dei totum salutis nostrae opus sit transscribendum; aliud acutius distinguens dicit servatos quidem nos non esse per corpus Christi pro nobis passum, sed per dolorem, quem senserit ille in corpore.[7] Quidam constanter affirmant mala pravaque ex ipso deo, omnium fonte, esse ipsumque deum non minus scelerate factis gaudere quam bonis et iis, quae cum virtute et bene fiant, quod nusquam non agunt atque disputant. Quorundam buccae nihil nisi praedestinationem crepant; hunc servari, etiamsi mala omnia operetur, contra illum non posse non damnari, credat, quicquid velit, atque etiam operetur bona omnia.[8] Non defuerunt, qui dicerent infernum esse nullum, etiamsi sint poenae malis constitutae, et in coelis hominum esse neminem praeterquam latronem illum, de quo in evangelio Lucae.[9] Huiusmodi disputare non puduit Calabrum[10] quendam in Ingadina in publico ad hoc convocato conventu.[11] Non desunt hodie ex iis, qui sunt concionatores, qui dominicam diem egre recipiant; sunt, qui articulos hic nostros de baptismo vehementer abominentur nec

[6] Es ist insbesondere an solche Italiener zu denken, die die Trinität ablehnten, wie z.B. Lelio Sozzini oder Camillo Renato (vgl. *Bonorand*, Emigration, 141–144. 153–157).

[7] Es sind vor allem Italiener angesprochen, die zum Opfertod Christi eine kritische Haltung einnahmen, wie z.B. Francesco Stancaro oder Francesco Negri (vgl. *Bonorand*, Emigration, 145–152).

[8] Damit sind verschiedene italienische Richtungen gemeint, die das göttliche Erbarmen nicht beschränkt sehen wollten, also eine eher universalistische Heilslehre vertraten, wie z.B. Celio Secondo Curione oder Giorgio Siculo (vgl. *Bonorand*, Emigration, 139–141, 157f.).

[9] Lk 23,43.

[10] Francesco Calabrese, der libertinische und täuferische Ansichten vertrat, kam 1542 in das Hoheitsgebiet der Drei Bünde und predigte in Ftan; seinetwegen fand schließlich in Susch eine Disputation statt, die zwar nur eine innerprotestantische Angelegenheit war, dennoch aber auch von katholischen Geistlichen aus dem Vinschgau besucht worden ist (vgl. *Pfister*, Konfessionskirchen, 120; *Dalbert*, Reformation, 17–19).

[11] Das Protokoll der Disputation von 1544 ist leider nicht mehr erhalten, so dass sich unser Wissen auf Campell stützt, der die Disputation selbst miterlebt hat: Auf der Disputation konnte zwar Francesco Calabrese seine Lehre verteidigen, doch seine Ansichten wurden nach zwei Tagen verworfen und er wurde durch die weltlichen Behörden aus den Drei Bünden und dem Tirol ausgewiesen (vgl. *Campell*, Historia Raetica, 296–307; *De Porta*, Historia, Bd. I/2, 67–76; Petrus Dominicus Rosius à Porta: Colloquium inferioris Oengadinae, Chur Staatsarchiv, B 1500 b, Nr. 2).

recipere velint. Certe eo redigi per nos non possunt, ut baptizantes nostra forma aut vestra, qua vos in ecclesia vestra utimini, utantur et ipsi; sed quilibet illorum proprium habet modum baptizandi, quem sectetur magno laicorum, ut loquuntur isti, scandalo.[12] Quidam esse nolunt in nostro consortio ac capitulo, ne videantur fidem et placita haec nostra recipere. Habemus etiam inter nos concionatores, qui nullam unquam scholam viderunt nec aliud in literis norunt bonis quam Italice legere, Latini autem sermonis aut Germanici ne verbum quidem intelligunt.[13] Istis qui favent, clamant: Apostolos etiam fuisse illiteratos et idiotas teste in Actis apostolorum Luca, ac spiritum requiri, ut quis bene doceat, non literam, quam dicat apostolus occidere.[14]

Et ne omnia persequamur: vix credis, quam quilibet ad nos veniens aliquid novi secum adferat, quo se commendet ac conspicuum faciat, et propriam confessionem unusquisque fere nobis offert, quam approbemus atque recipiamus, verbis conscriptas nonnunquam novis, ambiguis, captiosis et in universum non satis fidis. Huiusmodi igitur cum saepenumero pervenerint ad nos, visum est fidem et decreta nostra brevibus perscribere, ut, qui aliunde venerint ad nos, audiant fidem nostram necnon et causas singulorum a nobis decretorum, ad haec quid requiramus ab ipsis, si recipi velint in nostrum consortium.

Accipe et hoc: Magistratus in nostris Foederibus unius fidei non est;[15] quod in his statuendis in memoria nobis fuit habendum, ne

[12] Im Hintergrund steht unter anderem ein Vorfall aus Chiavenna, als Francesco Negri im September 1548 begehrte, dass sein soeben geborenes Kind von Mainardo auf sein, Negris eigenes Bekenntnis, das aber von Comander und Blasius gutgeheißen worden war, getauft werde – dies hatte Mainardo entschieden abgelehnt (vgl. Agostino Mainardo an Heinrich Bullinger, 22. September 1548, in: *Schiess*, Korrespondenz, Bd. 1, Nr. 102); vgl. *Bernhard*, Negri, 104f.

[13] Die Kenntnis der lateinischen und der deutschen Sprache waren im dreisprachigen Dreibündestaat für die synodale als auch bundstägliche Kommunikation essentiell. Am Bundstag wurde mehrheitlich in Deutsch verhandelt, an der Synode war die Verhandlungssprache bis zu Beginn des 19. Jahrhunderts das Lateinische. In der von Nikolaus Kesel angefertigten Abschrift der *Confessio Raetica* von 1584 wird dies bestätigend festgehalten: »In gratiam fratrum Italorum, omnes in veneranda Synodo, Latinam linguam callentes, latine. Si quid proponere voluerit, loquantur.« (Fides ac placita synodi [...], 1584, Chur Stadtarchiv, AB III/S 01.01, 23).

[14] Unter den reformatorischen Bewegungen Italiens waren spiritualistische Ansichten – begründet damit, dass auch die ersten Christen gemäß den Apostelakten keine Buchstabentreue gekannt hätten (vgl. Apg 2,6–12 und Apg 4,13) – recht verbreitet.

quam ansam calumniandi aut saeviendi daremus iis, qui nos nostraquc odio prosequuntur.

Tu itaque pro tua fide et integritate haec lege et corrige. Libellum autem nobis non remittas, donec ipsi certo nuntio eum a te repetierimus post octo vel quindecim dies. Interim tamen rogamus, ut rescribas aliquid hoc ipso nuntio, quo certi simus, reddita esse tibi haec nostra. Scripsimus ad te ante 15 dies; nescimus, an redditae sint tibi literae.

Petieramus, ut clam nobis scriberes, qualis vir esset Ioachimus Gachlinger; vestratem enim se esse gloriatur ac concionatorem egisse Campidonae;[16] huc venit non multos ante dies. Parce prolixitate; non potuimus non scribere haec ad te et curas nostras in tuum sinum velut in consultoris fidissimi effundere. Nova hic penitus nulla feruntur.

Vale in domino Iesu, vir maxime, una cum aliis doctissimis et optimis istic viris ac nos redamare non desine. Datum Curiae Rhetiarum, die 22. aprilis anni 1553.

Tui Ioannes Comander[17] et Philippus Gallicius iussi a fratribus Christum in Foederibus praedicantibus.

Accepimus literas a te missas, et hasce mittere digneris, si commode poteris, ad dominum Nicolaum Bernam.[18]

[15] Durch die Ilanzer Artikel (1526), die den Gemeinden das Recht einräumten, ihre Geistlichen zu wählen und zu entlassen, wurde die Parität geschaffen (vgl. oben S. 41).

[16] Joachim Gachnang, genannt Gachlinger, stammte aus Elgg, und nicht aus Kempten, wie er den Bündnern vorgegeben hatte. Er suchte eine Pfarrstelle in Bünden, bereitete den Bündnern aber nicht weniger Sorge als den Zürchern, wie Johannes Fabricius 1558, nachdem Gachlinger verstorben war, an Bullinger meldete: »[...] hat vylenmalen syn ee brochen, jaa, gar nie gehalten.« (Johannes Fabricius an Heinrich Bullinger, 9. Mai 1558, in: *Schiess*, Korrespondenz, Bd. 2, Nr. 82; vgl. HBBW, Bd. 6, Zürich 1995, 437).

[17] Die Unterschrift ist von Comander selbst, auch der Nachtrag stammt aus Comanders Feder.

[18] Nikolaus Baling (»Pfister«, gest. 1553) aus Württemberg konnte 1527 dank Zwinglis Empfehlung in Chur die Leitung der Stadtschule übernehmen, wechselte aber 1539 an die Lateinschule St. Nikolai; infolge einer Auseinandersetzung mit Simon Lemnius verliess er 1542 Chur und wirkte seit 1546 in Bern, das ihn bereits 1528 erstmals berufen hatte, als Vorsteher, später als Rektor des Barfüßerkollegiums (vgl. HBBW, Bd. 5, Zürich 1992, 408f.; *Jenny*, Comander, Bd. 1, 247–250; *Schiess*, Korrespondenz, Bd. 1, XXXVIII–XLII).

[Adresse:] Vere magno viro D. Heinrichcho Bullingero, domino ac fratri suo colendissimo.[19]

5 Philipp Gallicius an Heinrich Bullinger

Chur, 6. Juni 1553

Autograph: Zürich StA, E II 365, 143f. (Siegelspur)

Gedruckt:[1] *Schiess*, Korrespondenz, Bd. 1, 297f., Nr. 211/1

Die Synodalen lassen Bullinger für die Prüfung der Synodalordnung danken. Gallicius will die definitive Fassung erst schicken, wenn sie von allen gutgeheißen worden ist. Die Italiener haben zwar alle die Ordnung angenommen, obwohl sie bei drei Artikeln Kritik übten: beim ungesäuerten Brot [beim Abendmahl], bei den Taufzeugen bei der Taufe, und dass der Vater sein eigenes Kind nicht taufen dürfe. Die Synodalen haben die Italiener aber zu Eintracht und Frieden ermahnt. Darum mögen sie niemandem, der Taufzeugen erwünsche, es verwehren, mögen sie gesäuertes Brot essen, wenn sie ungesäuertes nicht mögen, schließlich dürfe aber ein Vater seine Kinder nur taufen, wenn es die Notwendigkeit erfordere. Zudem haben die Synodalen auch die Taufformel in die Ordnung aufgenommen, die in Zürich wie in den Drei Bünden gleich gebraucht werde. – Der neue französische Gesandte [Jean Moustiers Du Fraisse], der ein gelehrter und loquenter Mann ist, hat Comander und Gallicius zum Nachtessen eingeladen. Er las auch [reformierte] Bücher, so dass gleichfalls maßvoll über den Glauben diskutiert worden ist. Du Fraisse hat in Wittenberg bei Luther und Melanchthon gelebt; Gallicius kennt allerdings die heuchlerische Art der Höflinge, geht aber nicht davon aus, dass Du Fraisse gegen das Evangelium handle. – In Lyon sind am 16. Mai vier Personen, angeblich Berner, wegen ihres Glaubens verbrannt worden. – Lebewohl. Travers ist krank gewesen.

S. Fratres omnes, qui in his nostris nundinis hic congregati fuerunt,[2] gratias tibi egerunt ingentes, quod placita nostra dignatus sis legere, nosque super illis monueris tam humaniter.[3] Facis, quod humanum et pium virum decet. Exemplar nolui tibi scribere, donec prius esset denuo receptum ab omnibus; nunc describere incepi mittamque propediem. Itali omnes receperunt, videbantur tamen minus propenso animo recipere. Tribus tamen articulis aperte reclamarunt: azymo pani, compatribus in baptismo et quod pater

[19] Daneben von Bullingers Hand: »D. Ioan. Coma. Philip. Gallicii 1553«.

[1] Teildruck: *De Porta*, Historia, Bd. 1/2, 226f.

[2] Die Frühjahrssynode hat Ende Mai bzw. Anfang Juni stattgefunden (vgl. oben S. 50).

[3] Nicht erhalten.

infantis ipse eum non baptizet; hos recipere noluerunt. Nos monuimus homines, ut sequantur, quae sunt pacis et aedificationis, et ut resistere nolint ei, qui compatres accipere voluerit;[4] pane utantur cibario, si nolint azymo;[5] articulum denique, ne pater baptizet suos infantes, non temere esse positum à nobis neque praeter necessitatem, hoc maxime seculo.[6] Dimisimus tamen illos aequiores, nisi quod dicunt vestram baptizandi formam esse prolixiorem, quum nostra adhuc prolixior sit.[7] Manebunt tamen in officio; ita enim promiserunt nobis discedentes bono animo.

Legatus, qui hic nomine regis Gallorum,[8] invitavit ad coenam patrem Comandrum et me; ivimus, coenavimus, audivimus hominem satis loquentem, animadvertimus doctissimum esse virum atque etiam Grȩce peritum. Legit nostrorum libros etiam tenetque exactissime: de fide loquitur modeste et circumspecte. Olim iunior aliquandiu vixit Wittembergae admodum familiaris Lutero Melanchthonique et nunquam non testatur esse bonos viros. Scio aulicos esse vafros ac versipelles; attamen hunc pugnare contra evangelium persuaderi mihi non patiar. Quum plura scierimus, plura scribemus.

Audio regem Galliȩ die 16. Mai combussisse Lugduni quatuor christianos propter fidem; illi dicebant se esse Bernenses.[9]

[4] Die Einigung konnte dadurch erreicht werden, dass nicht formuliert wurde, dass Taufzeugen notwendig seien, sondern dass es lobenswert sei, Taufzeugen zu bestellen (vgl. Art. 44 der *Confessio Raetica*, in: *Busch*, Confessio Raetica, 271).

[5] Die Einigung konnte dadurch erreicht werden, dass formuliert wurde, dass das Abendmahl mit ungesäuertem Brot gefeiert werden soll, wenn solches irgendwie erhältlich sei (vgl. Art. 48 der *Confessio Raetica*, in: *Busch*, Confessio Raetica, 271).

[6] Hier ist deutlich zu Ungunsten der Italiener entschieden worden, nämlich dass der Vater seine Kinder nur taufen dürfe, wenn absolut kein anderer Geistlicher zu bekommen sei (vgl. Art. 39 der *Confessio Raetica*, in: *Busch*, Confessio Raetica, 270).

[7] Vgl. Art. 44 der *Confessio Raetica*, in: *Busch*, Confessio Raetica, 270.

[8] Jean des Moustiers Du Fraisse (gest. 1568), Bischof von Bayonne, war der neue französische Gesandte bei den Drei Bünden vom April 1553 bis Dezember 1554. Während dieser Zeit pflegte Bullinger eine rege Korrespondenz mit Du Fraisse (vgl. André *Bouvier*, Henri Bullinger: réformateur et conseiller oecuménique, d'après sa correspondance avec les réformés et les humanistes de langue française, Neuchâtel 1940, 227–244; *Schiess*, Korrespondenz, Bd. 1, XLVIII–L).

[9] Am 16. Mai 1553 wurden fünf aus Genf stammende Theologiestudenten – Gallicius spricht allerdings von vier aus Bern stammenden Personen – als Ketzer auf dem Scheiterhaufen verbrannt. Sie waren um Ostern 1552 nach Lyon gekommen, weil sie dort das Evangelium im Geist der Reformation verkündigen wollten. Die zahlreichen Gnadengesuche bei König Heinrich II. führten zwar zu einem Aufschub, konnten aber

Vale, vir observandissime. Salutat te Comander et amici. Traversus[10] se expurgat, quod diu invalidus fuerit; certe nos eum hic non vidimus multo iam tempore, nec usquam prorepit. Ex Curia, die 6. Iunii 1553.

Tuus totus Philippus.

[Adresse:] Vere magno viro D. Heinricho Bullingero, domino ac fratri suo colendissimo. Tiguri.

6 Philipp Gallicius an Heinrich Bullinger

Chur, 2. September 1553
Autographe Abschrift:[1] Chur SKA, B 1, 86f.
Ungedruckt

Gallicius schickt an Bullinger das bereits seit langem verlangte Glaubensbekenntnis und die Synodalordnungen. Diese sind von den Prädikanten und den Ratsboten gebilligt worden, insbesondere auch darum, weil Bullinger sie gutgeheißen hat. Dennoch erhebt sich Widerspruch von eigensinnigen Geistlichen, die aber die besonderen Umstände nicht bedenken. Wegen gewisser Kleinigkeiten machen sie einen großen Lärm, und bringen damit das ganze Werk in Gefahr. Bullinger wisse aber aus früheren Briefen von Gallicius, warum es notwendig war, ein Bekenntnis zu verfassen. Der Mangel an Eleganz möge Bullinger nicht verwundern, da er ja wisse, dass er, Philipp [Gallicius], der Verfasser sei, also kein Redner, sondern ein Theologe. Gallicius hält sich dabei an das Wort von Manilius, dass das Schmücken der Sache nicht notwendig sei, wenn nur die Sache unterrichtet werde. Lebewohl.

S. Fidei confessionem et placita synodi nostrae,[2] quae tibi à me descripta mitti petiisti, habes hic tandem vir maxime.[3] Nostratibus

die Verurteilung durch Kardinal François II. de Tournon nicht verhindern (vgl. Johann Jakob Wick: Sammlung von Nachrichten zur Zeitgeschichte, Zürich Zentralbibliothek, Ms F 24, 3f.).

[10] Siehe oben S. 61, Anm. 6.

[1] Wie bereits mehrfach erwähnt ist dieser Brief der ältesten Handschrift der *Fides ac placita synodi* (1555) nachgeordnet (vgl. Chur SKA, B 1, 86f.); gleichfalls ist eine Abschrift von Nikolaus Kesel aus dem Jahre 1584 in dem erwähntem Folio-Band des Stadtarchives Chur erhalten (vgl. Chur Stadtarchiv, AB III/S 01.01).

[2] Vgl. Fides ac placita synodi Evangelium Christi in tribus Rhetiae Foederibus praedicantium, Chur SKA, B 1, 1–84.

[3] Auch in den einleitenden Notizen zur Abschrift des Briefes hält Gallicius fest, dass er diesen Brief an Bullinger geschickt hätte, weil Bullinger die definitive Synodalordnung zu haben begehrt hätte: »Horum articulorum omnium exemplum privatum sibi describi

ecclesiastis nec non et primoribus[4] qui audierunt omnibus placent: vel eo etiam maxime quod tu non improbas. Refragantur tamen morosi[5] quidam, quos nosti, opinor, quod hic nihil placeat nisi quod sit aut immodicum, aut severitate et rigore illo stoico rigens et horrendum. Qui tamen si Locum perpenderent in quo sumus atque versamur, et auditores quos habemus, caeterasque circumstantiarum rationes, prudentibus in omni negotio considerandas,[6] huiusmodi inquam si cogitarent, his minus reclamarent: nec propter minutula quaedam non impia, magna commoverent, turbisque minime necessariis omnia miscerent, magno fortassis periculo rei totius perdenda. Quid nos coëgerit hoc constituere intellexisti ex prioribus meis litteris.[7] Quod elegantia non sint, non miraberis, si conscripta noris a Philippo tuo. Theologus esse volui, non orator.[8] Tuebor etiam inertiam meam, Manilii illo:[9] Ornari res ipsa negat, contenta doceri.[10] Vale Ex Curia die 2 sept: 1553.

mittique a me petiit Vere magnus ille Heinr. Bullingerus, descripsi ergo misique illi cum epistula hac.« (Chur SKA, B 1, 86).

[4] Auch Campell hält fest, dass im Herbst 1553 ein Bundstag die Synodalordnung bestätigt habe (vgl. *Campell*, Historia Raetica, 309). Zeitgenössische Akten und Urkunden, außer dem Brief von Gallicius, berichten darüber allerdings nichts (vgl. *Bundi*, Gewissensfreiheit, 51, 209).

[5] Vgl. oben S. 63, Anm. 5.

[6] Mit den besonderen Umständen meint Gallicius, dass die Drei Bünde inklusive Untertanenlande infolge verschiedener Sprachen und Talschaften mit unterschiedlichen Traditionen und Kulturen sich nicht mit anderen staatlichen Gegebenheiten vergleichen lassen würden. Eine gute Einführung in diese »besonderen Umstände« gibt Randolph C. *Head*, Jenatschs Axt: Soziale Grenzen, Identität und Mythos in der Epoche des Dreissigjährigen Krieges, Chur 2008 (Cultura alpina 5), 27–35.

[7] Es ist an die Briefe vom 12. Dezember 1552, 6. März, 22. April und 6. Juni 1553 zu denken.

[8] Das ist wohl eher falsche Bescheidenheit von Gallicius, denn es ist bekannt, dass, als Gallicius im Februar 1554 ins Engadin gerufen wurde, die Gläubigen aus dem ganzen Tal herbeiströmten, um seine Predigten zu hören (vgl. *Schiess*, Gallicius, 25f.); vgl. Philipp Gallicius an Heinrich Bullinger, 12. März 1554, in: *Schiess*, Korrespondenz, Bd. 1, Nr. 253.

[9] Marcus Manilius (1. Jh.) verfasste die *Astronomicon libri V*, ein Gedicht, das die aktuelle Sichtweise der Zeit über die Astronomie repräsentiert (vgl. Marcus *Manilius*, Astronomica – Astrologie. Lateinisch – Deutsch, hg. von Wolfgang Fels, Stuttgart 1990).

[10] Dieser Vers stammt aus Manilius' *Astronomicon* (III, 39) und ist unter Humanisten und Reformatoren häufig gebraucht worden. Giovanni Pico della Mirandola zitierte den Vers z.B. in seiner Schrift *De ente et uno*, und Zwingli hat in seiner persönlichen Ausgabe gar die betreffende Stelle unterstrichen (vgl. Irena *Backus*, Randbemerkungen Zwinglis in den Werken von Giovanni Pico della Mirandola, in: Zwingliana 18/4–5 [1990–1991], 303).

Jan-Andrea Bernhard, Dr. theol., Privatdozent für Kirchengeschichte, Universität Zürich

Abstract: The Raetian Confession of 1552/53 took shape during the Reformation in the context of Italian emigration to Grisons. The synod was obliged to write a binding order due to debates with the Italian non-conformists. Philipp Gallicius regularly consulted Heinrich Bullinger as he wrote the order. A hitherto forgotten letter from Gallicius to Heinrich Bullinger that is occasionally even considered to be fictitious, in addition to other important letters written between 1522 and 1552, shed new light on the formation, writing, and reception of the Raetian Confession, and challenges previous research conclusions.

Schlagworte: Philipp Gallicius, Pier Paolo Vergerio, Heinrich Bullinger, Confessio Raetica, Evangelisch-rätische Synode, Drei Bünde, Italien, Nonkonformismus, Reformatorische Emigration, Konfessionalisierung

ISSN 0254-4407 – Zwingliana 40 (2013), 73–99

Guy de Brès's »Le baston de la foy chrestienne«

From Personal Notebook to Patristic Anthology (1555–1565)

Erik A. de Boer

1. Introduction

Guy de Brès (c. 1520–1567) is best known as the primary author of the *Confession de foy*, published in 1561, translated into Dutch in 1562, which is also called »Confessio Belgica« or »Belgic Confession«. His very first, far less known publication is an anthology entitled *Le baston de la foy chrestienne*, whose first edition appeared in 1555. This work is a compilation of quotations from the Scriptures and the church fathers, organized thematically. Within a time span of no more than ten years, this work saw at least seventeen editions, all of which appeared during De Brès's lifetime. If a Dutch translation existed, as may indeed have been the case, it at any rate did not survive in publication.[1] In 1577 the book was translated into English as *The Staffe of Christian Faith* (although never reprinted). After the death of De Brès, *Le baston* was reprinted only a single time, in Saumur in 1601. Nevertheless, the work can be regarded as a French language bestseller, being

[1] See Erik A. *de Boer*, »Le baston« in Nederlandse vertaling?, in: Guido de Bres: Zijn leven, zijn belijden, ed. Emile *Braekman*, Erik A. *de Boer*, Utrecht 2011, 90–93.

published between 1555 and 1565 in Antwerpen, Geneva, Lyon, and Caen. As such, it was a popular handbook in the clash of the confessions.

The present study focuses on the genesis of *Le baston de la foy chrestienne*, investigating it in relation to the theological formation of the author of the Belgic Confession. The question regarding De Brès's theological training is all the more a pressing one since, as Johan Decavele has pointed out, the formation of all known preachers from the Southern *Pays Bas* (Nether Lands) in a religious order or university is known, with the one exception of Guy de Brès.[2] His second, larger work, entitled *La racine, source et fondament des Anabaptistes* (1565), also testifies to his intellectual maturity and later theological orientation in a dispute he held with the Anabaptists of his days, but it contains no patristic references. The letters of De Brès, which report the disputes held in prison in 1567 and were published in *Procedures tenues* (1568), do in contrast testify to his knowledge and handling of patristic sources. The present article, however, will look primarily at the first work of De Brès that testifies to his knowledge of the fathers of the church.

2. The Swiss connection

Most biographies relate the bare facts of De Brès's birth (c. 1520) in Bergen (Mons), in the Southern Low Countries, as the son of a glass painter, and of his flight to London around 1548.[3] Upon his return to the country of his birth, De Brès became minister of the Word in Rijssel (Lille) around 1550. In 1555 he published *Le baston de la foy chrestienne*, before travelling on to Lausanne and Geneva for further studies in 1556. But what can be said of De Brès's theological education? Is there a link between his earlier

[2] Johan *Decavele*, La place de Guy de Brès dans la Réforme et son époque, in: The Belgic Confession at 450, ed. Andreas J. *Beck* et al., Maastricht 2012 (Analecta Bruxelliana 15), 30–40.

[3] Biographies: L. A. *Van Langeraad*, Guido de Bray: Zijn leven en werken. Bijdrage tot de geschiedenis van het Zuid-Nederlandsche protestantisme, Zierikzee 1884; A. L. E. *Verheyden*, Anabaptism in Flanders 1530–1650, Scottdale, PA 1961 (Studies in Anabaptist and Mennonite History 9); *Braekman/De Boer*, Guido de Bres.

work on *Le baston* (which was probably finalized in Ghent) and his subsequent pursuit of theological studies?

The aforementioned facts concerning De Brès's whereabouts until 1556 are all found in one source, namely, the brief biographical account which Jean Crespin gave in the booklet *Procedures tenues* (1568) and later incorporated into his *Histoire des vrays tesmoins de la verité de l'Evangile* (1570). In the absence of further data from this period in his life, De Brès's subsequent biographers have tended to fill the lacunae by recounting who else was at work in those cities when he is thought to have been living there, and whom he therefore may have met or heard. But are there additional historical data which may substantiate Crespin's testimony and inform us on De Brès's theological formation?

In the long letter which Guy de Brès wrote from prison to his flock in Valenciennes, he reported on the interrogation he underwent in April 1567. The bishop of Arras, François Richardot, made an opening statement to which De Brès responded as follows:

> »Regarding my salvation, I dare say that I have been as eager to learn as any man. For that reason I have investigated the various sects and teachings which are found in Christianity, so that at least I could understand, travelling back and forth from one country to the other«.[4]

This statement in which De Brès mentions his travels is somewhat ambiguous, however. After all, it could refer either to the continuous journeys he undertook in serving the faithful in the southern Netherlands, or else, more specifically, to the *peregrinatio academica* on which he embarked through the German and Swiss territories.

Confirmation for Guy de Brès's Swiss connection comes from third party testimonies. The first is the long report on the confiscation of papers from De Brès's hiding place in Doornik (Tournai)

[4] Procedures ausquelles est deduit comme Guy du Bres et Peregrin de La Grange ont signé par leur sang la doctrine de l'Evangile, in: F. *Pijper* (ed.), Bibliotheca Reformatoria Neerlandica, vol. 8, 's-Gravenhage 1911, 561f. Cf. preface to *Le baston*: »L'un des jours nous avons la guerre contre les heretiques Anabaptistes, l'autre contre les Libertins et Epicuriens, contre les Arriens en contre les Davidistes en contre les dissimulateurs, et consequemment contre les venerateurs des Peres, par le zele desquels les enfans de Dieu sont mis à mort« (1558/1, 13).

on 10 January 1562. The report was written by the commissioners who were investigating the whereabouts of De Brès on behalf of the governess, Margaret of Parma. Among De Brès's papers, notes, and books, the officials also found a number of letters. The first letter, whose contents are unknown, is identified as being from the year 1556 and written by Jean Calvin.[5] The second one was by Petrus Dathenus, »who calls himself minister of the Word of God of the Flemish in Frankfort, and who addresses the said Guy as minister of the Word of God in the Netherlands«.

The next line in the officials' report to the governess contains the first evidence concerning De Brès's formative years: »We have also found out that the said Guy made the start to his aberrations in Lausanne and in Geneva«. Did the letters from Calvin and Dathenus reveal this specific information? This is in any case what the investigators concluded on the basis of the documentation they confiscated from De Brès's lodgings. They also describe a third letter in the report of their findings: »Also another letter to Jean Crespin from the year 1559, who requests from him the catalogue of martyrs who are amidst those who he knows are worthy of that title and honor, since he is making an account both in French as well as in Latin.«[6] The Genevan printer was thus building a network to obtain reliable sources for his work on Reformed martyrdom, and may have met De Brès in Frankfort during a visit to the book fair there.[7] The three confiscated letters thus establish a link to Geneva and Calvin in the second half of the 1550s.

But what is the bearing of the details which were later published by Jean Crespin? Guy de Brès and Pérégrin de la Grange were executed on 1 June 1567. The next year a booklet was published anonymously, written on the basis of the letters which De Brès sent

[5] *Van Langeraad*, Guido de Bray, 22: »[...] et entre icelles une lettre de Jan Calvin de l'an 1556, par lesquelles il respond à certaines questions, que luy avoit proposé ledt. Guy, dont nous envoions extraict à vostre Alteze«. Another point of contact between Geneva and Calvin is documented by the letter which the churches sent to Geneva, asking for approval of the Belgic Confession, see Erik A. *de Boer*, Calvijns brief over De Bres' belijdenis, in: *Braekman/De Boer*, Guido de Bres, 169–173, 181–183.

[6] Source: Papiers d'Etat, Correspondence de Tournay, 1561–1563, f. 136–138 (printed in *Van Langeraad*, Guido de Bray, 46).

[7] Jean-François *Gilmont*, Jean Crespin: un éditeur réformé du XVIe siècle, Geneva 1981 (Travaux d'Humanisme et Renaissance 186), 202, n. 65.

from prison to his congregation and which contain the documentation of his trial until the day of his execution: *Procedures tenues à l'endroit de ceux de la religion du Pais-Bas* (1568).[8] The introduction to this work includes a brief biographical sketch of De Brès, with the following data:

> »Concerning his erudition with which God had enriched him – after having made him study in Geneva and Lausanne – it is not necessary to dwell upon this aspect for a long time, since not only his last debates, which are found in this book, testify to it and give proof of his faithfulness, but also a Compilation he made of the Old Doctors, called *Le baston de la foy*, and what he assembled against the Anabaptists [...]«[9]

That Guy de Brès had studied theology in Geneva and Lausanne was thus knowledge preserved in the collective memory of his congregations in Lille, Tournai, and Valenciennes. The editor of this booklet, Jean Crespin, may in fact also have been the one to write these lines.

A third written testimony is found in Crespin's *Histoire des martyrs*. In the 1570 edition of his *Histoire des vrays tesmoins*, the learned editor incorporated the documentation of the trial and execution of Guy de Brès and Pérégrin de la Grange as it had earlier been published as the *Procedures tenues*. He concluded this account with the »specific tale of the life and death of the two said ministers«, together with some other short biographies. Crespin first described De Brès's birth in Mons (Flemish: Bergen), his flight to England, and the time he spent in his first congregation in Lille. In the wake of the trial against the Ogvier family, De Brès then left

[8] Gilmont identified Jean Crespin in Geneva as the editor (*Gilmont*, Jean Crespin, 257; Jean-François *Gilmont*, Bibliographie des éditions de Jean Crespin 1550–1572, vol. 1, Verviers 1981, 68/8; Jean-François *Gilmont*, Nouveau bilan bibliographique, in: Bulletin de la Société d'Histoire du Protestantisme Belge 7/2 (1977), 32.

[9] »Quant à l'erudition de laquelle Dieu l'avoit enrichi depuis l'avoir fait venir estudier à Geneve et Lausanne, il n'est besoin d'en tenir grand propos, par ce que non seulement ses dernieres disputes contenues en ce livre, en rendent tesmoignage, et font foy de sa fidelité, mais aussi un Recueil qu'il a fait des Anciens Docteurs, intitulé le Baston de la foy, et ce qu'il assemblé contre les Anabaptistes [...]« (Procedures ausquelles est deduit comme Guy du Bres et Peregrin de La Grange ont signé par leur sang la doctrine de l'Evangile, in: *Pijper*, Bibliotheca Reformatoria Neerlandica, vol. 8, 497). Crespin incorporated this booklet from 1568 in the 1570 edition of his Histoire des vrays tesmoins de la verité de l'Evangile, book 9, (ed. J.D. Benoit, vol. 3, 533–584).

Lille and travelled to Ghent where, according to Crespin, he compiled his first book, *Le baston de la foy*, »drawn from the old doctors«.

> »As he was eager to have a wider range of learning as required for the ministry, he then made his way to Lausanne and Geneva, to that end and also to learn the Latin language. After having lived there for some time he returned to the Netherlands and restored the churches in Lille, Tournai, and Valenciennes [...]«[10]

The fact that Crespin published the account of the oppression in Valenciennes and added it to his »History of the True Witnesses« tells us that he was in close touch with the congregation of De Brès and De la Grange.

One example may suffice to illustrate De Brès's involvement in Crespin's enterprise for an account of Reformed martyrdom. The latter began his account of the year 1556 in the *Histoire des martyrs* (1556) by relating the deaths of the four martyrs from Lille in Flanders, namely, the Ogvier household. In the letter written by the elder son Baudechon (and added to the 1564 edition), we find an exhortation to follow the narrow road, »as it has until now been shown to you very faithfully and with great ardour by our brother G[uy] who is well known to and respected by you all«.[11] According to the report, his younger brother Martin Ogvier too had stirred up some of his fellow prisoners, saying: »Be quiet, my brothers, take heart, it is finished: I have endured a last assault. I beseech you, do not forget the holy doctrine of the Gospel and the good lessons you have heard from our brother Guy«.[12]

[10] [Jean *Crespin*], Histoire des vrays tesmoins de la verité de l'Evangile, qui de leur sang l'ont signée, depuis Jean Hus jusques au temps present, [Geneva]: Jean Crespin, 1570: »Depuis, comme il estoit studieux de savoir plus amplement ce qui est requis au ministere, il s'achemina vers Lausanne et Genève, à ces fins et pour apprendre la langue Latine. Apres y avoit demeuré quelque temps, renevu qu'il fut au Pais-bas, redressa les eglises ã Lisle, Tournay, et Vallencennes, si bien qu'en servant ausdites villes Dieu le preserva, comme au milieu des feuz allumez, de ne tomer és mains des ennemis« (book 8, p. 690f.; photomechanical reprint 1964).

[11] Jean *Crespin*, Histoire des martyrs persecutez et mis à mort pour la verité de l'evangile, depuis le temps des apostres jusques à present, ed. Jean-Daniel Benoit, vol. 2, Toulouse 1887, 411.

[12] *Crespin*, Histoire des martyrs, ed. Benoit, vol. 2, 415.

The sum of our knowledge of De Brès's education therefore amounts to the following. The report of the commissioners after they had searched De Brès' house in 1561 was based on at least three letters, written to De Brès (by Calvin, Dathenus, and Crespin), proving his ties to Geneva. The second note on his theological formation dates from 1568 and comes from sources close to Crespin. The latter's expanded biographical account (1570) provided more detailed information. The sources therefore allow us to formulate the following initial conclusion: although Guy de Brès had already served as minister, he decided to pursue theological studies in order to improve his skills. His work on the first edition of *Le baston*, which was the fruit of his early ministry, made him aware especially of his lack of knowledge of Latin, the language in which the church fathers were primarily transmitted in the sixteenth century. To remedy this he travelled to the Reformed centres of learning that would have been most profitable to French-speaking students, namely, Lausanne and Geneva.

3. Theological training in London

One question that remains, of course, is how Guy de Brès became a minister of the Word in the first place. Crespin reported that he left Mons (Bergen), the village of his birth, and settled in London »at the time when the good king Edward VI had given harbour and access in the kingdom of Britain to all the faithful.«[13] Was he trained for the ministry of »prophecy« as it had been instituted there by John a Lasco?[14] It is quite likely that De Brès joined the French-speaking congregation in London (or in one of the villages

[13] *Crespin*, Histoire des martyrs, ed. Benoit, vol. 3 (1889), 581; cf. *Braekman/De Boer*, Guido de Bres, 52–62.

[14] Cf. Emile *Braekman*, Theological Training of Reformed Ministers of the Low Countries, in: Academic Relations Between the Low Countries and the British Isles 1450–1700: Proceedings of the First Conference of Belgian, British and Dutch Historians of Universities held in Ghent 1989, ed. H. *de Ridder-Symoens*, J. M. *Fletcher*, Gent 1989 (Studia Historica Gandensia 273), 89. On De Brès and the London »prophétie«, see Erik A. *de Boer*, The Genevan School of the Prophets: The Congrégations of the Company of Pastors and their Influence in 16th Century Europe, Geneva 2012 (Travaux d'Humanisme et Renaissance 512), 244–249.

on the coast), and visited »la prophétie« held every week on Tuesdays. His ability to translate a Dutch work into French in later years[15] suggests that he may earlier already have been able to understand the Dutch language. If this is true, it is also possible that he attended the Thursday prophecies organized by the Flemish theologian Marten de Cleyne (1523–1559), also known as Micron(ius).[16] But the Latin courses on the Old and New Testament given by Walter Delenus and John a Lasco may at that time still have been too difficult for De Brès to follow.

There is one point in his works at which De Brès seems to hint at his experience in such training centres of the early Reformed refugee churches. In a pamphlet entitled *Oraison au Seigneur* and attributed to Guy de Brès,[17] a section of the prayer is devoted to the ministry of the Word. The author beseeches the Lord to provide his gifts and grace »to us and our children, so that true teaching may be given to them such as it has been in former times in the early Church. We ask you that in all faithful assemblies teaching will be coupled with admonition and correction, and that your holy doctrine will be administered according to the right use of the keys, so that the training in holy propositions (*les exercices des sainctes propositions*) and *congrégations*, and also the schools, will be purely instituted and maintained«.[18]

The use of the term *congrégations* in this context suggests that de Brès is thinking back to the practice as it had been established in Geneva, the only place where this term was used at the time.[19] The *congrégation* was the weekly Bible study meeting of the Company of Pastors in Geneva where in lectio continua a biblical book was

[15] Close to »Le baston« is the translation into French which Guy de Brès made of a Dutch work in 1565: »The Remarkable History of the Betrayal and Imprisonment of Two Good and Faithful Persons in the City of Antwerp, that is Christophle Fabri, Minister of the Word in said city, and Olivier Bouck, Professor in Latin«. The margins contain many patristic and even scholastic quotations.

[16] See the description in Marten *Micron*, Christelicke ordinancien der Nederlantscher ghemeinten te London (1554), ed. W.F. Dankbaar, 's-Gravenhage 1956 (Kerkhistorische studiën 7), 37.

[17] J. *Lindeboom*, Een gebed van Guy de Brès, in: Archief van de Nederlandse Kerkgeschiedenis 20 (1924), 161–178.

[18] *Lindeboom*, Een gebed van Guy de Brès, 176; Guy de Brès: Pages choisies, ed. Emile *Braekman*, Brussels 1967, 27.

[19] See *De Boer*, The Genevan School of the Prophets.

expounded. All ministers were obliged to be present, but also lay members of the Church were welcome to attend and raise questions. In the refugee Churches abroad other forms developed, in which training and selection for the ministry became more central. In his *Le baston de la foy*, de Brès would include a chapter on »the assemblies and gatherings of the faithful« (*des assemblees et congregations des fideles*). Quoting from the New Testament, Hilary of Poitiers, Tertullian, Pliny's letter to Trajan, and the *Historia Tripartita*, De Brès instructed his fellow believers as to how they could defend the gatherings they held as a congregation on Sundays and during the week against the Roman Catholic insistence on attending the Mass. Therefore, the chapter on »assemblées et congrégations« in *Le baston de la foy*, written before the years of his study in Lausanne and Geneva, does not appear to use the term »congrégations« in its technical sense as referring to the kind of Bible study meetings held by pastors during the week (as in Geneva).[20] However, the later pamphlet *Oraison au Seigneur*, published in 1564, clearly does point to such meetings for biblical exposition and training for the ministry.

While in London, De Brès may have frequented the »prophétie« of the Walloon church there.[21] As has been noted, the aforementioned passage from *Oraison du Seigneur* of 1564 testifies to the practice maintained by the ministers of a region (e.g. the classis of Lausanne) or city to hold Bible study meetings, as it had developed in Geneva and was followed in the refugee churches in and around London. The synod of the »Churches under the Cross,« held in Antwerp in November 1564, adopted the following resolution:

> »Because the ministers have no opportunity to confer regularly on Christian doctrine except during synod, every time they come together for this matter the ministers who are present shall take turns at the end of every morning and after dinner to treat a passage from Scripture in order to express the unity of doctrine which is among them [...]«[22]

[20] [Guy *de Brès*], Le baston de la foy chrestienne, [Geneva]: Nicolas Barbier and Thomas Courteau, 1559, 260–263.

[21] Cf. *Braekman*, Guy de Bres: Pages choisies, 59f.

[22] »D'autant que les Ministres n'ont moyen de conferer souvent ensemble de la doctrine Chrestiene, sinon au Synode, que toutes les fois que l'on s'assemblera ensemble pour ceste affaire, les Ministres qui y assisteront, ayent tour-à-tour chaque matinee et apres disner, à traiter quelque passage de l'escriture saincte, pour tesmoigner de l'union

It is not known whether De Brès was present at that synod of November 1564.[23] But then again, he was not the only minister who had been trained abroad in »prophecy«.[24]

It is not possible to establish the level of training which men like the young Guy de Brès could have received in »la prophétie« in London. While such meetings focused on the exposition of the Scriptures, they lacked any kind of academic standard. De Brès's preparations for the ministry seem to have been limited to the training he received in London. Therefore, at the time he served the faithful during his first tour of duty in Lille from 1550 he 1555, he had to expand his knowledge through personal study. How intense his studies were is testified by the theological notebook which he published after his first five years in the ministry, namely, *Le baston de la foy chrestienne.*

4. Introducing »Le baston de la foy« (1555)

Le baston de la foy chrestienne is not a straightforward presentation of De Brès's own emerging theology, but a compilation from the works of other authors. As an anthology of quotes from the Bible and the church fathers, it is necessary to read between the lines in order to try and detect De Brès's own systematic theological thinking.[25] It may in fact be helpful to read this book as the kind of notebook students had more commonly, with De Brès keeping notes on the »loci communes« he detected in Scripture and the fathers when he turned to read them in his personal studies. After all, patristic authority played a large role in Reformation

de doctrine qui est entre eux, et pareillement les Diacres perpetuels, pour voir le profit qu'ils auront fait en l'exercice de leur vocation« (article 3 of the Synod held at la Vigne [Antwerp], 21 November 1564) (Livre synodal contenant les articles résolus dans le synodes des Églises Wallones des Pays-Bas, vol. 1 [1563–1685], 's-Gravenhage 1896, 10).

[23] *Braekman/De Boer*, Guido de Bres, 198.

[24] Cf. *Braekman*, Theological Training, 89.

[25] Jean-François *Gilmont*, Les écrits de Guy de Brès: Éditions des XVIe et XVIIe siècles, in: Bulletin de la Société d'Histoire du Protestantisme Belge 5/8 (1971), 265–275; *Gilmont*, Guy de Bres: Nouveau bilan bibliographique, 29–36; Emile *Braekman*, Les editions du »Baston de la foy chrestienne«, in: Revue d'Histoire et de Philosophie Religieuses 56 (1976), 315–345.

polemics.[26] *Le baston* came out in 1555, when De Brès had left his congregation in Lille and was working in Gand (Ghent) for a year. He dedicated the book to his flock, a written legacy to his training for defending the Reformed doctrine.

When Guy de Brès compiled the first edition of *Le baston de la foy*, he wrote it explicitly against a book written by a Roman Catholic author, the Parisian monk Nicole Grenier, which was first published in 1547 and widely disseminated since: *Le bouclier de la foy chrestienne* (»The Shield of Faith, in the Form of a Dialogue, taken from Holy Scripture«).[27] The *Bouclier* saw at least eighteen editions between the time of its initial publication and 1555, when De Brès published his response. To understand this latter response, it is necessary first of all to examine Grenier's own work. What points of Grenier's attack on the »Lutherans« had touched De Brès's theological sensitivities? In the *Bouclier*, Grenier had provided his readers with quotations from the church fathers in Latin, which he had also translated into French for the sake of his readership, for every point of doctrine that was in dispute between Rome and Reformation. The book had the form of a dialogue between Walker (»Le bien allant«) and Wanderer (»Le mal allant«), the first being an informed churchman and the other an erring spirit. The destiny of their long walk is Jerusalem – that is, Rome.

In order to counter this attack, De Brès decided to produce a better anthology of biblical and patristic quotations in French, which Protestant converts could read, memorize, and use in debate with parish priests or official inquisitors. To understand De Brès's mind, one must look at his choice of texts and quotes and their order, at the editorial lines he himself inserted between them, and

[26] Cf. the most recent work on editions of Augustine's works, Arnoud S.Q. *Visser*, Reading Augustine in the Reformation: The Flexibility of Intellectual Authority in Europe, 1500–1620, Oxford 2011 (Oxford Studies in Historical Theology). For a similar notebook, which was perhaps used as a catalogue of a personal library, see Martin *Bucer* and Matthew *Parker*, Florilegium patristicum, in: Martini Buceri Opera Latina, vol. 3, ed. Pierre Fraenkel, Leiden 1988.

[27] Andrew *Pettegree* et al., French Vernacular Books, vol. 1, Leiden/Boston 2007, nos 23578ff. See R.E. *Hallmark*, Defenders of the Faith: The Case of Nicole Grenier, in: Renaissance Studies 11/2 (1997), 123–140.

at the additions and the reorganization of material found in subsequent editions.

At the beginning of his dialogue, Grenier presented an alphabetical list of forty church fathers quoted in his book: »The names of the holy fathers and ancient doctors of the Church, whose sayings have been brought together in this book to confirm the articles of our faith contained therein – with the year in which they flourished or died in the Christian Church according to Trithemius in his *Book on the ecclesiastical writings*«.[28] One entry in Grenier's list is the general »various famous councils of the Church in different times«. When Guy de Brès compiled his own book in response, he listed the fathers in chronological order, and added to their names a list of fourteen councils. The chronology begins with the author Dionysius the Areopagite (now commonly known as Pseudo-Dionysius the Areopagite, a fifth- and sixth-century Christian theologian and philosopher), whom De Brès regarded as the convert of St. Paul mentioned in Acts 17:34, and who is thought to have died in 96 CE. Dionysius's name is then followed by Clement of Rome, who lived at the end of the first century. But whereas the last father on Grenier's list is Pope Gregory I, De Brès went much further in time and also included references to Thomas Aquinas and Jean Gerson. The names and quotations were thus chosen to have the most impact on the adversary in the confessional debate.

In 1555, De Brès may not have been aware that another man had already written a response to Grenier's *Le bouclier de la foy*. The first edition of that response seems to have been published in Paris, with nearly the same title as that of Grenier's book: *Bouclier de la foy chrestienne de forme de dialogue*, written by Barthélemy Causse and published in 1554 by Vivant Gaulterot.[29] Interestingly, Gaulterot himself had published ten editions of Grenier's *Le bouclier de la foy*, the first in 1547, the last in 1552. Of course, it is possible that the name of the editor and the place of publication for Causse's work were intentionally chosen as fakes. In fact, the second edition of Barthélemy Causse's book, which now bore the title *Le vray bouclier de la foy chrestienne*, appeared in Geneva in

[28] Nicole *Grenier*, Le bouclier de la foy chrestienne, Paris 1547. For the patristic facts he relied on Johannes *Trithemius*, Liber de scriptoribus ecclesiasticis (1531).

[29] *Pettegree* et al., French Vernacular Books, vol. 1, no 9459.

1557 from the presses of Jean Crespin, and in 1558 and onwards from the presses of Zacharie Durand.[30] There is one major difference between these two responses to Grenier's *Bouclier de la foy*. While Causse, like Grenier, cast his response in the form of a dialogue, De Brès compiled an anthology of quotations from the church fathers and organized them topically.[31]

5. Studies in Lausanne: Jeronime le Grand?

Even with the 1555 edition of *Le baston de la foy*, De Brès appears not to have considered himself a professional theologian, for he is reported to have travelled to Lausanne after the time of its publication. Apart from the testimonies discussed in the first section, no further sources have been found placing De Brès at Lausanne. The historian of the Reformation in the Pays de Vaud, Henri Vuilleumier, included the following entry in his list of students: »De Bray, Guy, de Mons, ancien boursier de LL. EE. de Lausanne«.[32] However, neither Karine Crousaz's research in the archives of Bern and Lausanne, nor her thorough study on the Academy of Lausanne, were able to corroborate this piece of information. No Guy de Brès or du Bray features in her lists of »extraordinary bursaries« for the period 1538–1560.[33] Yet there is one name in her list that may still link Guy de Brès to the academy. Listed as bursary recipient financed by the bailiff of Lausanne, there is a student who went by the name Jeronime le Grand.[34] He received financial aid for the academic years 1557–58 and 1558–59, which corresponds

[30] *Pettegree* et al., French Vernacular Books, vol. 1, no 9460–1.

[31] On such sixteenth-century anthologies, see Anthony N.S. *Lane*, Justification in Sixteenth-Century Patristic Anthologies, in: Auctoritas patrum: Contributions on the Reception of the Church Fathers in the 15th and 16th Century, ed. Leif *Grane* et al., Mainz 1993 (Veröffentlichungen des Instituts für Europäische Geschichte Mainz, Beiheft 73), 69–95, which lists a total of 22 other anthologies published until 1565.

[32] Henri *Vuilleumier*, Histoire de l'Église réformée du Pays de Vaud sous le régime Bernois, vol. 4, Lausanne 1933, 523.

[33] Karine *Crousaz*, L'Académie de Lausanne entre Humanisme et Réforme (ca. 1538–1560), Leiden/Boston 2012 (Education and Society in the Middle Ages and Renaissance 41), 518–527.

[34] *Crousaz*, L'Académie de Lausanne, 514.

precisely with the timeframe indicated by Crespin. Could this name be an alias for Guy de Brès?

In his later years, de Brès is known to have used the name Augustine du Mont, after the village of his birth, Mons or (in Dutch) Bergen.[35] Better known is the alias Jerom(m)e, which is mentioned in various depositions taken from interrogated witnesses.[36] While De Brès's use of the name Jerom(m)e is not well attested before 1561, it is entirely conceivable that Jerome or Jeronime – in Latin: Hieronymus – was the name by which Guy de Brès went about as one of the »heretical preachers« (*prescheurs hereticques*)[37] who was on the authorities' »most wanted« list. Moreover, De Brès is often described in various witness depositions as a man of »tall stature« (*hault de stature*).[38] When these details are put together, there is some ground for suggesting that Guy de Brès may have gone by the name of Jerome or Jeronime le Grand (i.e. the tall), and already used that name during the years of his exile and *peregrinatio* in the German and Swiss territories.

Braekman suggests that Guy de Brès left Lausanne at the time of Theodore Beza's departure for Geneva, »and followed him to Geneva in the autumn of 1558«.[39] Tensions between Lausanne and the Council of Bern caused all ministers in the Classis of Lausanne, together with the professors of the Academy, to leave the city. However, Beza's teaching obligations only ended in November 1558.[40] The split between the ministers of the Pays de Vaud and the Council of Bern was finalized in the spring of 1559. In March 1559, a number of the ministers, among whom Barthélemy Causse, the author of *Le vray bouclier de la foy*, arrived in Geneva »to receive lodging until they are employed elsewhere«.[41] To date,

[35] *Van Langenraad*, Guido de Bray, 15; Eduard *Poullet*, Correspondance du Cardinal Granvelle 1565–1586, vol. 2, Brussels 1877–1882, 353; Emile *Braekman*, Guy de Brès, vol. 1: Sa vie, Brussels 1960 (Collection Histoire du Protestantisme en Belgique et au Congo Belge 6), 61.

[36] *Van Langenraad*, Guido de Bray, 37–39, where he provides the testimony given by Gilles Espringalles of 15 November 1561 (Papiers d'Etat, Correspondence de Tournay, 1561–1563, 99r).

[37] *Van Langenraad*, Guido de Bray, 37.

[38] *Van Langenraad*, Guido de Bray, 39; cf. *Braekman*, Guy de Brès, 136.

[39] *Braekman*, Les editions du »Baston de la foy chrestienne«, 323.

[40] Alain *Dufour*, Théodore de Bèze: Poète et théologien, Geneva 2006 (Cahiers d'Humanisme et Renaissance 78), 59.

scholars have been unable to establish a special connection between Beza and De Brès. Nor do we know when the latter left Lausanne. Yet his contact with the Genevan team of publishers (Barbier and Courteau) may already have begun while he was still working in Lausanne.

Both the second and third editions of *Le baston de la foy* were published by Nicolas Barbier and Thomas Courteau in 1558, which Braekman has labeled BC 1558/1 and BC 1558/2, respectively.[42] The second edition closely followed the *editio princeps*, and added some material here and there (e.g. on marriage, see below § 9). The third edition shows a more extensive reorganization, and begins with three entirely new chapters. Chapter one is »On God and the properties attributed to Him by Holy Scripture« (p. 1–77), chapter two »On the properties of Christ« (p. 77–102), and chapter three »The properties of the Holy Spirit which are attributed to Him by Holy Scripture« (p. 102–112). The first chapter opens with a presentation of the knowledge of God »by inspiration of nature«, as well as an introduction to the testimonies from Holy Scripture which follow. This closely mirrors what De Brès would go on to write in article two of the Belgic Confession. The properties of God are presented by a multitude of quotations from the Old and New Testaments, some of which are taken from the apocryphal books. Chapter one closes with a discussion of the unity of God and the properties that distinguish the three Persons. This section mirrors much of what De Brès would write in article eight and nine of his confession.

It is especially the addition of these three chapters to *Le baston* late in 1558 which seems to reflect influence from Theodore Beza's *Confession de foi chrestienne*, which was composed in 1558 in Lausanne and appeared in 1559 in Geneva.[43] A striking feature is that Beza begins his confession with three chapters on Father, Son, and Holy Spirit, a feature which De Brès introduced in the second

[41] Ioannis Calvini Opera quae supersunt omnia, ed. Johann Wilhelm Baum et al., vol. 21, Braunschweig 1879 (Corpus Reformatorum 49), 712.

[42] *Braekman*, Les editions du »Baston de la foy chrestienne«, 315–345.

[43] Theodore *Beza*, Confession de foy chrestienne, [Geneva]: Conrad Badius, 1559, written in 1558, cf. Frédéric *Gardy*, Bibliographie des œuvres théologiques, littéraires, historiques et juridiques de Théodore de Bèze, Geneva 1960 (Travaux d'Humanisme et Renaissance 41), 60.

revision of *Le baston* in 1558. The Lausanne connection thus suggests that there may at that time already have been contact between De Bèze and De Brès, perhaps in the setting of the classroom of that city's academy prior to Beza's move to Geneva.

6. Preparing for the »Confessio Belgica«?

What is true of Lausanne is even more so for Geneva: no documentation has been found in support of De Brès's reported presence in the city or at the academy there, which opened its doors in 1559. The only evidence linking the author of *Le baston de la foy* to Geneva is the publishing house of Nicolas Barbier and Thomas Courteau, from whose presses (as noted above) the two editions from 1558, as well as further editions from 1559, 1561, and 1565, all appeared. Yet when Crespin noted that De Brès wrote the first edition while in Ghent,[44] and then travelled to Lausanne and later also to Geneva, he did not comment on the later editions of *Le baston*.

Two editions of *Le baston*, the second and third, thus appeared in Geneva within the same year, 1558, and from the same publishing house of Nicolas Barbier and Thomas Courteau.[45] A fourth edition came out in 1559. Could it be that De Brès himself was in Geneva while these new editions were being prepared and printed? As described above, the most striking difference between the two revisions of 1558 is the addition of the three first chapters on the Trinity. Also the fourth edition of 1559 shows the addition of several chapters. The production of three revised editions, which emerged from the same publishing house, thus suggests an intense period of study on the part of Guy de Brès while he resided in the cities of Lausanne and Geneva.

[44] The title page has »A Lyon. Anno. 1555«, but this may have been chosen to divert the Roman Catholic authorities. Suggestions for the place of publication include Antwerp, while for the printer Christopher Plantin has been proposed (cf. *Braekman*, Les éditions du »Baston de la foy chrestienne«, 321–323).

[45] *Braekman*, Les éditions du »Baston de la foy chrestienne«, 323–327; *Gilmont*, Nouveau bilan bibliographique, 30, 32.

But why would De Brès have another publisher produce a new edition of his first theological work, rather than Jean Crespin? Crespin, a learned and equally zealous editor, was De Brès's first connection to Geneva. Although Crespin's name and printer's mark are not found on the editions of *Le baston de la foy*, it turns out that he himself was the connection between De Brès and his real publishers Barbier and Courteau. From 1554 to 1558 Crespin associated himself with Nicolas Barbier, a printer who had come from Lyon.[46] Crespin's bio-bibliographer, Jean-François Gilmont, described the importance of this association »between a printer-editor and a bookseller-editor« as follows.[47] While Crespin took care of the Latin editions, Barbier would publish the French translation of a work, as happened, for example, with John Calvin's lectures on the minor prophets (1559–60). In 1558 Barbier associated himself with Thomas Courteau from the Picardy province. Together this duo published works under their own name: »Chez N. Barbier et Th. Courteau«. These books included reprints from works which had earlier been published by Crespin. Barbier and Courteau also acquired two bestsellers of their own: the illustrated French Bible, and Guy de Brès's *Le baston de la foy*.[48] It is possible that the acquisition of *Le baston* gave the Barbier-Courteau team a certain amount of independence. Whatever the case may have been, apart from the Genevan editions of *Le baston* there are no other historical data placing De Brès in that city.

Guy de Brès's marriage to Catharine Ramon is commonly used in order to establish a *terminus ad quem* for his stay in Geneva. Since the birth of their first son, Israel, dates to 31 August 1560,[49] this suggests that their marriage took place at the very latest in November 1559. This in turn corresponds with De Brès's remark in his farewell letter to his wife that »it pleased our good God to

[46] On Nicolas Barbier, see Hans Joachim *Bremme*, Buchdrucker und Buchändler zur Zeit der Glaubenskämpfe: Studien zur Genfer Druckgeschichte 1565–1580, Geneva 1969 (Travaux d'Humanisme et Renaissance 104), 108f.; on Thomas Courteau see *Bremme*, Buchdrucker, 144f.

[47] *Gilmont*, Jean Crespin, 91.

[48] *Gilmont*, Jean Crespin, 93.

[49] *Van Langeraad*, Guido de Bray, 97–103; Nicolaas H. *Gootjes*, The Belgic Confession: Its History and Sources, Grand Rapids, MI 2007 (Texts and Studies in Reformation and Post-Reformation Thought), 43–46.

allow us to live together for the time span of some seven years«. Their marriage was blessed with five children.[50] But where and when Guy and Catharine met remains unknown.

It is fair to assume that there may be a connection between De Brès's continuing work on *Le baston* until the 1561 edition, and his writing of *Le confession de foy* in 1561. Did he already contemplate the possibility of such a confession when he was in Geneva? A century later, Martinus Schoock stated on the basis of specific documents which are nevertheless unknown to us:

> »Already in the year 1559 Guido de Brès, a most faithful man (verily, as earlier he had opened up, he has sealed the truth of the Gospel by his blood), foremost because the raving Anabaptists were regarded as being on the same page as the Orthodox by the inquisitors, started to draw up some articles of the orthodox unanimity.«[51]

Schoock did not specify what his documentary basis for this claim was, and it has since been rejected by Van Langeraad and Gootjes.[52] It is quite possible that Schoock mistook De Brès's continuing work on *Le baston*, especially during his time in Geneva, for his work on a confession. *Le baston*, »which has been faithfully derived from the very books of the ancient teachers«, is preceded by the dedicatory epistle to the church of L[ille]. The author wrote: »When I offer the present book (in which nothing is from me, but everything from the Fathers) as a confession of my faith (*pour confession de ma foy*) to the enemies of the Fathers, I do not doubt that one day I will be condemned as a wicked heretic to be burned alive to ashes«.[53]

Even if Schoock confused De Brès's work on *Le Baston* with his preparations for the confession, his mention of the year 1559 calls to mind the drafting of the *Confession de Paris*, for which John Calvin in Geneva was asked to send a contribution that year.[54]

[50] *De Brès*, Procedures tenues, in: *Pijper*, Bibliotheca Reformatoria Neerlandica, vol. 8, 624; *Braekman*, Guy de Bres, vol 1: Sa vie, 118.

[51] Marten *Schoock*, Liber de bonis vulgo ecclesiasticis dictis, Groningen: Nicolai, 1651, 519–522, printed also in *Van Langeraad*, Guido de Bray, 97f.; *Gootjes*, The Belgic Confession, 213f.

[52] *Van Langeraad*, Guido de Bray, 47.

[53] *De Brès*, Le baston de la foy (1555), 7.

[54] See Erik A. *de Boer*, Confession de Foy, faite d'un commun accord par les Fran-

After all, it is possible that De Brès was in Geneva during those days and became aware of the need for a confession for the Reformed churches in the Netherlands as they lived under Spanish rule. In that sense, his continuing work on *Le baston* can be regarded as his preparation (albeit perhaps unconscious) for the composition of the *Confessio Belgica.*

7. Vir trilinguis

Having upgraded his theological skills in Lausanne and Geneva, De Brès returned to active duty and served as itinerant preacher to several congregations in northern France and the southern Low Countries. Although some ten other editions of *Le baston* would later appear, no substantial further revision took place in any of them. To assess De Brès's theological development it may be worthwhile first to depict him as he was at the end of his life, as a mature theologian. The very last documents testifying to De Brès's patristic learning are found in the letters he wrote from prison to his flock in Valenciennes. Two long letters read as a verbal report of the interrogation carried out on 16 and 17 May 1567 by a Franciscan monk, and on 22 May by the bishop of Arras, François Richardot.

Although he apparently had no reference books available to him, Guy de Brès was able to dispute detailed points of doctrine and to quote from memory. He refers expressly to the *De cura pro mortuis agenda* of Augustine, where the church father speaks of his mother Monica's inability to help him after her death.[55] Another point: »How the doctors of the Church are united, consecrating bread and wine against the bearing of the words of the Lord Jesus, one can see in the words of Scholasticus, who made a canon and lived around the time of Gregory«.[56] This is followed by a discus-

çois qui desirent vivre selon la pureté de l'Evangile de nostre Seigneur Iesu-Christ – 1559, in: Confessies: Gereformeerde geloofsverantwoording in zestiende-eeuws Europa, ed. M. te Velde, Heerenveen 2009, 353–394.

[55] *De Brès*, Procedures tenues, in *Pijper*, Bibliotheca Reformatoria Neerlandica, vol. 8, 503.

[56] Ibid., 509

sion of the meaning of the Latin and Greek terms, with reference to Erasmus's *Annotationes*. Also Peter Lombard and Peter Comester, John Duns Scotus (»in sententia II, lib. 4, quest. 3«) and Gabriel Biel (*In canone missae*, lect. 40) are referred to. There is thus good reason to trace De Brès's references and to investigate his quotes from the fathers and doctors of the church. After all, a comparison with his »database«, *Le baston de la foy*, may provide insight into the development of his learning.

The texts of the interrogations, published shortly after Guy de Brès and his colleague Pérégrin de la Grange were executed, remind us of the confiscation of De Brès's papers in 1561. When the Reformed citizens of Doornik publicly protested by marching through the streets while singing Psalms (*les chanteries*), the governess Margaret of Parma sent a committee to the city to investigate these events. The committee reported to the governess that a bundle of papers had been thrown over the castle wall, containing a letter and a confession. Concerning this letter they report: »Finally, they quote several lines in Latin, Greek, and Hebrew, taken from Scripture.«[57] Thus, the end of the letter which accompanied the Belgic Confession as an introduction ended with quotations taken from the Bible in the three languages of the original Scriptures and the ecclesiastical translation. When the confiscated letters were compared, the following investigation proved that the handwriting of the letter accompanying the confession was that of Guy de Brès. The Bible verses in the three languages were therefore also in his handwriting. That he could write in these languages should not surprise us, because the inventory of confiscated books mentions various books »in French and in Latin, with some books in Greek«.[58]

Crespin reported that Guy de Brès had travelled to Lausanne and Geneva in 1557–1558 »to learn Latin« (and, perhaps, the biblical languages). Only four years later, in 1561, the man who wrote the famous *Confession de foy* appears to have had a working knowledge of the Hebrew, Greek, and Latin languages. After his return from Geneva, De Brès adopted a false name for his

[57] The text of this report from 2 November 1561 is included in: *Gootjes*, The Belgic Confession, 191.

[58] *Gootjes*, The Belgic Confession, 15, 50, 197.

ministry in visiting the towns and villages of south-west Belgium. That name was Jerome. This was also the name of one of his brothers. But could De Brès also have decided upon it in an allusion to »Hierosme, prestre docteur Latin (†422)«, who is listed as one of his sources and authorities in *Le baston de la foy*? Hieronymus, or Jerome, was after all the true *vir trilinguis*, the great church father and biblical scholar who learned the biblical languages and composed the Vulgate.[59] The very fact that, contrary to the other preachers of the southern Low Countries, Guy de Brès is not known to have followed any ecclesiastical or academic formation before his turn to the Reformed cause, lends credence to the reports of his »peregrinatio academica« to Lausanne and Geneva and of his pursuit to study languages there[60].

8. Towards a critical edition

The development of Guy de Brès's *Le baston de la foy chrestienne* has never been studied in depth. A critical edition is now being prepared by the present author in cooperation with W.H.Th. Moehn and A.J. Kunz. This team intends to produce a digital edition (a) comparing the first edition and the Genevan editions of 1558/1–2, 1559, 1561, and 1565, (b) compiling a database of the church fathers, councils, and canons quoted, and (c) providing source references to sixteenth-century and modern editions. On the basis of this research, solutions may be found to answer the question how De Brès acquired his patristic expertise over the years.[61]

[59] Cf. the telling title of Dennis *Brown*, Vir trilinguis: A Study in the Biblical Exegesis of Saint Jerome, Kampen 1992.

[60] On his teachers in polemic against the Anabaptists he wrote: »Je ne veux taire aussi que je me suis grandement servi en cette oeuvre du labeur des saints personnages qui ont écrit contre ceste secte de notre temps, comme de ce grand serviteur de Dieu, feu de bonne et heureuse mémoire Maître Jean Calvin, Jean Alasko, Henri Bullinger, Martin Micron, à la moisson desquels j'ai comme recueillie les éspics après eux, pour servir aussi selon mon petit pouvoir à notre Seigneur, m'employant allègrement à offrir ce peu que je puis« (Guy *de Brès*, La racine, source et fondement des anabaptistes ou rebaptisez de nostre temps. Avec tresample refutation des arguments principaux, par lesquels ils ont accoustumé de troubler l'Eglise de nostre Seigneur Jesus Christ, et seduire les simples. Le tout reduict en trois livres, [Rouen]: Abel Clémence, 1565, 4).

[61] Samples of such research can be found in Erik A. *de Boer*, The Articles on Scrip-

There is one intriguing question in particular that begs for an answer: if De Brès had no command of Latin when he wrote his French language anthology in 1555, where did he find all these translated quotations? One of the earliest patristic anthologies, the *Unio dissidentium* by Hermannus Bodius (1527), had already been published in French translation in 1527–1528 by Martin Lempereur in Antwerp: *L'Union de toutes discordes, qui est un livre tres utile à tous amateurs de paix et de unité, extraict des principaulx docteurs de l'eglise chrestienne.*[62] Further editions we have been able to identify were published by Pierre de Vingle (1533), Jean Michel (1539), and Philibert Hamelin (1551) in Geneva. De Brès's work resembles that of Bodius in at least one important respect: every passage within a chapter begins with several quotes from Scripture on the doctrinal or ethical theme, followed by quotations from church fathers, using the systems of division found in the Latin editions of the sixteenth century.

Other sources of patristic facts and quotes can be identified by a careful reading of De Brès's texts. The following, concluding part of this essay provides a sample from our quest to track down the sources of De Brès's early knowledge of the *patres*.

9. A sample: De Brès on marriage

For the purposes of this article, we have chosen one of the smaller chapters in *Le baston* to illustrate our quest for its sources. The choice is as such random, although the theme ties in nicely with the story of De Brès's life. As we saw, after he left Geneva and headed

ture in the Confessio Belgica and in »Le baston de la foy chrestienne«, in: *Beck* et al., The Belgic Confession at 450, 105–122; Erik *de Boer*, Meester in de martial arts: De Bres' gebruik van de patres in »Le baston« en de »Confessio Belgica« over de doop, in: Geloofstaal trekt haar spoor: 450 Jaar Nederlandse Geloofsbelijdenis, ed. Frank *van der Pol*, Utrecht 2012, 153–161; Erik A. *de Boer*, Het offer van het lam: Het schriftberoep van Guido de Bres in artikel 34 van de Nederlandse geloofsbelijdenis, in: *van der Pol*, Geloofstaal trekt haar spoor, 162–172; Erik A. *de Boer*, De katholieke ecclesiologie van de »Confessio Belgica« in het licht van »Le baston de la foy«, in: Theologia Reformata 55/3 (2012), 264–277.

[62] For a description of the early editions, see Francis M. *Higman*, Piety and the People: Religious Printing in French, 1511–1551, Aldershot 1996 (St. Andrews Studies in Reformation History), nos. B 211–216.

for home, he married Catharine Ramon. So what were his thoughts on the marriage of a pastor or priest? De Brès chose to write on the topic of marriage when he was still a bachelor, and he treated it in a chapter entitled »Du marriage et des vo[e]ux« (1555, f. 128v–134v), although it is in fact followed by a distinct chapter on vows. The second edition corrected this error in the title (1558/1, p. 212). The quotation of Bible verses on marriage in the first edition was restricted to 1 Timothy 4:1–3 and Matthew 19:4–6, cited at the beginning of the chapter. In the margin De Brès also added references to Genesis 1 and 2, to Ephesians 5, and to 1 Corinthians 6. Later on in this chapter he also supplied long quotations from 1 Corinthians 7.

In the second edition, ten quotations – two from Genesis, and eight from the New Testament – are brought together and printed in full at the beginning of the chapter. Four later references from the 1555 edition are deleted in the 1558/1 edition. That section had originally read:

> »Solomon describes the praise of marriage, Proverbs 18.
> David describes God's blessing of married people, Psalm 128.
> The angel Raphael teaches Tobias how he should marry according to God['s command].
> The confirmation of marriage is found in Genesis 9« (f. 129v).

Having deleted these lines, De Brès also reordered his quotations from the church fathers. In the second revision which he undertook in 1558, he pushed the chapters on marriage, vows, and fasting towards the end of the book. The contents of the chapter on marriage, however, remained the same (1558/2, p. 402–409). After the second revision of 1558, the place and contents of this chapter were not revised again (1559–1565).

Having described the process of redaction in the chapter on marriage across the first editions of *Le Baston*, we now turn to examine the contents of the patristic quotations. The chapter constitutes a powerful defence of marriage, also for those who serve in the ministry of the Word. From Eusebius's *Histoire ecclesiastique*, De Brès used a passage from Clement of Alexandria on the apostles who travelled with their spouses. He further reads St. Paul's address to his *suzugos* in Philippians 4 as a reference to his wife.[63]

At two points De Brès introduces a quotation, and both times his text can easily be traced back to the French translation of Eusebius's *Histoire ecclésiastique* in the edition from Martin Lempereur (Merten de Keyser).[64]

The passage on the married apostles is followed by a reference to »Au quart des sentences« (i.e. book four of Peter Lombard's *Sentences*) which shows itself to have been taken and copied from a marginal reference in Calvin's *Institution de la religion chrestienne*.[65]

An examination of the remaining references reveals that De Brès further used three historical works:

- The *Historia tripartita*, which is a sixth-century compilation by Cassiodorus of the three church histories of Eusebius, Sozomen, and Theodoret from the fourth and fifth century.
- His source for the life of Sylvester I (pope, 314–335) is Bartolomeus Platina (Bartolomeo Sacchi, 1421–1481), *Liber de vita Christi et omnium pontificum*.[66]
- The chapter on marriage closes with a quotation from the work of the historiographer Jean le Maire de Belges, *Traicté de la différence des schismes et des conciles de l'Église*.[67]

The *Historia tripartita* was not translated into French until 1578. However, Eusebius's *Histoire ecclesiastique* in French translation was published in 1532, with editions produced in Antwerp by

[63] *Eusebius*, Historia ecclesiastica III 30.1; *De Brès*, Le baston de la foy (1555), 129v–130r.

[64] *Eusebius*, L'histoire ecclésiastique (transl. Claude de Seyssel), Antwerp 1533, 76r (book III, chapter xxvii as indicated also in *De Brès*, Le baston de la foy [1555], 129v).

[65] *De Brès*, Le baston de la foy (1555), 130r: »Au quart des sentences, distinction 17, Chapi[tre] 4 et au decret 27, question 2, Chapi[tre] qui se commence ›Cum societas‹«; cf. Jean *Calvin*, Institution de la religion chrétienne (1541), ed. Olivier Millet, Geneva 2008 (Textes littéraires français 598), 1476: »au quart des sen. Dist. 27 c. 4 et au decret 27 c. 2 c. Cum societas«.

[66] Modern edition: Bartolomeo *Platina*, Liber de vita Christi et omnium pontificum, ed. Giacinto Gaida, Città di Castello 1913–1932.

[67] Modern edition: Jean *Lemaire de Belges*, Traicté de la différence des schismes et des conciles de l'Église avec l'Histoire du Prince Sophy et autres oeuvres, ed. Jennifer Britnell, Geneva 1997 (Textes littéraires français), 170; also p. 237 (»roy Loys le Besque«); cf. Sacrorum conciliorum nova et amplissima collectio, ed. Giovanni Domenico Mansi, vol. 18, 121f. For a description of the editions of the »Traicté«, printed from 1511 to 1549, see *Lemaire de Belges*, Traicté, ed. Jennifer Britnell, 58–69.

Merten de Keyser (1533), who also published Bodius's *L'union de toutes discordes*, and in Paris by Vivant Gaulterot (1540), the publisher of De Brès's antagonist Nicole Grenier.[68] The work of Platina was published in French as *Les vies, faictz et gestes des sainctz peres papes, empereurs et roys de France*, and saw many editions between 1540 and 1551 produced in Paris.[69]

An intriguing reference, already found in the first edition of 1555, is the very last one to »St. Uldaric, bishop of Augsburg, in the letter which he sent to Nicolas I regarding the prohibition on marriage for priests«. Ulrich of Augsburg, however, lived from c. 890 to 973, whereas pope Nicolas I lived from c. 820 to 867. The first thus cannot have addressed a letter to the second, who had died decades before his birth. De Brès quoted at some length from this letter in which Ulrich, as he understood it, reproached the pope for prohibiting marriage for the clergy since it went »completely against the Word of God, the decisions of the Council of Nicaea, and the ancient church«. The author tells the story of Pope Gregory I who was forced to change his mind on the matter. For, on a fishing trip he is said to have seen six thousands heads of little children, tossed into the river after their illegitimate birth. The shock of this event caused Gregory to change his mind and to permit his priests to marry. De Brès brings this »coup de grâce« of his argument to a close as follows: »This Epistle has been found in a library in a town in Holland called Aldwater«[70]. The *Epistola divi Hulderichi Augustinensis Episcopi, adversus constitutionem de Cleri Coelibatum, plane referens Apostolicum Spiritum* had been published in Wittenberg in 1520, with a preface by Martin Luther.[71] At the end of the pamphlet, we also find the very same line on the origin of the manuscript, which De Brès quoted in French in *Le Baston*.[72] Apparently he was struck by the thought

[68] *Pettegree* et al., French Vernacular Books, vol. 1, 566.

[69] *Pettegree* et al., French Vernacular Books, vol. 2, 573–574.

[70] *De Brès*, Le baston de la foy (1555), 134r-v.

[71] D. Martin Luthers Werke: Kritische Gesamtausgabe (Weimarer Ausgabe), Briefwechsel vol. 12, no. 4217, 22 (n. 2).

[72] »Inventa est haec Epistola, in quadam Bibliotheca opidi veteris aquae Germanicae Aldwater in Hollandia Inferioris Germaniae provincia« (Epistola divi Hulderichi Augustinensis Episcopi, adversus constitutionem de Cleri Coelibatum, plane referens Apostolicum Spiritum [Wittenberg 1520], f. Aiiiiv). Aldwater seems to refer to Aduard

that this pamphlet could be verified as »ex antiqua codice excerpta« (as Luther had said in his preface) from somewhere in the Low Countries.

Whether De Brès used the Wittenberg edition or found a French translation elsewhere is not known, but the contents of the pamphlet in any case feature throughout his chapter on marriage in *Le Baston*. The following facts from early church history are found both in the pamphlet as well as in De Brès's chapter on marriage: the reference to Pope Sylvester, and another to the second book of the *Historia tripartita* (on the decision of the Council of Nicaea forbidding priests to marry, and the forceful reaction of Paphnutius, bishop of Egypt). The account regarding Pope Gregory I and his shock upon seeing so many dead babies ends in *Le baston* with the following words: »The Apostle said: It is better to marry than to burn. And I for my part say: it is better to marry than to create a reason for murdering« (illegitimate children). The same lines are found in the same place in the *Epistola*.[73]

In the short chapter on marriage, we thus find evidence for De Brès using four French language sources on theology and history: Calvin's *Institution de la religion chrestienne*, Jean le Maire's *Traicté*, the translation of Eusebius's *Historia ecclesiastica*, and Platina's *Les vies*. The quest to uncover De Brès's sources continues, however. One important question, especially relevant for the 1555 edition of *Le baston*, is this: does Crespin's remark that De Brès went to Lausanne and Geneva in order to study Latin imply that he knew no Latin prior to that time, and therefore had to rely on French language sources? If this was indeed the case, he must have used intermediate sources which provided him with French language quotes from books that had only been published in Latin. Comparison of the further editions of *Le baston* may allow us to uncover whether De Brès learned to handle Latin sources, or else

(close to Groningen) with its Benedictine abbey. I thank Wim Moehn for identifying this reference to the »Epistola«.

[73] »L'Apostre a dit, il vaut mieux se marier que brusler; et je dy aussi de ma part, qu'il vaut mieux se marier, que bailler occasion de mort« (*De Brès*, Le baston de la foy [1555], 134r). Cf. »Apostolicum illud laudavit consilium: Melius est nubere quam uri; addens ex sui parte: Melius est nubere quem mortis occasionem prebere« (Epistola divi Hulderichi [...], f. Aiiir).

relied on quotations which he found in other standard reference works.

Erik A. de Boer, Prof. Dr. theol., Theologische Universiteit Kampen, the Netherlands; Vrije Universiteit Amsterdam, the Netherlands; Free State University Bloemfontein, South Africa

Abstract: Guy de Brès, who would become the author of the »Confessio Belgica«, published his first work in 1555, »Le baston de la foy chrestienne«, a florilegium of quotes from the Bible and the Church Fathers, that was intended as a guide for the faithful who were engaged in dispute over Reformed doctrine. De Brès, a preacher in the South of the Low Countries, travelled to Lausanne and Geneva (1556–1559) to further study theology and improve his Latin. The connection between his studies at both institutions, his work on three more editions of his book, and the sources of his patristic knowledge are discussed. A critical edition of his work, that preceded the composition of the Belgic Confession, is being prepared.

Keywords: Guy de Brès, Théodore de Bèze, Jean Calvin, Confessio Belgica, Académie de Lausanne, Académie de Genève

ISSN 0254-4407 – Zwingliana 40 (2013), 101–111

Calvin's Interpretation of »Thy Kingdom Come«

John H. Mazaheri

Calvin translates and publishes his *Institutes* in French for the first time in 1541, that is five years after the first Latin edition. His commentary of the second petition of the *Lord's Prayer* remains basically the same in the following editions (till 1557), but for the definitive version of his work, that of 1560, he rewrites it entirely. First, I propose a close reading of the 1541–57 text; then I compare it with the last one. Why did the theologian decide to rewrite his text? How has his theology evolved? Is there any basic change in his view? These are the questions I am asking in this essay.[1]

[1] On our topic, see also the following studies: Donald K. *McKim*, Theological Turning Points: Major Issues in Christian Thought, Atlanta 1988, 151–165; Gunter *Zimmermann*, Die Vereinigung mit Gott und das Reich Christi nach Calvins »Institutio«, in: Zwingliana 18/3 (1990), 193–212; Wilhelm *Niesel*, Reformed Symbolics: A Comparison of Catholicism, Orthodoxy, and Protestantism, transl. by David Lewis, Edinburgh/London 1962, 292–301; J. H. van *Wyk*, John Calvin on the Kingdom of God and Eschatology, in: In die Skriflig 35/2 (2001), 191–205; I. John *Hesselink*, Calvin on the Kingdom of Christ, in: Religion without Ulterior Motive, ed. E. A. J. G. van der Borght, Leiden/Boston 2006, 139–158; Theodore *Plantinga*, Learning to Live with Evil, Grand Rapids, MI 1982, 135–143; G. *Brillenburg Wurth*, Calvin and the Kingdom of God, in: John Calvin: Contemporary Prophet. A Symposium, ed. Jacob T. Hoogstra, Grand Rapids, MI 1959, 113–126; Timothy *George*, John Calvin and Menno Simons: Reformation Perspectives on the Kingdom of God, in: Calviniana: Ideas and Influence of Jean Calvin, ed. Robert V. Schnucker, Kirksville, MO 1988 (Sixteenth Century Essays and Studies 10), 195–214.

1. The Institutes 1541–1557 (French) editions

Calvin starts by defining the notion of »Kingdom« with regard to God. He thus states that *His* Kingdom consists in two parts, both being readily observable, but of an abstract nature. 1. God rules through His Holy Spirit in the heart of every believer (»Car il règne premièrement en tant qu'il dirige et gouverne les siens par son S. Esprit«.[2]) The theologian uses three terms to define the role of the Heavenly King, since it is assumed that there is no kingdom without a king. Now the three verbs »règne« (rule), »dirige« (direct), and »gouverne« (govern) have specific meanings. *How* does He rule (»il règne«)? – The answer is that He *governs* (»il gouverne«), which means that He rules with *authority*. Indeed, one can rule but not necessarily govern, in which case he would be a king without authority. But God rules *with* authority. He also through His Spirit *directs* (»il dirige«) His children (»les siens«), i.e. He keeps them in »right order, controls, and governs their actions«.[3] Implicitly, He does that to prevent them from being tempted by the Devil. Thus God shows through the believers' works and words His goodness and abundant mercy (»pour en toutes leurs œuvres ou parolles manifester sa bonté et les richesses de sa miséricorde«). Therefore, one sign of God's Kingdom is that He is ruling through one's good deeds and words. So whenever we do good, we ought to know that we are acting under the rule of God, and that we are His obedient subjects or children. 2. But God rules also over the unbeliever. His Kingdom can indeed be seen through the punishment of the ungodly, already here on earth. For God destroys the evil-doers (»abysme les réprouvez«). The reprobate (»réprouvez«) are the ones rejected or disapproved by God, for they are disobedient subjects, wrong-doers, people who do not care about His rule (»qui ne le recongnoissent point pour leur Dieu et Seigneur, et ne luy veulent être subiectz«). God, in this case, throws them into the »abysme« (abyss), in other words, the »infernal pit« or »hell«[4]. The

[2] Jean *Calvin*, Institution de la religion chrestienne, ed. Jean-Daniel Benoît, Paris 1960, III, XX, 42. In the earlier editions, this text is the paragraph 36 in chapter XV.

[3] The Oxford English Dictionary [OED], 20 vols, Oxford [2]1989, under »to direct«, 3b.

[4] OED, »abyss«, 1c.

Heavenly Father humbles the proud and arrogant people who refuse to recognize Him as their ruler (»rabbat leur orgueil et arrogance«). The metaphor explains the fact that God punishes evildoers already in this world. One can witness His retribution every day, Calvin writes: »ces choses se font tous les jours devant noz yeux«. To sum up, God's Kingdom is revealed in two ways, through people's both good and evil deeds. That is how the Father shows His authority as the only King. Wrongdoing is punished, but is the opposite rewarded, according to the theologian? Yes, for even though it is not explicitly mentioned in his exegesis, the reward is perceived through God's goodness and mercy, which bring about happiness and joy.

After this spiritual definition of the Kingdom, Calvin stresses once more the fact that the latter is already right here on earth (»On peut veoir que ce Règne est mesmes en ce monde«), and mentions the power of it. Implicitly expressed is the idea that good people suffer by evil-doers, but God's Kingdom is not weakend for all that, for no power is able to resist God's power: »il n'y a nulle puissance qui puisse résister à la sienne«. God's good children suffer indeed in this world, but they must accept life's challenges and bear their crosses.[5] The good news is that the Lord gives them courage and does not forsake them: »notre Seigneur donne force et vigueur à sa parolle, ainsi érigée comme un sceptre, et la fait fructifier et régner, mesme soubs la croix, contemnement et ignominie du monde.« Two ideas are pointed out here: 1. He who follows the Word receives the power to resist all kinds of difficulties and miseries in this world, including the torture of the cross (»croix«), contempt (»contemnement«), and dishonor (»ignominie«); 2. The Word has a fructifying effect (Dieu »la fait fructifier et régner«). Another explanation is that, believing in the Word makes one powerful, for it is like a scepter (»comme un sceptre«), which symbolizes the King's authority and sovereignty.

In a third part of his commentary, the name of the Son is introduced: first God the Father was mentioned, then the Holy Spirit, and now Jesus-Christ. It is not that the Holy Spirit should come

[5] Indeed, as Timothy George writes, »The cross of Christ may in no wise be avoided, for the lamb will never be at peace with the wolf, the dove with eagle, Christ with Belial.« (*George*, John Calvin and Menno Simons, 207).

before the Son – Calvin's conception of Christ throughout the *Institutes* is very clear on this point. The Son is the Word of God, and so the Holy Spirit, being the power which instils the Word into one's conscience, cannot precede it. So the reason why in this exegesis the Son's name is mentioned after the Holy Spirit, is because the theologian first explains how the believer is *directed*. And now he points out that Christ has expressed the fact that the Kingdom is *within* us (»Pourtant aussi Christ dit que le Royaume de Dieu est en nous«). Two other ideas are then put forth: 1. Christ sometimes calls the Church »Kingdom of Heaven«, (Il »appelle aucunesfois l'Eglise le Royaume des cieux«). This church, of which Jesus is the ruler (»en laquelle vrayement il domine«) is not explained, but one understands that it is a spiritual place. It is a metaphor, neither a congregation, nor a building, nor an institution in the concrete sense, but rather the community of believers. 2. He also sometimes calls the predication of the Gospel »Kingdom of Heaven« (»aucunesfois la prédication de l'Evangile«). Christ rules by His Word (»par laquelle il establist sa domination« – to be understood in the etymological sense, from *dominus*, »Lord«). We perceive that the »Kingdom of God« is both a metaphor and a metonymy: as a metaphor, it is like a place, though a spiritual one – it is in one's heart. It could also be called »Eglise« (church) – from the Latin *ecclesia*, meaning »community of the faithful«. However, calling the predication or the spreading of the Word a »Kingdom« is a metonymy. The Kingdom is here the belief in the Word of God. If one does believe, one will preach the Gospel and spread it, and that is how it is related to the metaphoric kingdom. The citizens of this Kingdom consider themselves subjects of one king *only*, Christ. Indeed, the Kingdom without Him does not mean anything, for the Kingdom is his – it is where his Word rules and governs.

A fourth part of Calvin's exegesis, in the 1541 edition, concerns the justification of the request made in the prayer. First, after stressing again the spiritual nature of God's Kingdom (»il est *spirituel* et consiste en choses *spirituelles*«), he mentions the qualities of it: incorruptible and eternal (»il est incorruptible et éternel«). Second, the theologian explains the reason for this second petition, since God's Kingdom is already here, has always been, and will always be. Why, indeed, do we have to ask for its coming? There are two reasons for that, he asserts: 1. We pray for people who do not see God to be touched by His Grace; in other words we pray for the unbelievers to join the community of the faithful. We pray for the wrongdoers to become good. So we pray for the number of believers, who constitute the true church, to increase every day (»c'est à dire que de plus en plus tous les iours nostre Seigneur augmente le nombre de ses subiectz et fidèles«), and that God may be glorified in every way (»desquelz il soit en toutes manières glorifié«). 2. We pray for those, including ourselves, who *do* believe in Him to have our faith strengthened. We pray for receiving more and more of God's graces (»et qu'en ceux qu'il aura *désia* appellez en son Royaume il distribue et multiplie tousiours plus abondamment ses grâces«). I suppose that, since it is about the realm of spirit, the graces we are asking for must be of spiritual nature. We pray for everyone, therefore, to become some day united to God. We pray that God may live and reign in everyone's heart, and that He make everyone whole, or perfectly sound: that by his Grace, »de plus en plus continuellement il vive et règne en eux, iusques à ce que les ayant *parfaictement uniz à soy*, il les remplisse du tout«. This perfect unification of humanity with God somewhat reveals a mystical approach, but this requires a separate discussion, which is beyond the object of the present essay.

We reach the last part or the conclusion of Calvin's exegesis, which is about eschatology, first in the modern theological sense of the word, or eschatology pertaining to things of this world, then to eschatology in the traditional sense. In the last phase of human mental development, according to Calvin, the Devil will be destroyed. What is noteworthy is that this happens *gradually* in this world, according to the theologian. He thus repeats the expression »de plus en plus« (more and more); he means to emphasize the fact that there is an evolution in the human moral advancement. So one should not think of a sudden radical magical change at some vague point in the future, but consider a gradual process. Therefore, eschatology is being realized little by little.[6] It is in the here and now.

[6] Donald K. McKim points out that »While Calvin can say that ›the Kingdom of God increases, stage upon stage, to the end of the world‹, he does not believe in a gradual, evolutionary growth of the kingdom of God through the structures of the

We pray that »que *de plus en plus* il veuille illustrer sa lumière et sa vérité. Parquoy les ténèbres et mensonges du Diable et de ses suppostz s'évanouyssent, soient déchassées, confondues et annéanties«.[7] We pray for the progressive realization of the Kingdom, so that God's light (»lumière«) and truth (»vérité«) be revealed to everyone, and the Devil (or the evil principle) and its followers gradually vanish (»s'évanouissent«), be thrown out (»déchassées«), unmasked (»confondues«), and annihilated (»annéanties«). The evil will eventually completely disappear from this world. We pray for that and believe that it is happening a little more every day. This is certainly a happy and optimistic vision of humanity.

But Calvin also believes in eschatology in the traditional sense, and so in the following way he ends his interpretation: »En priant que le Règne de Dieu advienne ainsi, *pareillement* nous prions qu'il soit finalement consommé et accomply, qui sera *au iour de son Iugement*, quand toutes choses seront révélées. Auquel iour lui seul sera exalté et sera tout en tous, après avoir recueilly les siens en gloire, et avoir déprimé, subiugué et ruyné tout le règne du Diable.« Therefore, this concrete world on earth will end for the humans at some point in time. This last part of the exegesis, concerning the Day of Judgment, shows of course a theologian who also believes in a world after this material one, which is not surprizing, since this idea is present in the Bible. Calvin, as a faithful reader of the latter, believes that in that Day everything will be revealed and that God alone will be exalted. On that day, everybody will *only* see Him (»sera tout en tous«), referring to the First Corinthians 15:28.[8] That means that only the believers will re-

present world. The kingdom is not ours to win; it's God's to give [...]. The present reign of God is found where people both by denial of themselves and by contempt of the world and of earthly life, pledge themselves to God's righteousness in order to aspire to a heavenly life.« (*McKim*, Theological Turning Points, 163).

[7] As John Hesselink puts it, »Calvin also makes clear what was only implied before, namely, that God reigns in two ways: in the renewal of the lives of believers and in the overcoming of Satan and all God's ennemies. The goal in both cases is to restore order in a confused and disordered world, for ›disorder (*ataxia*) and confusion‹ are the ›opposite of the kingdom of God‹.« (*Hesselink*, Calvin on the Kingdom of Christ, 158).

[8] »When all things are subjected to him, then the Son himself will also be subjected to the one who put all things in subjection under him, so that God may be all in all« (New Revised Standard Version).

main. In the other world, the Devil will have no place at all, for his fragile kingdom (»le règne du Diable«) will have disappeared: it will be knocked down (»déprimé«), subdued (»subjugué«), and ruined (»ruiné«). It is noticeable that this last part, devoted to eschatology in the traditional sense, is but a small section of the exegesis, which is understandable insofar as nobody knows about the life beyond this one, but one can talk about the progressive eschatology in the present material world. So the main part of the commentary on Matthew 6:10 is about one's earthly life, i.e. on eschatolgy in the modern or, if I may say, existentialist sense of the word. Hope is the fundamental idea, for the Kingdom of God is being realized before our eyes on a daily basis; it is at our own hand. Our prayer helps us to appreciate it more and more as we see ourselves changing into better individuals and enjoying life better, and as we see others joining the community of the faithful. Although not explicit, these ideas are somehow suggested in Calvin's commentary.

2. The last version of the Institutes (the 1560 French edition)

We notice first that a few lines have been added to the beginning of the exegesis. In this introduction the commentator asserts that this second petition does not bring anything really new to the first. There is, however, a reason for the redundancy: »Car si nous pensons bien à nostre tardiveté et rudesse, il est besoin que nous ayons les oreilles battues souvent de ce qui doit estre tant et plus notoire«.[9] Two nouns are here stressed: »tardiveté« (slowness, dullness of intellect or comprehension) and »rudesse« (ignorance, or even absence of virtue)[10]. Because we are slow and ignorant, we need more explanation and repetition. We have ears but we do not hear, Calvin thinks, so we need to hear the Word of God over and

[9] »[f]or if we consider our languor in the greatest matters of all, it behooves us to extend our discussion in order to drive home something that ought to have been thoroughly known of itself« (Institutes of the Christian Religion, ed. John T. McNeill, transl. Ford Lewis Battles, Louisville, KY 1960, III, XX, 42).

[10] See OED, »rudeness«, 2b.

over again (»il est *besoin* que nous ayons les oreilles battues souvent de ce qui doit estre tant et plus notoire«). If we understand the first petition, it is »notoire« (from *notorius*, from *noscere*, »to know«), or »it ought to have been thoroughly known of itself«, that »Hallowed be Thy Name« includes »Thy Kingdom Come«, but we still need to say it again in a different way. Therefore, after we pray that God destroy all that stain his holy name (»Après doncques qu'il nous a esté ordonné de prier Dieu qu'il abbate, et finalement destruise tout ce qui souille son *sacré Nom* [...]«[11]), we pray for the coming of His Kingdom. We see that from the outset the theologian's tone is more critical in this last edition. Then he states that one can talk about God as one's King only when one renounces the material world and aspires to live spiritually by devoting oneself to God's justice: »Dieu est tenu pour Roy, quand les hommes, renonçans à eux mesmes et mesprisans le monde et ceste vie terrestre, s'addonnent à la justice de Dieu pour aspirer à la vie céleste«.[12] He also mentions the fact that he is repeating what he has already discussed elsewhere – referring to the *Institutes* III, III, 19. We realize that repetition is deliberate and has a didactic reason for Calvin. Repetition is also used by Jesus, as Calvin contends, in the Lord's Prayer.

From here the theologian goes back to his 1541 version and rewrites it, thus expressing in a new way the main idea of the kingdom on earth as being manifested through God's retribution. In the earlier editions, he had divided the kingdom into two parts, mentioning first God's goodness and mercy through his deserving children, then his punishment of the sinners. In the last edition, however, he uses a bitter tone saying: »Ainsi il y a deux parties de ce règne: c'est que Dieu corrige et abbate par la vertu de son Esprit toutes cupiditez de la chair, lesquelles se dressent à grand foulle pour batailler contre luy. Secondement, qu'il plie et forme tous nos sens pour les assuiettir à son empire«.[13] The emphasis is put on

[11] »Therefore, after we have been bidden to ask God to subject and finally completely destroy everything that casts a stain upon his holy name [...].«

[12] »God reigns where men, both by denial of themselves and by contempt of the world and of earthly life, pledge themselves to his righteousness in order to aspire to a heavenly life.«

[13] »Thus there are two parts to this Kingdom: first, that God by the power of his Spirit correct all the desires of the flesh which by squadrons war against him; second, that he shape all our thoughts in obedience to his rule.«

»correction«, and the distinction between reward and punishment, or good people and evildoers, is not made here. Everyone is equally concerned. The two following stages are indicated: 1. The destruction of evil tendencies and thoughts in humans. 2. The »the rule« of God.

Another point the theologian makes is that, in order to become a good subject of God as King, is to start with oneself. Before we wish to change the society, we must change ourselves: »Pourtant, quiconque veut tenir bon ordre en ceste requeste, il faut qu'il commence par soy, désirant d'estre purgé de toutes corruptions qui troublent en son cœur l'estat paisible du règne de Dieu, et en infectent la pureté.«[14] Self-criticism is an essential feature of the new version. In the 1541 version of the *Institutes*, the prayer stresses more God's action, whereas in the last edition, the theologian asks for more effort from humans. The human will and responsibility are, indeed, more strongly expressed in this edition. The fact that *all* are sinners is also better articulated here. Everyone, he insists, must follow His Word, which is like a scepter: »Au reste pource que la parolle de Dieu est comme un sceptre royal, il nous est ici ordonné de prier qu'il assuiestisse les esprits et les cœurs de *tous* à une obéissance *volontaire* d'icelle.«[15]

The concept of church is also differently conveyed in the new edition. The theologian is less abstract here and talks of church not as much as Jesus does, which corresponds more to the spirit of the first edition, but rather as Paul does. The church has become a more concrete group of Christians. The idea of mission is then conspicuous in the last edition. After we have reached – although not explicit, this idea is presupposed – a certain degree of maturity in our faith, we must go and rescue others: »Après nous pourrons descendre aux meschans qui résistent à son empire avec obstination et fureur désespérée,«[16] and »Nous avons à désirer que cela [God's retributive justice] se face chacun iour, afin que Dieu re-

[14] »Therefore, no others keep a lawful order in this petition but those who begin with themselves, that is, to be cleansed of all corruptions that disturb the peaceful state of God's Kingdom and sully its purity.«

[15] »Now, because the word of God is like a royal scepter, we are bidden here to entreat him to bring all men's minds and hearts into voluntary obedience to it.«

[16] »Afterward we should descend to the impious, who stubbornly and with desperate madness resist his authority.«

cueille des églises de toutes les parties du monde, qu'il les multiplie en nombre, qu'il les enrichisse de ses dons, qu'il y establisse bon ordre [...]«[17]

The following ideas are already clearly presented in the 1541 edition, but in 1560 they are simply rephrased: the perfect world will come with the coming of Christ, one must patiently bear one's Cross, etc. The idea of evolution, a gradual improvement of humans' understanding of God and morals, is also present. The ending is hopeful and somewhat similar to the first edition. I note, however, that the term »Antechrist« is used in 1560, instead of »Diable«, which is actually the last word of his commentary in 1541 – the Devil who will be completely destroyed. Moreover, in the first edition, Calvin calls the ending of our material world the Day of Judgment (»jour de son Iugement, quand toutes choses seront révélées«), whereas in 1560, the ending is presented as the Day when Antichrist is destroyed and that God has eliminated »toute impiété par la clarté de son advènement.«[18]

3. Conclusion

First, the fact that Calvin needed to write anew his text is significant. His interpretation has not changed so much, although a shift from Jesus' view of the church to Paul's view of it is in my opinion rather important. But, one might argue, since Jesus is being vague on this issue, it is hard to prove that there is a real difference between Paul and him. Furthermore, it seems that Calvin has psychologically changed: he is less optimistic, and needs to blame ourselves more for our shortcomings. He does not exclude himself of course. It is self-criticism at the same time. Finally, the fact that the theologian wants to say in a different and longer way basically the same things, justifies what he considers redundancy in Jesus, since,

[17] »We must daily desire that God gather churches unto himself from all parts of the earth; that he spread and increase them in number; that he adorn them with gifts, that he establish a lawful order among them [...].«

[18] »at last he slays Antichrist with the Spirit of his mouth, and destroys all ungodliness by the brightness of his coming.« He thus refers to II Thess. (2:8): »And then the lawless one will be revealed, whom the Lord Jesus will destroy with the breath of his mouth, annihilating him by the manifestation of his coming.«

according to Calvin, the first petition should also make the second one obvious (»notoire«).

John H. Mazaheri, PhD, Professor of French, Auburn University (Auburn, AL, USA)

Abstract: In this article I compare Calvin's exegesis of the Second Petition of The Lord's Prayer in the 1541–57 editions of the Institutes with the one he offers in the last edition of his work (1560). My close reading is based on the French editions only with a rhetorical approach. First, it is interesting to note that for the last edition Calvin rewrote his paragraph on the Second Petition entirely, which he had also done with the First Petition. Second, the formal structures as well as the content are somewhat different. In the 1541–57 editions, the paragraph is divided into two parts: (1) He explains the reason why we pray that God be considered our only king – implicitly no other (earthly) ruler should be accepted. (2) He explains why right here on Earth already we are punished, if we do not accept this principle and follow another ruler. Therefore, »Thy Kingdom come« is not only about the future, but also about now. It is an existential issue. In the 1560 edition, Calvin divides his paragraph into three parts: (1) He claims that the First and the Second Petitions say basically the same thing. So the reason for the repetition is just because we are too slow to understand God. Besides, if we believe in Him, we have to deny ourselves and despise our earthly life, and consider the Lord our only ruler and king, right here and now. (2) We pray that God destroy the Evil that is in everyone. (3) We pray that we live according to God's rule alone. To conclude, two important differences are stressed: (1) In the last edition, Calvin puts more emphasis on the evil spirit in humans. (2) Although in all the editions of the Institutes the crucial role of the Holy Spirit is mentioned, it is only in the last edition that the name of Christ appears, the Son without whom we cannot live in God's Kingdom.

Keywords: John Calvin, Lord's Prayer

ISSN 0254-4407 – Zwingliana 40 (2013), 113–126

Faculty Recruitment and Retention in the Early Modern Era

The Zurich Lectorium, c. 1560–1610

Carrie Euler

In her book *Teaching the Reformation: Ministers and Their Message in Basel,* Amy Nelson Burnett declares that the hiring of university faculty at Basel between roughly 1530 and 1630 was driven by »a mixture of parochialism, parsimony, and political influence.«[1] One example she offers is the difficulty the university and city officials faced in finding a replacement for Andreas Karlstadt, who died suddenly of disease in 1541. Karlstadt was a refugee from Wittenberg who had been hired based on the recommendation of Heinrich Bullinger in Zurich. Yet his time in Basel had been marred by controversy. In particular, he was often at odds with Basel minister and professor Oswald Myconius over revisions to the university statutes. After his death in 1541, Bullinger once again tried to steer Basel towards hiring a foreign refugee, Peter Martyr Vermigli, who had recently fled Italy for religious reasons and arrived in Switzerland. As Burnett recounts, the Basel magistrates balked at Bullinger's suggestion for two reasons. First, »The potential parallels between Karlstadt and Vermigli were only too clear, and it is unlikely that either the professors or the Senate

[1] Amy Nelson *Burnett,* Teaching the Reformation: Ministers and their Message in Basel, 1529–1629, Oxford 2006 (Oxford Studies in Historical Theology), 81.

would willingly risk hiring another outsider.«[2] Second, the Senate also liked the idea of saving money by paying the current Hebrew professor one salary for doing two jobs, his own and that of Karlstadt's. Eventually they did hire a replacement for Karlstadt, Martin Cellarius, who, Burnett explains, was not necessarily the best candidate but was related by marriage to two Basel senators. Hence, her statement about »parochialism, parsimony, and political influence.«

Twenty years later a strikingly similar scenario played out in Zurich, and the Basel faculty and Senate may have shared a laugh at Heinrich Bullinger's expense. Peter Martyr Vermigli – having held positions in Strasbourg and England in the meantime – was hired by the Zurich theological academy or Lectorium in 1556.[3] By 1560, disagreements between Vermigli and long-standing Old Testament professor Theodor Bibliander had led to controversy and to Bibliander's early retirement. In 1562 Vermigli died, and a struggle ensued over his replacement.[4] Bullinger and the rest of the faculty wanted to hire another foreign scholar of international renown; specifically, they suggested Jerome Zanchi, another former Italian who was currently working in Strasbourg but looking to move. The Zurich city council balked, however, at the prospect of hiring another foreigner. They refused Zanchi on the grounds that he had signed the Augsburg Confession and then passed a law requiring citizenship for all future professors. The faculty's suggestion for a homegrown candidate – Ludwig Lavater – humbly demurred, protesting that his Hebrew skills were not good enough. Ultimately, Josias Simler, the other Old Testament professor, was moved into Vermigli's position, while Johannes Wolf, pastor of Zurich's second largest church (the Fraumünster), was put in Simler's place. Wolf continued serving as pastor while also taking on the Old Testament job.

[2] *Burnett,* Teaching the Reformation, 82.

[3] On Vermigli's hiring, see Michael *Baumann*, Petrus Martyr Vermigli: Doctor, Lehrer der Heiligen Schrift und Zürcher. Hinweise zu Vermiglis Tätigkeit in Zürich, in: Peter Martyr Vermigli: Humanism, Republicanism, Reformation, ed. Emidio Campi, Geneva 2002 (Travaux d'Humanisme et Renaissance 365), 212–224.

[4] Most of the evidence for this article is taken from three volumes of *Acta Scholastica* held in the Zurich Staatsarchiv, E II 458, 459, and 466. The notes regarding Vermigli's replacement are found in E II 458, 32–38. Hereinafter, all references to documents that begin E II or G I refer to documents in the Zurich Staatsarchiv.

This incident reveals that Zurich, like Basel, was guided by parochialism in its faculty hiring. The story also reveals the political influence the city magistrates had in hiring. In terms of parsimony, Vermigli had enjoyed relatively comfortable terms of employment – higher than average pay and light teaching duties. It is likely that the magistrates knew they would not have to pay a local candidate as much as a famous foreign scholar. In order to investigate some of these issues more thoroughly, this article surveys the faculty at the Zurich Lectorium from the time of Vermigli's death through the first decade of the seventeenth century.

The Lectorium had its roots in Zwingli's reorganization of education in Zurich in the 1520s.[5] In addition to reforming the Grossmünster and Fraumünster Latin schools, Zwingli instituted daily public biblical lectures in the nave of the Grossmünster. These lectures, which were more like interactive discussions, became famous in the Reformed world; in the 1520s and 30s, they were often attended by foreign students and guests, and the fruits of the discussions resulted in the publication of the Zurich German Bible. By 1560 this lively tradition of public lectures had developed into a more formal institution of higher education. The Lectorium still had a close relationship with the Latin schools, but it had a set number of professors and its own classroom; lectures and exams were given in theology, languages, and natural philosophy.[6] It also had a fairly impressive record-keeping system, which makes it a rich subject for historians. This article is based on those records, now housed in the cantonal archives (Staatsarchiv) of Zurich. These archives have been known to historians of Zurich for some

[5] For Zwingli's reorganization of Zurich's schools and the origins of the Lectorium, see Ulrich *Ernst*, Geschichte des Zürcherischen Schulwesens bis gegen das Ende des sechzehnten Jahrhunderts, Winterthur 1879; Hans *Nabholz*, Zürichs Höhere Schulen von der Reformation bis zur Gründung der Universität, 1525–1833, in: Die Universität Zürich 1833–1933 und ihre Vorläufer, ed. Ernst Gagliardi et al., Zurich 1938, 1–164; Kurt *Spillman*, Zwingli und die Zürcher Schulverhältnisse, in: Zwingliana 11 (1962), 427–448; Karin *Maag*, Seminary or University?: The Genevan Academy and Reformed Higher Education, 1560–1620, Aldershot 1995 (St. Andrews Studies in Reformation History), 131–139.

[6] The school is referred to (in the archives and by modern historians) using many different names, including Pfarrerschule, Carolinum, Collegium, Schola Tigurina, and Lectorium. I have chosen the latter because it seems to be the name used the most by recent historians.

time. In the last ten to fifteen years, scholars Karin Maag and Anja Silvia Göing have published a few short pieces looking at different aspects of the Zurich schools.[7] In 1999, a publication produced to accompany an exhibit at the Zentralbibliothek contained brief studies of several of the scholars teaching at the school circa 1550.[8] But no one, as of yet, has produced a longitudinal study of Zurich's faculty or students similar to Burnett's in Basel, a study that attempts to assess developments and changes over the confessional age.[9] This article offers a small start in that direction. First it will provide an overview of the structure and recruitment of the faculty between 1560 and 1610; second, a look at some individual faculty members will illuminate further the kinds of men who taught at the Lectorium; and third, examples of problems faced by the faculty and the city council in maintaining a qualified teaching staff will reveal the pressures and changes that affected institutions of higher education in the post-Reformation era.

For most of the period in question (1560–1610), there were seven professors appointed to teach at the Lectorium. Three were in biblical theology: two Old Testament and one New. Records towards the end of the century sometimes distinguish between the two Old Testament chairs, calling one a professor of Old Testa-

[7] Karin *Maag,* Financing Education: the Zürich Approach, 1550–1620, in: Reformations Old and New: Essays on the Socio-Economic Impact of Religious Change, c. 1470–1630, ed. Beat A. Kümin, Aldershot 1996 (St. Andrews Studies in Reformation History), 203–216; Anja-Silvia *Göing,* Die Zürcher Hohe Schule, 1525–1560, als Bildungsinstitution, in: Zeitschrift für pädagogische Historiographie 8 (2002), 29–83; Anja-Silvia *Göing* and Hans-Ulrich *Musolff,* Anfänge und Grundlegungen moderner Pädagogik im 16. und 17. Jahrundert, Köln 2003 (Beiträge zur historischen Bildungsforschung 29); Anja-Silvia *Göing,* Die Zürcher Schulprotokolle 1563: Spezifika einer Gattung, in: Konfession, Migration und Elitenbildung: Studien zur Theologenausbildung des 16. Jahrhunderts, eds Herman J. Selderhuis and Markus Wriedt, Leiden 2007 (Brill's Series in Church History 31), 141–170.

[8] Schola Tigurina: Die Zürcher Hohe Schule und ihre Gelehrten um 1550, ed. Hans Ulrich Bächtold et al., Zurich 1999.

[9] *Ernst,* Geschichte and *Nabholz,* Zürichs Höhere Schulen do look at Zurich's schools over long periods of time, but they do not fill this lacuna in the historiography for a couple of reasons. Ernst wrote over a century ago; his work contains some errors and does not address more recent historigraphical issues, such as confessionalization. Nabholz wrote over seventy years ago and was mostly concerned with the eighteenth and nineteenth centuries; he offers very little analysis of the second half of the sixteenth century.

ment *in prophetis* and the other *in lege,* of the prophets and of the law, but it is not clear how strictly this division was upheld.[10] Initially, one of the Old Testament professors doubled as the Hebrew professor, but with the coming of Peter Martyr Vermigli in 1556 that changed, and a separate line was created for Hebrew. In addition to the three theology positions there were three in languages: Hebrew, Greek, and Latin. (The Latin position was sometimes referred to by other names – Rhetoric, Logic, or Dialectic). The seventh was in *Physica*, which meant natural philosophy and medicine. In 1600, a new position in History was added by creating a new line. With the new school ordinance of 1609, however, the number of professors dropped from eight to six. One of the Old Testament positions was dropped, and the Greek and Hebrew lines were combined into one.[11]

This shifting around of positions in the early seventeenth century is significant, for it shows that the second half of the sixteenth century was a distinct period in the history of the Zurich academy. The faculty first took on this shape in the 1550s, as the Lectorium grew out of its earlier more spontaneous form into a more formal institution of higher education, and it retained this shape for fifty years. In 1600, this stability began to break down, and with a new school ordinance in 1609 things changed even more. The privileged status that the two Old Testament positions held in this period of stability might also be significant. The Old Testament professors were always placed first in lists of the faculty, and, though men were frequently promoted up from another faculty position to Old Testament, no one ever went from Old Testament to something else. This is intriguing, because it demonstrates that the heavy emphasis put on the Old Testament by theologians like Zwingli in their theology had an impact on the organization of the school, but that by 1600, this influence was waning. Around 1600 one also sees an increase in the use of Latin in the school records, which, up until this point, had been almost entirely in German. This may be interpreted as a sign of the increasing professionalization of the clergy. This phenomenon of the clergy becoming more of a sepa-

[10] For example, see the list for the year 1592 in Catalogi Scholae Tigurinae, E II 497, 24.3. Compare with the list for 1594 in E II 459, 28.

[11] Acta Scholastica, E II 459, 49; E II 466, 95.

rate professional group – an educated elite – has been observed elsewhere in Europe during the age of confessionalization.[12]

There seems to have been two approaches to finding professors after the 1562 law that required their citizenship. The first and most obvious was that the city hired men already citizens of Zurich, often sons of earlier professors and teachers, almost always men who had been local preachers and pastors before (and often during and after) becoming professors. The second solution was to hire men from outside of Zurich – but never too far outside, usually from territories surrounding Zurich – and to grant them citizenship before they assumed the position at the Lectorium. A result of both of these strategies was that, increasingly over the years, men whose names initially appear as students in the records later appear as faculty. The academy, whose primary function had always been to educate and train clergy for Zurich and its environs, became a fairly insular place that also educated and trained its own faculty.

It is important to add, however, that most of the former students who became faculty had indeed studied outside of Zurich, thanks to a program of travel bursaries from the city for students to study at academies and universities abroad. As the research of Karin Maag has demonstrated, roughly half of the students who came up through Zurich's Latin schools and the Lectorium spent a year or two in places like Basel, Heidelberg, Geneva, Wittenberg, or Marburg.[13] The *Acta Scholastica* contain many references to students abroad – who was studying where each year – and to what happened to them upon their return. When they arrived back home, students were to provide school authorities with a thorough account of where they had been, with whom they had resided, and what lectures they had heard. Faculty were also advised to watch and make sure that the students had not picked up any foreign habits or fashions while away.[14] This system of foreign exchanges is significant to the history of the Lectorium, because it allowed Zurich students to learn from internationally-renowned faculty, to

[12] Rosemary *O'Day,* The English Clergy: The Emergence and Consolidation of a Profession, 1558–1642, Leicester 1979.

[13] *Maag,* Financing Education.

[14] Acta Scholastica, E II 458, 157v.

bring ideas and training back with them, while the schools in Zurich still remained relatively local and self-contained.

Individual examples of faculty at the Lectorium will help to illuminate the kinds of men who taught there and what their backgrounds were. A good person to start with is Josias Simler, because he was part of the solution to the problematic situation left by the death of Peter Martyr Vermigli, and because he was probably the most prolific, internationally-known scholar among the second generation of professors. Simler was Heinrich Bullinger's godson; he was born in the 1520s, educated at Zurich, Basel, and Strasbourg.[15] He became professor of the New Testament in Zurich in the 1550s; in 1560 he moved up to one of the Old Testament positions, working alongside Vermigli. When Vermigli died, Simler moved to the other Old Testament position, taking Vermigli's place, and Johannes Wolf took the other. Simler went on to be widely known, at least in the Germanic world, for his scholarly works, including his magisterial survey of the Swiss republic, *De Republica Helvetiorum*.

Two interesting third-generation professors were Markus Bäumler and Kaspar Waser. Bäumler was born in 1555 in a small town within the canton of Zurich. He attended the Lectorium and is mentioned in the records as a student abroad in Tubingen in 1580.[16] Before returning to Zurich, he served for about eight years as a teacher and pastor in Germany. In 1594 he was granted Zurich citizenship and brought in to be archdeacon and assistant preacher at the Grossmünster; at the same time, he taught grammar in one of the Latin schools and served a stint as Schulherr (more about that position below). He gave up his preaching post in 1600 or 1601, however, to become a full-time professor of either New Testament and Latin language or Greek at the Lectorium (the manuscript records disagree on the exact year and which position); from 1607 until his death in 1611, he was professor of Old Testament theology[17] During his teaching career, Bäumler published se-

[15] Much of the biographical information for faculty in this study – especially things like birth dates that are not found in the Acta Scholastica – was taken from Emanuel *Dejung* and Willy *Wuhrmann*, Zürcher Pfarrerbuch, 1519–1952, Zurich 1953.

[16] Album in Tigurina Schola Studentium, E II 479, 58.

[17] Evidence of these appointments can be found in various manuscripts: Verzeich-

veral German religious texts and one Latin grammar. Kaspar Waser was born in the 1560s in Zurich, educated there and at Heidelberg.[18] From approximately 1598 to 1625, he taught Hebrew, Greek, and finally Old Testament at the Lectorium, all the while also serving as pastor in the nearby town of Witikon. He also served a stint as Schulherr around 1609.[19] One of his sons, Heinrich Waser, went on to be Burgermeister of Zurich in the seventeenth century.

Bäumler and Waser are good examples of how a local boy, or, in Bäumler's case, a nearly-local boy, could work his way through the Zurich school system and rise to the top. Their respective careers illustrate some interesting points about the Lectorium in this period. First, the fact that Bäumler taught in one of the Latin schools while also serving as Schulherr is significant, because it demonstrates the close relationship between the Lectorium and the Latin schools during this period. The Schulherr was the head administrator and record-keeper of the schools.[20] The position rotated every two years, but not only through the professors of the Lectorium. As often as not, the serving Schulherr was not a professor, but held a different position, such as teacher at one of the Latin schools or head pastor at the Fraumünster. The *Acta Scholastica*, the name for the main collection of documents used for this study, were recorded by the Schulherr. They are essentially records of faculty regular faculty meetings held by the faculty at all the schools and sometimes attended by one or two city magistrates. They contain mainly information about the faculty and students of the Lectorium, but also a fair amount about the Latin schools. That, combined with the common trajectory of students like Bäumler – from student in a Latin school, to attending the »public

nisse der Inhaber von geistlichen und Schulpfründen in Stadt und Landschaft Zürich und in Landfrieden, G I 179, 6r, 10v, 11v; Acta Scholastica, E II 459, 36r–37r, 42r, 57a v.

[18] For Waser as a student in Zurich and his time abroad, see Acta Scholastica, E II 458, 372b r, 401r. Waser travelled extensively as a young man as the *Hofmeister* for J.P. Hainzel of Degerstein (*Dejung*, Zürcher Pfarrerbuch, 599).

[19] Acta Scholastica, E II 459, 85a r; Verzeichnisse der Inhaber, G I 179, 10v–11v.

[20] There is not a perfect English translation for this title. The most obvious, »superintendent,« was a title used sometimes for the head of each of the Latin schools, so I do not want to use it here.

lectures« for a year or two, then to study abroad, then home to take exams and teach in the Latin school, then to a pastorate and/or professorship – reminds us that the Zurich Lectorium was less of an independent theological academy than just one step in a more complex system of pastoral education and training in Zurich.[21]

Waser, unlike Bäumler, did not give up his pastoral position in the city when he became a professor. His career brings up the issue of how professors were paid. In the 1520s, Zwingli established that the faculty would be paid through the foundations of the pre-Reformation Grossmünsterstift, or chapter. As the old canons (Chorherren) died, faculty took over their livings; these were then passed down, much like tenure lines today. For example, the records of 1563 indicate that Josias Simler inherited Peter Martyr Vermigli's living when he took over the latter's Old Testament position.[22] One of the Grossmünster livings was specifically attached to the post of »deacon of the Silvershield.« The Silvershield was an old house by that name located just up the street from the Grossmünster. Since before the Reformation, this house had been the dwelling place of one of the deacons of the Grossmünster chapter. Around 1560, the position became associated with the academy, and from that point forward, with the exception of two years between 1578 and 1580, it was always held by the professor of Hebrew. Kaspar Waser was deacon of the Silvershield and raised his family at the house in the early seventeenth century.[23]

The story behind the two years in which the deacon of the Silvershield was not the Hebrew professor reveals how the Zurich faculty and magistrates did sometimes run into difficulties finding and paying faculty for each of the seven professor lines. One reason seems to be that a professorship in the Lectorium was not considered all that desirable or prestigious compared to pastoral positions in Zurich's churches. In this specific case in 1578, there

[21] As Karin Maag explains, both the Genevan and Zurich academies went by various names in the sixteenth century, names that sometimes referred only to the higher level theology school and sometimes indicated the theology school *and* the lower Latin school or schools combined as one institution. *Maag,* Seminar or University?

[22] Acta Scholastica, E II 458, 32v; Verzeichnisse der Inhaber, G I 179, 11r.

[23] *Dejung,* Zürcher Pfarrerbuch, 599.

seems to have been some difficulty filling the position of New Testament theology. In 1575, the New Testament professor, Heinrich Bullinger's son, left the position to become head pastor of St. Peter's church in Zurich. Rudolph Körner was chosen to replace him in 1576, but he only lasted about a year. Körner was a former student who was only twenty-five at the time and serving as a deacon in the Fraumünster; it is likely that his year of teaching was unsuccessful due to his youth and inexperience.[24] Instead, Felix Trüb, the current Hebrew professor and deacon of the Silvershield, was moved to New Testament. Another young former student, Heinrich Wolf, son of the aforementioned Johannes Wolf, was put in the Hebrew position, but Trüb was allowed to keep the Silvershield living. Two years later, however, Wolf and Trüb switched positions, putting Trüb back in Hebrew and Wolf in New Testament.[25] The notes in the records suggest that the move was not considered necessarily permanent, and that Wolf and the Schulherr would reconsider every year how things were going. They also indicate that the faculty hoped to fill the New Testament position with young men who had recently completed their studies at the Lectorium itself.[26] Four years later, in 1584, Wolf is nowhere to be found in the records, and it is not clear who was teaching New Testament. Wolf appears again in 1587 back in the Hebrew position and as deacon of the Silvershield. This move was made possibly because Trüb was able to take over the recently deceased Ludwig Lavater's position archdeacon in the Grossmünster. Five years later Wolf also gave up teaching to take over his father's position as head pastor of the Fraumünster.

Although it might take some further research to work out exactly what was happening between Wolf and Trüb, it appears as though they both preferred to have the Hebrew position, probably because it came with the house of the Silvershield, or possibly because they both felt more comfortable in the subject of Hebrew than that of New Testament theology (which is interesting in itself and again speaks to Zurich's focus on Old Testament theology and

[24] Verzeichnisse der Inhaber, G I 179, 9r, 13v. Although this record indicates that Körner started in 1575, other sources suggest it was not until the following year.

[25] Ibid., 13r–v.

[26] Acta Scholastica, E II 458, 308r.

language). The main lesson to draw is that both of them eventually left to became pastors in city churches. In fact, from the early 1580s forward, the New Testament position was filled with recent graduates of the Lectorium, graduates who soon advanced into more prestigious positions, either Old Testament or Hebrew teaching positions or pastoral posts in the city. Rudolf Körner, the youth first put in the New Testament position in 1576, never went back to teaching at the Lectorium. He became head pastor at St. Peter's in 1583, but he continued to be involved with the schools as superintendent of the Fraumünster school from 1591 to 1594 and, for a brief time in 1594, as Schulherr.[27]

This leads back once again to the issue of money, or parsimony. Not all the professors had full livings from the chapter, and even when they did, the pay was not great. Most faculty members had to supplement their living with preaching positions either in the city or in outlying towns and villages. Kaspar Waser is once again an example; even though he was deacon of the Silvershield, he remained pastor of Witikon the entire time he was a professor. Johannes Wolf remained pastor of the Fraumünster the whole time he was professor of the Old Testament. Jacob Ulrich, professor of Latin from 1576 to 1605, was also the pastor at Schwamendingen, another small town nearby. There are many more similar examples. The case of Markus Bäumler, who held no other positions besides professor during his years at the Lectorium, is fairly rare for this time period.

Another professor who lasted a long time at the Lectorium and did not take on other pastoral duties was the Professor of Physica from 1546 to 1563, Conrad Gessner. Gessner was a true scholar who published several books known to scientists and doctors throughout Europe.[28] At first he was paid a stipend of forty florins by the city; in 1558, he received one of the canon (Chorherr) stipends in the Grossmünsterstift. In 1563, the faculty and magistrates became concerned that Gessner's teaching load was too heavy. They offered to relieve him of some of his lectures – putting in place two young graduates, Georg Keller and Caspar Wolf – but

[27] Acta Scholastica, E II 458, 429r; E II, 459, 29r.

[28] For more on Gessner, see Urs *Leu,* Konrad Gessner: Naturforscher und Lehrer, in: Schola Tigurina: Die Zürcher Hohe Schule und ihre Gelehrten um 1550, 38–41.

Gessner refused the offer, claiming that it would not look right to have him receive his stipend without doing the work.[29] Two years later, he died, and Keller and Wolf did, in fact, take over.

Soon after Gessner's death, a situation arose that demonstrates how the boundaries between the Lectorium and the Latin schools were not hard and fast, and how teaching duties could be shuffled between faculty. In 1566, Ludwig Lavater and Rudolph Funk, teachers at the Fraumünster school, were asked to take on Friday morning Latin exercises for the Lectorium students, in addition to their other teaching duties.[30] They did this for a year, but in 1567, they asked to be relieved and were replaced by Georg Keller, professor of physics, and Huldrych Zwingli the Younger, professor of New Testament. Twenty-five years later, the faculty seem to have adopted a more systematic approach to relieving the burdens of teaching. In the 1590s, the names of assistant professors (*coadjutores*) start to appear in the records, regularly listed after the names of the »ordinary« professors.[31] The hiring of assistants is a significant sign of both the overburdened state of the Lectorium and also its increasing institutionalization or bureaucratization. The school had come a long way from the 1520s when the leading lights of the Zurich Reformation would hold dynamic, interactive lectures in the nave of the Grossmünster.

The overburdened state of the schools becomes very clear in the records in the year 1591, when the professors petitioned the city council for a revision to the – then thirty-one years old – school ordinance (Ordnung). In this petition, the faculty argued that while the number of students and the general workload of the professors had increased over the years, the pay was poor, and many students and teachers had difficulties supporting their families.[32] Their concerns focused around the money in the old chapter foundation (Stift), and how it was going to run out if things were not changed. They pointed out that many of the preachers in and around Zurich were getting old and dying, and they feared there would be no one to replace them.

[29] Acta Scholastica, E II 458, 53v; *Ernst*, Geschichte, 105.

[30] Acta Scholastica, E II 458, 75r.

[31] Acta Scholastica, E II 459, 28v; Catalogi Scholae Tigurinae, E II 497, 24.3r–v.

[32] Acta Scholastica, E II 458, 431r–432v.

In addition to shedding light on the financial straits of Zurich higher education, this document provides a fascinating glimpse into the mindset of the educators themselves and how they viewed the recent history of city's schools. The faculty referred in one place to the »Reformation of this church« and in another to »the time of the Reformation.«[33] It is clear that they recognized that they were living at some chronological distance from the time when the academy and the Zurich Reformed church were founded in order to spread the »teaching of the holy gospel.« They looked back with longing to the time of Zwingli and still held strongly to his original belief that higher education was crucial to the maintenance of the Reformed faith. They wrote of the praise that had been heaped on Zurich by others for its superior school system and clearly believed that their city had inspired other territories and cities to establish churches and schools as well. »This Christian and praiseworthy ordinance,« they declared, »has brought with it such great use, not only to the city of Zurich with its many churches and schools in the city and territory, but also other territories, cities, churches, and communities.«[34] Nevertheless, they believed the Zurich schools were in trouble, that many serious problems had developed with finance, teaching, and administration since the time of Zwingli. They begged the city council to revise the ordinance so that »scholarship and teaching and also true religion may be maintained.«[35]

In conclusion, it does appear that »parochialism, parsimony, and political influence« did guide the hiring of faculty at Zurich's Lectorium between 1560 and 1610. The evidence also suggests that the increasing burdens of teaching and administration affected the caliber and prestige of the faculty. In this time period, thirty-two different men filled the seven permanent faculty positions at the Lectorium. Only two or three of these men stayed more than fifteen years at the academy. More and more, it seems as if professorships were treated as stepping stones to the more prestigious preaching positions at city churches.

[33] Ibid., 431r.
[34] Ibid., 431r.
[35] Ibid., 432v.

One of the most famous seventeenth-century Zurichers will serve as a final example. Johann Jacob Breitinger taught Latin for a few years before going on to be pastor of St. Peters and then Antistes at the Grossmünster. Breitinger became an internationally known scholar, author of many works, and was a member of the Zurich delegation at the Synod of Dort. It is significant, however, that almost all of his scholarly works appeared during his time as Antistes, not as professor. While the Lectorium enjoyed a period of relative stability between 1560 and 1610, in general, Zurich's theology professors in this period were, by and large, overworked, underpaid, and did not have as much time for scholarship.

Carrie Euler, PhD, Associate Professor, Central Michigan University (Mount Pleasant, MI, USA)

Abstract: Using records from the Zurich Staatsarchiv, this article investigates the faculty of the Zurich Lectorium between 1560 and 1610. The author argues that this period was important as an epoch of both stability and transition for the school, a time when the memory and influence of Zwingli was still strong, but when the school was also developing into a formal institution of higher learning. Most professors in this era taught at the school while also holding pastoral positions in and around the city. Consequently, many were overworked, underpaid, and had little time for scholarship.

Keywords: Zurich, Reformed Academy, Faculty, Education

ISSN 0254-4407 – Zwingliana 40 (2013), 127–141

Teufelsspuk und Feuerflammen

Pfarrer Josua Finsler (1525–1602) über Unglaubliches aus Biel und Umgebung

Hans Rudolf Lavater-Briner

1. Anzeichen des Jüngsten Tages in Biel

»1572. Von einem unerhörtem, doch warhafftem wunder und zeichen, welches an ettlichen fürnemmen personen zů Biel gesähen, wie fhürflammen und gneist [Funken] von innen ussgangen, und doch das fhür sy nütt gebrent, und kein sonderen schmerzen dardurch empfangen.« Diesen exklamatorischen Titel setzt der Zürcher Archidiakon und Chorherr Johann Jakob Wick[1] über eine Nachricht, die er, wie Tausende zuvor, im 21. Band seiner 1559 begonnenen illustrierten Sammlung zum Zeitgeschehen ablegt.[2]

In Zürich, notiert er, sei die unglaubliche Nachricht aus dem 850-Seelen-Städtchen am Jurafuß mit großer Skepsis aufgenommen worden, was ihn veranlasst, der Sache auf den Grund zu gehen. Nach der Befragung von mehreren Augenzeugen in den letzten Märzwochen kommt Wick zum Schluss, »dass leyder nun [nur] zvil« an dieser Geschichte sei. Ein Händler aus Biel hat ihm erzählt,

[1] Johann Jakob Wick (1522–1588), von 1552 bis 155 Pfarrer an der Predigerkirche, dann Chorherr und zweiter Archidiakon am Großmünster. Biographisch-Bibliographisches Kirchenlexikon, Bd. 17, Herzberg 2000, Sp. 1536–1540.

[2] Zürich Zentralbibliothek, Ms. F 21, 154r–156r. Franz *Mauelshagen*, Wunderkammer auf Papier: Die »Wickiana« zwischen Reformation und Volksglaube, Epfendorf 2011 (Frühneuzeit-Forschungen 15) (Lit.).

erst seien zwei Knaben, dann der Großweibel[3] und weitere Personen von »fhürflamenn und gneist« befallen worden, »wie ein blauw schwäbel [Schwefel] fhür, hinden zum naken uss und zum mul und nasen uss«, und dies alles ohne Schaden zu nehmen. Vereinzelt sei es zu Ohnmachtsanfällen gekommen, »als ob sy verscheiden [sterben] wöllend, kömmend aber hernach widerum zerächt«. Von Solothurn her kommend, hat Hauptmann Lucius Angelberger von Maienfeld Kenntnis, »das[s] nun mehr in die 30 mans personen werind, an denen man dise fhürflammen heyter sähe und gspüre«. Diese Aussagen ergänzt Hans Schwarz, Burger und Krämer zu Biel, dahingehend, »das[s] mertheils die fürnempsten personen, insonders des rhads, auch dess meyers[4] sun (den wir den burgermeyster nennend) ankommen sye«.

Wie so häufig angesichts solcher und ähnlicher Phänomene lautet Wicks Erklärungsversuch:

> »Was der Allmechtig Gott darmit anzeigen und bedüten wölle, ist im alleyn zewüssen, aber mines erachtens, so hab ichs für ein gwüssen vorbott dess allgemeinen iüngsten und letsten tags, uff welchen Gott durch sinen sun, unseren Herren Jesum Christum, mit fhür kommen, 2. Pet. 3 [2Petr 3,7], und den ganzen erdbodem richten wird. Der trüw lieb Gott gebe uns allen gnad, das wir in warem glauben und sinem willen erfunden werdint.«[5]

Eine ganzseitige farbige Federzeichnung, vielleicht von eigener Hand, versucht die Glaubwürdigkeit des Geschehens zu erhöhen (Abb. 1).

2. Johann Jakob Wick (1522–1588)

Ein schillerndes Porträt Johann Jakob Wicks zeichnete Ricarda Huch 1895 in ihrer Studie »Die Wicksche Sammlung von Flugblättern und Zeitungsnachrichten«,[6] der ersten ernsthaften Dar-

[3] Gerichts- und oberster Ratsdiener.

[4] Der bischöfliche Meier amtete als Stellvertreter des Bischofs. Er führte in Rat und Gericht den Vorsitz. Paul *Bloesch*, Die Rechtsquellen der Stadt Biel, Basel 2003 (Die Rechtsquellen des Kantons Bern 13/1), XXIV.

[5] Zürich Zentralbibliothek, Ms. F 21, 155v.

[6] Ricarda *Huch*, Die Wicksche Sammlung von Flugblättern und Zeitungsnachrichten aus dem 16. Jahrhundert in der Stadtbibliothek Zürich, Zürich 1895.

Abb. 1: Von Panik ergriffen, flüchten sechs lichterloh brennende Bieler aus dem Städtchen ins offene Feld, Lavierte Federzeichnung von Johann Jakob Wick (?), Zürich Zentralbibliothek, Ms. F 21, 155r.

stellung dieses wohl bedeutendsten und mit 13 000 Seiten umfänglichsten Epochenarchivs des 16. Jahrhunderts, das der Zürcher Pfarrer in den Jahren 1559 bis 1588 zusammengestellt hatte, um künftige Leser »sich grösslich verwunnderen« zu lassen »ab der trůbseligen zyth«,[7] so der Generaltitel über alle 24 Foliobände. Als ein »Kind seiner Zeit«, einer »abergläubischen und wilden, [...] durch ihre Phantasie gepeinigten Zeit«,[8] kommt ihr Wick vor, der, nicht anders als das wundersüchtige Volk, ein spontanes Eingreifen Gottes ins Weltgeschehen für jederzeit möglich gehalten habe. Zwar fällt ihr auf, wie bei dem Theologen mitunter »eine natürlichere, vernünftigere Art zu denken aufkommt und um sich greifen möchte«, doch findet sie den nur allzu raschen Rückfall in vorwissenschaftliche Denkmuster gleichermaßen »unterhaltend und belehrend«. Bei einer Kometenerscheinung etwa sei Wick durchaus in der Lage, die »naturales rationes [vernünftigen Erklärungen]« der »physici [Naturkundigen]« zu würdigen, doch bezeuge seine Erfahrung vielmehr, »dass die Kometen kommen, um Blutvergießen anzuzeigen.«[9]

Gegenwärtige Untersuchungen, die sich mit dem umfangreichen frühneuzeitlichen Sammelschrifttum beschäftigen, lesen die »Wickiana« vor dem Hintergrund der seit Mitte des 16. Jahrhunderts zur Hochblüte entfalteten Mirabilien-, Prodigien- und Ostentaliteratur, als deren Exponent die 1557 erschienene Weltchronik der Prodigien, das mit zahllosen Holzschnitten ausgestattete *Prodigiorum ac ostentorum chronicon* des Conrad Lycosthenes gelten kann.[10] Seine Kompilation von abnormen Himmelserscheinungen und Geburten, von katastrophalen Naturereignissen und von Hexen- und Teufelswerk versteht der Diakon zu St. Leonhard in Basel als ein Kontinuum von endzeitlichen Mahnungen Gottes zur Umkehr.[11] Dieses auch der Flugschriftenliteratur eigene moralisierende

[7] Zürich Zentralbibliothek, Ms. F 12, 1r (Titelblatt).

[8] *Huch*, Sammlung, 3.

[9] *Huch*, Sammlung, 7.

[10] Conrad *Lycosthenes*, Prodigiorum ac ostentorum chronicon, Basel: Heinrich Petri, 1557 (Verzeichnis der im deutschen Sprachbereich erschienenen Drucke des XVI. Jahrhunderts, Stuttgart 1983–2000 [VD16], Nr. W 4314); deutsch: Wunderwerck, oder Gottes unergründtliches vorbilden, Basel: Heinrich Petri, 1557 (VD16 W 4315). Zu Lycosthenes (Wolfhart) vgl. Heinrich Bullinger Briefwechsel, Bd. 14, Zürich 2011, 243f.

Deutungsmuster führt die einschlägige Forschung auf ein geschärftes Krisenbewusstsein in einer Zeit konfessioneller und politischer Verunsicherung zurück.[12]

Anders jedoch als das *Chronicon* des Lycosthenes war und blieb die *Wickiana* eine private Unternehmung. Wenn sich auch beide Theologen von jener eschatologischen Unruhe erfasst zeigen, die zur Signatur der Zeit gehört, so erscheint der Zürcher mehr als sein Basler Kollege darum bemüht, die Zeichen und Hinweise Gottes geschichtstheologisch zu reflektieren. Die gesuchte »Schau auf die vom Funken des Jenseits getroffene Zeit«,[13] beziehungsweise auf den providentiellen Weltenlauf, konnte Wick im »prophetischen« Geschichtsbild finden, wie es in Zürich seit Zwinglis Zeiten *communis opinio* war: Gott offenbart sich in der Geschichte, die Gegenwart ist somit von der Vergangenheit wie auch vom Ende her zu bedenken. Insofern konnte es sinnvoll sein, »Zeitzeichen« zusammen zu tragen, wenn man auch deren revelatorischen Wert gegenüber der Schrift deutlich geringer einstufte. Zürichs prominenteste Prodigiensammler neben Wick waren Ludwig Lavater mit seinem Kometenkatalog, namentlich aber Antistes Heinrich Bullinger,[14] dessen beeindruckendes historiographisches Schaffen dem Nachweis von Gottes Wirken in der Geschichte dienen will.[15] Nirgends gib er diese seine Absicht klarer bekannt als im Vorwort zu seiner 1567 abgeschlossenen Reformationsgeschichte, wo er erklärt, nichts anderes als die »wunderwerche Gottes«, »die herrli-

[11] »Prodigium« ist »eine staunenswerte, ungewöhnliche und von Gott absichtlich bewirkte Naturerscheinung, die auf kommendes Unheil hinweist und zur Einkehr mahnt«, Rudolf *Schenda*, Die deutschen Prodigiensammlungen des 16. und 17. Jahrhunderts, in: Archiv für Geschichte des Buchwesens 4 (1963), Sp. 637–710, hier Sp. 646.

[12] Barbara *Bauer*, Die Krise der Reformation: Johann Jakob Wicks Chronik außergewöhnlicher Natur- und Himmelserscheinungen, in: Wahrnehmungsgeschichte und Wissensdiskurs im illustrierten Flugblatt der Frühen Neuzeit (1450–1700), hg. von Wolfgang Harms und Alfred Messerli, Basel 2002, 193–236.

[13] Gottfried W. *Locher*, Das Geschichtsbild Huldrych Zwinglis, in: *id.*, Huldrych Zwingli in neuer Sicht, Zürich/Stuttgart 1969, 75–104, hier 91f.

[14] Franz *Mauelshagen*, Die »portenta et ostenta mines lieben Herren vnsers säligen ...«: Nachlassdokumente Bullingers im 13. Buch der Wickiana, in: Zwingliana 28 (2001), 73–117.

[15] Christian *Moser*, Die Dignität des Ereignisses: Studien zu Heinrich Bullingers Reformationsgeschichtsschreibung, 2 Bde., Leiden/Boston 2012 (Studies in the History of Christian Traditions 163), vor allem 292–301.

che werke Gottes, gůte leeren und fürträffenliche exempel« darstellen zu wollen: »Hierinn wirt der Läser so wunderbare ding finden, das er gwüßlich und offt daran erstunen und schwärlich sömliche wunder glouben wird.«[16] Nicht anders würde Wick die von ihm gesammelten »wunderzeichen« und »vorzeichen« als gnädige Willenskundgaben Gottes verstehen, nur dazu angezeigt, um die Menschen rechtzeitig zu Umkehr und Besserung des Lebens zu bewegen.

3. Aus der Bieler Gerüchteküche

Als Chorherr war Wick an das erstaunlich dichte Nachrichtennetz der Zürcher Kirchenleitung[17] angeschlossen. Seine wichtigsten regelmäßigen Informationsvermittler waren die Chorherren,[18] allen voran Heinrich Bullinger, der mit ganz Europa von Schottland bis Weißrussland in Korrespondenz stand, wovon noch heute 12000 Briefe zeugen, dann dessen Nachfolger Burkhard Leemann[19] sowie der Universalgelehrte Konrad Gessner.[20] Daneben verfügte Wick über eine Vielzahl von Korrespondenten, die ihn mit Gelegenheitsnachrichten belieferten.

Die »nüwen zyttungen« aus Biel und Umgebung verdankte Wick dem aus Zürich stammenden Bieler Pfarrer Josua Finsler,[21] dessen Informationen jedoch mehrheitlich zuerst an Burkhard Leemann gingen. Dass Finsler mit der Weitergabe seiner Nachrichten an Wick rechnete, geht aus einem Brief vom 24. Juni 1567 an Leemann hervor. Nach fünf Zeilen mit den üblichen lateinischen Höflichkeiten und einem untertreibenden »Nil apud nos novi« wechselt der Bieler unvermittelt in den gemeinverständlichen Schreibdialekt:

[16] Heinrich Bullingers Reformationsgeschichte. Nach dem Autographon hg. von J[ohann] J[akob] Hottinger und H[ans] H[einrich] Vögeli, 3 Bde., Frauenfeld 1838–1840, Bd. 1, 1f.

[17] Leo *Weisz*, Die Bullinger Zeitungen [...], Zürich 1933.

[18] *Mauelshagen*, Portenta, 74; *Mauelshagen*, Wunderkammer, 168–177.

[19] Historisches Lexikon der Schweiz [HLS], Bd. 7, Basel 2008, 733.

[20] HLS, Bd. 5, Basel 2006, 352f.

[21] Werner *Bourquin* und Marcus *Bourquin*, Biel: Stadtgeschichtliches Lexikon, Biel ^{2}2008, 141.

»Inn Bärn biet, nit wyt von Thun, hat J[unker] Gladi Mey ein herschafft.[22] Da hand ettlich puren einem andern puren verwyßen, er könne nit bätten. Der ander hat sich verschworen, er könne bätten, und wo das nit sye, solle der tüfel kommen und in hin fůren. Von Stund an kumpt der tüfel inn einer windbrutt, erwüscht und erhept den puren und schleickt inn dahin über ettlich matten und väld. Die ander louffend nach, letstlich findend sy inn in einem zun dermaßen mit thörnen verwicklet, daß sy [ihn] heruß hand můßen houwen, und also mit dem läben darvon bracht. Biennæ raptim. 24. Iunij Anno 67.«[23]

Diese Nachricht Finslers schrieb Wick wortgetreu und unter Angabe der Quelle ab: »Am 27, Junij schrybt herr Iosue Vinsler, pfarrer zů Biel, an m[eister] Burkart Lemann, dieneren der kilchen Zürich also: [...]«. Darüber setzte er die Schlagzeile »Ein erschrokenliche historia, die sich dieser tagen in Berner piett zůgetragen.«[24]

Abb. 2: Der Teufel holt einen Bauern, der nicht beten kann. Lavierte Federzeichnung von Johann Jakob Wick (?), Zürich Zentralbibliothek, Ms. F 17, 255v.

Ähnlich wird man sich den Informationsfluss und die redaktionellen Vorgänge bei den nachfolgenden Mitteilungen Finslers denken:

[22] Glado (Claudius) May, Sohn des gleichnamigen Freundes Zwinglis, war »Herr zu Strättligen und Twingherr zu Toffen«, Bern Staatsarchiv, F. Stift (13.03.1555).

[23] Zürich Staatsarchiv, E II 344, 11r.

[24] Zürich Zentralbibliothek, Ms. F 17, 255r.

1572 In Biel gehen von mehr als 30 Personen Feuerflammen aus.[25]

1576 Auf dem Weg von Biel nach Büren springt am 27. April eine als Hexe verurteilte Frau vom Henkerskarren und ertrinkt in der Aare. Ihr Denunziant, der dem Teufel ergebener Freiämtler Michael Jaussi endet am 1. Mai auf dem Scheiterhaufen.[26]

1577 In Murten erhängt sich ein Mann aus Kummer über den Pesttod von Frau und Tochter; in Biel wird dem Hans Lamprandt ein missgestaltetes Kind tot geboren; auch über Biel zeigt sich der blutrote Komet.[27]

1579 Im katholischen Le Landeron erschlägt ein Sohn seine Mutter mit der Hacke und versucht den Leichnam zu verbrennen. Er wird gerädert und verbrannt (29. Dezember 1579).[28]

4. Josua Finsler

An Josua Finsler erinnert in Biel nur noch der gleichnamige Weg im Kreis 4. Rasch aufgezählt sind die biografischen Eckdaten des Namensgebers: 1538 als Pfarrersohn in Stäfa am Zürichsee geboren, seit 1555 Pfarrer in Witikon und Weiach, 1556 als Vikar seines Vaters in Otelfingen, seit 1562 in Meilen,[29] vom 20. Februar 1566 bis zu seinem Tod am 19. Januar 1602 als Nachfolger von Jakob Funcklin[30] Erster Stadtpfarrer und Dekan des Pfarrkapitels Biel

[25] Zürich Zentralbibliothek, Ms. F 21, 154r–156r (Finsler an Leemann, 25. Juni 1567).

[26] Zürich Zentralbibliothek, Ms. F 25, 80r-v.

[27] Zürich Zentralbibliothek, Ms. F 25, 225r-v (Finsler an Leemann, 16. November 1577). Der auch von Tycho Brahe beschriebene sogenannte »Große Komet C/1577 V1« war tagsüber hell am Himmel zu erkennen und wurde in verschiedenen Flugblättern abgebildet. Clarisse Doris *Hellman*, The Comet of 1577: Its Place in the History of Astronomy, New York 1944.

[28] Zürich Zentralbibliothek, Ms. F 28, 211r.

[29] Georg *Finsler*, Genealogie der Familie Finsler, Basel 1891, 7f.

[30] Hans Rudolf *Lavater*, Lignea Aetas: Der Bieler Dekan Jakob Funcklin und die Anfänge der »Holzsparkunst« (1555–1576), in: Schweizer Kirchengeschichte – neu reflektiert: Festschrift für Rudolf Dellsperger, hg. von Ulrich *Gäbler* et al., Basel 2011 (Basler und Berner Studien zur historischen und systematischen Theologie 73), 63–145.

und Erguel. Als solcher bewohnte der am 18. Dezember 1594 Eingeburgerte bis 1597 mit seiner Familie das Haus Obergasse 20.[31] »War ein guter Poet«, urteilte Johann Jakob Hess 1829,[32] doch Finslers schriftlicher Nachlass ist heute weitgehend *terra incognita.*[33] Zwei handschriftliche Folianten mit lateinischen Gedichten aus den Jahren 1572–1589, *Josua Vinsleri Tigurini Ecclesiæ Biennensis Pastoris poëmata* bieten Gottlieb E. von Haller 1765 zufolge »sehr viel Schweizerische, besonders aber Bernerische und Bielische Sachen.«[34] Während eine den Bernern gewidmete *Expositio Christiana* des Berner Katechismus bisher gänzlich unbeachtet blieb,[35] hat Hans Bloesch sein Porträt des Burgermeisters Hans Hugi[36] ganz auf Finslers Darstellung der *Unrůw der Burgeren zů Biel* abgestützt.[37] Diese trotz ihrer 472 Quartseiten nur unvollständig erhaltene Geschichte des sogenannten Bieler Tauschhandels 1598–1600 beschreibt »niemant zů lieb, ouch niemant z'leyd, allein der Warheit zů bescheyd« den hinterhältigen Versuch Berns, Biel zu seinem Untertanengebiet zu machen.

Von Finslers lebenslänglicher Verbundenheit mit der Heimatstadt zeugt eine noch kaum bearbeitete umfangreiche Korrespondenz, die der Heimwehzürcher regelmäßig mit dem Kürzel »I·V·T« für Iosua Vinslerus Tigurinus unterzeichnete. Hauptsächliche Adressaten sind Heinrich Bullinger (42 Briefe 1566–1575)[38] und Burkhard Leemann (mindestens 40 Briefe 1567–1601).[39] Bullinger ehrte er 1575 mit einer Trauerode,[40] Leemann 1592 mit einem

[31] *Bourquin*, Biel, 141.

[32] Johann Jakob *Hess*, Lebensgeschichte M. Heinrich Bullingers, 2 Bde., Zürich 1828–1829, Bd. 2, 508.

[33] Biel Stadtarchiv; Bern Burgerbibliothek; Zürich Staatsarchiv, Zürich Zentralbibliothek.

[34] Gottlieb Emanuel von *Haller*, Bibliothek der Schweitzer-Geschichte und aller Theile, so dahin Bezug haben, 7 Bde., Bern 1785–1787, Bd. 4, 521.

[35] Bern Burgerbibliothek, Cod. A 34.1

[36] Hans *Bloesch*, Hans Hugi, der Burgermeister von Biel, nach der Chronik Josua Vinslers, in: Blätter für Bernische Geschichte, Kunst und Altertumskunde 21 (1925), 145–157.

[37] Bern Burgerbibliothek, Mss.h.h.XV.160A (1). *Haller*, Bibliothek, Bd. 5, 675.

[38] Gemäß Kartei der Heinrich Bullinger-Briefwechseledition am Institut für Schweizerische Reformationsgeschichte Zürich.

[39] Zürich Staatsarchiv, E II 344 (Originaltitel *Literae Finsleri past. Biennens. civ. Tig, aliorumve*).

[40] Carmina syncharistica, in honorem religione doctrina, aetate et meritis praestan-

Festgedicht.[41] Weitere wichtige Briefempfänger sind Rudolf Gwalther in Zürich und Theodor Beza in Genf.

5. Josua Finslers Darstellung der Bieler Feuererscheinungen von 1572

Angesichts der noch zu leistenden Quellenarbeit ist eine angemessene Würdigung Josua Finslers derzeit kaum möglich. Der Glücksfall indessen, dass Johann Jakob Wick seinem Bericht über die Bieler Feuererscheinungen vom Frühjahr 1572 einen diesbezüglichen Brief Finslers beifügte (Abb. 3), kann dazu beitragen, die Konturen des Bieler Dekans etwas zu schärfen.

Aus der Briefanrede geht hervor, dass Finslers Adressat wiederum Burkhard Leemann war. Leider ist die Abschrift, die Wick in seine Chronik einklebte, am rechten Rand teilweise stark beschädigt, auch bricht sie gegen das Ende hin unvermittelt ab. Umso mehr verdient sie es, so gut wie möglich ergänzt, an dieser Stelle mitgeteilt zu werden:

»Eerwirdiger, wolgeleerter, insunders günstiger lieber herr und pr[aeceptor]. Ich han diser tagen ein schryben von minem l[ieben] brůder Helia emp[fangen], inn wellichem er mich under anderem berichtet, wie üch ettwas st[...] nüwer zyttungen sye fürckommen, dz hie by uns zů Byell [...] personen ein böße plag anckommen, dz inen ire höupter brün[nen], derhalben ir begärind, deße von mir ein eigentlichen bericht [zů] empfahen. Diewyl ich dann üch und anderen m[inen] g[nädigen] h[erren] zed[ienen] geneigt billichen bin, so han ich mich nit wellen beschwëren [nit ?] üch zůzeschryben, damit ir und villicht andere meer dem w[hon an ?] ein ënd kommind (wiewol dz gschrey gar unglych und vil g[rößer] ist, dann die sach an iro selber). Es hat sich hie zů Byell [zů]tragen vor ettlichen monaten bißhar, und insunders in verschyner kelte, dz ettliche junge knaben gredt, wënn sy sich zů nacht abz[iehind], so fhürind inen ire höupter und hëmbder. Dz hat man ein [wyl und?] anfangs für narrenwärch und ein whon gehalten, iedoch, die[wyl] sy immerdar dz beharret, hat man es für gwüß also syn erfa[ren].

tissmi viri Dn. M. Burckhardi Leemanni, Zürich: Johannes Wolf, 1592 (VD16 C 1185), 4v–5r.

[41] Carmina doctorum virorum in obitum D. Henrici Bullingeri, ecclesiae Tigurinae pastoris fidelissimi, scripta, in: Josias *Simler*, Narratio de ortu, vita et obitu reverendi viri D. Henrici Bullingeri, Tigurinae Ecclesiae pastoris, Zürich: Christoph Froschauer d.J., 1575 (VD16 S 6507), 72v.

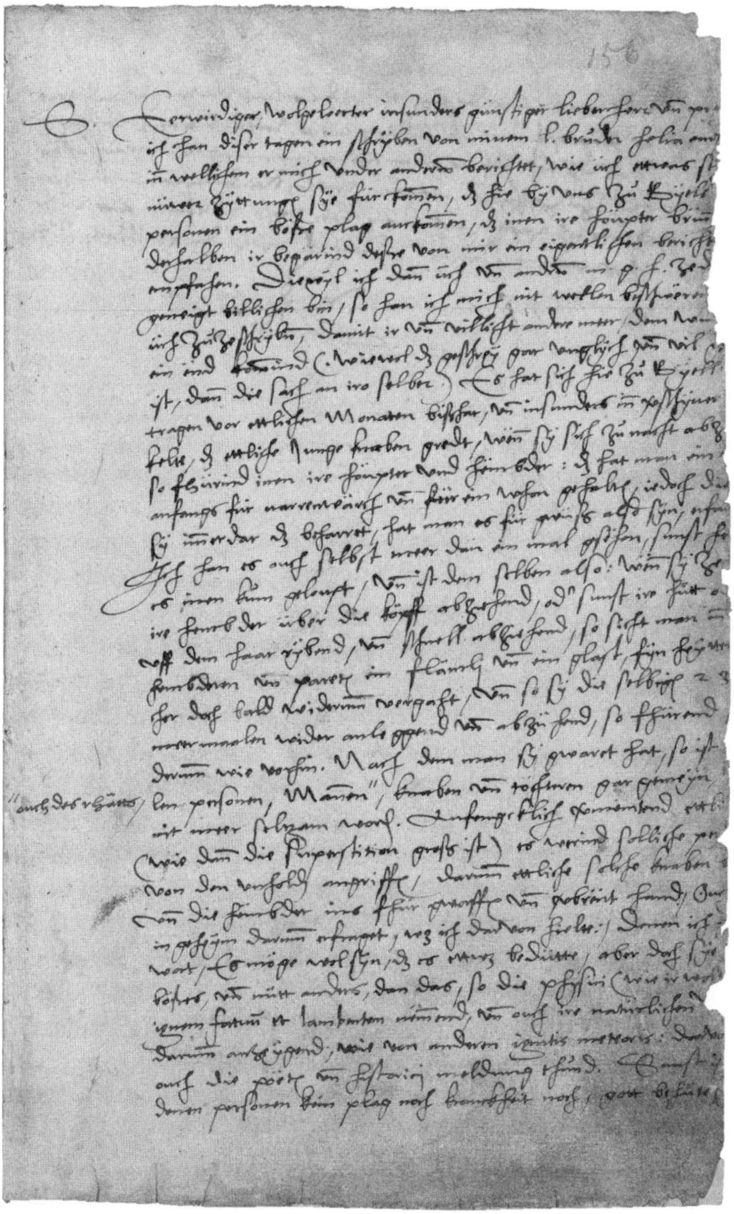

Abb. 3: Brief Josua Finslers an Burkhard Leemann über die Bieler Feuererscheinungen vom Frühjahr 1572 (Abschrift von unbekannter Hand), Zürich Zentralbibliothek, Ms. F 21, 156r.

Ich han es ouch selbst meer dan ein mal gsëhen, sunst he[tt ich] es inen kum geloupt. Und ist dem selben also: Wënn sy ze [abend] ire hembder über die köpff abziehend oder sunst ire hůtt [...] uff dem haar rybend und schnell abziehend, so sicht man inn [iren] hembderen und pareten ein flämli und ein glast, fyn heytter, [wel]cher doch bald widerumb vergaht. Und so sy die selbigen 2, 3 [oder] meermaalen wider anleggend und abzühend, so fhürend [sy wi]derumb wie vorhin. Nach dem man sy gwaret[42] hat, so ist [das ? vi]llen personen, mannen, ouch des rhatts, knaben und töchteren, gar gemeyn [und] nit meer seltzam worden. Anfengcklich vermeintend ettli[che] (wie dann die superstition groß ist), es werind solliche pe[rsonen] von den unholden angriffen, darumb ettliche solche‹n?› knaben [die hůt] und die hëmbder ins fhür gworffen und verbrënt hand, ou[ch] in geheym darumm erfraget, wz ich darvon hielte. Denen ich [geant]wort, es möge wol syn, dz es ettwz bedütte, aber doch sye [es nüt] bößes und nüt anders dann das, so die *physici* (wie ir woh[l wüsst]) *ignem fatuum et lambentem* nemmend, und ouch ire natürlichen [gründ] darumb anzeygend wie von anderen *ignitis meteoris*, darvo[n] ouch die poëten und historici meldung thůnd. Sunst i[n] denen personen kein plag noch kranckheit, noch, gott behüte, [der Tod festgestellt wurde ?].«[43]

6. Ältere Deutungen

Nirgends deutlicher als im letzten Briefabschnitt tritt bei Josua Finsler eben jene »natürlichere, vernünftigere Art zu denken« zutage, die Ricarda Huch bei Johann Jakob Wick insgesamt vermisst hatte. Den Versuch, die Bieler Phänomene mit dem Wirken des Teufels in Verbindung zu bringen, bezeichnet Finsler als abergläubisch, doch ebenso strikt vermeidet er es, Gott ins Spiel zu bringen. Wick kann sich nicht helfen: »Was der allmächtige Gott damit anzeigen und ›bedeuten‹ will, weiß Er allein«. Finsler dagegen: »Es könne sein, dass es etwas bedeute, doch sei es nichts Böses und nichts Anderes als das, was die Naturkundigen, wie Ihnen sicher bekannt ist, ein ›Irrlicht‹ und ein ›züngelndes Feuer‹ nennen, wofür sie ebenso eine vernünftige Erklärung haben wie für andere ›feurige Lufterscheinungen‹.«

Damit steht Finslers Deutung auf der Höhe der Naturwissenschaften seiner Zeit – einer Wissenschaft allerdings, die die Schwel-

[42] Zürich Zentralbibliothek, Ms. A 26 (Hallersche Chronik), 60r: »gwarntt«.
[43] Zürich Zentralbibliothek, Ms. F 21, 156r.

le zur Moderne noch nicht überschritten hat. Ihre Beobachtungen dienen weniger der physikalischen Theoriebildung als vielmehr dem übergeordneten Ziel, Gottes Gegenwart in der Natur zu beweisen, doch ist ihre Argumentation nicht mehr supranatural, sondern bereits »natürlich«. Auffällig übrigens auch Finslers selbstverständlicher Gebrauch der wissenschaftlichen Terminologie, die vermutlich von seiner Auseinandersetzung mit früheren Kometenerscheinungen (1531, 1558, 1572) herrührt. Das einschlägige Werk des Simon Grynaeus, *Commentarii duo, de ignitis meteoris unus, alter de cometarum causis atque significationibus* erschien freilich erst 1579.[44] Die von Finsler verwendeten Begriffe finden sich alle wieder in der berühmten *Physicæ Synopsis* von 1633 des Jan Amos Comenius:

> »Feurige Lufterscheinungen (*meteora ignita*) entstehen aus fetten Rauchen, die sich in der Luft entzünden. Davon gibt es namentlich sieben Arten: Fallender Stern, Fliegender Drache, Blitz, Fliegende Funken, Irrlicht (*ignis fatuus*), Fackel und Leckendes Feuer (*ignis lambens*).«[45]

Weitere Beobachtungen, in die sich auch die Bieler »Feuererscheinungen« einreihen ließen, lieferte ein gewisser Johannes Müller in seiner Wittenberger Dissertation 1676:

> »Das *züngelnde Feuer* gehört zu den *meteorischen Feuern*. Es haftet den Haaren und Kleidern des Menschen, den Mähnen der Pferde, den Mastbaumspitzen der Schiffe und anderen Dingen an, ohne Schaden anzurichten.«[46]

In der *Beschreibung der Natur-Geschichten des Schweizerlands* spricht der Zürcher Arzt und Naturtheologe Johann Jakob

[44] Simon *Grynaeus*, Commentarii duo, de ignitis meteoris unus, alter de cometarum causis atque significationibus, Basel: Leonhard Ostein, 1579 (VD16 E3671).

[45] »Meteora ignita sunt, quæ oriuntur è fumis pinguibus in aëre accensis, quorum præcipuæ species septem sunt: stella cadens, draco volans, fulmen, scintillae volantes, ignis fatuus, fax et ignis lambens«, zitiert nach Jan Amos *Comenius*, Physicæ Ad Lumen Divinum Reformatæ Synopsis, Amsterdam: Jan Jansson, 1663, 108.

[46] Johannes *Müller*, De meteoris ignitis et aqueis, Wittenberg: Matthäus Henckel, 1676 (Verzeichnis der im deutschen Sprachraum erschienenen Drucke des 17. Jahrhunderts [elektronische Ressource], Nr. 3:018289B), A4r: »Ignis lambens est Meteorum Ignitum, hominum capillis ac vestimentis, jubis equorum, navium malis, atque aliis sine noxa adhærens. Lambens dicitur, locutione Poëtis familiari, quia leviter tangit res, quibus adhæret, non urit.«

Scheuchzer 1707 nicht ohne frühaufklärerischen Spott die Bieler Feuererscheinungen von 1572 an:

»Von der Lechzenden Flamm. Es lasset sich diese Feuer-Geschicht sehen etwann an den Kleideren und Haaren under Menschen und Thieren zu nicht geringem Schrecken der Zuseheren. Die alte Heidenschaft hielte dergleichen *Ignes Lambentes* oder Lechzende Flammen vor sonderliche Wunderzeichen und von den Götteren herrührende bezeugung künftiger Dingen. [...] Ich were ohne grosse Mühe zu bereden, daß in denen mittleren Jahr hunderten mancher bey Anlaß einer um sein Haupt erschienenen Flamm in die Zahl der Heiligen aufgenommen worden. Wenigstens hat man auß disen lechzenden Flammen allerhand Geheimnussen gemachet, wie dann nebst anderen An. 1572 gesehenen Wunderzeichen Haller Chron. MSC. Lib 38. cap 16. auch setzet dergleichen lechzende Feure, so an verschiedenen Kinderen in der Statt Biel an ihren Hembderen, Haaren und Hüten gesehen worden.«[47]

Das von Scheuchzer zitierte Manuskript ist die vom Zürcher Bäcker und Militärtechniker Johannes Haller als Fortsetzung von Heinrich Bullingers Reformationsgeschichte gedachte und 1620 abgeschlossene »Chronik«,[48] die bei der angegebenen Stelle eine ins Wörtliche gehende Kurzfassung des Finslerbriefs bringt.[49]

7. Heutige Deutung

Ein befreundeter Physiker, Dr. Alfred Roulier in Neuenegg, der das Interesse und die Freundlichkeit hatte, Wicks und Finslers Berichte durch die Brille des heutigen Naturwissenschaftlers zu lesen, steuert folgenden Kommentar bei:

»Wick beschreibt sogenannte Spitzenentladungen. Bei Gewitterlagen kann die Feldstärke der ionisierten Luft grösser als 100 Kilovolt pro Meter werden. Die Feldlinien laufen an Spitzen (Masten, Eispickel, Gipfelkreuze aber auch Finger, Haare) zusammen. Die Funkenentladung ist bläulich; es ist dies die Spektralfarbe der Sauerstoff- und Stickstoff-Ionen. Die Funkenlän-

[47] Johann Jakob *Scheuchzer*, Beschreibung der Natur-Geschichten des Schweizerlands, 3 Bde., Zürich: Christoph Hardmeyer und Michael Schaufelberger, 1706–1708, Bd. 2, 82f. – Zu Scheuchzer vgl. HLS, Bd. 11, Basel 2012, 52f.

[48] *Moser*, Dignität, 387–390.

[49] Zürich Zentralbibliothek, Ms. A 26, 59v–60r, unter dem Titel »Was sich dieser zytt zů Biel an ettlichen jungen knaben zůgetragen, deßglychen hie zů Zürich am Balgrist ouch mit einem.«

ge liegt im Bereich 10 bis 50 cm, und die Erscheinung kann Minuten dauern. Die Stromstärken sind klein, die Erscheinung daher ungefährlich. Aber es drohen Blitzentladungen mit tödlichen Folgen. Es seien auch vornehme Personen betroffen gewesen: Seide und Pelz begünstigen die elektrostatische Aufladung. Fragwürdig sind die Entladungsstellen. Mund und Ohren sind keine ›Spitzen‹. Die Funken entstehen vielmehr an Fingern und Haaren. In Finslers Bericht steht dagegen die Reibungselektrizität im Fokus, die beim Ausziehen der Hemden bzw. beim Reiben von faserigem, wollenen Material gegenüber den Haaren entsteht. Wie bei den Spitzenentladungen muss die Luft trocken und stark ionisiert sein. Die Personen müssen gegenüber dem Boden isoliert stehen (auf dem Bett?).«

Dieser überzeugenden Analyse ist höchstens noch beizufügen, dass Finsler ausdrücklich feststellt, die Phänomene hätten sich »insunders in verschyner kelte« ereignet, d.h. in einem Milieu trockener Luft, die bekanntlich das Auftreten von luftelektrischer Erscheinungen begünstigt. Einen genaueren zeitlichen Anhalt geben weder Wick noch Finsler. Wick sagt nur, dass die Nachricht 1572 »in disem Merzen« nach Zürich gelangt sei. Unter der Voraussetzung vergleichbarer Wetter- und Temperaturverhältnisse in Biel und Zürich, lässt sich diese Zeitangabe unter Zuhilfenahme der vom Zürcher Pfarrer Wolfgang Haller von 1543 bis 1576 minutiös nachführten Witterungstagebücher[50] noch etwas einengen: Den Eintragungen in den *Kalender uff das M.D. und LXXII. Jar* zufolge wies der Februar insgesamt 22 Eistage auf mit Spitzenwerten zwischen dem 19. und dem 26., die Haller »gar grimm kalt« und »gar grusam kalt« vorgekommen waren.[51]

Hans Rudolf Lavater, Dr. theol. h.c., Gymnasiallehrer i.R. in Erlach

Abstract: The chorherr (canon), Johann Jakob Wick of Zurich drew the material for his voluminous collection of news (*Wickiana*) from a dense network of intelligence. The information from Bern and Biel was provided here and there by the lesser known citizen of Zurich, deacon Josua Finsler, who lived in Biel. The article spotlights the »Miraculous Sign« of February 1572 in Biel and the diverse interpretations of the event by these two contemporaries. The »Reformed« eschatological understanding of Wick is compared to Finsler's more rationalist worldview coloured by science.

Schlagworte: Johann Jakob Wick, Josua Finsler, Biel, Zürich, Prodigien, Geschichtsbild, Naturwissenschaft

[50] Zürich Zentralbibliothek, Ms. D 269, 270, 271.
[51] Zürich Zentralbibliothek, Ms. D 271, 4.

ISSN 0254-4407 – Zwingliana 40 (2013), 143–164

Die Katechismen in der Schaffhauser Kirche

Erich Bryner

1. Die Anfänge des Religionsunterrichtes: Die ersten Schaffhauser Katechismen

Es soll auf Geheiß der Regierung »geschechen, das ain sölcher latozissung in statt und land gehalten werde«.[1] Diese Bestimmung findet sich in den Erlassen der Schaffhauser Räte an die Geistlichkeit aus den Jahren 1536/1537. Vorausgegangen war das Begehren der Pfarrerschaft der jungen Schaffhauser reformierten Kirche einige Jahre nach der Einführung der Reformation 1529, es sei notwendig, »dass ein catechismus, daß ist gloubensleer, angericht werde uff dem land al sontag nach imbiss, damit iung und alt [...] underricht werdind, waß der gloub, welchs die Artickel des gloubens, was bätt [Gebet] und wie man bätten sölle, item welchs die gebott gottes und was yr inhalt und verstand sye, erclert werdind [...]«[2] Auch solle jedermann wissen, was er zu tun und wie er zu handeln habe. Die Regierung erklärte ihr Einverständnis. Um was es sich bei einem solchen »catechismus« handle, hatte sie genau verstanden, doch der Begriff »Katechismus« kannte sie nicht und verballhornte ihn eben zu »latozissung«.

Dies war die Geburtsstunde der katechetischen Tätigkeit in der Reformierten Kirche Schaffhausens. Die öffentliche Katechisation

[1] Hans *Lieb*, Karl *Schib*, Beschwerden und Sorgen der Schaffhauser Geistlichkeit um 1540, in: Schaffhauser Beiträge zur vaterländischen Geschichte 48 (1971), 159.

[2] *Lieb/Schib*, Beschwerden, 155.

fand jeweils an den Sonntagen um 15 Uhr statt. Als Lehrmittel wurde zuerst der große Katechismus von Leo Jud aus dem Jahre 1534, dann auch der mittlere Katechismus Juds von 1541 verwendet. Doch bald verfiel die öffentliche Katechisation immer mehr. In einzelnen Gemeinden wurde nur noch der kleine Katechismus Juds »für gar junge Kinder« verwendet, der mechanisch auswendig gelernt und hergesagt werden musste, in vielen Gemeinden gab es überhaupt keinen Unterricht mehr. Als Johann Konrad Ulmer 1566 sein Amt als Pfarrer der Stadtkirche St. Johann antrat, lag der Katechismusunterricht völlig im Argen. »Als ich noch ein Knabe war«, berichtete der gebürtige Schaffhauser in einem Brief an Heinrich Bullinger, »nahm ich zusammen mit meiner Mutter und mit meiner Großmutter mit großer Lernbegierde an den Katechisationen teil. Hätte man diesen Brauch behalten, wäre das Antlitz unserer Kirche jetzt ein anderes [...] Doch dieser Brauch hielt sich nicht lange.«[3] Katechesen habe es bald nur noch an Weihnachten, Ostern und Pfingsten sowie an den ersten Sonntagen nach diesen Feiertagen gegeben.

Bereits an der ersten Synode, an der Ulmer teilnahm, derjenigen vom 7. November 1566, forderte er, dass die Katechesen wieder aufgenommen werden sollten. Sein Vorstoß blieb ergebnislos. An der Mai-Synode 1567 wiederholte er seine Forderungen »heftiger und energischer«.[4] Mit viel Elan führte er selber die öffentlichen »Kinderlehren« am St. Johann wieder ein, schrieb dafür ein »deutsches Gedicht über das Mahl des Herrn«, das er Bullinger zusandte[5] – kurz vorher hatte er eines über den Dekalog gedichtet – und verfasste 1568 einen eigenen Katechismus, den er der Herbstsynode 1568 vorlegte und in der ganzen Schaffhauser Kirche einführen wollte: »Brevis et succinta tamen Catechismi formula conscripta in usum parvulorum Christi in schola et Ecclesia Scaphusiana«,[6] bzw. in deutscher Sprache: »Summarischer und in Gottes Wort

[3] Johann Konrad Ulmer an Heinrich Bullinger, 7. April 1569, Zürich Staatsarchiv [StA], E II 362, 85r–v.

[4] Zürich StA, E II 362, 86r.

[5] »Mitto Carmen Germanicum, quod ante aliquot dies concinnatum a me de Coena Domenica [...] Nam et paulo ante Decalogum, ex textu scripturae in rhythmos Germanicos transtuli [...]« Johann Konrad Ulmer an Heinrich Bullinger, 2. Oktober 1567, Zürich StA, E II 362, 67.

[6] Schaffhausen Staatsarchiv [StA], Abschriften 4/8, Spleiss 8, 66–73.

gegründeter kinderbericht für einfältige hausvätter und Kinder in Frag und Antwort gestellet«.[7] In knappen, aber gut durchdachten und klar formulierten Fragen und Antworten legte Ulmer die Grundzüge des reformierten christlichen Glaubens in sechs Kapiteln dar: Dekalog, Glaubensbekenntnis, Unser Vater, Taufe, Abendmahl und »Die Worte Christi über die Schlüssel des Himmelreiches oder über den Dienst des Evangeliums«. Ulmers entschlossenes und forsches Vorgehen rief eine heftige Kontroverse hervor: Einige Schaffhauser Pfarrer beanstandeten, dass die Sprache des neuen Katechismus zu neuhochdeutsch sei und auf die lokale Sprache zu wenig Rücksicht nehme. Dann wurden die Knappheit und die Kürze der Fragen und Antworten kritisiert, weil sie zu Missverständnissen Anlass geben könnten, und schließlich fanden findige Leser Reste lutherischer Theologie in Ulmers Abendmahlslehre. Darauf entstand ein heftiger und mühseliger Streit in der Schaffhauser Kirche.[8] Heinrich Bullinger, mit dem Ulmer seit seinem Amtsantritt in Schaffhausen eine rege Korrespondenz vor allem über kirchenpolitische Angelegenheiten führte, hatte Ulmers Katechismus gelobt: »Was dein Katechismus betrifft, missfällt er mir nicht. Mit knappen Worten und Gedanken fasst er die Prinzipien unserer Religion zusammen. Er weicht nicht von unserem gemeinsamen Bekenntnis ab.«[9] Bald darauf erfuhr er vom Schaffhauser Katechismusstreit und schrieb am 25. März 1569 sehr besorgt an Ulmer: »Ich möchte dir kundtun, dass es mich sehr schmerzt, wenn wahr ist, was ich höre, dass Uneinigkeit und Streit unter den Brüdern wegen des Katechismus überhandnehme«, und wenn es so sei, so riet er ihm, wäre es besser, die alte Form zu bewahren, d.h. weiterhin den Kleinen Katechismus Leo Juds zu gebrauchen, als wegen einer neuen sich zu zanken und die Kirche zu verwirren.[10] In seiner detaillierten Antwort an Bullinger vom 7. April 1569 legte

[7] Schaffhausen StA, Abschriften 4/8, Spleiss 8, 75–83.

[8] Jakob *Wipf*, Reformationsgeschichte der Stadt und Landschaft Schaffhausen, Zürich 1929, 353–357; Eduard *Scherrer*, Der erste Schaffhauser Katechismus von Johann Konrad Ulmer und der Kampf um denselben (1567–1569), in: Schaffhauser Beiträge zur vaterländischen Geschichte 16 (1939), 179–198.

[9] Heinrich Bullinger an Johann Konrad Ulmer, 12. Dezember 1568, Schaffhausen StA, Abschriften 4/8, Spleiss 8, 66.

[10] Heinrich Bullinger an Johann Konrad Ulmer, 25. März 1569, Schaffhausen StA, Abschriften 4/8, Spleiss 8, 106f.

Ulmer die ganze Geschichte und Problematik des Schaffhauser Katechismusstreites dar, klagte darüber, wie viel Mühe und Anstrengungen ihn diese Auseinandersetzung kosteten, bat Bullinger um Unterstützung dort, wo er den Katechismus überarbeiten müsse und versicherte: »Die Übereinstimmung mit dem Brüdern werde ich mit allen Kräften zu pflegen versuchen«.[11] In seinem ausführlichen Schreiben vom 25. April hielt Bullinger fest:

»Gerade die weisesten Menschen urteilten immer so, dass jede Veränderung des Staates gefährlich sei. Und noch gefährlicher ist es, in den Kirchen etwas zu verändern und aus dem Gebrauch zu ziehen, an das man sich als freie Menschen gewöhnt hat. Von hier aus entstehen unheilvolle Verdächtigungen, dass man früher nicht richtig unterrichtet worden wäre und dass nun unter dem Vorwand einer notwendigen Veränderung darüber hinaus etwas verlangt wird, das jetzt, zu dieser Zeit hervorgebracht werde. [...]

Wenn das die Übereinkunft eurer Kirche ist, dass eine neue Form (des Katechismus) eingeführt werden müsse, dann muss dies aus der gemeinsamen Übereinstimmung der Brüder geschehen, und es ist nützlich, sie (die neue Form) an die alte Form, die bis dahin verwendet wurde, so gut wie möglich anzunähern, damit nicht jene vor den Kopf gestoßen werden, die das Alte errichtet hatten und nicht eine hasserfüllte Verdächtigung gegenüber dem Neuen entsteht.«[12]

Bullinger vertrat hier eine sehr vorsichtige, diplomatische, konservative Ansicht. Man soll keine unnötigen Reformen vornehmen und wenn man am Bisherigen etwas ändern wolle, solle es unbedingt in Übereinstimmung mit allen Beteiligten durchgezogen werden. Sonst könnte leicht eine Feuersbrunst entstehen, der schwer zu löschen wäre. Bullinger ermahnte energisch zur Gemeinsamkeit und zu innerem Frieden zu Gunsten des Aufbaues der Kirche. Im Einzelnen überließ er es Ulmer, wie er vorgehen möchte. Die Synode vom 6. Mai 1569 beschloss, »daß der alte damals gebräuchliche Catechismus[13], auß dem neugestellten des Herrn Decani sollte, wo von nöten, gebessert und vermehrt werden«.[14] Eine Fünferkommission tat dies in rund vier Wochen, Bullinger und Gwalther

[11] Zürich StA, E II 362, 85–89, das Zitat Bl. 89r; Responsio Ioan. Conradi Ulmeri ad proximum Bullingeri Epistolam, 7. April 1569, Schaffhausen StA, Abschriften 4/8, Spleiss 8, 108.

[12] Heinrich Bullinger an Johann Konrad Ulmer, 25. April 1569, Schaffhausen Stadtbibliothek, Ulmeriana 6, Codex 130, 5–8.

[13] Also der kleine Katechismus Leo Juds.

[14] Zitiert aus *Scherrer*, Der erste Schaffhauser Katechismus, 197.

in Zürich überprüften die Arbeit und hießen sie gut.[15] Noch im selben Jahr erschien der neue Katechismus bei Froschauer in Zürich im Druck: »Catechismus oder Kinderbricht für die kirchen in der Statt und Landschafft Schaffhusen«.[16] In der Vorrede legte Ulmer dar, welche Stücke er dem bisherig verwendeten kleinen Katechismus Leo Juds beigefügt habe:

»So habend wir derwegen / angsehen die nodturfft unnd gelegenheit unserer gemeinden / ouch vom bruch deß gsatzes / von der gråchtigkeit deß gloubens / von deß gloubens früchten und gůten wercken / vom Touff und Nachtmal des Herren etc. / ein summarische und gar kurtze leer hinzůsetzen wôllen / damit ouch dise stuck also mit gewüssen dütlichen worten begriffen / sampt den anderen / durch embsige / ståte ůbung und widerholung / einfeltigen Christen yngebildet werden môgind.«[17]

Der Haupttext beginnt so:

»Der Leermeister fragt. Das Kind gibt antwort. Leermeister: Weß gloubens bist du? Kind: Ich bin ein rechter Christ. L[eermeister]: Was ist ein rechter Christ? K[ind]: Ein rechter Christ ist ein solcher mensch / der den rechten waaren Gott durch den glouben an Jesum Christum / sinen eingebornen sun / uß sinem heiligen wort / und yngesetzten Sacramenten / in krafft deß heiligen geistes / recht erkennt und anfrůfft / unnd jm allein zů eeren / und dem nåchsten zů nutz / in einem nüwen låben / dienet.«[18]

Es folgen ganz kurze und einfache Fragen und Antworten über die drei Grundtexte, die jeweils in Katechismen behandelt werden: die zehn Gebote, das Apostolische Glaubensbekenntnis, das »Unser Vater«. Theologiegeschichtlich interessant ist die Aufnahme der Bundestheologie fast am Anfang des Katechismus: Vor die Behandlung der zehn Gebote stellte Ulmer Fragen über Gott (»Was ist Gott?«) und über den Bund Gottes mit den Menschen (»L[eermeister]: Was ist der pundt unnd verheissung Gottes? K[ind]: Daß er

[15] »Probatur ea nobis plurimum, quia breviter et dilucide religionis et doctrinae Christiane capita praecipua comprehendit, neque aliquid continet, quod non sit ex Scripturae Sacrae libris desumptum.« Heinrich Bullinger an Johann Konrad Ulmer, 10. Juli 1569, Schaffhausen StA, Abschriften 4/8, Spleiss 8, 144.

[16] Catechismus oder kinderbericht für die Kirchen unnd Schulen in der Statt und Landtschafft Schaffhusen, Zürich: Christoph Froschauer d.J., 1569 (Verzeichnis der im deutschen Sprachbereich erschienenen Drucke des XVI. Jahrhunderts, Stuttgart 1983–2000 [VD16], Nr. K 160).

[17] Catechismus oder kinderbericht, A2r–v.

[18] Catechismus oder kinderbericht, A4r.

unser Gott woͤlle syn / und uns alle gnuͤge woͤlle geben«[19]). Im Jubiläumsjahr des Heidelberger Katechismus ist bemerkenswert, dass Ulmer die Frage und Antwort Nr. 21 des Heidelberger Katechismus wörtlich übernommen hat. Er stellte sie aber in einen anderen Kontext. Lehrer: »Was ist warer gloub / der vor Gott allein geraͤcht und saͤlig macht?« – Kind: »Es ist nit allein ein gewüsse erkanntnuß / damit ich alles für waar halt [...] sonder ouch ein hertzlich vertruwen unnd zůversicht [...]«[20] Im Heidelberger steht diese Schriften *vor* den Fragen zum Apostolischen Glaubensbekenntnis und leitet dessen Auslegung ein; Ulmer behandelt im Hauptteil »Vom Glauben« zuerst das Apostolische Glaubensbekenntnis und bringt erst *danach* Fragen zur Bedeutung des Glaubens generell: »Was lernest du in einer summa / uß den articklen deß gloubens?«, »Wie gedenckst du dann vor Gott geraͤcht und saͤlig zů werden?« Und dann: »Was ist warer gloub / der vor Gott allein geraͤcht und saͤlig macht?«

Auf die drei klassischen Katechismustexte folgen Fragen und Antworten zu Taufe und Abendmahl, am Schluss Kindergebete für den Morgen, den Abend, bei Tisch, usw. Die im Katechismusstreit beanstandete Kürze erwies auch ihre pädagogischen Vorteile. Im Anhang bot Ulmer – wie schon in seinem ersten Katechismus – eine ganze Reihe von Liedern, die gut zum Katechismusstoff passten, und dies in einer Zeit, als man zum Beispiel in Zürich den Kirchengesang noch gar nicht kannte. Auf dem Titelblatt zum Druck von 1569 heißt es: »Mit angehenckten reinen Kirchengesangen / auff yede houptstuck deß Catechismi gerichtet«. Zu diesen Liedern gehörten das bekannte Lied Martin Luthers über den Text des »Unser Vaters« »Vatter unser im himmelrych [...]«, Lieder von Paulus Speratus, Nikolaus Hermann und anderen. Wo Ulmer keine guten Vorlagen gefunden hatte, dichtete er selber, so ein Lied über

[19] Catechismus oder kinderbericht, A4v. Diese beiden Fragen und Antworten übernahm Ulmer aus dem kleinen Katechismus Leo Juds.

[20] Catechismus oder kinderbericht, B1v. Frage und Antwort 21 des Heidelberger Katechismus war schon in den handschriftlichen Entwürfen aufgenommen worden: Ulmer an die Ministri der Stadt Schaffhausen, 12. Dezember 1568: »Q[uaestio]: Quod est fides vera? R[esponsio]: Est non tantum notitia certa qua omnia vera esse credo, quae Deus in verbo mihi suo patefuit, sed etiam firma cordis fiducia [...]«, Schaffhausen StA, Abschriften 4/8, Spleiss 8, 69, deutsche Fassung Bl. 79.

die zehn Gebote: »Nun hőrt mit ernst die zehen Gebott [...]« und über die Taufe: »Als Christus unser Herr und Gott / war uferstanden von dem tod [...]« Ulmers Abendmahlslied »Nun hőrt deß Herren testament / das er ufricht am letsten end« hielt sich in den Schaffhauser Gesangbüchern bis ins 19. Jahrhundert hinein. Ulmer hat den katechetischen Stoff theologisch gut durchdacht, klar strukturiert und pädagogisch geschickt dargeboten, wie er es auch in anderen Schriften jeweils tat. Interessant ist ferner, dass Ulmer die Lutherübersetzung der Bibel und nicht die Zürcher gebrauchte.

2. Der Heidelberger Katechismus in den Ausgaben von 1643 und 1699

Der Katechismus Ulmers (1. Auflage 1569, weitere Auflagen 1579, 1596, 1607) wurde in der Kinderlehre und in der Schule Schaffhausens jahrzehntelang gebraucht. Er gehört zu den großen Leistungen Ulmers zur Festigung und Bewahrung der Reformierten Kirche Schaffhausen. 1642 wurde – wieder durch Synodalbeschluss – der Katechismus Ulmers durch den Heidelberger Katechismus abgelöst. Nachdem die Synode von Dordrecht 1618/1619 den Heidelberger Katechismus zur Bekenntnisschrift des reformierten Protestantismus erklärt hatte, drang er zunehmend auch in die Schweizer reformierten Kirchen ein. Wegen seines reichhaltigen Inhaltes und seiner Ausführlichkeit wurde er sehr geschätzt, auch in der Schaffhauser Kirche. Mit seiner sehr differenzierten Darstellung der Glaubensinhalte entsprach er den Anforderungen an ein Lehrmittel im Jahrhundert der protestantischen Orthodoxie. Die Abgrenzungen gegen die römisch-katholische Kirche – im Heidelberger die Frage 80 mit der Verurteilung der katholischen Eucharistiefeier als einer »vermaledeiten Abgötterei« – wurden besonders in Gebieten in der Nähe der Konfessionsgrenze geschätzt; Schaffhausen gehörte zu ihnen. Gleich an den Beginn der Ausgaben wurde jeweils die Autorität Bullingers gestellt, sein Urteil über den Heidelberger Katechismus von 1563: »Arbitror meliorem Catechismum editum non esse«, stärkte seinen Einfluss. Im Bernbiet, in Schaffhausen und St. Gallen verdrängte der Heidelberger die einheimischen Katechismen.[21] In Schaffhausen blieb er bis weit ins 19.

Jahrhundert hinein obligatorisches Lehrmittel in Kirche und Schule und diente somit vielen sehr Generationen von Kindern als Lesebuch und als Glaubensunterweisung.

Die Schaffhauser ließen ihren Katechismus von der Basler Offizin Georg Decker drucken. Der Titel lautete: »Catechismus Oder Kurtzer Unterricht Christlicher Lehr / wie der in Kirchen und Schulen Reformierter Evangelischer Religion getriben wird. Mit nutzlichen Rand-fragen kürtzlich erklärt / und mit Zeugnissen der heiligen Schrifft bestätiget. Übersehen und in komlichere [bekömmlichere] form gebracht / für die Statt Schaffhausen Kirchen und Schulen. Gedruckt zu Basel bey Georg Decker / Im Jahr 1643«.[22] Schaffhausen besaß damals keine eigene Druckerei. Auf dem Titelblatt musste aber ausdrücklich vermerkt werden, dass es sich um ein Schaffhauser Lehrmittel handelt. Der Anhang im Umfang von 56 Druckseiten mit seinen Ausführungen über die Unterrichtsweise, mit den Verzeichnissen der biblischen Bücher und der neutestamentlichen Kernstellen sowie einem Gebet für die Schuljugend wurden von Johann Christian Rothfuchs, »Gymnas. Scaph. Rect.« gestaltet und unterzeichnet. Dem Katechismustext waren verschiedene Vorbemerkungen vorausgestellt worden, darunter das bereits zitierte Urteil Bullingers über die hohe Qualität des Heidelbergers, die Versicherung, der Text von 1563 sei unverändert abgedruckt worden, nur Druckfehler seien beseitigt worden. Dann hieß es: Die Jugend soll den Katechismus »nicht allein außwendig / sondern auch verstehen lernen«. »Die Kinder müssen fleissig abgerichtet werden«. Und nochmals: Sie sollen das Gelernte »auch recht verstehen«. Die Texte über die kurfürstlichen Schulverhältnisse wurden in den Vorbemerkungen abgedruckt samt ihren Bemerkungen über die »Churfürstlichen Paedagogia« bis hin zu den »geringen schlechten Schulen in Flecken und Dörfern«. Spezielle Hinweise auf die Kirchen und Schulen Schaffhausens wurden hier nicht gegeben. Der Hauptteil des Buches enthält den vollständigen Text des Heidelberger Katechismus mit Randbemerkungen und Anmerkungen. Es ist eine schöne, sorgfältig gestaltete Ausgabe.

[21] Paul *Wernle*, Der schweizerische Protestantismus im 18. Jahrhundert, Bd. 1, Tübingen 1923, 57.

[22] Der Originaltitel »Catechismus oder christlicher Underricht, wie der in Kirchen und Schulen der Churfürstlichen Pfaltz getrieben wirdt«, wurde so adaptiert.

1655 erhielt Schaffhausen eine eigene Druckerei.[23] Der Zürcher Buchdrucker und Jungunternehmer Johann Caspar Suter (1635–1673) eröffnete mit obrigkeitlicher Genehmigung eine Offizin. Er brachte aus Zürich eine Probe seiner Kunst mit, die Waldenserchronik, eine »erste Trucker-prob«, die er dem Rat zu Schaffhausen als Dank widmete, da er ihm die Möglichkeit verschaffte, ihn »mit einhelligem gutachten zu Ihrer loblichen Statt (als) Buchtrucker anzunehmen«. In der zweiten Hälfte des 17. Jahrhunderts wurde ziemlich viel theologische und geistliche Literatur in Schaffhausen gedruckt. Darunter befanden sich die erste Schaffhauser Reformationsgeschichte des Schaffhausers Leonhardt Meyer (1627 – nach 1684) »Loblicher Statt Schaffhausen Reformation« und eine Märtyrergeschichte desselben Autors »Denckwürdige Reden und Thaten vieler H. Märtyrer« (1664). Die ganze kirchliche Gebrauchsliteratur konnte jetzt in Schaffhausen gedruckt werden, auch die Neuauflagen der Heidelberger Katechismus. Zu einer solchen Neuauflage kam es im Jahre 1699: »Getruckt zu Schaffhausen / Bey Alexander Rieding. In Verlegung Alexander Zieglers sel. Erben«. Der Titel war derselbe wie in der Ausgabe von 1643. Um aber die Autorität Schaffhausens zu bekräftigen wurde am Anfang des Buches eine graphische Darstellung beigegeben. Sie enthält den Titel »Catechismus.« Dann den Wahlspruch der Schaffhauser Kirche in einem Schriftband: »Deus spes nostra est« und dann das Schaffhauser Wappen (Schaffhausen Reich: Doppelköpfiger Adler, darüber Kaiserkrone, darunter zweimal der Schaffhauser Bock). Im Vorwort steht, es sei »nichts geändert«, die Darstellung ist aber neu und übersichtlich gestaltet worden.

3. Der Heidelberger Katechismus in Versen

Der Heidelberger Katechismus war im ganzen 17. und im 18. Jahrhundert *das* katechetische Lehrmittel. Er wurde auswendig gelernt. Es wurde ein eigentlicher Katechismusdrill ausgeübt und der Stoff

[23] Johann *Oethiker*, Der Werdegang der Buchdruckereien und Zeitungen im Kanton Schaffhausen, in: Typographia Schaffhausen: Festschrift zur Jubiläumsfeier anlässlich des fünfzigjährigen Bestandes 1872–1922, Schaffhausen 1922, 2.

mit unendlich vielen Wiederholungen und »oft mit kräftigem Gebrauch des Prügelstocks« eingetrichtert.[24] Im 18. Jahrhundert, dem Zeitalter von Pietismus und Aufklärung, wurde der Heidelberger Katechismus oft als zu gelehrt, zu theoretisch und zu trocken empfunden – und die Lehrmethoden als unzeitgemäß. Der Schaffhauser Münsterpfarrer und Antistes Johann Wilhelm Meyer (1690–1787), ein Vertreter der reformierten Orthodoxie, der aber auch vom Pietismus zinzendorfscher Prägung beeinflusst war, kam auf die Idee, den Heidelberger in Verse umzuarbeiten und als Lieder für die 52 Sonntage des Jahres zu gestalten. Katechismuslieder waren an sich nichts Neues. Man kannte sie auch in Schaffhausen. Ulmer hatte, wie oben erwähnt, mehrere Katechismuslieder geschrieben, darunter über die Themen Taufe und Abendmahl. Vielerorts versuchten sich Versemacher damit, allerdings mit unterschiedlichem Talent und auch mit unterschiedlichem Erfolg. Paul Wernle schreibt von »schauerlichen Versifizierungen«, denen man begegnen konnte.[25] Meyer gelangen viele gute und interessante Formulierungen. Vieles von seiner Umdichtung empfindet man heute aber als kitschig und ungenießbar.

»Die Haupt-Summ der wahren Christlichen Religion in LII Liedern. Nach Ordnung der Sonntagen des Heidelberger Catechismi abgefasset, und auf außerlesene Melodeyen der Lobwasserschen Psalmen gerichtet« wurde 1728 (weitere Auflagen 1734, 1740, 1742, 1755, 1821) innerhalb des Psalmenbuches, das der Kantor Johann Caspar Deggeler (1695–1776)[26] herausgab, gedruckt. Frage und Antwort Nr. 1 des Heidelberger Katechismus lauteten in der Nachdichtung Meyers:

1. Strophe (zum 1. Sonntag)
»Es ist nur eins in disem leben, Das meine Seele tröst,
Nur eins kan mir erquickung geben, Wann ich werd aufgelößt;

[24] *Wernle,* Der schweizerische Protestantismus, 59.

[25] *Wernle,* Der schweizerische Protestantismus, 58.

[26] Erwin *Bührer*, Johann Caspar Deggeler, Kantor und Praeceptor, in: Schaffhauser Biographien des 18. und 19. Jahrhunderts. Erster Teil, Thayngen 1956, 32–34. Sein Werk, das 1728 zuerst privat herausgegeben wurde, enthält vier Teile: 1. Die Psalmen Davids, 2. Hymnen oder Lobgesänge, 3. Die »Haupt-Summ« Meyers und 4. Texte zur Abendmahlsfeier. Zu Meyer vgl. Hans-Alfred *Girard*, Johann Wilhelm Meyer, Antistes, in: Schaffhauser Biographien des 17., 18., 19. und 20. Jahrhunderts. Dritter Teil, hg. vom Historischen Verein des Kantons Schaffhausen, Thayngen 1969, 196–200.

und das ist nicht in dir zu finden, Du trugesvolle welt!
Nichts hilfft im tod, in angst und sünden,
Pracht, wollust, gut und geld.«

2. Strophe (zum 1. Sonntag)
»Herr Jesu! Du, du bists alleine, Du bist das Höchste Gut,
Mit leib und seel bin ich der deine, Dein theures Gottes-blut.
Ist die bezahlung meiner sünden, Der seelen ranzion,
Tod, teuffel, höll kann mich nicht binden.
Du hilffst mir frey davon.«

Die Strophen zu den beiden ersten Fragen werden mit der Melodie von Psalm 38 des Lobwasserschen Psalters gesungen.

Strophe 3 beginnt so:

»Du waltest auch mit starcken armen, Herr Jesu, über mir,
Du hörst nit auf dich zu erbarmen. Du trägst mich für und für. [...]«[27]

Die Dreieinigkeit (Fragen 24 und 25 zum 8. Sonntag) wird so umschrieben (zu singen nach der »Melodey« von Psalm 134):

»Gott Vatter wird zuerst gemeldt, Der uns erschaffen und erwehlt.
So dann Gott Sohn, der Heyland heisst, und uns aus dem verderben reißt.
Gott heilger Geist, der lehrt und tröst macht heilig , die der Sohn erlößt [...]
Die drei sind eins und unzertrennt, In allem wird ein Gott bekennt,
Jedoch sind der Personen drey. Diß zeuget Gott, da bleibt es bey [...]«[28]

In der Nachdichtung der Fragen 69–71 über die Taufe heißt es:

»[...] Durchs blut sind alle Schulden / Der sünden ausgethan
Dass sich die seel in hulden / Bey Gott verspühren kan;
Der geist gibt neue stärcke / Dass man in heiligkeit
Zum anbefohlnen wercke / mit lust und freude schreit [...]«[29]

Der Abschnitt mit den Fragen 80–82 über das Abendmahl (Melodey von Psalm 36) beginnt mit den Worten: »Das Abendmahl ist von der meß / Was himmel-weit Verschidenes [...]« Das Abend-

[27] Johann Wilhelm *Meyer*, Die Haupt-Summ der wahren Christlichen Religion; bestehend in LII. Liedern: Nach Ordnung der Sonntagen des Heidelbergischen Catechismi abgefasset, Schaffhausen 1752, 1. Das Buch ist beigebunden zu: Johann Caspar *Deggeler*, Die Psalmen Davids, Durch Dr. Ambrosium Lobwasser in teutsche Reimen gebracht, Schaffhausen 1752.

[28] *Meyer*, Die Haupt-Summ, 9.

[29] *Meyer*, Die Haupt-Summ, 26.

mahlsverständnis wird nach reformierter Lehre geschildert, die scharfe Polemik im Original gegen die römisch-katholische Kirche ist jedoch gemildert. Die vierte Strophe mahnt mit pathetischen Worten zu ernsthafter innerer Einstellung:

> »Laß Jesu! Mich im feyer-kleid / des heyls, und der gerechtigkeit, / Bey deinem tisch erscheinen.
> Laß mich in heil'ger hertzens-schaur / Vor dir, gleich in schwartzer traur / Der sünden schuld beweinen.
> Mein glaub an deines opfers blut / Sey gegen tod und höllen-wuth / Mein rothes siges kleide [...]«[30]

Die Texte Meyers waren natürlich nicht wortwörtliche Übertragungen des Katechismustextes in Verse. Sie wurden inhaltlich an die Theologie und den Geschmack der ersten Hälfte des 18. Jahrhunderts angepasst. Auffällig ist, dass manche Texte Gebetscharakter haben, dass Gott oder Christus häufiger angerufen wird als im Originaltext, und dass eine ganze Reihe von Texten pädagogisch oder spirituell ausgerichtet sind. Theologisch ist Manches vereinfacht.[31] Meyers Arbeit scheint einzigartig gewesen zu sein. Ähnlich umfangreiche Versbearbeitungen des Heidelberger Katechismus sind mir nicht bekannt. Meines Wissens wurde Meyers Verskatechismus nicht außerhalb der Schaffhauser Kirche benutzt, von ihr aber mehrere Male nachgedruckt; einzelne Teile hielten sich als Katechismuslieder bis gegen das Ende des 19. Jahrhunderts in den Schaffhauser Gesangbüchern.

4. Biblische Geschichten

Auch die frühe Aufklärung beeinflusste die Katechetik in Schaffhausen, vor allem durch das hochberühmte, in ganz Europa verbreitete Werk des Hamburger Pastoren Johannes Hübner (1668–1731): »Zweymahl zwey und fünffzig Auserlesene Biblische

[30] *Meyer*, Die Haupt-Summ, 30.

[31] Heike und Udo *Wennemuth*, Gesungene Lehre – Katechismus in Liedern: Katechismuslied und Heidelberger Katechismus, in: Martin *Heimbucher* et al. (Hg.), Zugänge zum Heidelberger Katechismus: Geschichte – Themen – Unterricht, Neukirchen-Vluyn 2012, 81–85.

Historien, Aus dem Alten und Neuen Testament. Der Jugend nützlich und zu Besten abgefasset«, erschienen in erster Auflage in Hamburg 1714.[32] Innert kürzester Zeit eroberte dieses Buch die ganze protestantische Welt und wurde in unzähligen Auflagen nachgedruckt; bis 1857 sollen es deren 107 gewesen sein.[33] Auch in der reformierten Schweiz war es äußerst populär. 1744 wurde in Schaffhausen eine eigene Druckausgabe herausgebracht, gedruckt und verlegt vom Pietisten Benedict Hurter.[34] In seinem für damalige Zeiten bahnbrechenden Werk ging es Hübner darum, »eine Werkstatt Gottes«, eine christliche Schule darzubieten, »darinnen die noch unmündige Jugend in der Gottseligkeit, in der Gelehrsamkeit und in der Ehrbarkeit unterwiesen werde«.[35] Es ging also um Spiritualität, Theologie und Moral (in dieser Reihenfolge). Biblische Geschichten werden hier erzählt, nach einer von Hübner entwickelten »Zergliederungsmethode« strukturiert und mit Fragen und Antworten für Lehrer und Schüler, außerdem mit Merkgedichten und Illustrationen versehen. In den einzelnen Kapiteln wurde jeweils zuerst der biblische Text gedruckt, dann wurden – in kleineren Lettern – »Deutliche Fragen« geboten und schließlich »Nützliche Lehren« und »Gottselige Gedanken« in deutscher und lateinischer Sprache sowie eine Illustration angefügt. Frühe Aufklärung (Hübner) und Pietismus (Benedict Hurter) waren damals keine Gegensätze, sondern gingen Hand in Hand miteinander. Die programmatischen Begriffe Gottseligkeit, Gelehrsamkeit und Ehrbarkeit sind typische Ausdrücke einer frommen Aufklärung. In der Vorrede zu seinem Buch hielt Hübner fest: »Ein jedwedes Kind hat von seinem Schöpffer empfangen erstlich ein Gedächtniß / daß es etwas auswendig lernen kann; darnach einen Verstand / daß es

[32] Es waren 52 Geschichten aus dem Alten und 52 Geschichten aus dem Neuen Testament, für jeden Sonntag des Jahres auf zwei Jahre hinaus bestimmt. Nachdruck der Ausgabe Leipzig 1731, hg. von Rainer Lachmann, Hildesheim 1986.

[33] Die Religion in Geschichte und Gegenwart, 3. Aufl., Bd. 5, Tübingen 1961, 1002.

[34] Die Ausgabe enthielt eine Widmung und eine Widmungsvorrede an drei Pfarrer in der Schweiz, die die Ausgabe förderten, mit der Bitte, »dieses Büchlein bestens [zu] recomandiren«, die Vorrede Hübners an die »ministri« der Stadt Hamburg, die Vorrede des Autors über die Ziele des Buches und dann den ganzen Text.

[35] Johannes *Hübner*, Zweymahl zwey und fünfftzig Auserlesene Biblische Historien Aus dem Alten und Neuen Testamten, Der Jugend nützlich und zum Besten abgefasset [...] Schaffhausen / Druckts und verlegts Benedict Hurter, wohnhaft zum Roßmarin auf dem Platz. 1744, Vorrede Des Autoris, Bl. 1v.

einer Sache nachdencken kann: – und endlich einen Willen / daß es sich einen Vorsatz fassen kann.«[36] Über die Methode schrieb Hübner: »Wenns aber gleich mit der Memoria [i.e. dem Auswendiglernen] seine Richtigkeit hat, so ist das Kind deswegen noch nichts klüger, und also muß man bey diesen Fragen nicht bewenden lassen. Sondern nunmehr muß der Verstand des Kindes geübet werden, daß es einer solchen Geschichte nachdencken, und die darinn verborgenen Wahrheiten durch den Gebrauch seiner Vernunft heraus suchen lernt.«[37] Auch das Gebet, das ein Kind vor dem Hören und Lernen von biblischen Geschichten beten soll, weist auf die frühe Aufklärung mit ihrer Betonung von Wissen und Moral hin: »[...] Schärffe doch mein Gedächtniß , daß ich dein Wort recht fassen und begreiffen könne! Erleuchte doch meinen Verstand, daß ich dich, GOtt Vater, und den du gesandt hast, JEsun Christum daraus erkenne! Heilige doch endlich auch meinen Willen, daß ich das Böse verwerffen, und das Gute erwählen, und also nicht nur ein Hörer, sondern auch ein Thäter deines Worts seyn möge!«[38] Die biblischen Geschichten wurden von Hübner mit einem »moralischen Schwänzchen« versehen, wie aus der Nacherzählung des Gleichnisses vom verlorenen Sohn hervorgeht, die folgende Belehrung enthält:

> »Der ungerathe Sohn muss endlich Treber fressen
> Nachdem er Hab und Gut mit Huren hat verpraßt.
> So läuffts mit Kindern ab, die das Gebot vergessen,
> Das GOTT den Eltern hat zu Ehren abgefaßt:
> Ach GOTT! Wie will ich mich vor dieser Sünde hüten,
> Daß ich bei Schweinen mich nicht darff zu Gaste bitten?«[39]

Hübners Buch war ein bedeutender Fortschritt in der Religionspädagogik. Es wurde im Laufe des 18. Jahrhunderts zur verbreitetesten Kinder- und Jugendbibel und wurde gegen Ende des Jahrhunderts in der ganzen Schweiz gebraucht.[40] Das mechanische Auswendiglernen von abstrakten theologischen Formulierungen

[36] *Hübner*, Zweymahl, 2v.
[37] *Hübner*, Zweymahl, 3v.
[38] *Hübner*, Zweymahl, 6v.
[39] *Hübner*, Zweymahl, 5r–v und S. 324–329.
[40] Paul *Wernle,* Der schweizerische Protestantismus, 442.

wurde damit ergänzt, aber nicht abgelöst. Die Kinder sollten die biblischen Geschichten hören, verstehen und durch die Gliederung, die Illustrationen und die Verspartien leicht aufnehmen und damit auch lieben lernen.

1758 erschien eine französische Übersetzung »Histoire de la Bible« für die welschen Kantone. Ostervald verfasste ein ähnliches Buch wie Hübner. 1785 erschien eine Berner Druckausgabe von Hübners »Biblischen Geschichten«, also 41 Jahre nach der Schaffhauser Edition.[41] Hübners Buch wurde in 15 europäische Sprachen übersetzt. Aus der Biographie des russischen Dichters Fjodor Dostojewski (1821–1881) wissen wir, dass er und seine Geschwister mit der russischen Fassung von Hübners Buch Lesen lernten.[42] Im Roman »Die Brüder Karamazov« lässt Dostojewski den Starzen Zosima aus seiner Kindheit und Jugend erzählen:

> »Zu meinen Erinnerungen an das Elternhaus zähle ich auch die Erinnerungen an die Biblische Geschichte, die, obgleich ich noch ein Kind war, mein größtes Interesse weckte. Ich hatte damals ein Buch, biblische Geschichte, mit wunderbaren Bildern, es hieß ›Hundertundvier biblische Geschichten aus dem Alten und Neuen Testament‹, und nach diesem Buch habe ich lesen gelernt. Heute liegt es bei mir hier auf dem Bord, ich bewahre es als ein kostbares Andenken.«[43]

5. Der Heidelberger Katechismus in Schaffhausen gegen Ende des 18. und im 19. Jahrhundert

»Wie in Bern so regierte in Schaffhausen und St. Gallen der Heidelberger bis ins 19. Jahrhundert hinein«, stellte Paul Wernle in seinem Werk »Geschichte des schweizerischen Protestantismus im 18. Jahrhundert« fest.[44] Allerdings wurde der Heidelberger Katechismus vor allem von der jüngeren Generation scharf kritisiert: Er

[41] Rudolf *Pfister,* Kirchengeschichte der Schweiz, Bd. 3, Zürich 1984, 208.

[42] Konrad *Onasch*, Der verschwiegene Christus: Versuch über die Poetisierung des Christentums in der Dichtung F.M. Dostojewskis, Berlin (Ost) [1975], 20. In Russland wurde Hübners Buch in einer von M. Sokolov übersetzten und bearbeiteten Fassung von Hauslehrern in Adelsfamilien als Lehrbuch benutzt.

[43] Fjodor *Dostojewski*, Die Brüder Karamasow. Aus dem Russischen von Swetlana Geier, Zürich 2003, 467.

[44] Paul *Wernle*, Der schweizerische Protestantismus, 653.

sei veraltet, man brauche jetzt ein neues, kürzeres und leichter fassbares Lehrmittel für den Religionsunterricht. Die Hauptargumente gegen den Heidelberger Katechismus lassen sich in fünf Punkten zusammenfassen:[45]

1. Der Heidelberger Katechismus wurde als zu schwer für die Kinder beurteilt, seine Sprache als ein »Hebräisch-Deutsch« bezeichnet. Der Katechismus werde von den Lehrkräften auf oft »marterhafte Art« eingetrichtert und von den Schülern mechanisch und ohne Verständnis auswendig gelernt. Das bringe auch eine grundsätzliche Abneigung gegen die Religion mit sich.

2. Die Anordnung des Stoffes sei für das heutige Verständnis von Theologie und Glauben unnatürlich, ja verkehrt. Vermisst wurden einleitende Ausführungen über die Heilige Schrift als Erkenntnisquelle, kritisiert wurde, dass die Lehre von Gott zu spät im Gesamtduktus behandelt werde. Ulmers Katechismus von 1569 übrigens hatte diese Forderungen erfüllt.

3. Beanstandet wurde, dass das irdische Leben und Wirken Jesu Christi im Heidelberger nicht einmal erwähnt wird und über Jesus Christus nur abstrakte theologische Ausführungen geboten werden. Die Kritiker wiesen darauf hin, dass bereits im Apostolischen Glaubensbekenntnis zwischen »geboren aus der Jungfrau Maria« und »gelitten unter Pontius Pilatus« nichts steht. Was im 16. und 17. Jahrhundert offensichtlich wenig gestört hatte, wurde im Zeitalter von Pietismus und Aufklärung zu einem theologischen Problem.

4. Die Wahl der Beweisstellen und die Gestaltung der Randglossen wurden als »öfters elend« kritisiert.

5. Schließlich betrachtete man viele theologische Begriffe und Ausführungen im Heidelberger Katechismus als für das aktuelle Verständnis von Religion zu hart. Frage und Antwort 5, der natürliche Mensch sei geneigt, Gott und seine Nächsten zu hassen, die Ausführungen über die ewigen Strafen für die Sünde (zu Frage 11), die Formulierungen über den Zorn Gottes (zu den Fragen 14, 17, 37) entsprachen überhaupt nicht dem Menschen- und Gottes-

[45] Vgl. Johann Georg *Müller*, Bedenken über den Heidelbergischen Catechismus, Schaffhausen 1828, 1–16.

verständnis der Zeit. Es wurde festgestellt, dass vieles deutlich über den Gesichtskreis der Jugendlichen hinaus ging, so die Passagen über die Satisfaktion (12–17), die Vereinigung der beiden Naturen Jesu Christi (47–48) und anderes mehr. Die polemischen Formulierungen etwa gegen die römisch-katholische Kirche würden nicht zu einem Unterricht in einer Religion der Liebe passen.

Auf der andern Seite wurde an der Wende vom 18. zum 19. Jahrhundert und weit darüber hinaus der Heidelberger heiß geliebt und als unentbehrlich bezeichnet. Viele Schaffhauser verteidigten ihren »Katikismus« energisch und waren offensichtlich bereit, für ihn auf die Barrikaden zu steigen. Johann Georg Müller, ein treuer Anhänger des Heidelbergers, erhielt 1789 von hoher Stelle aus die Zusicherung: »Ihr sollt euren Katikismus zu Stadt und Land wie bis dahin ohne alle Vernunft und Verstand fernerhin traktieren [...] damit nicht auf den ehrsamen Zünften ein unerhörtes Gepolter und Aufruhr und Blutvergiessen auf der Landschaft entstehe.«[46]

In seiner Schrift »Theophil oder Unterhaltungen über die christliche Religion mit Jünglingen von reiferem Alter« (1801)[47] setzte sich der soeben genannte Schaffhauser Theologe Johann Georg Müller (1759–1819) ausführlich mit den Kritikern des Heidelberger Katechismus auseinander, unternahm es, ihre Argumente zu widerlegen und die hohe Qualität des seiner Meinung nach sehr bewährten Buches zu verteidigen. Das Auswendiglernen sei gerechtfertigt, auch wenn man nicht alles verstehe. »Ich musste ihn auch, und freilich oft mit Pein und Marter auswendig lernen, aber ich erinnere mich gar wohl, schon in den untersten Classen zwar nicht alle, doch die wichtigsten Fragen und Antworten recht gut verstanden, und noch mehr, gefühlt und empfunden zu haben.«[48] Die sogenannte »hebräisch-deutsche Schreibart« sei der Sprache der Bibel angemessen, mit ihr könne »der Verstand der Kinder ungemein geübt« werden.[49] Die Anordnung des Stoffes sei natür-

[46] Johannes Büel an Johann Georg Müller, 28. Dezember 1789, zitiert aus Paul *Wernle*, Der schweizerische Protestantismus, 653, Anm. 5.

[47] Zürich 1801, auszugsweiser Nachdruck mit dem Titel »Bedenken über den Heidelbergischen Catechismus«, Schaffhausen 1828 (hieraus wird im Folgenden zitiert).

[48] *Müller*, Bedenken, 5.

[49] *Müller*, Bedenken, 6.

lich, psychologisch und ein »Hauptvorzug dieses Lehrbuches«.[50] Das Fehlen von Ausführungen über »die Umstände des Lebens Jesu« sei allerdings ein Mangel, doch man solle sich an das bestehende Unterrichtsmittel halten, in der Theologie sei dazu noch vieles im Fluss.[51] Beweisstellen und Randglossen müssten überarbeitet werden. »Endlich wünschte ich auch einige harte Ausdrücke, die in die damalige Dogmatik aufgenommen waren, und ihren eigentlichen Ursprung in den Vorstellungsarten der Scholastiker hatten, ausgemerzt und mit solchen vertauscht, die milder sind und häufiger in der Schrift vorkommen.«[52] Verbesserungen sind nach Johann Georg Müller also notwendig, doch, so versichert er am Schluss seiner Ausführungen, das Urteil Heinrich Bullingers, »arbitror meliorem Catechismum editum non esse«, sei weiterhin gültig.[53]

Zu den entschlossenen Verteidigern des Heidelberger Katechismus gegen die Kritik aus rationalistischer und aufklärerischer Sicht gehörte der Schaffhauser Pfarrer Friedrich Hurter (1787–1865, 1844 Konversion in die römisch-katholische Kirche). In seiner Schrift »Für den heidelbergischen Katechismus. Ein öffentliches Votum Oktober 1828«, behandelte er aus seiner konservativen Sicht die verbreitetesten Einwände: Der Heidelberger Katechismus enthalte zu viel Polemik, sei pädagogisch nicht geeignet, Form und Sprache seien nicht zeitgemäß, es fehle eine Moral oder Pflichtenlehre, von der heiligen Geschichte und vom Leben und Wirken Jesu sei nur wenig zu erfahren. Hurter stellte sich entschlossen gegen die modernen Geistesströmungen seiner Zeit. Er wetterte gegen die »Menschheits-Emancipatoren«, die »Glaubens Aus- und Abklärer«, gegen die, welche das Christentum »verzeitgemässleren« wollten[54] und kam zum Schluss, dass der Heidelberger Katechis-

[50] *Müller*, Bedenken, 8.

[51] *Müller*, Bedenken, 12.

[52] *Müller*, Bedenken, 14.

[53] *Müller*, Bedenken, 16.

[54] Kleinere Schriften von Friedrich Hurter, Bd. 1, Schaffhausen 1844, 4. – Über Hurter: Karl *Schib*, Hurter, Friedrich Emanuel (1787–1865), in: Schaffhauser Biographien des 18. und 19. Jahrhunderts. Erster Teil, hg. vom Historischen Verein des Kantons Schaffhausen, Thayngen 1956, 210–227; Peter *Vogelsanger*, Weg nach Rom: Friedrich Hurters geistige Entwicklung im Rahmen der romantischen Konversationsbewegung, Zürich 1954.

mus auf alle Fälle beibehalten werden müsse. Wenn wir das tun, »dürfen wir freudig alle jene Verunglimpfungen über uns ergehen lassen, und nimmer es bereuen, das theure Kleinod der Väter bewahrt zu haben.«[55] 1828 wehrte sich Hurter gegen die geplante Streichung des Heidelberger Katechismus aus dem Lehrplan des Gymnasiums, polemisierte dabei wiederum gegen Rationalismus, Liberalismus und Umsturzpläne und kämpfte für den weiteren Gebrauch des Altbewährten, jedoch vergeblich.[56]

Der Heidelberger Katechismus wurde im Laufe des 19. Jahrhunderts immer wieder kritisiert, aber von maßgebenden Lehrern und Pfarrern auch energisch verteidigt, so von Johannes Kirchhofer, Religionslehrer an der Realschule Schaffhausen in einem Vortrag 1853[57] oder von Johannes Lang, Pfarrer in Osterfingen 1863[58]. Kirchhofer urteilte: Er meine, dass die heilsame Lehre des evangelischen Glaubens im Heidelberger Katechismus »köstlich« dargelegt sei und die Vorzüge des Katechismus seine zugegebenermaßen vorhandenen Mängel überwiegen. Allerdings müsse sehr viel geschickter unterrichtet werden als es meistens geschehe. »Durch unmässige Pensen, durch Unerklärtlassen des Inhaltes, durch Einbläuen mit dem Stock oder durch Püffe und Stösse wird ein Religionsbuch weder eingeübt noch beliebt«, erklärte er.[59] Modernisierungen seien immer notwendig, auch heute: »Wenn unsere Zeit mit Eisenbahnen und andern materiellen Verbesserungen vorwärts schreitet, so wollen wir mit den religiösen nicht träge dahinter bleiben.«[60]

[55] Friedrich *Hurter*, Für den heidelbergerischen Katechismus, in: Kleinere Schriften von Friedrich Hurter, 31.

[56] Friedrich *Hurter*, Gegen Entfernung des heidelbergischen Katechismus aus dem Gymnasium (Bemerkungen, an den damaligen Schulrath gerichtet; Juni 1828), in: Kleinere Schriften von Friedrich Hurter, 32–42.

[57] Johannes *Kirchhofer*, Über den Heidelberger Katechismus und das Memorieren desselben, Schaffhausen 1853.

[58] Johannes *Lang*, Der Heidelberger Katechismus: Seine Verfasser und Hauptzüge seiner Geschichte. Zur 300jährigen Gedächtnisfeier, Schaffhausen 1863.

[59] *Kirchhofer*, Über den Heidelberger Katechismus, 26.

[60] *Kirchhofer*, Über den Heidelberger Katechismus, 32.

6. Ausblick auf das 20. Jahrhundert

Der Heidelberger Katechismus wurde in den Schaffhauser Schulen bis in die Mitte des 19. Jahrhundert, in der Reformierten Kirche des Kantons Schaffhausen bis weit ins 20. Jahrhunderts hinein gebraucht. 1935 wurde er von der Evangelischen Gesellschaft in Schaffhausen nachgedruckt. Die letzte Ausgabe wurde von Willy Meyer (1903–1987), damals Pfarrer in Neuhausen am Rheinfall, bearbeitet und herausgegeben und erschien 1963 im Verlag und Buchhandlung der Evangelischen Gesellschaft Schaffhausen. Der äußere Anlass war der 400. Jahrestag des Erscheinens der Erstausgabe. Meyer verteidigte vehement die Bedeutung des Heidelbergers und schrieb im Vorwort, dass sprachliche Wendungen zwar veralten, der Inhalt aber nicht veralten könne,[61] und wiederholte das altbekannte Urteil Heinrich Bullingers, dass noch kein besserer Katechismus herausgegeben worden sei. Der Verlag blieb auf der Auflage weitgehend sitzen. Der Heidelberger kam damals im kirchlichen Unterricht immer seltener zur Anwendung. Als ich selber Pfarrer in einer Schaffhauser Kirchgemeinde (in Dörflingen) war (1979–1989) hat kaum noch jemand im Konfirmandenunterricht mit dem Heidelberger Katechismus gearbeitet, und ich selber nahm ihn auch eher als einen Katechismus für Erwachsene als für Jugendliche wahr, den man allenfalls im Konvertitenunterricht, nicht aber im Konfimandenunterricht gebrauchen konnte.

7. Zusammenfassung

Die Geschichte der Katechismen in der Schaffhauser Kirche ist weitgehend eine Geschichte des Heidelberger Katechismus. Die Reformierte Kirche Schaffhausens war neben derjenigen St. Gallens die einzige, die ihn jahrhundertelang, von der Mitte des 17. Jahrhunderts bis weit ins 20. Jahrhundert, fast ausschließlich verwendete. Unmittelbar nach der Einführung der Reformation hatte man für kurze Zeit die Katechismen Leo Juds aus Zürich ge-

[61] Heidelberger Katechismus: Jubiläumsausgabe zum 400jährigen Bestehen des Heidelberger Katechismus, hg. von Willy Meyer, Schleitheim 1963.

braucht. Nachdem der Unterricht sehr rasch verfallen war, führte ihn Johann Konrad Ulmer, der zweite Reformator Schaffhausens, wieder ein und schuf 1568 einen eigenen Katechismus, der im Katechismusstreit, der kurz darauf ausbrach, nicht akzeptiert wurde. Die Synode von 1569 nahm eine von Ulmer überarbeitete und ergänzte Fassung des Kleinen Katechismus Juds an. Dieser stand jahrzehntelang in hohem Ansehen, wurde 1643 jedoch vom Heidelberger abgelöst. Der Heidelberger wirkte im Einflussbereich der Reformierten Kirche Schaffhausen jahrhundertelang nachhaltig und prägend. Als der Heidelberger im Laufe des 18. Jahrhunderts zu abstrakt und schwierig erschien, wurde er von Johann Wilhelm Meyer in Versen nachgedichtet und mit Johannes Hübners »Zweimal zweiundfünfzig biblischen Geschichten« ergänzt. Trotz scharfer Kritik moderner Theologen und Pädagogen verteidigten ihn namhafte Persönlichkeiten aus Kirche und Schule wie Johann Georg Müller und Friedrich Hurter vehement. Er wurde aus den Gymnasien ausgeschlossen. Doch er hielt sich in der Kirche durch das ganze 19. Jahrhundert hindurch bis weit ins 20. Jahrhundert hinein und wurde von vielen Schaffhauser Reformierten außerordentlich geschätzt. Da er oft mit Druck und Prügelpädagogik eingetrichtert wurde, hat er allerdings nicht nur Freunde gefunden. Doch er hat während Jahrhunderten sehr viel dazu beigetragen, die Jugend in den evangelischen Glauben einzuführen.

Erich Bryner, Dr. phil., Titularprofessor für osteuropäische Kirchengeschichte, Universität Zürich

Abstract: When Johann Konrad Ulmer took up his pastorate in Schaffhausen in 1566, the traditional practice of religious training according to the catechism of Leo Jud, which had been taught ever since the reform had been accepted, was in trouble. Ulmer wrote his own catechism, however, the pastors in Schaffhausen did not accept it. Bullinger's mediation ended the conflict about the catechism in Schaffhausen, whereby the synod accepted the »Catechism for the Church and Schools of the City and Countryside of Schaffhausen«, which was a combination of Ulmer's own work and Jud's Small Catechism. The Heidelberg Catechism replaced it in 1642. Schaffhausen printed its own printouts. The Heidelberg Catechism remained the tool for religious training for a long time and was highly praised. In the eighteenth century, Johann Wilhelm Meyer modeled a collection of literary verses after the text. Johann Hübner's »Zweimal zweiundfünfzig biblische Geschichten« (printed in Schaffhausen in 1744) was a supplement to the instruction. The Heidelberg Catechism underwent sharp criticism at the end of the eighteenth century; critics argued the text was too difficult for children because its style was old fashion, its theology too dogmatic and not contemporary enough. Noteworthy theologians and educators passionately defended the Heidelberg Catechism, its form, language and theology, as well as the method of learning it by heart. The Heidelberg Catechism remained in the Schaffhausen Church well into the twentieth century as a useful tool for introducing Evangelical faith to the youth.

Schlagworte: Johann Konrad Ulmer, Heinrich Bullinger, Schaffhauser Katechismusstreit, Heidelberger Katechismus, Johann Wilhelm Meyer, Johannes Hübner, Johann Georg Müller, Friedrich Hurter, Katechismuslieder

ISSN 0254-4407 – Zwingliana 40 (2013), 165–187

Lavaters Rezeption von Spaldings »Ueber die Nutzbarkeit des Predigtamtes« und Herders »An Prediger« in seiner Predigtreihe zur Apokalypse

Daniela Kohler

Von Mai bis Oktober des Jahres 1779 hat Johann Caspar Lavater (1741–1801) als Diakon am St. Peter in 44 »Abendgebeten« die 22 Kapitel der Apokalypse erläutert. Für Lavater hatte diese Predigtreihe eine besondere Bedeutung, bot sich ihm darin doch die Möglichkeit, die heilsgeschichtliche Bedeutung Jesu Christi, die in der aufgeklärten Theologie seiner Zeit eine in seinen Augen bedenkliche Abwertung erhielt, wieder in das richtige Licht zu rücken. Einen gewichtigen Beitrag zu dieser Abwertung lieferte Johann Joachim Spalding (1714–1808) in seiner Schrift »Ueber die Nutzbarkeit des Predigtamtes« (1772), der Lavater trotz der großen Wertschätzung für Spalding kritisch gegenüberstand und die ihn dazu führte, ernsthaft über die angemessene Weise der Christusverkündigung nachzudenken. Welche Aspekte ihn an Spaldings Schrift besonders störten, in welchen Bereichen er sich von Johann Gottfried Herders (1743–1804) Predigtauffassung und dessen affektiven Zugang zu biblischen Zeugnissen im Allgemeinen und der Johannes-Offenbarung im Besonderen anregen ließ, sollen in Bezug auf Lavaters in der Apokalypse-Gebetsreihe zum Ausdruck gebrachtes Verständnis der Christuspredigt erörtert werden. Im Zentrum stehen dabei nicht nur unterschiedliche Auffassungen von den Aufgaben und Pflichten eines Predigers, sondern auch grundsätzliche theologische Differenzen, die sich vor allem auf exegetische und dogmatische Aspekte konzentrieren und deren Dreh- und Angelpunkt die Bedeutung Jesu Christi ist.

Zur besseren Einordnung der Predigtreihe in Lavaters berufliche Tätigkeit soll einleitend sein Werdegang als Pfarrer kurz nachgezeichnet werden.

1. Lavaters beruflicher Werdegang

Nach seiner Ausbildung am Zürcher Collegium Carolinum, die etwas mehr als vier Jahre dauerte, wurde Lavater 1762 ordiniert und in der Herbstsynode desselben Jahres als Exspektant, d.h. als Geistlicher, der auf sein erstes Amt wartet, eingeführt. Da er aus wohlhabendem Elternhaus stammte, musste er sich nicht wie andere Exspektanten als Hauslehrer sein Geld verdienen.[1] Stattdessen begab er sich ins Ausland auf eine Bildungsreise. Diese führte ihn über Berlin nach Barth in Schwedisch Pommern, wo er sich mehrere Monate im Haus von Spalding aufhielt. Während dieses Aufenthalts setzte er sich intensiv mit der neologischen Theologie auseinander, was seine eigenen theologischen Ansichten prägte; zuerst, indem er ihr Gedankengut übernahm, später, indem er sich davon abgrenzte.

1764 kehrte Lavater nach Zürich zurück, wo er fünf weitere Jahre, in denen er sich vor allem schriftstellerisch betätigte,[2] als Exspektant zubrachte, bis er 1769 als Diakon an die Waisenhauskirche gewählt wurde.[3] Dort übernahm er 1775 die Pfarrstelle. 1778 wurde Lavater Diakon an der zu den vier Zürcher Hauptkirchen gehörenden Kirche St. Peter, als deren Pfarrer er ab 1787

[1] Klaus Martin *Sauer*, Die Predigttätigkeit Johann Kaspar Lavaters (1741–1801), Zürich 1988, 116.

[2] Lavater gab die Zeitschrift »Der Erinnerer« heraus, in der er selbst viele Artikel verfasste, 1768 und 1769 erschienen die ersten beiden Bände seiner »Aussichten in die Ewigkeit«, und 1769 verfasste er seine Übersetzung von Charles Bonnets (1720–1793) »La Palingénésie Philosophique, ou idées sur l'état passé et l'état futur des êtres vivans« (1769).

[3] *Sauer*, Predigttätigkeit, 131.

bis an sein Lebensende amtete und somit zu der Spitze der Zürcher Geistlichen gehörte.

Zu seiner Aufgabe als Prediger hatte sich Lavater nicht nur in seinem Studium am Carolinum und in der unter Aufsicht eines Inspektors stehenden Exspektantenzeit mit eingängigen Schriften vorbereitet.[4] Auch nach seiner Wahl als Diakon interessierte sich Lavater für Neuerscheinungen auf dem Gebiet der Theologie. So auch für Spaldings »Von der Nutzbarkeit des Predigtamts«, das bei Zürcher Pfarrern ein großes Echo auslöste.

2. Lavaters Kritik an Spaldings »Ueber die Nutzbarkeit des Predigtamtes«

In dem regen, leider bis anhin unedierten Briefwechsel zwischen Lavater und Spalding, in dem nahezu jedes Problem und Phänomen des damaligen geistigen und geistlichen Lebens diskutiert wurde, finden sich auch Äußerungen zu Spaldings »Ueber die Nutzbarkeit des Predigtamtes.«[5] Spalding erörtert in dieser 1772 erschienen Schrift ausführlich die Pflichten und Aufgaben, die seiner Meinung nach einem Prediger zukommen. Er geht dabei auf homiletische Aspekte ein, bei denen seine theologischen Überzeugungen eine wichtige Rolle spielen und klarer zum Ausdruck kommen als in anderen Schriften. Gleichzeitig versucht er aber auch, das in der zweiten Hälfte des 18. Jahrhunderts im Zuge der kritischen Aufklärungstheologie nicht mehr unhinterfragt akzeptierte Amt des Predigers als für die Gesellschaft und den Staat nützlich darzustellen und somit zu legitimieren. Spaldings Schrift ist dadurch Homiletik, theologische Abhandlung und Apologie gleichermaßen.[6]

Bereits kurz vor Erscheinen seiner »Nutzbarkeit« kündet Spalding seinem Zürcher Freund eine Schrift an, die ihm viel bedeute, von der er aber nicht wisse, ob er »manche Seite der abgehandelten

[4] Eine Liste der Werke, mit denen sich Lavater in der Exspektantenzeit auseinandergesetzt hat, findet sich in: *Sauer*, Predigttätigkeit, 121.

[5] Johann Joachim *Spalding*, Ueber die Nutzbarkeit des Predigtamtes und deren Beförderung (^{1}1772, ^{2}1773, ^{3}1791), hg. von Tobias Jersak, Tübingen 2002.

[6] *Spalding*, Nutzbarkeit des Predigtamtes, XVII.

Dinge übersehen habe, die nicht sollten übersehen werden.«[7] Er wünsche sich daher diesbezügliche Ratschläge für künftige Auflagen.[8] Lavater entspricht diesem Wunsch in seinem Brief vom 5. Mai 1772 in Form einer ausführlichen Kritik.

Nach anfänglichem Lob, in dem er seinem Berliner Lehrer und Amtskollegen das Ausräumen vieler Vorurteile attestiert, kommt er zu den seiner Meinung nach wichtigen Kritikpunkten. Zunächst allerdings stimmt er Spalding darin zu, dass der Mensch als Bestimmung und Erfüllung seines Daseins nach Glückseligkeit strebe. Die damit grundsätzlich bejahte Glückseligkeitslehre, wie sie in der »Nutzbarkeit« vertreten wird, hat ihren Ursprung in Spaldings erstmals 1748 erschienenen Schrift »Bestimmung des Menschen.«[9] Ausgehend von der Frage, zu welchem Zweck der Mensch da sei und was er, als vernunftbegabtes Wesen, sein soll, entwickelt Spalding seine Theorie über die menschliche Glückseligkeit. Der Mensch ist, so Spaldings programmatisch für die Aufklärung vertretenes Menschenbild, nicht, wie die traditionelle »Erbsündenlehre« formuliert, »von Natur aus« unfähig, das Gute zu tun und anzustreben. Vielmehr hat er in sich die Veranlagung, Moral und Tugend zu erkennen, was ihn zur Besserung und Entwicklung befähigt. Diese Kapazität entspringt im Wesentlichen der Vernunftbegabung; durch die ratio vermag der Mensch über seine Bestimmung zu reflektieren. Die erste Erkenntnis dabei besteht darin, so führt es Spalding in seinem epochemachenden Werk vor, dass die Befriedigung von sinnlichen und materiellen Lüsten resp. Gütern lediglich vergängliche Glückseligkeit verschaffen.[10] Spalding geht davon aus, dass dem menschlichen Geist »ein natürlicher Begriff von einem Anständigen und Schändlichen, von einem Schönen und Hässlichen, von Recht und Unrecht eingedrückt«[11] ist, was ihn seine Bestimmung zu einem moralischen, tugendhaften Leben er-

[7] Spalding an Lavater, 28. April 1772, Zentralbibliothek Zürich, FA Lav. Ms. 527.24.

[8] Spalding an Lavater, 28. April 1772, Zentralbibliothek Zürich, FA Lav. Ms. 527.24.

[9] Johann Joachim *Spalding*, Die Bestimmung des Menschen (^{1}1748; ^{2}1748; ^{3}1749; ^{4}1752; ^{5}1754; ^{6}1759; ^{7}1763; ^{8}1764; ^{9}1768; ^{10}1774; ^{11}1794), hg. von Albrecht Beutel et al., Tübingen 2006.

[10] *Spalding*, Bestimmung des Menschen, 4.

[11] *Spalding*, Bestimmung des Menschen, 8.

kennen lässt. Darüber hinaus sei der Mensch von einem Streben nach Wissen und Wahrheit erfüllt, was ihn zur Gewissheit führe, dass sein gegenwärtiges Leben und die darin verwirklichte Moralität, Tugend und Religiosität den Anfang einer Entwicklungsleiter hin zur Vollkommenheit seien, die im jenseitigen Leben weitergehe und dort ihre Vollendung finde. Spaldings Meinung nach erkennt der Mensch in seiner tugendhaften, gottgefälligen Veranlagung die Heilsgewissheit, die ihn glückselig macht.[12] In der »Bestimmung des Menschen« schreibt er dazu:

> »Ich bin also für ein anderes Leben gemacht. Die gegenwärtige Zeit ist nur der Anfang meiner Dauer; es ist meine erste Kindheit, worin ich zu der Ewigkeit erzogen werde; Tage der Zubereitung, die mich zu einem neuen und edlern Zustande geschickt machen sollen.«[13]

Auch in der »Nutzbarkeit des Predigtamtes« werden Moral, Tugend und Religiosität als menschliche Veranlagung festgelegt, die den Ausgangspunkt darstellen für die heilsgeschichtliche Gewissheit, für die Entwicklung zur eigentlichen menschlichen Bestimmung, der höchstmöglichen Annäherung an Gott im Jenseits. Der Prediger müsse nun besagte Veranlagungen im Menschen wecken und deren Entwicklung fördern:

> »Jenes ist also das erste Augenmerk und die erste Pflicht unsers Amtes, nehmlich die Menschen in ihrer Beziehung auf Gott, auf ihr Gewissen und auf die zukünftige Welt glücklich zu machen.«[14]

Lavater stimmt zwar mit Spalding überein, dass sich Glückseligkeit durch ein moralisches, tugendhaftes Leben konstituiert, als dessen Motivation er die Annäherung an Gott bis zu seiner Ebenbildlichkeit festlegt.[15] Dass sich daraus aber Heilsgewissheit ergebe, akzeptiert Lavater nicht, fehlt ihm doch die dabei seiner Meinung nach unerlässliche Voraussetzung; für Lavater führt jede Annäherung an

[12] Peter *Opitz*, Der (unge)treue Schüler: Religiöse Selbstthematisierung bei Johann Joachim Spalding und Johann Caspar Lavater, in: Christentum im Übergang: Neue Studien zu Kirche und Religion in der Aufklärungszeit, hg. von Albrecht Beutel et al., Leipzig 2006 (Arbeiten zur Kirchen- und Theologiegeschichte 19), 118.

[13] *Spalding*, Bestimmung des Menschen, 22.

[14] *Spalding*, Nutzbarkeit des Predigtamtes, 87.

[15] Lavater an Spalding, 5. Mai 1772, Zentralbibliothek Zürich, FA Lav. Ms. 581.74.

Gott und jede damit verbundene Hoffnung und Verheißung über Jesus Christus:

> »Gott selbst, der ewige Vater, der in jedem Sinn unendlich ist, und keine Proportion zu unserer Erkenntniß und Empfindungskräften hat – kann nicht unmittelbar (wenigstens im Anfang nicht unmittelbar) von uns erkannt werden. Er muss sich also in ein sichtbares, gedenkbares überschaubares Ebenbild befassen und concentrieren, in welchem er sich der ganzen Geister Welt offenbaren, mittheilen, durch welches er mit ihr eine Relation, Unterhaltung, Verbindung eintreten kann. Dieß Ebenbild Gottes ist Jesus Christus. Er ist der Abklang seiner Herrlichkeit der Sohn Gottes. Wer ihn siehet, siehet den Vater; des Vaters Macht – Weisheit – Güte – Herrlichkeit –. In ihm leuchtet die Herrlichkeit Gottes.«[16]

Anders als Spalding, der in seiner Schrift vor allem darum bemüht ist, die menschlichen Anlagen zu Tugend und Moral zu erklären und Jesus diesbezüglich als absolutes Vorbild bezeichnet, betont Lavater den Christus der Evangelien und alle daran gebundenen Lehren, die der Prediger dem Volk zu erläutern habe. Genau dies aber unterlasse Spalding, so Lavaters Kritik:

> »Ob Sie nicht viele hundert Lehren mehr erbaut, gewonnen, und ihnen alle Ausflüchte, die sie nun haben, abgeschnitten hätten, wenn Sie Christo mehr Gerechtigkeit hätten widerfahren lassen; wenn Sie den Glauben an Christum von dieser Seite wichtiger gemacht hätten.«[17]

Was Lavater hier als »Ausflüchte« anspricht, ist Spaldings als pädagogisches Konzept für den Prediger getarnte Kritik an zentralen christlichen Dogmen, die ihren Ausgangspunkt in der losgelöst von der Heilsbotschaft gelehrten Heilsgewissheit hat. Für Lavater steht außer Frage, dass es nicht lediglich, wie Spalding es postuliert, eines gottgefälligen Lebens bedarf, um sich der Annäherung an Gott und des ewigen Heils gewiss zu sein. Obschon Lavater sich in seiner Christologie in vielen Punkten an Spalding anlehnt und insbesondere dessen Vergleich von Christus mit einem Linderung und Rettung bringenden Arzt oder Arzneimittel verwendet,[18] verliert er die soteriologische Bedeutung nicht aus den Augen. Erst durch das

[16] Lavater an Spalding, 5. Mai 1772, Zentralbibliothek Zürich, FA Lav. Ms. 581.74.

[17] Lavater an Spalding, 5. Mai 1772, Zentralbibliothek Zürich, FA Lav. Ms. 581.74.

[18] Peter *Opitz*, »Fortgekämpft und fortgerungen...«: J.C. Lavaters Verkündigung der Gnade im Rahmen seiner Christusreligion, in: Zwingliana 33 (2006), 175f.

Opfer Gottes in Christi Tod am Kreuz ist die Voraussetzung gegeben, dass der Mensch überhaupt fähig ist, seine guten Eigenschaften zu entfalten und sich Gott anzunähern. Dem Volk müsse also nicht nur das tugendhafte Leben Jesu gepredigt werden, sondern auch dessen Leid und Auferstehung und die damit verbundene Lehre von der Gnade und Gerechtigkeit Gottes, die als einzigen Weg zur Heilsgewissheit führen:

> »Mein einziges Ziel ist, Spalding, die Menschen, die Würde der Menschheit fühlen zumachen – oder – Sie Gottes und der Unsterblichkeit zuversichern. Und das kann ich schlechterdings besser nicht als durch Darstellung des Gott und Unsterblichkeit in sich fassenden Christus.«[19]

Anders sieht dies Spalding. Die vom Prediger zu beachtende Differenz von Volk und Gelehrten,[20] die einhergeht mit der neologischen Differenzierung von Religion und Theologie, macht Spalding eine kritische Distanznahme zu den christlichen Dogmen möglich, ohne diese direkt anzugreifen oder sie gar aus dem Christentum verbannen zu wollen. Spalding geht von zwei verschiedenen Arten von christlichen Lehren aus. Die einen würden konkrete, auf das alltägliche Leben ausgerichtete Anweisungen geben. Indem sie den Menschen zu moralischen und tugendhaften Handlungen anleiten, vermitteln sie ihm den Weg zu Gott und zur ewigen Glückseligkeit, die Spalding, wie bereits erläutert, als Hauptinhalt des Christentums festlegt. Daneben gebe es aber auch Lehren, die dieser Absicht im alltäglichen Leben keinen Dienst tun würden. So die Lehre vom satisfaktorischen Strafleiden. Sie führe dazu, dass ein falsches Gottesbild vermittelt werde. Der christliche Gott erwarte nicht zürnend das Blut- und Sühneopfer Jesu, sondern sei

> »ein Gott voller Erbarmung, ein Vater, der seine Kinder darum gerne tugendhaft und gut haben will, weil es ihr Glück ist [...], der durch die liebreichsten Verheißungen seiner Verzeihung auch dem Verschuldeten Muth und Freudigkeit zur Rückkehr giebt.«[21]

Die »liebreichen Verheißungen seiner Verzeihung« schließen das mit Leid verbundene Opfer Jesu am Kreuz aus. So betont denn

[19] Lavater an Spalding, 4. Juni 1777, Zentralbibliothek Zürich, FA Lav. Ms. 581.86.
[20] *Spalding*, Nutzbarkeit des Predigtamtes, 146.
[21] *Spalding*, Nutzbarkeit des Predigtamtes, 128f.

Spalding auch, dass sich die Bedeutung Jesu für das Christentum nicht aus dem Kreuztod erschließt, sondern aus der Moral und Tugendhaftigkeit; wer diese predige, predige Jesus, so formuliert es Spalding nachdrücklich und meint:

> »Darum, dass eine Aussage in der Bibel stehet, wird sie nicht zu einer eigentlichen Glaubenslehre, zu einem Theile der Religion, in so ferne diese den Weg zu einer wahren und ewigen Glückseligkeit enthält.«[22]

Ähnlich verhält es sich laut Spalding mit der Gnadenlehre. Diese sei für den gemeinen Christen nur schlecht verständlich und führe zur Gefahr, dass er keinen Wert mehr auf das moralische Tun legt, so Spaldings Gründe dafür, sie in der Predigt nicht zu erwähnen:

> »Er [der Christ] wird dadurch noch immer gar leicht in den Gedanken erhalten, dass er ohne heilsame Aenderung seines Gemüths und seines Lebens Gott wohlgefällig und in seiner Gnade einer ewigen Glückseligkeit fähig werden könne.«[23]

Dass damit der Gedanke einer dem Menschen nur durch Gottes Gnade ermöglichte Rechtfertigung, der Kernpunkt der evangelischen Rechtfertigungslehre, nicht nur in Bezug auf die Predigt, sondern grundsätzlich eine Sinnentleerung erfährt, ist nicht zu leugnen.

Spalding versteht seine Dogmenkritik als Folge der pädagogischen Aufgabe, die er, ganz im Sinne der Aufklärung, dem Prediger überantwortet: Der Pfarrer soll das ungebildete Volk erziehen und bilden. Die religiöse Erziehung hat denn auch, so Spaldings legitimatorisch eingesetzte Relation zum gesellschaftlichen Leben, Auswirkungen auf den Staat: Ein durch die Religion zu Tugend und Moral angespornter und erzogener Mensch hat nicht nur in Gottes Augen, sondern auch in denjenigen des Staates einen Mehrwert. In der Kirche wird also auch bürgerliche Erziehung betrieben, was sie als Institution und damit verbunden das Amt des Predigers unbedingt notwendig macht, so Spaldings Argumentation.[24]

[22] *Spalding*, Nutzbarkeit des Predigtamtes, 141.

[23] *Spalding*, Nutzbarkeit des Predigtamtes, 189.

[24] Albrecht *Beutel*, Reflektierte Religion: Beiträge zur Geschichte des Protestantismus, Tübingen 2007, 217.

Indem Spalding seine Dogmenkritik auf dem Feld der Homiletik vorträgt und sie mit der pädagogischen Aufgabe des Predigers, der das Volk mit dem Verstand nachvollziehbaren Lehren erziehen soll, begründet, distanziert er sich von einer radikaleren Dogmenkritik, wie sie beispielsweise Johann Salomon Semler (1725–1791) vertritt. Explizit alle nicht »vernünftigen« biblischen Ereignisse und Lehren als den historischen Umständen entsprungen und darum nicht als immergültige christliche Wahrheiten zu bezeichnen widerspricht dem gemäßigten Spalding. Der Verdacht aber, dass in ihrer Verbannung aus dem Bereich der empfohlenen Predigtinhalte nicht auch eine versteckte grundsätzliche Kritik mitschwingt, kann nicht von der Hand gewiesen werden.

Genauso muss auch Lavater empfunden haben. Umso mehr, als Spalding ihm auf seine Kritik erst ein Jahr später anlässlich des Erscheinens der zweiten Auflage antwortete:[25]

> »Von der Leipziger Messe erhalten Sie die vermehrte Auflage des kleinen Buchs vom Predigtamte. Was soll ich davon sagen? Ich habe ehrlich und gewissenhaft vor Gott untersucht und geschrieben, wenn anders jemal ein Mensch sich dies Zeugniß geben darf; und weiter kann ich freylich für nichts stehen. Gott gebe mir mehr Erleuchtung, wenn sie mir nöthig ist!«[26]

Trotz Spaldings deutlich zum Ausdruck gebrachter, als ehrliches Zeugnis vor Gott ausgezeichneter Überzeugung, christliche Theologie auch ohne eine von Christus ausgehenden Soteriologie zu lehren, versuchte Lavater in seinem Briefwechsel immer wieder, die richtige Darstellung von Jesus Christus zu thematisieren. So schreibt er 1776:

> »Der Christus, den wir predigen, ist nicht Christus der lebende, würkende, nahe, den die Apostel predigten. Der Christus unserer Zeit ist nicht der der Vorzeit. Er ist ein Antichrist. Wir stossen ihn zur Bibel heraus. Die Apostel thaten alles mit Christus. Die Theologen des Jahrhunderts, alles ohne ihn.«[27]

[25] Zwischen Lavaters Brief vom 5. Mai 1772 und Spaldings Brief vom 16. April 1773 sind keine Briefe von Spalding erhalten. Lavater hat in dieser Zeit zweimal an Spalding geschrieben; im zweiten Brief beklagt er sich über Spaldings Stillschweigen.

[26] Spalding an Lavater, 16. April 1773, Zentralbibliothek Zürich, FA Lav. Ms. 527.25.

[27] Lavater an Spalding, 2. Aug. 1776, Zentralbibliothek Zürich, FA Lav. Ms. 581.85.

Und ein Jahr später meint er zu seinem Berliner Freund, »dass ich Sie für einen der besten, vortreflichsten Menschen und dennoch vieles in Ihren Meynungen für höchst antievangelisch halte.«[28]

Seit dem Erscheinen von Spaldings Schrift »Ueber die Nutzbarkeit des Predigtamtes« versuchte Lavater also, Spalding von der wahrhaftigen, anhand des Evangeliums zu verkündenden Darstellung Jesu Christi zu überzeugen, stieß aber dabei auf keine Resonanz. Was ihn zu einer düsteren Einschätzung der Theologie seiner Zeit brachte und ihn nach neuen Wegen und Mitteln suchen ließ, um Jesus zu predigen. Auf dieser Suche wandte sich Lavater an Herder.

3. Herders Ansicht über das Amt des Predigers und seine affektive Bibelexegese

1772, im Erscheinungsjahr von Spaldings »Nutzbarkeit«, schrieb Lavater Herder in einem Brief: »O Herder – ich beschwöre Dich – hilf mir ihn [Christus], ihn darstellen.«[29]

Einen ersten für Lavater relevanten Versuch in dieser Darstellung von Jesus Christus lieferte Herder mit seiner 1774 veröffentlichten Schrift »An Prediger. Funfzehn Provinzialblätter«, in der er die Funktion und Aufgabe des Predigers erläutert. Herders Schrift ist eine Antwort auf Spaldings »Nutzbarkeit« und sollte gleichzeitig die Grundlage bilden für die erhoffte, jedoch nicht erfolgte Berufung an die Universität Göttingen auf den Lehrstuhl für Praktische Theologie.[30]

Obschon Herder im ersten Teil heftig gegen Spalding polemisiert,[31] hat er, wie Lavater, wichtige theologische Impulse von ihm empfangen. Dass er sich dessen bewusst ist und Spalding trotz der

[28] Lavater an Spalding, 4. Juni 1777, Zentralbibliothek Zürich, FA Lav. Ms. 581.86.

[29] Aus Herders Nachlass: Ungedruckte Briefe von Herder und dessen Gattin, Goethe, Schiller, Klopstock, Lenz, Jean Paul, Claudius, Lavater, Jacobi und andern bedeutenden Zeitgenossen, hg. von Heinrich Düntzer, Bd. 2, Frankfurt a.M. 1857, 28.

[30] Johann Gottfried Herder: Theologische Schriften, hg. von Christoph Bultmann, und Thomas Zippert, Frankfurt a.M. 1994, 917.

[31] Neun der insgesamt fünfzehn Stücke beginnen mit einem Zitat aus Spaldings »Nutzbarkeit.«

Kritik immer noch große Wertschätzung entgegenbringt, kommt in seinem Vorwort zum Ausdruck:

> »Man kann uneinig in Meinungen sein, und doch die Denkart eines Mannes, selbst mit dem, was uns Mangel oder Irrtum dünkt, sehr ehren, und vielleicht als Mensch sich gar die Denkart mit allen Fehlern wünschen.«[32]

Herders Kritik an Spaldings Schrift richtet sich auf dieselben Punkte wie diejenige Lavaters. Neben Spaldings Versuch, das Predigtamt für den Staat nutzbar darzustellen,[33] nimmt er Anstoss an dessen sich lediglich auf die Morallehre und nicht mehr auf die Evangelien beziehenden Verkündigungsauftrag des Predigers. Als »Krankheit Zweifelsucht«[34] bezeichnet Herder die neologische Herangehensweise an theologische Fragen nach den Grundsätzen der vernünftigen Philosophie und polemisiert heftig gegen die »Lehrer der Weisheit und Tugend«,[35] als welche die Prediger nun wirken sollen. Der ironisch-polemische Ton, der den gesamten ersten Teil seiner Abhandlung durchzieht, wird ersichtlich, wenn er die Meinung seiner Amtskollegen zum Abendmahl und zur eigenen Funktion als Moralprediger in der zynischen Aufforderung »Haltet Abendmahl, leidiges Andenken an einen guten Mann, der freilich lange nicht so vollständig als wir, Wahrheit und Tugend lehrte, und Gottlob, so lange schon todt ist«[36] wiedergibt. Wie Lavater kritisiert Herder, dass die neuere Theologie jeder christlichen Grundlage entbehre. Es sei bedenklich, »dass da jetzt andre Zeit sei; dass da die Philosophie sich einiger sehr gehäßigen und unbewiesnen Artikel von Dreieinigkeit, Sohn Gottes, Erlösungswerk angenommen, sie unbewiesen zum Christenthume hinaus gebannet« habe.[37] Eine nicht mehr auf die christlichen Wahrheiten fokussierte, »ra-

[32] Johann Gottfried *Herder*, An Prediger: Funfzehn Provinzialblätter, in: Johann Gottfried Herder: Theologische Schriften, 69.

[33] So schreibt Herder Ende Dezember 1773 an Lavater: »Ihr Spalding ärgert mich von Tag zu Tag mehr. Seine zweite Auflage des Predigers. – kein Wort, was ein Prediger vor Gott und Menschen sein soll! alles nur, was er in den Staaten Sr. glorwürdigsten Majestät, des Königs von Preussen höchstprivilegirtermaßen sein darf und sein möchte«, in: Johann Gottfried *Herder*, Briefe: Gesamtausgabe 1763–1803, hg. von der Klassik Stiftung Weimar, Weimar 1977–2009, Bd. 3, 59f.

[34] *Herder*, An Prediger, 71.

[35] *Herder*, An Prediger, 73.

[36] *Herder*, An Prediger, 74.

[37] *Herder*, An Prediger, 77.

tionale« Predigt verliere ihren eigentlichen Zweck; es gehe nicht darum, das Volk mit philosophischen Lehren zu bilden, sondern es zu stärken, zu erbauen. Diese Erbauung erfolgt Herders Meinung nach durch Gefühle, die der Prediger, anstelle zu belehren, zu wecken hätte. »Die sogenannte Predigttheorie, die darauf eingerichtet ist, mit ihrem Nichterregen der Leidenschaft, mit ihrem Nichterregen heller Ideen, mit ihrem andächtigen Schwunge zu erbauen und zu lähmen«[38] erfüllt diese Anforderung seiner Meinung nach nicht. Anders verhalte es sich mit den biblischen Zeugnissen. Die Bibel schildere in bildhafter Sprache die Leidenschaften, die den Menschen in ihrer Erfahrung mit dem sich offenbarenden Gott bewegten. In der zeitgleich mit den »Provinzialblättern« erschienenen »Ältesten Urkunde des Menschengeschlechts« erläutert Herder anhand von Gen. 1 seine Theorie von der Bibel als ältestem Zeugnis von der affektiv-sinnlichen Annäherung zwischen Mensch und Gott.[39] Im Zentrum von Herders Theorie steht die Rezeption der göttlichen Offenbarung. Um die biblische Botschafte zu verstehen, dürfe nicht nach der direkten Aussage gesucht werden, die Gott darin vermitteln wollte. Vielmehr seien sie zu erschließen durch die Gefühle, die den Empfänger bewegten und die er in sinnlicher, bildhafter Sprache zum Ausdruck brachte. Herders Bibelhermeneutik geht von der Anschauung und Erfahrung des Göttlichen und nicht vom sich offenbarenden Gott aus – der Rezipient ist nicht von Gott inspiriert, sondern emotional von ihm ergriffen.[40] Diese anthropozentrische Exegese erinnert an die Aufklärungstheologie, die Herder mit ihrer von den menschlichen Veranlagungen, Bedürfnissen und Lebensumständen ausgehenden Theologie beeinflusst hat. Anders aber als die aufgeklärten Theologen, die sich auf der Grundlage der Perfektibilität damit auseinandersetzen, wie der Mensch in seiner Moral und Tugend gestärkt werden und dadurch größtenteils aus eigener Kraft zur Glückseligkeit gelangen kann, bringt Herder seine anthropozentrische Theologie in direk-

[38] *Herder*, An Prediger, 73.

[39] Grundlegend zu Herders Genesis-Interpretation: Rudolf *Bultmann*, Die Biblische Urgeschichte in der Aufklärung: Johann Gottfried Herders Interpretation der Genesis als Antwort auf die Religionskritik David Humes, Tübingen 1999 (Beiträge zur historischen Theologie 110).

[40] *Bultmann*, Biblische Urgeschichte, 137.

ten Zusammenhang mit der göttlichen Offenbarung. Seine Überlegungen zielen darauf ab, wie der Mensch diese verstehen und ihr in seinem gegenwärtigen Leben eine Bedeutung geben kann, und rücken dabei nicht den Verstand, sondern die Sinnlichkeit und seelische Bewegtheit in den Mittelpunkt: »Geht nicht alles bei uns auf Sinnlichkeit zurück, bau'n tausenfach mehr auf Glauben, als auf aufgeklärte Regungen, Bewegungsgründe, und wie der Triumpfkram weiter laute.«[41]

Vor diesem Hintergrund ist es verständlich, dass Herder denjenigen neologischen Theologen, welche die Bibel vornehmlich als historisches Zeugnis veralteter Vorstellungen betrachteten, kritisch gegenüberstand. Zwar betont auch er, dass die Bibel in ihrem geschichtlichen Kontext betrachtet werden müsse; man dürfe aber nicht lediglich vernünftige Morallehren daraus abstrahieren und die diesen Anforderungen nicht entsprechenden Zeugnisse als historisches Kolorit erklären. Denn dadurch wäre die Bibel nur mehr dazu da, »Erkenntnis zu geben, wie man sie etwa aus einem andern bessern, Historienbuche auch besser und pragmatischer sammlet.«[42] Stattdessen gehe es darum, in der reichen Bildsprache nach den theologischen, durch die Affekte des Empfängers erschließbaren Botschaften zu suchen. Daraus erklärt sich die besondere Rolle, die Herder der biblischen Symbolik beimisst. Die Bibel »gibt [...] nur Beispiele, Muster, Bilder! Da spricht Empfindung unmittelbar zum Herzen, zum Sinn, zur Nachahmung.«[43] Dem in seinem Zeitalter konstatierten »Tugend-Antidogmatismus, und Antisymbolismus«[44] stellt Herder die in der Bibel bildhaft und symbolisch dargestellten Empfindungen gegenüber. Dementsprechend solle ein Prediger, statt sich mit homiletischen Anleitungen zu befassen, die Bibel nicht lediglich als »Nebengerüst«[45] betrachten, sondern sie als Fundament des Christentums studieren und verkünden: »Glaubenslehre, im edelsten Verstande, das ist reine Summe der Bibel.«[46] Im Zentrum dieser Glaubenslehre steht für Herder Jesus Christus.

[41] *Herder*, An Prediger, 86.
[42] *Herder*, An Prediger, 90.
[43] *Herder*, An Prediger, 103.
[44] *Herder*, An Prediger, 77.
[45] *Herder*, An Prediger, 79.
[46] *Herder*, An Prediger, 89.

Die Wahrheit des Christentums drehe sich um die im Evangelium bezeugte soteriologische und eschatologische Botschaft, so kontert Herder Spaldings auf Moral und Tugend basierende Heilsgewissheit. Die Offenbarung ist für Herder »Gebäude der Entwickelung des Menschengeschlechts in die Ewigkeit hinüber!«[47] Und einem richtigen Christen ist »Jesus nicht etwa auch ein guter Mann und Lehrer guter Moral, sondern Erlöser der Welt! Mittelpunkt des Menschlichen Geschlechts! Vorbild Christlicher Vollkommenheit in die Entwickelung der Ewigkeit hinüber!«[48]

Lavater setzte große Erwartungen in Herders Schriften in Bezug auf die adäquate Darstellung Jesu Christi, wie er an Johann Georg Schlosser (1739–1799) in Erwartung der »zwei oder drei Büchelchen und Aufsätze«,[49] die Herder ihm angekündigt hatte, schrieb: »Nur von Herdern erwart' ich das erste Buch über die Religion, wie ichs wünsche. Es wird in wenigen Tagen da seyn!«[50]

Obschon sich Lavater schliesslich in der Korrespondenz mit Herder nur knapp zu den »Provinzialblättern« äußert – die Briefe Lavaters an Herder aus dem Jahr 1774 sind sehr kurz, was Lavater mehrfach mit seiner Arbeitsüberbelastung entschuldigt – ist davon auszugehen, dass er sich von Herders Schrift angesprochen fühlte. Herders Betonung des Predigers, der von einer gefühlten Glauben ausgehen und die biblischen Berichte als Zeugnisse vom wahrhaftigen Christus verkünden sollte, entsprachen Lavaters Vorstellungen mehr als Spaldings Ansichten, wie er diesem mitteilte:

> »Das müssen Sie wissen, dass kein Herz Sie aufrichtiger und zärtlicher lieben kann, als das meinige – aber gestehen muss ich, muss es vor aller Welt geschehen – Ich glaube: ›Herder hat den Geist des christlichen Predigers wahrer dargestellt als Spalding.‹«[51]

Dass Lavater aber trotzdem von Herder enttäuscht wurde, hängt mit einer anderen Schrift zusammen, von der er sich die Erfüllung

[47] *Herder*, An Prediger, 91.

[48] *Herder*, An Prediger, 91.

[49] Herder an Lavater, 26. Oktober 1773, in: *Herder*, Briefe, Bd. 3, 48.

[50] Lavater an Schlosser, 26. März 1774, Zentralbibliothek Zürich, FA Lav. Ms. 580.43.

[51] Lavater an Spalding, 3. Dez. 1774, Zentralbibliothek Zürich, FA Lav. Ms. 581.83.

seines Wunsches einer wahrhaftigen Darstellung Jesu Christi erhoffte: Herders Paraphrase der Apokalypse.

4. Herders Auseinandersetzung mit der Johannes-Offenbarung

Zeitgleich mit den Provinzialblättern beschäftigte sich Herder damit, die Johannes-Offenbarung in einer eng an die Originalsprache angelehnten Paraphrase zu bearbeiten. In der Apokalypse sieht Herder alles ausgedrückt, was die biblischen Zeugnisse auszeichnet: sich in sinnlicher Sprache äußernde Affekte, symbolische Bildhaftigkeit und die christliche Hoffnung auf Erlösung. In zwischen 1773 und 1778 verfassten sechs Manuskript gebliebenen Vorstufen und dem 1779 gedruckten Werk »Maran Atha« erzählt Herder die Visionen des Johannes nach. Und zwar dergestalt, wie er es in den Provinzialblättern als Verkündigungsauftrag für den Prediger postuliert: Als möglichst nah am Text bleibende Paraphrase, deren zwischen die Verse eingebauten Kommentare die Bildhaftigkeit als Ausdruck der Empfindungen, die Johannes beim Empfang der Visionen überkommen, erklärt.

Herders Exegese basiert auf einer Synthese zwischen emotionaler Gotteserfahrung und historischer Tatsachenbeschreibung. Der entweder durch die bereits erlebte oder noch bevorstehende Zerstörung Jerusalems traumatisierte Johannes findet in einer symbolischen, zum Teil nur durch die damaligen Umstände entschlüsselbaren Bild- und Affektsprache eine Ausdrucksform, um die Zerstörung der irdischen Welt zu prophezeien:

> »Schöne Probe, wie Gott offenbahret. Er verrückt nicht den Kopf: Johannes hatte gesehen: er kannte die Bilder, konnte in ihnen den höhern Sinn der Weissagung fassen und weil er davon gewiss innig gerührt war, auch schildern.«[52]

Als Antwort auf die Frage nach der Kanonizität, die im Zuge der historisch-kritischen Bibelexegese insbesondere von Semler stark

[52] Johann Gottfried *Herder*, Johannes Offenbarung: Ein heiliges Gedicht ohn' einzelne Zeichendeutung verständlich, in: Herders sämmtliche Werke, hg. von Bernhard Suphan, Berlin 1877–1913, Bd. 9, 32.

angezweifelt wurde, wollte Herder die Johannes-Offenbarung als sowohl historisch belegbar wie auch theologisch bedeutsam auslegen. Auf den römisch-jüdischen Geschichtsschreiber Flavius Josephus (37/38-ca. 100) rekurrierend, deutet Herder die apokalyptischen Visionen als Ereignisse aus der Zeit des jüdischen Kriegs gegen die Römer, der im Jahr 70 mit der Eroberung Jerusalems und der Zerstörung des Tempels sein Ende fand. Dabei soll aber die theologische Bedeutung der Heilsbotschaft nicht aus den Augen gelassen werden: »Nur Ein Wort im doppelten Sinne Jesu war der Schlüßel: der Herr kommt.«[53] Wer sich dies gewiss sei, werde ewige Glückseligkeit erlangen, so Herders im Gegensatz zu Spalding auf Christus bezogene Lehre der Heilsgewissheit und ewigen Glückseligkeit: »Sie [die Offenbarung des Johannes] betrift Dinge, die seinen Knechten wissenswerth sind, darüber sie, wenn sie sie lesen, hören, bewahren, Preis der Glückseligkeit empfangen.«[54]

Lavater wartete begierig auf Herders Arbeit zur Apokalypse, die dieser, nach zwei als ungenügend erachteten Vorstufen, in einem dritten Versuch als handschriftliches Manuskript unter seinen Bekannten zirkulieren ließ und in dessen Besitz schließlich auch Lavater gelangte. Das Resultat genügte jedoch seinen Vorstellungen nicht. Er fand Herders Paraphrase zwar »erquicklich«,[55] die eschatologische Botschaft aber war ihm zu wenig stark zum Ausdruck gebracht und auf Grund der seiner Meinung nach zu umfangreichen historischen Erklärungen in den Hintergrund gerückt. Der sinnlich-affektive Zugang zu den biblischen Zeugnissen und die damit verbundene, über das Gefühl und den Glauben zu vermittelnde Erkenntnis Jesu Christi fand Lavater in Herders Paraphrase nicht. Er musste erkennen, dass sein Freund die Hoffnungen auf eine seinen Ansprüchen entsprechende Darstellung von Jesus und dem Christentum – »O Herder – wie viel erwart' ich von Dir – nein! Wahrlich! nicht von Dir – von Gott durch Dich«[56] – nicht erfüllen konnte.

Herder antwortete ihm zwar, dass er seine Apokalypse-Paraphrase umarbeiten wollte, erklärte aber zugleich, dass er von sei-

[53] *Herder*, Johannes Offenbarung, 32.
[54] *Herder*, Johannes Offenbarung, 5.
[55] Lavater an Herder, 8. Nov. 1775, in: Aus Herders Nachlass, Bd. 2, 149.
[56] Lavater an Herder, 4. Nov. 1773, in: Aus Herders Nachlass, Bd. 2, 87.

nem exegetischen Grundkonzept der affektiven Bildsprache und historischen Einordnung nicht ablassen werde.[57] Aus der danach folgenden zweijährigen Korrespondenzpause ist die große Enttäuschung erkennbar, die Herders Apokalypse-Paraphrase bei Lavater ausgelöst hat. Nach dem erneut fehlgeschlagenen Versuch aus dem Jahr 1779, mit Herder zu exegetischen Übereinstimmungen zur Johannes-Offenbarung zu gelangen,[58] brach der Kontakt fast völlig ab – obschon sich Lavater intensiver denn je mit der adäquaten Darstellung Jesu Christi und der Johannes-Offenbarung auseinandersetzte.

5. Lavaters Abendgebetsreihe zur Apokalypse

Als Lavater 1779 dem Predigtzyklus folgend in seinen Abendgebeten die Apokalypse erläutern musste, ergab sich für ihn die Möglichkeit, seine Vorstellungen von einem gefühlten, wahrhaftigen Christentum anhand von demjenigen Zeugnis zu erläutern, das seiner Meinung nach Christus in seiner höchsten, wenn auch rätselhaftesten Erhabenheit zeigte. Um seine Absicht umzusetzen, schienen ihm einige Veränderungen bei der Gestaltung und Durchführung der Abendgebete nötig.

Die Zürcher Tradition der zweimal wöchentlich stattfindenden Abendgebete geht auf das Jahr 1610 zurück.[59] Im Sinne einer Lectio continua wurden mittwochs und freitags bzw. samstags je ein halbes Kapitel aus dem Neuen Testament besprochen, und zwar als kurze Predigt, die gegebenenfalls auch auf die sonntägliche lange Predigt vorbereiten sollte. Diese Gebete wurden, im Gegensatz zu den am Sonntag stattfindenden Predigten, vom Diakon gehalten.[60]

Lavater maß diesen Abendgebeten eine besondere Bedeutung zu, waren sie doch seiner Meinung nach hervorragend dazu geeignet,

[57] Herder an Lavater, 30. Dez. 1776, in: *Herder*, Briefe, Bd. 3, 241.

[58] Lavater an Herder, 26. Juni 1779, in: Aus Herders Nachlass, Bd. 2, 182; Herder an Lavater, Juli 1779, in: *Herder*, Briefe, Bd. 4, 98.

[59] Johann Jacob *Wirz*, Historische Darstellung der Urkundlichen Verordnungen, welche die Geschichte des Kirchen- und Schulwesens in Zürich, wie auch die moralische und einiger Massen die physische Wolfahrt unsers Volks betreffen, 1. Teil, Zürich 1793, 37.

[60] *Wirz*, Historische Darstellung, 38.

in besonderer Nähe zur Gemeinde über die biblischen Zeugnisse zu reflektieren. Er verglich diese Zusammenkünfte mit denjenigen der Apostel in den Anfängen des Christentums; wie diese dienten sie seiner Ansicht nach der Erbauung, Bestärkung und der Hinführung zu Gott in Christus. So verlangte er von seiner Gemeinde »andächtige Aufmerksamkeit«,[61] um das von Gott Gewünschte – »Licht, Salbung, Leitung, und alles was unter dem Worte: Seegens – Begriffe seyn mag«[62] – zu empfangen.

Die Idee von an apostolische Gemeinschaften erinnernde Zusammenkünften hatte Lavater bereits früher umzusetzen versucht. Angelehnt an pietistische Erbauungsstunden gründete er 1777 in Zürich zwei Gesellschaften mit der Absicht, jungen Theologen seine gefühlsbetonte Christologie näherzubringen und so Verbündete in seinem Kampf gegen die Aufklärungstheologie zu rekrutieren.[63] In seinen Abendgebeten bot sich ihm nun die Gelegenheit, sich mit demselben Anliegen direkt an seine Gemeinde zu wenden. Gerne hätte er sie allabendlich dazu zusammengerufen,[64] was ihm aber wohl durch die Zürcher Predigtordnung untersagt wurde. Inhaltlich jedoch erlaubte er sich, seinem Verkündigungsauftrag gemäß nicht einfach eine kurze Predigt auf der Grundlage des Bibeltextes zu halten, sondern diesen als Botschaft Jesu Christi zugänglich machen. Lavater wollte seinen Zuhörern die Offenbarung als fortlaufendes Zeugnis der christlichen Heilsbotschaft in einer eng an die biblische Vorlage angelehnten Interpretation erläutern, mit einem Ziel, wie er es in seinem ersten Abendgebet an St. Peter ausdrückt: »Verherrliche Deinen Sohn durch das Evangelium, und lass uns alle Deiner durch ihn und ihm herzlich frohwerden. Amen.«[65]

Um sich noch stärker von der rationalen Predigt abzusetzen, versuchte Lavater, die Abendgebete wieder in ihre ehemalige Form, in

[61] Erstes Abendgebet am St. Peter, 8. Juli 1778, Zentralbibliothek Zürich, FA Lav. Ms. 67 l.4.

[62] Erstes Abendgebet am St. Peter, 8. Juli 1778, Zentralbibliothek Zürich, FA Lav. Ms. 67 l.4.

[63] Georg *Gessner,* Johann Kaspar Lavaters Lebensbeschreibung von seinem Tochtermann Georg Gessner, 3 Bde., Winterthur 1802/03, Bd. 2, 169f.

[64] »Ich gesteh' aufrichtig, dass ich herzlich gerne täglich solche gemeinschaftlichen öffentlichen Abendgebethe wünsche.« (Erstes Abendgebet am St. Peter, 8. Juli 1778, Zentralbibliothek Zürich, FA Lav. Ms. 67 l.4).

[65] Erstes Abendgebet am St. Peter, 8. Juli 1778, FA Lav. Ms. 67 l.4.

diejenige des Gebets, zu bringen, wie er seinen Zuhörern im ersten an St. Peter gehaltenen Abendgebet erläuterte. Aus dem ursprünglichen Zweck, »ein gemeinschaftliches Abendgebeth zu verrichten«[66], seien im Verlaufe der Zeit »Predigt-Stunden, deren wir ohnedem genug haben«[67], entstanden, was er nun ändern wolle: »Des Predigens ist so viel, und des Bethens so wenig. [...] O dass wir weniger predigten und mehr betheten!«[68]

Die Kraft des Gebets ist ein wichtiger Aspekt in Lavaters Theologie. Auf seine damit verbundene Hoffnung, mit übersinnlichen Kräften begabt zu werden, kann im Rahmen dieses Beitrags nicht weiter eingegangen werden. Wichtig ist in unserem Zusammenhang das Beten in der Gemeinde, in dem Lavater die gemeinschaftliche Vereinigung mit Gott als besonders eindrucksvolle affektive Gotteserfahrung gestalten wollte. Er würde darum, so teilte er es seiner Gemeinde mit, dem Predigen nicht viel Platz einräumen. Sein Anliegen war es, »dem Bibelforscher mit kurzen Erklärungen und Anmerkungen nachhelfen, und die Andacht durch untermischte leicht mitzubethende Gebethe zu unterhalten.«[69]

Dass Lavater durchaus Erfolg hatte mit seiner Umgestaltung der Abendgebete, zeigt die große Besucherzahl. Nicht nur in seinen sonntäglichen Predigten, bei denen auf Grund der die Kapazitäten von St. Peter sprengenden Besucherströme regulierend eingegriffen werden musste,[70] sondern ebenfalls in den Abendgebeten erfreute er sich großen Zulaufs.[71]

Seine Apokalypse-Gebetsreihe wurde aber nicht nur rege besucht, sondern bereits im Vorfeld mit Spannung erwartet, wie einem anonymen Brief, den Lavaters Freund Johann Konrad Pfenninger (1747–1792) in dem von ihm herausgegebenen »Christlichen Magazin« abdruckte, zu entnehmen ist:

> »In unserer Stadt (Zürich) wird nun in den Mittewoch- und Samstäglichen Abendgebetstunden der Ordnung nach die Offenbarung Johannes erklärt.

[66] Erstes Abendgebet am St. Peter, 8. Juli 1778, FA Lav. Ms. 67 l.4.
[67] Erstes Abendgebet am St. Peter, 8. Juli 1778, FA Lav. Ms. 67 l.4.
[68] Erstes Abendgebet am St. Peter, 8. Juli 1778, FA Lav. Ms. 67 l.4.
[69] Erstes Abendgebet am St. Peter, 8. Juli 1778, FA Lav. Ms. 67 l.4.
[70] *Gessner*, Lebensbeschreibung, 216f.
[71] Elisa von der *Recke*, Tagebücher und Brief aus ihren Wanderjahren, hg. von Paul Rachel, Bd. 2, Leipzig 1902, 96.

Diß geschieht nach einer alten Einrichtung, nach welcher die Diakonen der Stadt das Neue Testament von Anfang zu Ende wöchentlich ein Kapitel zu erklären und anzuwenden gehalten sind. Da nun die Reihe die Offenbarung Johannis trift, so kannst du leicht denken, in welcher Verlegenheit sie sich da bisweilen finden müssen! Jedennoch hoff ich dir das eine und andere von dem besten, was sie vorbringen werden, mitzutheilen, besonders von meinem näheren Freunden Hess und Lavater.«[72]

Die angesprochene Verlegenheit, in die der Exeget der Offenbarung zuweilen komme, ist im Zusammenhang mit der durch die Rätselhaftigkeit der Visionen gestellten Kanonizitäts-Frage zu sehen. Neben Semlers zwischen 1769 und 1776 erschienenen drei Schriften, in denen er für den Ausschluss der Johannes-Offenbarung aus dem biblischen Kanon plädiert, haben sich auch Friedrich Andreas Stroth (1750–1785), Jeremias Friedrich Reuss (1700–1777) und Christian Friedrich Schmidt (1741–1778) mit einschlägigen Abhandlungen in das literarisch ausgetragene Streitgespräch eingeschaltet und Semler in seiner Kritik (Stroth) unterstützt oder apologetische Gegenschriften (Reuss, Schmidt) verfasst.

Obschon Lavater keinerlei Zweifel an der Kanonizität der Apokalypse hegte, hatte auch er Schwierigkeiten bei deren Deutung. Diese sollten aber einen auf Gottes Hilfe vertrauenden Exegeten nicht abschrecken, wie er es in den einleitenden Worten zur Apokalypse-Gebetsreihe deutlich macht:

»Nach meinem Gefühl ist dies Buch einerseits das allermerkwürdigste, heiligste, unnachahmlichste Buch; anderseits aber das Geheimnissvollste, schwerste, räthselhafteste, alle menschlichen Geistes Kräfte weit übersteigende Buch. Auf der einen Seite erhebt es uns weit über die Erde, weit über die Menschheit, und versezt uns gleichsam in weite offne Himelshohen, und auf der andern Seite drükt es den Menschen mit allen seinen Geisteskräften und Fähigkeiten tief in den Staub zurük, macht ihn verstumen, und bringt ihn an die Grenzen alles Wissens, und alles Lichtes. Aber wie nun sollen wir darum, da es uns auf der einen Seite tief darnieder drükt gänzlich darüber schweigen, oder absprechen, und es dem spottenden Wiz des Leichtsinns nach länger preis geben? Sollen wir nicht vielmehr um seiner Erhabenheit willen Muth fassen, und mit aller Bescheidenheit nach dem Licht, das Gott uns gibt, darüber reden?«[73]

[72] Christliches Magazin, hg. von Johann Konrad Pfenninger, 1. Bd., 2. Stück, Zürich 1779, 203.

[73] Abendgebet 5. Mai 1779, Zentralbibliothek Zürich, FA Lav. Ms. 68a.

Seinem Vorsatz gerecht werdend, die Apokalypse im gemeinschaftlichen, affektiven Gebet zu erschließen und deren Wahrhaftigkeit im Glauben zu fühlen und nicht mit dem Verstand zu erkennen – »Ich fühle, dass die erhabne Gottheit Geheimnisse hier in diese Gegend einschloss, die nur Er, und kein Menschenverstand aufschließen kann«[74] –, bemühte sich Lavater um eine adäquate Herangehensweise an das schwierige letzte Buch des Neuen Testaments, bei der er sich an Herders affektiven Zugang anlehnte. Wo es Herder aber vor allem darum geht, die Empfindungen als Erklärungsansatz für die Sprache und die Bilder der Bibel, die dem zeitgenössischen Leser nicht mehr direkt zugänglich sind, zu erläutern, will Lavater über die Vermittlung seiner eigenen Gefühle die Gemeinde in seelische Bewegung und dadurch in Bereitschaft, die göttlichen Geheimnisse zu erahnen, versetzen:

> »Wenn ich jemahl die heilige Kanzel mit Ehrfurcht und Gefühl meiner Ohnmacht und Unwürdigkeit betrette, so betrett ich sie jetzt, wie noch nie mit heiligem Schauer, mit Furcht und Zittern, mit Demuth und Ohnmacht, da ich über das Wichtigste, Geheimnissvollste, erhabenste Buch der ganzen Bibel mit euch reden soll.«[75]

Doch Lavater äußerte sich nicht nur über seine Empfindungen, er trug sie auch dem Inhalt entsprechend vor, wie verschiedene seiner Predigtbesucher festhielten. So meinte Elisa von der Recke (1754–1833) nach einem Besuch von Lavaters Abendgebet: »Es ist rührend, mit was für einer Inbrunst der Mann betet«,[76] und Christoph Friedrich Rinck (1757–1821), der 1783 auf seiner Studienreise ein Abendgebet von Lavater besuchte, hält in seinem Tagebuch fest: »Sein Vortrag ist deutlich, nachdruksvoll, eindringend, oft lebhaft und hinreisend, auch überzeugend, [...]. Sein Stil ist angenehm, sinnlich ausgeschmückt, aber ganz natürlich und verständlich.«[77] Obschon oder vielleicht gerade weil Lavater aufgrund seiner großen Arbeitsbelastung seine Predigten nur noch selten

[74] Ibid.

[75] Ibid.

[76] *Recke*, Tagebücher, 96.

[77] Tagebucheintrag vom 30. August 1783. In: Christoph Friedrich *Rinck*, Studienreise 1783/84, unternommen im Auftrage des Markgrafen Karl Friedrich von Baden. Nach dem Tagebuche des Verfassers herausgegeben von Dr. Moritz Geyer, Altenburg 1879, 10.

wörtlich ausformulierte – so ist auch die Apokalypse-Gebetsreihe nicht als sein eigenes Predigt-Manuskript erhalten, sondern als Mitschrift einer begeisterten Zuhörerin –, vermochten seine emphatischen, bewegenden und die Gefühle ansprechenden Predigten zu überzeugen und verfehlten ihre Wirkung nicht, wie der Theologiestudent Johann Georg Müller (1759–1819) berichtet: »Herr Lavater hat leztern Samstag die lezte Abendpredigt über die Offenbarung Johannis gehalten. Ohne Rührung gingen gewiss wenige weg. Ich gewiss auch nicht.«[78]

Lavater konnte also in seinen Abendgebeten erfolgreich gegen das von Spaldings »Ueber die Nutzbarkeit des Predigtamts« ausgelöste, sich im Verlaufe der 1770er Jahre verstärkt auch in seinem Umfeld beobachtete Predigen ankämpfen, das die Förderung des Christusglaubens durch die »Verbesserung« der Moralität der Hörer zu ersetzen suchte. Er beließ es aber nicht dabei, lediglich predigend Jesus Christus anhand der evangelischen Zeugnissen darzustellen. Wie Herder versuchte er, den Verkündigungsauftrag im Medium der Dichtung weiterzuverfolgen. So verfasste er zeitgleich mit seiner Abendgebetsreihe zur Apokalypse und auch zeitgleich mit dem Erscheinen von Herders Apokalypse-Paraphrase »Maran Atha« (1779) sein Epos »Jesus Messias, oder die Zukunft des Herrn« (1780), das in vierundzwanzig hexametrischen Gesängen die Visionen des Johannes nacherzählt. Lavater hatte sich also auch dichterisch von Herder anregen lassen, diese Anregung und gegenseitige Beeinflussung aber wie beim Predigen in eine eigene Richtung entwickelt. Nahe an der biblischen Vorlage bleibend, diese aber in hexametrische Verse umdichtend, hat Lavater die Bibel in ein neues, seiner Meinung nach einprägsames und emotional ergreifendes Werk gekleidet, das nicht wie Herders Paraphrase zu stark auf historische Erklärungen dringt, sondern die christliche Botschaft in den Mittelpunkt stellt.

Ausgelöst durch Spaldings Schrift und beeinflusst von Herders Ansichten über die biblischen Zeugnisse als Hauptinhalt der Predigt und dessen Beschäftigung mit der Apokalypse als affektive erhabene Bibelpoesie, hat Lavater seinen eigenen Weg gefunden, zu

[78] Johann Georg Müller an Anna Maria Müller, 28. Okt. 1779, in: Johannes von Müller, Johann Georg Müller: Briefwechsel und Familienbriefe 1766–1789, hg. von André Weibel, Bd. 2, Göttingen 2010, 98.

predigen, zu beten und zu dichten und damit den evangelischen Christus zu verkünden.

Daniela Kohler, lic. phil., Institut für Schweizerische Reformationsgeschichte, Universität Zürich

Abstract: After Joachim Spalding's oeuvre, »Ueber die Nutzbarkeit des Predigtamtes« was published in 1722, Johann Caspar Lavater challenged Spalding's view of the duties and benefits of the clerical minister. Above all, Lavater criticized Spalding's focus on the moral aspects of religion, arguing that Spalding failed to concentrate on the true center – Christ and all Christian dogma. Lavater felt that Johann Gottfried Herder had furnished a better interpretation of ministerial responsibilities in »An Prediger. Funfzehn Provinzialblätter« (1774). Intrigued by Herder's proclamation of the evangelical Christ, Lavater thought that he had found support for his own Christianity in Herder. His assumption was destroyed by Herder's work on the Apocalypse in »Maran Atha« (1779). In accordance, Lavater in his sermons about the Book of Revelation sought to provide an example, not only of how to understand the last book of the New Testament, but also by emphasizing where a minister should focus his attention in order to function as a prophet of the evangelical Jesus.

Schlagworte: Johann Caspar Lavater, Johann Joachim Spalding, Johann Gottfried Herder, Apokalypse, Homiletik, Christologie, Eschatologie

ISSN 0254-4407 – Zwingliana 40 (2013), 189–198

Neue Literatur zur zwinglischen Reformation

Hans Ulrich Bächtold

Berücksichtigt sind wissenschaftliche und wissenschaftsrelevante Publikationen zu Themen und Personen der Reformation in der Eidgenossenschaft und zu deren Umfeld bis um 1650; Rezensionen, Lexikonartikel und kleinere Kapitel in Überblicksdarstellungen werden im Allgemeinen nicht aufgenommen. Die Bibliographie ist in vier Abteilungen gegliedert: Sammelschriften, Bibliographien, Quellen und Darstellungen. Die Titel der Sammelschriften erscheinen unter der jeweils angegebenen Kurzform in den übrigen Abteilungen. Außer den kursiven Nachbemerkungen stammen auch die in eckigen Klammern gesetzten Zusätze vom Autor der Bibliographie. Gedankt sei allen aufmerksamen Lesern und Leserinnen, die auf entlegene Titel hingewiesen haben.

1. Sammelschriften

Dichtung – Gelehrsamkeit – Disputationskultur: Festschrift für Hanspeter Marti zum 65. Geburtstag, hg. von Reimund B. Sdzuj, Robert Seidel und Bernd Zegowitz, Wien: Böhlau, 2012.
[Zit.: Dichtung]

Johannes Calvin 1509–2009: Würdigung aus Berner Perspektive, im Auftrag der Theologischen Fakultät hg. von Martin Sallmann, Moisés Mayordomo und Hans Rudolf Lavater, Zürich: Theologischer Verlag Zürich, 2012.
[Zit.: Calvin aus Berner Perspektive]

Johannes Calvin und die Prägekraft des Protestantismus, hg. von Emidio Campi, Peter Opitz und Konrad Schmid, Zürich: Theologischer Verlag Zürich, 2012.
[Zit.: Calvin und die Prägekraft]

Die Marburger Artikel als Zeugnis der Einheit, hg. von Wolf-Friedrich Schäufele, Leipzig: Evangelische Verlagsanstalt, 2012.
[Zit.: Die Marburger Artikel]

Orbis Helveticorum. Das Schweizer Buch und seine mitteleuropäische Welt, hg. von Viliam Čičaj und Jan-Andrea Bernhard, Bratislava: Historický ústav Slovenskej akadémie vied, 2011.
[Zit.: Orbis Helveticorum]

Reformierte Bekenntnisse: Ein Werkbuch als Grundlage für eine Vernehmlassung zum reformierten Bekennen in der Schweiz und zugleich als Geschenk für Jean Calvin zum 500. Geburtstag am 10. Juli 2009, hg. von einer interkantonalen Initiativgruppe unter Leitung von Matthias Krieg, Zürich: Theologischer Verlag Zürich, 2009.
[Zit.: Bekenntnisse]

Sierszyn, Armin. Evangelium und Kulturrevolution: 17 Vorträge und Aufsätze, Bäretswil: A. Sierszyn, 2012.
[Zit.: Sierszyn, Evangelium]

2. Bibliographien

Bächtold, Hans Ulrich. Neue Literatur zur zwinglischen Reformation, in: Zwingliana 39 (2012), 145–154.

Beyer, Michael. Lutherbibliographie 2012, in: Lutherjahrbuch: Organ der internationalen Lutherforschung 79 (2012), 345–386.
S. 374: »Schweizer und Oberdeutsche«.

Zürcher Bibliographie 2011: Bibliographie zur Geschichte, Landes- und Volkskunde zur Orts- und Personengeschichte von Stadt und Kanton Zürich, hg. von der Zentralbibliothek Zürich, Zürich 2012.
Vgl. bes. S. 22–27: »Religion« und 89–139: »Personen und Familien«.

Handbuch der historischen Buchbestände in der Schweiz – Répertoire des fonds imprimés anciens de Suisse – Repertorio dei fondi antichi a stampa della Svizzera, 3 Bde., hg. von der Zentralbibliothek Zürich, bearb. von Urs B. Leu et al., Hildesheim: Olms-Weidmann, 2011.

Wriedt, Markus et al. Literaturbericht, in: Archiv für Reformationsgeschichte, Beiheft 41 (2012).
S. 44–46: »Täufertum und heterodoxe Richtungen«.

3. Quellen

Calvin-Studienausgabe, hg. von Eberhard Busch et al., Bd. 8: Ökumenische Korrespondenz: Eine Auswahl aus Calvins Briefen, Neukirchen-Vluyn: Neukirchener, 2011.
Enthält im Kap. 3 Calvin-Briefe an Bullinger, 1544 und 1556, an Brenz in Basel, 1548, und in Kap. 10 an die evangelischen Flüchtlinge in Zürich, 1554.

De' conviti degli antichi: Opera adespota, hg. von Damiano Acciarino, Padua: Il poligrafo, 2012 (Humanitas 19).
Kritische Edition einer zeitgenössischen italienischen Übersetzung von Johann Wilhelm Stuckis »Antiquitatum convivialium libri tres«.

Correspondance de Théodore de Bèze, Bd. 36 (1595), hg. von Alain Dufour, Hervé Genton, Monique Cuany, unter Mitarbeit von Béatrice Nicollier, Genf: Droz, 2012 (Travaux d'Humanisme et Renaissance 500).
Der Band enthält u.a. Briefe von und an Jakob Grynäus, Raphael Egli, die Pfarrer von Schaffhausen.

Döpp, Siegmar. Neulateinische Wissenschaftspoesie: Ioannes Fabricius Montanus (1527–1566) über Engadiner Heilquellen, Speyer: Kartoffeldruck-Verlag, 2012.
Enthält S. 39–41 des Fabricius' Gedicht »Descriptio Fontium Engadinae inferioris prope Scultinum«, 42–45 dessen Übersetzung ins Deutsche.

Heinrich Bullinger: Kommentare zu den neutestamentlichen Briefen. Röm – 1Kor. – 2Kor., hg. von Luca Baschera, Zürich: Theologischer Verlag Zürich, 2012 (Heinrich Bullinger Werke III/6).

Kunz, Ralph. Confessio Helvetica posterior, in: Bekenntnisse, 99–105.
S. 102–104: Edition von Kap. 17 des Bekenntnisses in neuhochdeutscher Übersetzung.

Melanchthons Briefwechsel, Band T 13: Texte 3421–3779 (1544), bearb. von Matthias Dall'Asta, Heidi Hein und Christine Mundhenk, Stuttgart-Bad Cannstatt: Frommann-Holzboog, 2012
Enthält u.a. von Briefe von und/oder an Bullinger, Schaffhausen, Eberhard von Rümlang, Oswald Myconius, Johann Konrad Ulmer, Vadian. Vgl. auch die (Teil-)Edition einschlägiger Briefe gemäß Verzeichnis der Fremdstücke (604f).

Moser, Christian. Die Dignität des Ereignisses: Studien zu Heinrich Bullingers Reformationsgeschichtsschreibung, 2 Bde., Leiden/Boston: Brill, 2012 (Studies in the History of Christian Traditions 163).
Bd. 2 »Editorischer und beschreibender Anhang«: 1. Heinrich Bullinger: Vorrede zur Reformationsgeschichte; 2. Inhaltsverzeichnis von Heinrich

Bullingers Reformationsgeschichte; 3. Heinrich Bullinger: Materialien über die Jahre 1523–1528; 4. Heinrich Bullinger: Aufzeichnungen über den Zweiten Kappelerkrieg; 5. Heinrich Bullinger: »Consignatio temporum«: Aufzeichnungen über die Jahre 1518–1529; 6. Heinrich Bullinger: Aufzeichnungen über die Jahre 1531/1532; 7. Heinrich Bullinger: Aufzeichnungen über die Jahre 1524–1529; 8. Heinrich Bullinger: Materialien zum Marburger Religionsgespräch; 9. Heinrich Bullinger: Über die Rechtmäßigkeit der reformatorischen Veränderungen in Zürich, Antwort an Johannes Cochläus (»Ad Ioannis Cochlei libellum responsio«); 10. Ludwig Lavater: Konzept einer Reformationsgeschichte (1559); 11. Ludwig Lavater an Johannes Pontisella d.J. (1579/1580); 12. Heinrich Bullinger: Annotationen zu Juan Luis Vives' »De disciplinis libri XX«; 13. Handschriftenbeschreibungen.

Reformation Commentary on Scripture. Old Testament I: Genesis 1–11, hg. von John L. Thompson, Downers Grove, IL: IVP Academic, 2012.
Einbezogen sind Werke von u.a. Wolfgang Musculus, Oekolampad, Pellikan, Vermigli und Zwingli.

Reformation Commentary on Scripture. Old Testament XII: Ezekiel, Daniel, hg. von Carl L. Beckwith, Downers Grove, IL: IVP Academic, 2012.
Einbezogen sind u.a. Werke von Bullinger und Oekolampad.

Ramstein, Christoph. Das Basler Bekenntnis, in: Bekenntnisse, 69–76.
S. 73–75: Edition des Bekenntnisses in Neuhochdeutsch.

De ratione communi omnium linguarum et literarum commentarius: Theodore Bibliander, hg. und übers. mit einer Einleitung von Hagit Amirav und Hans-Martin Kirn, mit einem Vorwort von Irena Backus, Genf: Droz, 2011 (Travaux d'Humanisme et Renaissance 475).

Schäufele, Wolf-Friedrich. Der Text der Marburger Artikel: Faksimile – Transkription – Übertragung, in: Die Marburger Artikel, 13–30.

Schäufele, Wolf-Friedrich. Die Schwabacher und die Marburger Artikel: Eine Synopse, in: Die Marburger Artikel, 31–42.

Sallmann, Martin. Die Berner Thesen, in: Bekenntnisse, 57–62.
S. 61: Edition der Thesen in Neuhochdeutsch.

Sallmann, Martin. Die Ilanzer Schlussreden, in: Bekenntnisse, 51–56.
S. 55: Edition der Schlussreden in Neuhochdeutsch.

Wälchli, Philipp. Reformationsmandat für den Thurgau 1530, in: Zwingliana 39 (2012), 51–77.

Zeindler, Matthias. Fidei Ratio, in: Bekenntnisse, 63–68.
S. 65–67: Edition von Kap. 7 und Teil von 8 in Neuhochdeutsch.

4. Darstellungen

Arend, Sabine. Hugo von Hohenlandenberg und die Landpfarrer der Diözese Konstanz vor der Reformation, in: Ein feiner Fürst in einer rauen Zeit: Der Konstanzer Bischof Hugo von Hohenlandenberg, hg. von Peter Niederhäuser, Zürich: Chronos, 2011, 59–70.

Backus, Irena. Zwingli und der Beginn der Schweizer Reformation, in: Calvinismus: Die Reformierten in Deutschland und Europa [Ausstellungskatalog], hg. von Ansgar Reiß et al., Dresden: Sandstein, 2009, 104–109.

Bächtold, Hans Ulrich. Eine herrliche Gnade und Gabe Gottes – Heinrich Bullinger als Publizist, in: Orbis Helveticorum, 63–67.

Bahr, Petra. Von der Befreiung der Bilder – ein etwas anderer Blick auf den reformierten Bildersturm, in: Calvin und die Prägekraft, 45–56.
Betrachtungen zum Thema ausgehend von den Zürcher Ereignissen 1524.

Balserak, Jon. »We need Teachers today, not Prophets«: Peter Martyr Vermigli's Exposition of Prophecy, in: Archiv für Reformationsgeschichte 103 (2012), 92–116.

Barbieri, Laura de. Das Orbis Helveticorum von Matthias Borbonius aus Borbenheim, in: Orbis Helveticorum, 167–173.

Baschera, Luca. Independent Yet Harmonious: Some Remarks on the Relationship between the Theology of Peter Martyr Vermigli (1499–1562) and John Calvin, in: Church History and Religious Culture 91/1–2 (2011), 43–57.

Baumann, Maurice. Calvin und Castellio: Eine theologische Kontroverse anlässlich der Hinrichtung von Michel Servet, in: Calvin aus Berner Perspektive, 121–138.

Bernhard, Jan-Andrea. Die Bedeutung des Basler Humanismus für Ungarn: Warum ungarische Adelshöfe zu Förderern der Reformation helvetischer Richtung wurden, in: Orbis Helveticorum, 113–142.

Bernhard, Jan-Andrea. Ungarische Studenten disputieren über die *Confessio Helvetica posterior* (1566) im Vorfeld der *Formula consensus* (1675): Ein theologie- und kommunikationsgeschichtlicher Beitrag, in: Dichtung, 511–539.

Bôbová, Mária. Helvetica aus dem 16. Jahrhundert in Neusohl, in: Orbis Helveticorum, 273–276.
Betr. Drucke aus Basel und Genf.

Birmelé, André. Das reformatorische Evangelium: Sünde und Rechtfertigung (Marburger Artikel 4–7), in: Die Marburger Artikel, 105–114.

Bryner, Erich. Die Reformation in Schaffhausen und ihre Besonderheiten, in: Zwingliana 39 (2012), 79–92.

Bundi, Martin. Zur Führungsrolle des Grauen Bundes und der Stadt Ilanz in der frühen Reformbewegung Graubündens, in: Zwingliana 39 (2012), 23–50.

Caldwell, Amy R. »A True and Certain Means to Peace«: Small State Diplomacy and Reformation in Zurich 1515–1526, Diss. University of California, Santa Barbara, März 2011, Ann Arbor: UMI, 2011.

Campi, Emidio. Probing Similarities and Differences Between John Calvin and Heinrich Bullinger, in: Calvinus clarissimus theologus: Papers of the Tenth International Congress on Calvin Research, hg. von Herman J. Selderhuis, Göttingen:Vandenhoeck & Ruprecht, 2012 (Reformed Historical Theology 18), 94–117.

Čičaj, Viliam. Das Schweizer Buch und die Privatbibliotheken der Stadtbürger in der Frühen Neuzeit, in: Orbis Helveticorum, 161–165.

Fejtová, Olga und Jiři *Pešek*. Reformierte Literatur in frühneuzeitlichen Bürgerbibliotheken der böhmischen Städte, in: Orbis Helveticorum, 143–159.

Felici, Lucia. L'immensa bontà di Dio: diffusione e adattamento dell'idea erasmiana in Italia e in Svizzera, in: Religione e politica in Erasmo da Rotterdam, hg. von Enzo A. Baldini und Massimo Firpo, Rom: Edizioni di storia e letteratura, 2012 (Studi storici e politici 6), 129–158.

Flückiger, Fabrice. Le choix de religion: Le rôle de l'autorité politique dans les disputes religieuses des années 1520, in: Schweizerische Zeitschrift für Geschichte 60/3 (2010), 277–301.

Freudenberg, Matthias. »... und Zwingli vor mir wie eine überhängende Wand«: Karl Barths Wahrnehmung der Theologie Huldrych Zwinglis in seiner Göttinger Vorlesung von 1922/23, in: Matthias Freudenberg. Reformierter Protestantismus in der Herausforderung: Wege und Wandlungen der reformierten Theologie, Berlin: LIT Verlag, 2012 (Theologie: Forschung und Wissenschaft 36), 314–332.
Wiederabdruck eines Aufsatzes aus: Zwingliana 33 (2006), 5–27.

Friesen, Abraham. Reformers, Radicals, Revolutionaries: Anabaptism in the Context of the Reformation Conflict, Elkhart, IN: Institute of Mennonite Studies, 2012.

Gemeinhardt, Peter. Das Erbe der Alten Kirche: Gott und Christus (Marburger Artikel 1–3), in: Die Marburger Artikel, 69–103.

George, Timothy. Reading Scripture with the Reformers, Downer Grove, IL: IVP Academic, 2011.

Gordon, Bruce. »In my Father's House There Are Many Mansions«: Heinrich Bullinger on Death and the Afterlife, in: A Linking of Heaven and Earth: Studies in Religious and Cultural History in Honor of Carlos M. N. Eire, hg. von Emily Michelson et al., Farnham: Ashgate, 2012 (St. Andrews Studies in Reformation History), 159–173.

Grimmsmann, Damaris. Heinrich Bullingers Deutung der Türkengefahr und des Islam, in: Archiv für Reformationsgeschichte 103 (2012), 64–91.

Gutmann, Andre. Die Schwabenkriegschronik des Kaspar Frey und ihre Stellung in der eidgenössischen Historiographie des 16. Jahrhunderts, 2 Teile, Stuttgart: Kohlhammer, 2010 (Veröffentlichungen der Kommission für geschichtliche Landeskunde in Baden-Württemberg B 176/1–2).

Haberland, Detlef. Der Druckort Basel und Ostmitteleuropa – Spuren geistiger Verbindungen, in: Orbis Helveticorum, 11–21.

Hauswirth, René. Die »Hackordnung«: Untersuchungen zur informellen Sozialstruktur einer politischen Elite in der frühen Neuzeit, in: Schweizerische Zeitschrift für Geschichte 59 (2009), 159–190.
Über die sozialen Strukturen im Zürich der Reformationszeit.

Hein, Martin. Der bleibende Auftrag von Marburg 1529. Was heißt heute »evangelisch«? in: Die Marburger Artikel, 197–207.

Hitz, Florian. Campell als Wunderzeichendeuter, in: Bündner Monatsblatt 2012/1, 3–27.

Hoffmann, Gottfried. Kirchenväterzitate in der Abendmahlskontroverse zwischen Oekolampad, Zwingli, Luther und Melanchthon: Legitimationsstrategien in der innerreformatorischen Auseinandersetzung um das Herrenmahl, Göttingen: Edition Ruprecht, 2011.
Teilweise überarbeitete Dissertation von 1972.

Jehle, Frank. Fritz Blanke – Lehrer und Forscher: Vortrag an der Mitgliederversammlung des Zwinglivereins 2012, in: Zwingliana 39 (2012), 131–144.
Betrifft Fritz Blanke vor allem auch als Reformationshistoriker.

Kim, Min Soon, Huldrych Zwingli and Heinrich Bullinger on Covenant Theology: Was Bullinger the Successor of Zwingli in Covenant Theology? in: Jurnal Teologi Reformed Indonesia 2/2 (2012), 113–133.

Komorová, Klára. Helvetica in einer Adelsbibliothek, in: Orbis Helveticorum, 257–265.
Zürcher und v.a. Basler Drucke des 16. Jh.s in der Privatbibliothek Krupek.

Lanfranchi, Arno. Conflitti confessionali a Poschiavo nel Cinquecento, in: Bollettino / Società storica Val Poschiavo 15 (2011), 3–14.

Letsch, Walter. Der Zolliker Palmesel, in: Zolliker Jahrheft 35 (2012), 61–70.

Leu, Urs. Der Zürcher Buchdruck des 16. Jahrhunderts im europäischen Kontext unter besonderer Berücksichtigung Ostmitteleuropas, in: Orbis Helveticorum, 23–32.

Leu, Urs. The Book and Reading Culture in Basle and Zurich During the 16th Century, in: The Book Triumphant: Print in Transition in the Sixteenth and Seventeenth Centuries, hg. von Malcolm Walsby und Graeme Kemp, Leiden/Boston: Brill, 2011 (Library of the Written Word 15), 295–319.

Leu, Urs B. Häresie und Staatsgewalt: Die theologischen Zürcher Dissertationen des 17. Jahrhunderts zwischen Orthodoxie und Frühaufklärung, in: Reformierte Orthodoxie und Aufklärung: Die Zürcher Hohe Schule im 17. und 18. Jahrhundert, hg. von Hanspeter und Karin Marti-Weissenbach, Wien: Böhlau, 2012, 105–145.

Leu, Urs B. Die Privatbibliothek des Hebraisten und Theologen Konrad Pellikan, in: Dichtung, 58–75.

Lexutt, Athina. Das Abendmahl: Die lutherische Position (Marburger Artikel 15), in: Die Marburger Artikel, 151–174.

Matejková, Adriana. Bücher schweizerischer Provenienz in der Lyzeumsbibliothek von Schemnitz, in: Orbis Helveticorum, 277–284.
S. 25 Werke des 16. Jahrhunderts stammen aus der Schweiz.

Maurer, Esther. Wie beeinflussen Protestantismus und Sozialismus die Arbeitswelt einer Politikerin? in: Calvin und die Prägekraft, 125–136.
Über das Wesen des Zürcher Reformiertentums.

Mente, Michael. »Von dem Amt eines verordneten Decani«: Einblicke in die Geschichte des Dekanenamtes in der Evangelisch-reformierten Landeskirche des Kantons Zürich, in: Zwingliana 39 (2012), 93–129.

Monok, István. Der Basler Buchdruck und die Gelehrtenbibliotheken in Ungarn im 16. Jahrhundert, in: Orbis Helveticorum, 33–39.

Moser, Christian. Die Dignität des Ereignisses: Studien zu Heinrich Bullingers Reformationsgeschichtsschreibung, 2 Bde., Leiden/Boston: Brill, 2012 (Studies in the History of Christian Traditions 163).

Niederhäuser, Peter. Ein Leben im Umbruch: Die Zürcher Äbtissin Katharina von Zimmern, in: Mäzene, Sammler, Chronisten: Die Grafen von Zimmern und die Kultur des schwäbischen Adels, hg. von Casimir Bumiller et al. [Ausstellungskatalog], Stuttgart: Belser, 2012, 119–129.

Opitz, Peter. The Authority of Scripture in the Early Zurich Reformation (1522–1540), in: Journal of Reformed theology 5 (2011), 296–309.

Opitz, Peter. Die Marburger Artikel als Zeugnis der Einheit. Artikel 15: Das Abendmahl – die reformierte Perspektive, in: Die Marburger Artikel, 175–196.

Opitz, Peter. Das Evangelium als Befreiung zum Vertrauen bei Huldrych Zwingli, in: Gottvertrauen: Die ökumenische Diskussion um die fiducia, hg. von Ingolf U. Dalferth und Simon Peng-Keller, Freiburg i.Br.: Herder, 2012 (Quaestiones disputatae 250), 182–208.

Piirainen, Ilpo Tapani. Luther-Nachdruck mit einem Glossar in der Offizin des Adam Petri, in: Orbis Helveticorum, 69–73.

Piłaszewicz-Łopatecka, Marta. Ulrich Zwingli: zwiastun słowa, przeciwnik obrazów [Ulrich Zwingli als Gegner von Gemälden als Einrichtungselemente von Kirchenräumen], in: Studia nad Reformacją [Studium der Reformation], red. von Elżbieta Bagińska, Piotr Guzowski, Marzena Liedke, Białystok: IH UWB, 2010.

Rohls, Jan. Glaube und Leben: Die evangelische Ethik (Marburger Artikel 10–13), in: Die Marburger Artikel, 137–149.

Saktorová, Helena. Helvetica in der Bibliothek des Palatins Georg Thurzo, in: Orbis Helveticorum, 251–256.

Sallmann, Martin. Glaube als Geschenk: Predigt und Taufe (Marburger Artikel 8–9, 14) oder: Die Zuordnung von Wort und Geist als Dreh- und Angelpunkt der Marburger Artikel, in: Die Marburger Artikel, 115–135.

Sallmann, Martin. Bern und die Reformation in Genf, in: Calvin aus Berner Perspektive, 11–23.

Schäufele, Wolf-Friedrich. Bündnis und Bekenntnis: Die Marburger Artikel in ihrem dreifachen historischen Kontext, in: Die Marburger Artikel, 43–68.

Scheidegger, Christian. »Wider die unsinnigen Widertäufer«: Ein unbekanntes Briefgedicht von Jörg Syz an Hans Brennwald (um 1527), in: Zwingliana 39 (2012), 1–21.

Schmidt, Heinrich Richard. Inquisition im Reformiertentum? Die Bekämpfung von Täufern und Pietisten in Bern, in: Tribunal der Barbaren? Deutschland und die Inquisition in der Frühen Neuzeit, hg. von Albrecht Burkardt und Gerd Schwerhoff, Konstanz/München: UVK Verlagsgesellschaft, 2012 (Konflikte und Kultur – Historische Perspektive, 25), 335–358.

Schreiner, Susan. Are You Alone Wise? Oxford: Oxford University Press, 2010 (Oxford Studies in Historical Theology).
Kap. 2 (S. 37–77) über die theologischen Debatten um die Heilsgewissheit anhand von Luther, Zwingli und Calvin.

Schulthess-Rechberg, Gustav von. Luther, Zwingli und Calvin in ihren Ansichten über das Verhältnis von Staat und Kirche, überarb. Nachdruck der Ausgabe 1909, hg. und mit einem Vorwort versehen von Christiane Beetz, Hamburg: Severus Verlag, 2012 (ReligioSus 12).

Sibylová, Michaela. Helvetica in der Adelsbibliothek der Familie Pálffy, in: Orbis Helveticorum, 267–272.
Betr. Basler und Zürcher Drucke des 16. Jahrhunderts.

Sierszyn, Armin. Heinrich Bullinger: Vater der Reformierten Kirche, in: Sierszyn, Evangelium, 32–41.

Sierszyn, Armin. Zur Täuferbewegung im Grüninger Amt, in: Sierszyn, Evangelium, 108–140.
Erstpublikation in Zwingliana 34 (2007), 37–60.

Stephens, William Peter. The Interpretation of the Bible in Bullinger's Early Works, in: Reformation & Renaissance Review 11 (2009), 311–333.

Szeghy, Andrej. Helvetica des 16. Jahrhunderts in den Beständen der Wissenschaftlichen Staatsbibliothek in Kaschau, in: Orbis Helveticorum, 285–291.
Betrifft v.a. Werke aus Basel und Genf.

Van den Belt, Henk. Heinrich Bullinger and Jean Calvin on the Authority of Scripture (1538–1571), in: Journal of Reformed Theology 5 (2011), 310–324.

Vásárhelyi, Judit P. Die Wirkung der Schweizer Bibel im Lebenswerk von Albert Szenci Molnár, in: Orbis Helveticorum, 185–191.

Verók, Attila. Das schweizerische Buch bei den Siebenbürger Sachsen vom 16. bis 18. Jahrhundert, in: Orbis Helveticorum, 299–305.

Zibritová, Gabriela. Schweizerische Bücher in den ältesten Bibliotheken von Leutschau und Bartfeld, in: Orbis Helveticorum, 237–249.

Zientara, Wlodzimierz. Schweizer alte Drucke in den Thorner Buchbeständen, in: Orbis Helveticorum, 207–212.

Zmeták, Igor. Jost Ammanns Habitus im mitteleuropäischen Kontext, in: Orbis Helveticorum, 201–203.

Hans Ulrich Bächtold, Dr. phil., Zug

ISSN 0254-4407 – Zwingliana 40 (2013), 199–247

Buchbesprechungen

Maximilian von Habsburg, Catholic and Protestant Translations of the Imitatio Christi, 1425–1650: From Late Medieval Classic to Early Modern Bestseller, Farnham: Ashgate, 2011 (St. Andrews Studies in Reformation History), 355 S. – ISBN 978-0-7546-6765-0.

»Lieber möchte ich Reue und Leid im Herzen empfinden, als eine Definition abgeben können«, heißt es in der *Imitatio Christi*. In dieser anonym überlieferten Sammlung von geistlichen Sprüchen und Reden wird betont, dass Christus nachfolgen keine Frage der Schultheologie, sondern eine Herzenssache und ein Lebensstil primär für Ordensleute und dann auch für alle Geistlichen und Laien ist.

Während sich bisherige Untersuchungen mehr mit der Verfasserfrage und dem Entstehungskontext der *Imitatio* beschäftigt haben, stellt Maximilian von Habsburg in seiner Studie vorwiegend die Rezeption im protestantischen und katholischen Umfeld bis zur Mitte des 17. Jahrhunderts auf einer bibliographischen Grundlage dar. Die präsentierten Zahlen sind eindrücklich: 800 überlieferte Handschriften bis zum Beginn des 16. Jahrhunderts und 740 gedruckte Ausgaben in den verschiedensten Sprachen bis 1650 (mehr als 4 Auflagen pro Jahr) zeigen, dass die *Imitatio* nicht nur zu den klassischen Texten der europäischen Erbauungsliteratur gehört, sondern vom Spätmittelalter bis in die frühe Neuzeit nach der Bibel auch den zweiten Platz auf der Bestsellerliste belegt.

Von Habsburg versucht die Vermittlung und den Erfolg der *Imitatio* in der frühen Neuzeit vor dem Hintergrund ihrer Entstehung und frühen Wirkungsgeschichte zu verstehen. Wie andere Texte der Devotio moderna kam die *Imitatio* anonym heraus, was dem Demutsideal dieser christlichen Erneuerungsbewegung entsprach. Thomas a Kempis (gest. 1471), von dem ein Autograph existiert, gilt als mutmaßlicher Verfasser. Der Text ist geprägt von einem engen Bezug zur Bibel, einer starken Betonung der Innerlichkeit und einer kritischen Distanz sowohl zur Schultheologie als auch zu vielen äußeren Religionsformen. Seine frühe Verbreitung war mit der Devotio moderna aufs engste verknüpft. Die Brüder vom gemeinsamen Leben und die Windesheimer Kongregation stellten unermüdlich und mit Hingabe Abschriften her, welche die schnell wachsende Nachfrage weit über die eigenen Einrichtungen hinaus befriedigten. Denn die Devotio moderna erfasste verschiedene geistliche Vereinigungen wie zum Beispiel die mehr als 300 Klöster, die unter Windesheimer Aufsicht reformiert wurden.

Die Rezeption der *Imitatio* im 16. Jahrhundert ist verbunden mit Personen und Kreisen in den damaligen kirchlichen Randzonen. Namentlich sind dies Pedro Ruiz de Alcaraz, Caspar Schwenckfeld, Leo Jud, Sebastian Castellio, Hendrik Niclaes oder Ignatius von Loyola, der zu jenem Zeitpunkt Probleme mit der Inquisition bekam.

Nach einer merkwürdigen Lücke ohne eine deutsche Ausgabe in den Jahren 1515 bis 1530 erschien 1531 die deutsche Übersetzung des Reformators und Spiritualisten Caspar Schwenckfeld, der damit die erste evangelische Version der *Imitatio* und zwar ohne das vierte Buch über die Eucharistie vorlegte. Nach Meinung des Autors übersetzte Schwenckfeld in Straßburg nicht zufällig nur die ersten drei Bücher, denn 1529 sei in Straßburg die Messe abgeschafft worden. Diese Begründung leuchtet nicht besonders ein, zumal Schwenckfeld die leibliche Gegenwart Christi im Abendmahl schon zuvor abgelehnt und eine Abendmahlsschrift verfasst hat, die Huldrych Zwingli 1528 in Zürich drucken ließ. Auch die aus der Sekundärliteratur übernommene Vermutung, Schwenckfeld sei von den Täufern zur Übersetzung der *Imitatio* angeregt worden, muss bezweifelt werden, da die christliche Nachfolge bei den Täufern im Gegensatz zu Kempis viel mit dem Äußeren und Sichtbaren zu tun hatte.

In Zürich entstand die zweite protestantische Übersetzung der *Imitatio*. Sie ist das Werk von Leo Jud. Ob sein vorübergehender Kontakt zu Schwenckfeld dabei eine Rolle gespielt hat, bleibt unklar. Seine deutsche Übersetzung erschien 1539 in Zürich und erlebte nur zwei weitere Auflagen, während Schwenckfelds Übersetzung im untersuchten Zeitraum immerhin elfmal gedruckt wurde.

In Basel übertrug der Humanist Sebastian Castellio die *Imitatio* in ein klassisches Latein und passte den Text vermutlich auf der Grundlage der deutschen Übersetzung Schwenckfelds für eine protestantische Leserschaft an. Die Erstausgabe erschien dort 1563, fünf weitere Ausgaben folgten bis 1620. Castellios lateinische Fassung wurde weit bekannt und diente als Grundlage für verschiedene protestantische Übersetzungen. Zum Beispiel benutze Edward Hake Castellios Textausgabe für seine englische Übersetzung, die 1567 erschien. Eine neue englische Übersetzung fertigte Thomas Rogers 1580 im Auftrag des Druckers Henry Denham an. Beide Übertragungen erlebten bis 1650 gemeinsam 22 Auflagen. Die *Imitatio* wurde so zu einem bedeutenden Werk für den englischen Protestantismus.

Die protestantischen Übersetzer haben die ursprüngliche Textgestalt mit verhältnismäßig geringen Eingriffen für ihre Leserschaft angepasst mit dem Resultat, dass es im revidierten Text nur Himmel und Hölle (kein Fegefeuer) und Christus als einzigen Mittler (keine Heiligen) gibt; die Tugenden und guten Werke sind im Gegensatz zum Original nicht mehr intrinsisch oder verdienstvoll, sondern allein eine Wirkung der göttlichen Gnade. Auch fehlt in allen protestantischen Ausgaben das vierte Buch, weil die Übersetzer die darin vertretene Transsubstantiationslehre ablehnten. Weiter mieden sie die monastische Terminologie und ersetzten das Kloster durch die Gemeinde, den Mönch durch den wahren Christen und das Klosterleben durch ein Leben in stiller Abgeschiedenheit. Monastische Begriffe fehlten allerdings bereits in den vorreformatorischen Ausgaben, wenn sie für ein Laienpublikum bestimmt waren. Trotz diesen Eingriffen blieb der Text theologisch flexibel, weshalb Schwenckfelds Übersetzung auch in Jesuitenkollegien gelesen werden konnte. Auch mag es erstaunen, dass der katholische Übersetzer Georg Witzel die Vorrede zu Schwenckfelds Übersetzung verbatim übernommen hat. Bewusste irenische oder ökumenische Absichten hat es jedoch zu keinem Zeitpunkt gegeben.

Die protestantische Vermittlung der *Imitatio* stand ganz im Zeichen, die biblische Botschaft zu erklären und zu popularisieren. Bei Leo Jud ist dies angesichts seiner umfangreichen Übersetzungsarbeit und seiner pastoralen Tätigkeit besonders deutlich erkennbar. Ähnlich wollten Edward Hake und Thomas Rogers mit ihren englischen Übersetzungen das geistliche Leben im Rahmen der sakramentalen Kirche Englands fördern.

Ausführlich geht von Habsburg auch auf die jesuitischen Ausgaben und deren Rezeption ein. Der Erfolg der *Imitatio* als Bestseller in der ersten Hälfte des 17. Jahrhunderts hat wesentlich mit dem starken Wachstum der Jesuiten zu tun. Dieser weltweit vernetzte und missionarisch aktive Orden übte allgemein einen großen Einfluss auf die katholische Bildung und auf die frühneuzeitliche Gesellschaft aus. Wichtig waren die lateinischen Ausgaben von Henricus Somalius und des Bollandisten Heribert Rosweyde, die den Text beide auf der Grundlage einer Originalhandschrift des Thomas a Kempis herausgaben. Insgesamt erschienen davon im untersuchten Zeitraum 49 Auflagen, zwei davon in Luzern. Die Jesuiten übersetzten die *Imitatio* ins Englische, Französische, Deutsche, Katalanische, Spanische, Japanische, Polnische, Tschechische, Ungarische, Georgische, Griechische und Chinesische. Dabei betont von Habsburg, dass die jesuitische Spiritualität selbst von der *Imitatio* geprägt worden ist und die innere Erneuerung als Voraussetzung für das Apostolat aufgefasst wurde.

Nützlich ist das Verzeichnis aller bekannten gedruckten Ausgaben bis 1650 im Anhang. Noch besser wäre natürlich eine kommentierte Bibliographie mit genauen Titelbeschreibungen. In diesem Zusammenhang müsste auch überprüft werden, ob es die nicht belegten Ausgaben (L1481a, L1487b, L1488b und L1489a) überhaupt gegeben hat. Der Umfang des Buches hat es außerdem nicht erlaubt, alle gedruckten Ausgaben zu untersuchen; auf protestantischer Seite sind dies die von Johann Arndt und die englischen Übersetzungen von John Preston, William Page und John Worthington. Trotz dieser plausiblen Mängel und einigen redundanten Abschnitten füllt die besprochene Untersuchung, die als Arbeit im Rahmen eines Doktorats am St. Andrews Reformation

Studies Institute entstanden ist, eine Forschungslücke. Die vielseitige und wertvolle Studie zeigt zudem wie andere Untersuchungen der letzten Jahre und Jahrzehnte, dass die Reformation und die katholische Reform keineswegs losgelöst von der spätmittelalterlichen Zeit betrachtet werden dürfen. Gerade im Bereich der Frömmigkeit scheinen die Verbindungen besonders stark gewesen zu sein.

Christian Scheidegger, Zürich

Karine Crousaz, L'Académie de Lausanne entre humanisme et Réforme (ca. 1537–1560), Leiden/Boston: Brill, 2012 (Education and Society in the Middle Ages and Renaissance 41), XVIII & 610 p. – ISBN 978-90-04-21038-7.

L'auteure d'un très bon mémoire de Licence publié sous le titre »Erasme et le pouvoir de l'imprimerie« (Lausanne 2005), »récidive« en présentant à la communauté des seiziémistes une très belle thèse en Histoire sur un sujet qui s'imposait depuis longtemps déjà. L'Académie de Lausanne, créée au lendemain de l'annexion (1535/36) par les Bernois des régions situées autour du lac Léman, allait, au cours du XVIe s., former de nombreux jeunes gens francophones, dont une bonne partie étaient originaires de France. L'un des objectifs de cette Académie fut la formation de pasteurs pour la Romandie, sachant qu'au cours des premières années de l'occupation bernoise une grande partie du corps pastoral a dû, à défaut d'un nombre suffisant de candidats locaux, être recrutée comme à Neuchâtel et à Genève parmi des étrangers – à signaler à propos du corps pastoral genevois l'excellente étude de Scott M. Manetsch, Calvin's Company of Pastors: Pastoral Care and the Emerging Reformed Church, 1536–1609 (Oxford 2013). Qui fréquente les correspondances d'époque sait toutefois que l'Académie de Lausanne forma aussi bon nombre de jeunes gens originaires de la partie germanophone des cantons confédérés suisses. Ainsi, pendant des siècles, l'aristocratie bernoise ne manqua pas d'envoyer sa descendance à Lausanne, dont l'Académie avait le mérite d'être protestante et où, bien que l'enseignement y fût dispensé en latin, les jeunes germanophones pouvaient au contact des hôtes assurant leur entretien et par la fréquentation d'un environnement francophone, d'autres étudiants, de sermons et peut-être aussi de cours privés (voir p. 410) apprendre la langue des territoires occupés et du coup celle du royaume de France avec lequel les confédérés entretenaient depuis longtemps des relations diplomatiques complexes. Les correspondances des Amerbach (11 tt. en 14 volumes, dont l'édition a été provisoirement »arrêtée« à la mort de Bonifacius Amerbach en 1562) et de Heinrich Bullinger (dont le tome 15 comportant les lettres de l'année 1545 vient de paraître) attestent, elles aussi, l'envoi régulier à Lausanne de jeunes adolescents bâlois et zurichois.

L'Académie de Lausanne fit par le passé l'objet de plusieurs études, répertoriées dans la bibliographie exhaustive de Crousaz, sauf que celles-ci ne consacraient généralement à l'époque de la Réforme que quelques pages ou n'en traitaient que certains aspects bien définis. Le mérite incontestable du travail de Crousaz est d'avoir exploité ces travaux, et surtout d'avoir entrepris de nouvelles recherches dans des fonds d'archives conservés non seulement à Lausanne et à Berne, mais aussi ailleurs, tout en recourant également à des correspondances d'époque publiées et aux transcriptions manuscrites (réalisées en 1767 par Johannes Müller) des correspondances de Wolfgang et d'Abraham Musculus, conservées à Zofingue. Depuis la parution du travail de Crousaz, une nouvelle source importante, celle des lettres restées jusqu'ici inédites de Pierre Viret, éditées par Michael W. Bruening, a vu le jour: Epistolae Petri Vireti: The Previous Unedited Letters and a Register of Pierre Viret's Correspondence (Genève 2012).

Après avoir retracé dans son introduction l'historiographie de l'Académie de Lausanne et précisé et les sources employées et sa méthode de travail, Crousaz retrace dans un premier chapitre le contexte politique, religieux et éducatif de l'époque en soulignant l'importance de la conquête bernoise et en faisant ressortir l'impact général que les humanistes et les réformateurs exercèrent alors sur le développement de l'instruction, avant de présenter en quelques mots la situation, après l'adoption de la Réforme, des systèmes éducatifs de Bâle, Zürich, Berne et Genève. Dans un deuxième chapitre, Crousaz s'arrête à la naissance et au développement de l'Académie de Lausanne en présentant les règlements dont cette

Académie se dota et en montrant que celle-ci fut à la fois un lieu de reconversion professionnelle du clergé vaudois et de débats théologiques aux composantes politiques, permettant une confrontation avec le nouveau pouvoir en place. Ce faisant Crousaz retrace l'histoire du bras de fer qui en 1558 et 1559 opposa les professeurs de l'Académie au Magistrat bernois et la détermination dont celui-ci fit alors preuve. Dans un troisième chapitre, Crousaz étudie de plus près les finances et d'autres aspects matériels liés à la nouvelle institution. On y trouve des renseignements sur les salaires des professeurs (avec des graphiques et un tableau illustrant l'évolution de ces salaires), sur les bourses accordées aux étudiants et sur l'évolution des frais de pension (là encore de nombreux graphiques). Pour son enquête, Crousaz s'est essentiellement appuyée sur les *Ratsmanuale* conservés aux Archives de l'Etat de Berne et sur les *Comptes du baillage de Lausanne* conservés aux Archives cantonales vaudoises, ainsi que sur des correspondances d'époque, encore que la correspondance de Bullinger eût pu fournir quelques renseignements supplémentaires, en particulier sur le coût des pensions. Crousaz étudie également la question intéressante des contreparties auxquelles les jeunes s'engageaient en acceptant une bourse et s'arrête à l'infrastructure matérielle de l'école (à ses bâtiments et à sa bibliothèque), pour terminer le chapitre en se penchant sur la question du financement par les autorités des frais liés à cette institution. Le chapitre quatre est consacré aux professeurs. Crousaz passe en revue les modalités de leur recrutement, leur provenance et la durée de leur enseignement. Le chapitre cinq s'arrête aux étudiants. Il traite de la sélection des boursiers, de leur âge, de leur niveau scolaire antérieur, de leur provenance, de leur destin, pour ensuite se tourner vers les étudiants non-boursiers et examiner leur origine. Le dernier chapitre s'intéresse à l'enseignement, à son déroulement, aux horaires et aux vacances, aux programmes et aux matières enseignées (dont le grec et l'hébreu), au contrôle des connaissances, à l'exercice des disputes académiques, aux activités hors programme (telle la représentation de pièces de théâtre dans un but didactique) et enfin à l'analyse, par le biais des *Colloques* de Maturin Cordier, des exigences éthiques rattachées à l'Académie.

Le fil de la pensée de l'auteure est clair; son style agréable. Crousaz cite dans son texte ses sources à l'aide de traductions françaises élégamment élaborées, reproduisant en note le texte original latin ou allemand des passages cités: ce qui assure à la lecture confort et fluidité.

En annexe Crousaz édite plusieurs documents intéressants, entre autres des textes latins accompagnés de traductions françaises et deux lettres inédites, tous de l'enseignant Celio Secundo Curione; les *Leges scholae Lausannensis* de 1547 (également accompagnées d'une traduction française); des extraits inédits d'un dossier important, conservé aujourd'hui à la Bibliothèque nationale de France (Ms. Lat. 8641; digitalisé par Gallica), provenant à l'origine des archives de l'enseignant Jean Ribit – une source dont Louis Junod et Henri Meylan avaient déjà en 1947 publié deux pièces dans leur ouvrage intitulé »L'Académie de Lausanne au XVIe siècle: Leges scholae Lausannensis 1547. Lettres et documents inédits«; un tableau synchronique des six principaux postes de l'Académie; une liste chronologique des professeurs, pasteurs et baillis de Lausanne pour la période allant de 1536 à 1560; et une annexe comportant sur une douzaine de pages des notices biographiques consacrées à des »personnages importants«. Deux petites remarques à propos de cette dernière annexe: Gessner quitta probablement Lausanne déjà en août ou au début du mois de septembre 1540 (voir Die Amerbachkorrespondenz, t. XI/2, p. 988); et à propos d'Eustache Du Quesnoy, un absent non seulement de cet annexe, mais curieusement aussi de l'index (alors qu'il est bel et bien mentionné aux p. 528s. par exemple), on se reportera à Heinrich Bullinger Briefwechsel, t. XV, p. 253s.

Je souhaiterais souligner ici l'importance de l'une de ces annexes. En 1937 Louis Junod publia le tome 2 d'un ouvrage intitulé de façon prometteuse: »Album studiosorum Academiae lausannensis, 1537–1837, dressé d'après les registres officiels et d'autres documents«. Seul ce tome, consacré aux années 1602 à 1837, vit le jour. Personne n'a osé depuis s'attaquer à la tâche titanesque et délicate de la reconstruction d'un inventaire (qui restera forcément lacunaire) des jeunes qui étudièrent à Lausanne entre 1537 et 1601. Par son annexe 9, d'une vingtaine de pages, une liste des boursiers financés par le bailli de Lausanne, Crousaz a fourni une première contribution non négligeable à la reconstitution de cet *Album* fictif. L'idéal serait la création, sur un site web accessible à tous, d'une banque de données nourrie déjà, pour commencer, de tous les noms identifiés par Crousaz – une banque de données que les seiziémistes, et surtout les éditeurs de correspondances, pourraient alimenter en faisant parvenir à un webmaster, par le biais de mails au format prédéfini (dont il suffirait de remplir certaines cases), les précisions telles que le nom de l'étudiant, la date attestée du séjour lausannois de ce dernier et la source à l'origine du renseignement.

A signaler enfin, à propos de l'appel adressé par les Bernois en 1559 à Andreas Hyperius et du séjour lausannois, en mars 1550, du Portugais Luis Nuñez (qu'il ne faut pas confondre avec Pedro Nuñez, qui enseigna plus tard le Grec à Lausanne), les publications suivantes: Andreas Gerhard Hyperius: Briefe, 1530–1563, éd. par Gerhard Krause (Tübingen 1981); et Francisco de Enzinas: Epistolario, éd. par Ignacio J. García Pinilla (Genève 1995). Peut-être qu'une consultation et exploitation du livre de raison de Jean Hollard ou Houllard (1491–1569) conservé dans les archives régionales de Maastrich aux Pays-Bas, une source dont la redécouverte a été signalée par Frank Claessen (»Surprises dans un livre de raison, le *Liber Houlardi*«, dans: Revue historique Vaudoise, t. 119 [2011], p. 228–257), permettra-t-elle non seulement de préciser le prénom de l'étudiant signalé par Crousaz à la p. 177, mais aussi d'obtenir d'autres informations relatives à l'Académie de Lausanne et à ses étudiants.

Pour terminer, il reste à espérer qu'il ne faille pas à nouveau attendre un demi-siècle avant que quelqu'un ne poursuive l'histoire de cette Académie entre 1560 et 1600: une période encore moins étudiée (voir p. 126) que celle que Crousaz vient de traiter avec succès. Cela permettrait entre autres d'appréhender les différences majeures entre l'Académie d'avant la crise de 1558/59 et celle postérieure à cette crise et contemporaine à la nouvelle académie de Genève, créée quant à elle comme par hasard en 1559.

Reinhard Bodenmann, Zurich

Registres du Consistoire de Genève au temps de Calvin, Tome IV (1548), avec extraits des Registres du Conseil, 1548–1550, hg. von Isabella M. Watt und Thomas A. Lambert, Genf: Droz, 2007 (Tra-

vaux d'Humanisme et Renaissance 429), XXVI & 294 S. – ISBN 978-2-600-01169-3.

Registres du Consistoire de Genève au temps de Calvin, Tome V (20 février 1550 – 5 février 1551), hg. von Thomas A. Lambert und Isabella M. Watt, Genf: Droz, 2010 (Travaux d'Humanisme et Renaissance 468), XXXIV & 372 S. – ISBN 978-2-600-01429-8.

Registres du Consistoire de Genève au temps de Calvin, Tome VI (19 février 1551 – 4 février 1552), hg. von Robert M. Kingdon et al., Genf: Droz, 2012 (Travaux d'Humanisme et Renaissance 496), XXXII & 280 S. – ISBN 978-2-600-01567-7.

Über die von Robert M. Kingdon unter aufwendigen und mühevollen Vorarbeiten ins Leben gerufene und von ihm geleitete Edition der »Registres du Consistoire de Gèneve au temps de Calvin« ist Mehreres an verschiedener Stelle geschrieben worden. Zuletzt hat Robert M. Kingdon auch selbst über die Entstehung und die Arbeit an der Edition berichtet sowie eine Begründung für das Projekt gegeben, und zwar in seinem zusammen mit Thomas A. Lambert herausgegebenen und postum erschienenen Buch »Reforming Geneva: Discipline, Faith and Anger in Calvin's Geneva« (Genf 2012), Kapitel 1: »The Genesis of the Consistory Project« (ebd., S. 1–8). Man vergleiche auch die Einleitung von Thomas A. Lambert und Isabella M. Watt zum ersten Band, der im Jahr 1996 erschien. Deshalb sei hier auf allgemeine Bemerkungen über die Edition verzichtet. Aber auch eine Wiedergabe persönlicher Schicksale nach den Akten soll hier nicht erfolgen. Vieles kann in der grundlegenden und ausführlichen Darstellung von Walther Köhler (Zürcher Ehegericht und Genfer Konsistorium, Bd. 2, Leipzig 1942, 540–674) nachgelesen werden, wo auch juristische Zusammenhänge erörtert werden. Hier seien vielmehr kurze Notizen zum zeitgeschichtlichen Horizont und zu Genfer Ereignissen angesprochen, die auch in den Einführungen zu den einzelnen Bänden zu finden sind.

Die in den drei zu besprechenden Bänden edierten Archivalien umfassen die Zeiträume 1548 und Februar 1550 bis Februar 1552. Für Band 4 ist ein Umstand zu erwähnen, auf den schon Peter Opitz in seiner Besprechung dieses Bandes (in: Zeitschrift für Kirchengeschichte 122 [2011], 393f.) aufmerksam machte: »Er deckt das Jahr 1548 ab, genauer: den Zeitraum vom 16. Februar bis zum 15. November 1548, dem Zeitpunkt der Suspendierung des Sekretärs Jean-Louis Favre. Die Lücke, welche das Fehlen der Protokolle seines Nachfolgers Jean de Ripha hinterlässt (November 1548 bis Februar 1550), haben die Herausgeber mit Auszügen aus den Ratsprotokollen dieser Zeit, welche sich auf Angelegenheiten des Konsistoriums beziehen, nach besten Möglichkeiten zu füllen versucht.« In Band 4 werden – wie auch aus dessen von Thomas A. Lambert verfasster Einführung hervorgeht – Dokumente aus einem Jahr präsentiert, in dem die Niederlage der Protestanten im Schmalkaldischen Krieg (April 1547) noch nicht lange zurücklag und das Augsburger Interim durch die Aufnahme in den Reichsabschied vom 30. Juni 1548 gesetzlich in Kraft getreten ist. Calvin hat gegen das Interim schriftlich protestiert, »verbunden mit einem Ratschlag, wie die christliche Kirche in Wahrheit befriedet und reformiert werden könnte« (Peter Opitz, Leben und Werk Johannes Calvins, Göttingen 2009, 136). Des Weiteren näherten Calvin und Heinrich Bullinger sich in den Jahren 1547 und 1548 in ihrer Abendmahlsauffassung immer mehr aneinander an, und im Mai 1549 kam es zur Unterzeichnung des *Consensus Tigurinus*, den man als die höchste Leistung der Schweizer Theologie im 16. Jahrhundert ansieht. Wie nun der Einleitung zu Band 4 weiter zu entnehmen ist, brach in Genf selbst im Jahr 1548 eine Kontroverse über die Taufnamen aus und vergiftete die Beziehungen zwischen den Pfarrern und den Gemeindemitgliedern (s. Bd. 4, S. XII).

Der in Band 5 dokumentierte Zeitraum vom 20. Februar 1550 bis zum 5. Februar 1551 ist geprägt von drei Ereignissen, wie der von Thomas A. Lambert geschriebenen *Introduction* unter Verweis auf Theodor Bezas *Vita Calvini* entnommen werden kann: Von der Entscheidung, die Pfarrer auf Hausbesuche zu schicken, um vor dem österlichen Abendmahl des Jahres 1550 jedes Gemeindemitglied in Glaubensfragen zu prüfen; von der Verkündigung eines Edikts, dass Feste nur noch an Sonntagen gefeiert werden dürfen; und von der Publikation von Calvins *De scandalis*, einer Auseinandersetzung mit Vorwürfen seitens einiger Humanisten (man könnte zahlreiche weitere Publikationen dieses Zeitraums hinzufügen, die etwa in der Bibliographie »Bibliotheca Calviniana« verzeichnet sind, so zum Beispiel etliche Kommentare zu Büchern des Neuen

Testaments oder *De vita hominis christiani*, ein Separatdruck des 21. Kapitels aus der *Institutio christianae religionis*). Ferner wird in der Einleitung unter anderem darauf aufmerksam gemacht, dass dieser Band der erste in derjenigen Ära ist, die man als »le premier refuge« betrachtet, in der eine Genfer Reaktion auf die Zunahme von Flüchtlingen zu beobachten war, die auch einen Niederschlag in den Konsistorialprotokollen gefunden hat, wenn auch nicht in vergleichbarer Intensität wie in den Jahren zuvor (s. die Einleitung, S. XVIII).

Band 6, der die Protokolle aus dem Zeitraum vom 19. Februar 1551 bis zum 4. Februar 1552 umfasst, setzt mit einem von Lee Palmer Wandel verfassten Vorwort ein, in welchem sie die Verdienste Robert M. Kingdons um die Edition würdigt. Die Einleitung zu diesem Band, geschrieben von Jeffrey R. Watt, trägt den Titel: »Genève et le Consistoire en 1551«. Unter den in Band 6 dokumentierten Ereignissen ragt der Prozess gegen Jérôme (Hieronymus) Bolsec heraus (s. dazu Bd. 6, S. IX–XII). Als Schwerpunkte dieses Bandes kommen hinzu der Widerstand gegen die Genfer Pfarrer (ebd., S. XII–XIV) sowie die Reform der Sitten, denn Prozesse gegen Personen, die weiter dem Katholizismus anhingen, waren im Abnehmen begriffen, da diese zumeist die Stadt verlassen hatten; aber auch deshalb, weil die Zahl derjenigen, die sich vor dem Konsistorium erklären mussten, zunehmend aus Menschen bestand, die aus Glaubensgründen nach Genf geflohen waren (s. ebd., S. XV). Weiter geht es in der Einführung um »La paillardise et le blasphème« (ebd., S. XVII–XIX) sowie um »Disputes conjugiales, querelles et réconciliation« (S. XIX–XXII). Für den genannten Zeitraum ist außerdem der Druck des *Consensus Tigurinus* im März 1551 in Zürich und in Genf zu vermerken, der ein »endgültiges enges Zusammenrücken der beiden Städte« bewirkte (Opitz, Leben und Werk, 126).

Die Einrichtung der Bände entspricht dem hohen Standard des Verlagshauses Droz. Nach dem *Preface* folgt eine *Introduction*, danach werden *Sources et Bibliographie* aufgeführt. Es schließt sich die Wiedergabe der Protokolle an. Die Transkription der mittelfranzösischen Akten erfolgte unter behutsamen Modernisierungen gemäß den Regeln für die Edition von Texten des 16. Jahrhunderts, wie man etwa der *Introduction* zu Band 5 (ebd., S. XXI, mit Anm. 82) entnehmen kann. In den Texten selbst finden sich einige wenige nicht aufgelöste Abkürzungen (led. = ledit; lad. = ladite), die wohl auch von einem ungeübten Leser des Mittelfranzösischen recht leicht mit Hilfe eines größeren Wörterbuchs erschlossen werden können. Die Texte sind annotiert bzw. kommentiert. Die Kommentare zu den vor das Konsistorium zitierten Personen und Zeugen *(tesmoings)* sind häufig sehr ausführlich, was mitunter dadurch begünstigt wird, dass das Genfer Bürgerbuch (»Le livre des Bourgeois«) und das Einwohnerbuch (»Livre des habitants«) erhalten geblieben (und auch ediert) sind. Die Bände enden mit einem *Glossaire*, einem *Index des metiers*, einem *Index des sujets* und einem *Index des noms de personnes et de lieux*.

Schließlich soll in gebotener Kürze noch auf einige Akzentuierungen in zwei früher erschienenen Rezensionen zur Edition der Konsistorialprotokolle aufmerksam gemacht werden. Im Jahr 1996 war der erste Band der »Registres du Consistoire« publiziert worden, die mit dem Jahr 1542 einsetzen. Wie William E. Monter in seiner Rezension schrieb, dokumentiert dieser Band einen »abrupt shift from matrimonial court to early instrument of confessionalization« (in: The Catholic Historical Review 90/3 [2004], 550; mit Verweis auf ebd. 83/2 [1997], 332), da die Einwohner Genfs von dem Konsistorium mehrheitlich in ihrer Kenntnis der christlichen Lehre und in ihrem Verhältnis zur Reformation geprüft wurden. William E. Monter schloss seine Besprechung mit dem Satz: »Further volumes will trace the Consistory's subsequent evolution from a doctrinal tribunal to a morals tribunal« (ebd. 83/2 [1997], 333). Man vergleiche damit etwa die Ausführungen von Philip Benedict (Christ's Churches Purely Reformed: A Social History of Calvinism, New Haven 2002, bcs. S. 97), dic wohl, zumindest nach Ansicht der Rezensentin, gleichfalls auf eine mit den Jahren erfolgte Zunahme von Verhandlungen in moralischen gegenüber religiösen Angelegenheiten hindeuten. Einen weiteren Akzent setzte Peter Opitz in der oben schon erwähnten Rezension des vierten Bandes (in: Zeitschrift für Kirchengeschichte 122 [2011], 394): »Über weite Strecken hat das Konsistorium aber wohl weniger als Instanz zur Durchsetzung rigoroser, dem Volksempfinden fremder protestantischer Moralnormen gewirkt, denn als Schlichtungsinstanz im Dienst des Ausgleichs und der Versöhnung im Rahmen der geltenden Rechtstradition.« Gewiss wird es zu den Aufgaben der künftigen Forschung gehören, anhand der fortschreitenden Erschließung der Konsistorialakten sich mit dem Genfer Konsistorium zur Zeit Calvins zu beschäftigen.

Judith Steiniger, Zürich

Jon Balserak, Establishing the Remnant Church in France: Calvin's Lectures on the Minor Prophets, 1556–1559, Leiden: Brill, 2011 (Brill's Series in Church History 50), 224 p. – ISBN 978-90-04-19144-0.

John Calvin's lectures on the minor prophets between 1556–1559 are here shown, persuasively, to be much more than mere exegesis. In this volume Balserak makes a powerful case for seeing Calvin as – in his own estimation – a prophet.

More specifically, in the chapters which follow the introduction, Balserak unpacks Calvin's lectures on the minor prophets by first spelling out Calvin's audience and the context of the lectures (chapter 2); then he turns to an evaluation of Calvin's self-understanding as authoritative interpreter and Reformer (chapter 3). From that point B. shows from Calvin's lectures precisely how he exegeted those writings (chapter 4) and how those texts lead Calvin to the conclusion that it is his »prophetic« task to overthrow the Roman Catholic church and establish a new Remnant church (chapter 5).

Balserak brings the book to a close with a brief »Concluding Thoughts: Calvin's Vision of the Church in This Age« (chapter 6). He offers as well a bibliography and the requisite index.

Balsarek states his thesis clearly and concisely, writing: »...Calvin reads the Minor Prophets as a mirror of his own day. Accordingly, he sees the French evangelicals as the faithful remnant and himself as the prophet who, like Hosea, Micah and Zechariah before him, condemns the idolatrous church and seeks to call out from it, and to comfort, the tiny remnant of the faithful, whose lives are so difficult given their present circumstances« (p. 2–3).

The entire book's purpose and goal is to prove this thesis correct. Once more, Balsarek is, in this reviewer's estimation, completely successful in so doing. Alongside, though, providing proof for his case, Balserak also opens a window on Calvin's life and thought unavailable to those less familiar with his lectures and lesser known tractates and books. For instance: »When in 1544 the pope rebuked the emperor for daring to presume that he was able, or possessed the authority, to call a general council ... without consulting his holiness, Calvin wrote this reply *Admonitio paterna Pauli III. Romani pontificis ad invictissimum.* It is full of sharp criticism, name-calling, and sarcasm« (p. 43).

Balserak is so familiar with the whole range of Calvin's works that he draws from every genre (from the Institutes to the Commentaries to the Lectures to the Tractates to the Polemical Works and everything else) in bolstering his case. And he does it by citing the Latin or French originals. If ever a historian/theologian truly appreciated the Reformation cry *Ad fontes*, it is Balsarek as demonstrated by his reliance not on translations but originals.

Balserak includes, therefore, a great number of direct quotations as evidence for his thesis. Indeed, page after page and paragraph following paragraph include citations such as: »There are some today who say: ›There's Calvin who makes himself a prophet, when he says that one will know that there is a prophet among us. He's talking about himself.‹ Is he a prophet? Well, since it is the doctrine of God that I am announcing, I have to use this language« (p. 90).

But the volume is not just a series of quotations strung together »like pearls on a string«. Our author combines these citations with incisive observations concerning their significance and meaning for Calvin's program of establishing the »true church« in the French speaking world. To wit: »... Calvin must have seen himself as possessing a remarkable, God given authority; indeed the authority of a prophet and the authority which moved him to take radical steps to endeavor to preserve the church throughout Europe, and additionally and especially, in his beloved France« (p. 107). And again: »... Calvin was under the conviction that the age in which he lived was like that of the prophets and that he and his small band were the modern day equivalent of the remnant of the faithful – those who worship God in truth but who dwelled amongst a corrupt body whose worship was characterized by blatant idolatry. Of this identity between his own and the prophets's age, Calvin was absolutely convinced as were other of the Swiss (like Zwingli, for instance)« (p. 211).

However, a careful reading of Balserak's contribution does reveal a number of typographical errors which need to be addressed in future editions.

Balserak is to be congratulated for his incredible work and his important contribution to our understanding of the great Reformer of Geneva. All those engaged in Calvin research will benefit from a reading of it.

Jim West, Petros, TN, USA

Epistolae Petri Vireti: The Previously Unedited Letters and a Register of Pierre Viret's Correspondence, ed. Michael W. Bruening, Geneva: Droz, 2012 (Travaux d'Humanisme et Renaissance 494), 654 p. – ISBN 978-2-600-01553-0.

The larger part of Pierre Viret's correspondence had already been published either in the *Calvini opera*, Herminjard's *Correspondance des réformateurs*, or in Barnaud's *Quelques lettres inédits de Pierre Viret*. Now the remaining twenty percent have found their capable editor in Michael Bruening. The chronological register in the back of this book gives an overview of all of Viret's correspondence providing for each of the 759 letters archival locations, publication details for the original text or translation, the incipit, and – if necessary – corrections and additions.

The 155 letters edited here date from 1541 to 1565, fifty of them are addressed to Viret, the rest is authored by him. They expand our knowledge of his life, family, and work. We can follow him from Lausanne, via Geneva to Nîmes and Lyon. The letters inform about the progress, difficulties, and conflicts in the city and classe of Lausanne, and during the last few years, about developments in France. Apparently, Viret is glad to report the steadily growing number of participants in the Lord's Supper and the growth of the Lausanne Academy.

More than half of these letters were exchanged between Viret and Guillaume Farel. This will make it possible now to value the better the mutual friendship they had apart from their shared friendship with John Calvin. These letters contain the usual news and rumors regarding the Council of Trent, the reformation in Frisia, developments in Germany, their publications, etc. Other important correspondents of Viret in this edition are the magistrates and ministers of Bern, the ministers of Lausanne, Rudolph Gwalther, and Heinrich Bullinger. As can be expected, these letters shed light on several key issues then in dispute: Eucharistic theology, predestination, the role of the secular magistrate especially of Bern, and ecclesiastical discipline. Eventually the debates about predestination and ecclesiastical discipline – to which the 25 letters in the Appendix are related – led to the banishment of Viret from Bernese territory.

For this edition of Viret's correspondence Bruening mainly follows the editorial principles of the new edition of Calvin's works and letters. The Latin letters are prefaced by an English summary, however not the letters in French. The line numbering is lacking too. However, for all letters footnotes provide a wealth of detailed information by identifying persons, explaining relationships and the important historical facts mentioned. Sometimes they provide corrections to literature; references to archival sources are included as well. The short biographical notice in the front of the book is helpfully referenced to the edited letters.

In almost every publication, some minor points can be criticized. The handful of tiny typographical errors is not worth mentioning. Sometimes one could wish for more fully elaborated Biblical allusions. Footnotes occasionally come too late. For example in note 4 to Ep. 152 Bruening informs the reader about the fact that Gwalther understood French, though this was already apparent from Ep. 23 on p. 129. The index fully lists personal and geographical names as well as titles of books. Unfortunately, it includes only a few keywords. For example, »marriage« has no entry, but compare Ep. 75. Going through this edition one soon gets the impression that the deacons mentioned hold an office different from the Genevan deacons, but more like the reformed deacons in mid-sixteenth-century France. However, the index contains no relevant entry and one has to wait for clarification until p. 484.

This last example shows how this edition can make us the better aware of the fact that the reformation in the Pays de Vaud, however intimately connected to Genevan theology it may have been, is not identical to the Genevan reformation, nor are Pierre Viret's ideas regarding church order to John Calvin's. Michael Bruening has served us very well with his excellent addition to the ongoing publication of the correspondence of Swiss reformers. One can only hope that these resources will once be fully searchable in something like an integrated Swiss Reformation Letter database on the internet.

Kees de Wildt, Dordrecht

Erik de Boer, The Genevan School of the Prophets: The congrégations of the Company of Pastors and their Influence in 16th Century Europe, Genf: Droz, 2012 (Travaux d'Humanisme et Renaissance 512), 330 S. – ISBN 978-2-600-01611-7.

Der vorliegende Band, der einer langjährigen Beschäftigung des Autors mit der Geschichte der *congrégations* in Genf erwachsen ist, ist in drei Teile gegliedert. Im ersten Teil lernt der Leser die Natur der Zusammenkünfte kennen, die ab 1536 jeden Freitag stattfanden und bei denen sich die Geistlichen der Stadt Genf sowie der ihrem Herrschaftsgebiet angehörenden Dörfer trafen, um die Heilige Schrift zu studieren. Nach dem Modell der *lectio continua* wurden bei den *congrégations* ganze biblische Bücher gelesen und kommentiert, wobei ein Teilnehmer jeweils eine Passage erläuterte, um dann das Wort den anderen zu überlassen, die seine Auslegung ergänzten (47f.). Auf diese Weise wurden die Pfarrer einer steten Weiterbildung unterzogen, von der sie in ihrem Amt als »Propheten« – d.h. Prediger des Wortes Gottes – nur profitieren konnten (vgl. den Titel des Bandes »The Genevan School of the Prophets«).

Anders als in Zürich – wo die gemeinsame Auslegung biblischer Schriften im Rahmen der sogenannten »Prophezei« in lateinischer Sprache erfolgte – wurden die *congrégations* auf Französisch durchgeführt, was ab 1541 auch die Teilnahme von »Laien« ermöglichte. Die Frage nach Präsenz und Partizipation der »Laien« wird im vierten Kapitel anhand einer besonders gut dokumentierten *congrégation* erläutert. Dabei handelt es sich um das Treffen vom 16. Oktober 1551, an dem Jérôme Bolsec erstmals die calvinische Prädestinationslehre öffentlich kritisierte. Auf die Bolsec-Kontroverse konzentriert sich auch das fünfte Kapitel. Darin wird dargestellt, wie eine außerordentliche *congrégation* abgehalten wurde (18. Dezember 1551), um die von Bolsec aufgeworfenen Fragen zu klären. Die Resultate der Diskussion wurden von Calvin in seiner Schrift *De aeterna Dei praedestinatione* (1552) zusammengefasst, welche nicht zufällig als »consensus« der Genfer Pastoren in Sachen Prädestinationslehre präsentiert wurde. Erst 1562 erschien auch der vollständige Text der *congrégation* in französischer Fassung (125–127).

Dass der Fall Bolsec im Rahmen einer *congrégation* behandelt wurde, macht deutlich, zu welchem Zweck diese Treffen in erster Linie eingerichtet worden waren: die Bewahrung der reinen Lehre und der Eintracht unter den Pastoren in Genf (39; 185). Darüber hinaus dienten sie aber auch der Prüfung von Kandidaten zum Pastorenamt (62–66). Schließlich stellt De Boer einen engen Zusammenhang zwischen den *congrégations* und der Auslegungstätigkeit Calvins fest, dessen Kommentare zu einem bestimmten biblischen Buch häufig in direktem Anschluss an die Behandlung desselben Buches in den *congrégations* erschienen. Ließ Calvin tatsächlich – wie De Boer vermutet – die Ergebnisse der Diskussionen mit seinen Kollegen in seine Kommentare einfließen, so dürfen Letztere nicht nur als das Werk eines Einzelnen, sondern sollten vielmehr als Resultat gemeinsamer theologischer Arbeit sowie als Ausdruck eines exegetischen Konsenses unter den Genfer Pastoren betrachtet werden.

Während der ganze zweite Teil des vorliegenden Bandes der Frage nach dem chronologischen Zusammenhang zwischen der Auslegeordnung in den *congrégations* und dem Erscheinen der Kommentare Calvins gewidmet ist, geht De Boer im dritten Teil auf den Einfluss des Genfer Modells auf die Praxis reformierter Gemeinden in Frankreich, Großbritannien und der Niederlande ein. In all diesen Ländern wurden zwar regelmäßige Treffen unter den Pfarrern einer territorialen Einheit zum Zwecke des gemeinsamen Bibelstudiums abgehalten, aber diese Praxis erwies sich aus unterschiedlichen Gründen als relativ kurzlebig. Nur in Genf pflegte man sie – mit einigen Veränderungen – weiter bis ins 19. Jahrhundert hinein.

Im vorliegenden Band gelingt es Erik de Boer, Entstehung, Natur und Entwicklung der Genfer *congrégations* auf detaillierte und klare Weise zu schildern und somit ein Thema zu beleuchten, das bislang kaum beachtet wurde. Dabei erweist er sich einmal mehr als profunder Kenner und passionierter Erforscher der Geschichte des reformierten Protestantismus.

Luca Baschera, Zürich

Matthias Freudenberg, Aleida Siller (Hg.), Was ist dein einiger Trost? Der Heidelberger Katechismus in der Urfassung, Neukirchen-Vluy: Neukirchener Theologie, 2012, 64 S. – ISBN 978-3-7887-2595-2.

Matthias Freudenberg (Hg.), Heidelberger Katechismus-Brevier, Neukirchen-Vluy: Neukirchener Theologie, 2012, 64 S. – ISBN 978-3-7887-2594-5.

Paolo Ricca, La fede cristiana evangelica: Un commento al Catechismo di Heidelberg, Turin: Claudiana, 2012, 384 S. – ISBN 978-88-7016-668-2.

Karla Apperloo-Boersma, Herman Selderhuis (Hg.), Macht des Glaubens: 450 Jahre Heidelberger Katechismus, Göttingen: Vandenhoek & Ruprecht, 2012, 460 S. – ISBN 978-3-525-55048-9.

Martin Heimbucher, Christoph Schneider-Harpprecht, Aleida Siller (Hg.), Zugänge zum Heidelberger Katechismus: Geschichte, Themen, Unterricht. Ein Handbuch für die Praxis mit Unterrichtsentwürfen auf CD-ROM, Neukirchen-Vluyn : Neukirchener Theologie, 2012, 255 S. – ISBN 978-3-7887-2596-9.

Georg Plasger, Glauben heute mit dem Heidelberger Katechismus, Göttingen: Vandenhoek & Ruprecht, 2012, 212 S. – ISBN 978-3-525-55044-1.

Christoph Strohm, Johannes Ehmann, Albert de Lange (Hg.), Heidelberg und die Kurpfalz, Leipzig: Evangelische Verlagsanstalt, 2013 (Orte der Reformation 6), 96 S. – ISBN 978-3-374-03144-3.

Evangelische Theologie 72/6 (2012). – ISSN 0014-3502.

Im Jahr 2013 jähren sich zum 450. Mal zwei große kirchengeschichtliche Ereignisse, welche die westliche Christenheit der Neuzeit bis heute maßgeblich beeinflusst haben: der Abschluss des

Konzils von Trient und die Veröffentlichung des Heidelberger Katechismus (HK). Während dem Tridentinum eine bewundernswerte Neuordnung der katholischen Kirche gelang, wurde der »Heidelberger« der wohl weltweit am häufigsten gelesene reformierte Bekenntnistext. An vielen Orten im In- und Ausland wurde an das Erscheinen des HK erinnert. Insbesondere sei hier das Anfang Mai von der Universität Heidelberg unter großer internationalen Beteiligung organisierte Symposium zum Thema »Profil und Wirkung des Heidelberger Katechismus« erwähnt. Das Jubiläumsjahr 2013 brachte nicht nur Kongresse, sondern auch viel beachtete Ausstellungen sowie eine beträchtliche Anzahl neuer Editionen und Studien. Die folgende Sammelbesprechung soll über mehrere Neuveröffentlichungen und ihre Bedeutung für die aktuelle Forschung informieren. Bei einem Jahrbuch wie der Zwingliana kommt das verhältnismäßig große Interesse am HK nicht überraschend. Das liegt zum Teil an dem eminenten historischen Einfluss des HK auf die reformierte Konfessionsbildung, aber auch daran, dass die Entstehung des Katechismus ein deutlicher Beweis für die Ausstrahlung der schweizerischen Reformation darstellt. Denn wie bereits Kaspar Olevian, einer der Mitverfasser des Werkes, in einem Brief vom 14. April 1563 an Bullinger schrieb: »Gewiss, wenn irgendeine Klarheit in ihm sich findet, so haben wir das zu einem guten Teil Dir und den hellen Geistern der Schweiz zu verdanken.«

Matthias Freudenberg hat sich mit zwei unscheinbaren Büchlein verdient gemacht, die jedoch in Kirchgemeinden, Schulen und in der Erwachsenenbildung zweifelsohne helfen werden, die komplexe theologische Welt des Katechismus zu verstehen. *Was ist dein einiger Trost?* bietet eine Übertragung des ursprünglichen Textes von 1563 in eine hochdeutsche Fassung. Dabei werden die Wortwahl und der Satzbau so weit wie möglich beibehalten. Leider hat der Herausgeber die verdienstvolle Edition nicht mit dem Abdruck der beigegebenen Bibelstellen ausgestattet, sodass man sie mühsam in anderen Ausgaben suchen muss. Erfreulich ist allerdings, dass dem Katechismustext die wichtige (aber in neueren Ausgaben ausgelassene) Vorrede von Kurfürst Friedrich III. vorangestellt ist, die der Zweck des Katechismus erklärt. Das *Heidelberger Katechismus-Brevier* befragt einzelne Aussagen des Katechismus auf ihre gegenwärtige Bedeutung hin. Diese wurden mit biblischen Versen und neueren Liedstrophen aus dem Evangelischen Gesangbuch (Ausgabe Rheinland-Westfalen-Lippe) sowie einer Kurzerklärung versehen, um dadurch das eigene Nach- und Weiterdenken anzuregen. Ein ebensolches Ziel verfolgt Paolo Ricca mit seinem Band *La fede cristiana evangelica: Un commento al Catechismo di Heidelberg*. Eine knappe Einführung orientiert über die Abfassung sowie über den theologischen und pädagogischen Charakter des Katechismus. Dabei dürfte der Hinweis auf eine bisher unbekannte italienische Übersetzung des frühen 17. Jahrhunderts (S. 16, Anm. 17) als Erkenntnisgewinn gelten. Es folgen Kommentare unterschiedlicher Länge zu allen 129 Fragen des Katechismus. Ricca ist eine plausible Darstellung der Theologie des »Heidelberger« gelungen, als deren zentrales und integrierendes Motiv die Dankbarkeit gedeutet wird. Sie überzeugt durch profunde Quellenkenntnis, nachvollziehbare Interpretation und stringente Gedankenführung.

Im Jubiläumsjahr fand eine Ausstellung an drei Standorten statt: im Schloss Heidelberg, im Kurpfälzischen Museum der Stadt Heidelberg und im Paleis Het Loo in Apeldoorn (NL). *Macht des Glaubens: 450 Jahre Heidelberger Katechismus* ist der von Karla Apperloo-Boersma und Herman Selderhuis herausgegebene Katalog zur gleichnamigen Ausstellung. Die Gliederung des Werks, das gleichzeitig auf Deutsch, Englisch und Niederländisch erscheint, ist klar und übersichtlich. Wie bei solchen Katalogen üblich und von der Sache her fast schon unvermeidlich, bilden die wissenschaftlichen Beiträge den ersten Teil. Der zweite Teil umfasst die Abbildungen und Beschreibungen von nahezu allen Exponaten der Ausstellungen in Heidelberg und Apeldoorn. Die wissenschaftlichen Beiträge im ersten Teil sind von Fachleuten verfasst und obwohl sie sich an ein breites Publikum wenden, sind sie auch für den akademischen Bereich geeignet. Sie konzentrieren sich auf drei Themen. Begonnen wird mit »Geschichte und Theologie des HK«. Dieser Abschnitt enthält gehaltvolle Aufsätze: »Die weltweite Ausstrahlung des HK« (Herman Selderhuis); »Die Ursprünge der Dreiteilung des HK« (Lyle Bierma); »Der HK und die konfessionellen Debatte des 16. Jh.s« (Irene Dingel); »Die Verbreitung des HK in gedruckter Form« (August den Hollander); »Der HK, Schweizer Wurzel, Schweizer Verbreitung« (Peter Opitz); »Hercules Collins und sein ›An Orthodox Catechism‹« (Michael Haykin / Steve Weaver). Man kann nur staunen, was in einem wahrlich beackerten Feld doch noch Neues herauskommen kann. Im zweiten Abschnitt »Die Pfalz, Heidelberg und der HK« richten die Verfasser ihre Aufmerksamkeit auf die Erkundung des breiten Kontexts der Kurpfalz im 16. Jahrhundert, vom höfischen Leben bis zur Entwicklung der Stadt Heidelberg zu einem international bedeutenden Zentrum der Wissenschaft. Die Aufsätze behandeln Themen wie »Strategien des Konfessionswechsels im 16. Jh.« (Frank Engehausen); »Der HK im Kontext des Calvinismus des 16. und 17. Jh.s.« (Christoph Strohm); »Der HK in seinem Territorium« (Johannes Ehmann); »Die Heidelberger Hofkapelle zwischen Gotteslob und fürstlicher Repräsentation« (Klaus Winkler); »Kurfürst Friedrich IV: Politik und Lebenslust in der Kurpfalz um 1600« (Frieder Hepp); »Kurpfalz und Universität zur Zeit des HK« (Eike Wolgast); »Astrologiekritik und reformierte Theologie in Heidelberg« (Barbara Mahlmann-Bauer). Die erzielten Ergebnisse sind zwar nicht ganz neu, aber noch nie so stringent und präzise ausgearbeitet worden. In den Niederlanden fand und findet der HK Beachtung, vielleicht sogar mehr Beachtung als in deutschsprachigen Ländern, wie der dritte Abschnitt »Der HK in den Niederlanden« deutlich dokumentiert. In den Beiträgen von Arie Baars (»Eine kurze Geschichte der Katechismuspredigt in den Niederlanden«), Wim Verboom (»Katechismus-Unterricht in den Niederlanden«); Johan ter Molen (»Das Haus Oranien-Nassau: Kunst und Religion«); Paul Rem (»Ehrengestühl für das Haus Oranien-Nassau in den Kirchen der Niederlande«) kommt nicht nur die große Verbreitung des HK zum Ausdruck, sondern wird den Lesenden zugleich ein Stück Kirchen- und Kulturgeschichte jenes Landes geboten. Der Band besticht nicht nur durch seinen Reichtum an wissenschaftlichen Beiträgen, sondern auch durch die Schönheit seiner Ikonographie und die umfangreichen Kommentare, die von einem Team anerkannter Experten von hoher wissenschaftlichen Kompetenz verfasst wurden. Bilder sind ja schwieriger zu deuten als Texte und die rund 450 Abbildungen im zweiten Teil des Katalogs sind überreichlich. Sie fordern den Leser auf, Religion und Politik in Mitteleuropa in der Frühen Neuzeit quer zu etablierten Deutungen, zu Chronologie und Epochenlogik auf eigene Faust zu entdecken. Wer sich verirrt, findet wieder Halt im Text durch die knappen aber präzisen Bildlegenden. Schließlich enthält der Band eine umfassende Literaturliste zum HK, ein detailliertes Personen- und Ortsregister sowie ein knappes Sachregister, die eine enorme Hilfe für die Benutzer und Benutzerinnen darstellen. Niemals zuvor hat der »Heidelberger« eine vergleichbar gründliche und umfassende theologische sowie historische und kunsthistorische Bearbeitung erfahren. Wer die aktuelle Diskussion über den HK verstehen will, dem sei der zum Standardwerk tendierende Band sehr empfohlen.

Für die Union Evangelischer Kirchen in der EKD, den Reformierten Bund und die Evangelische Landeskirche in Baden, war das HK-Jubiläum der Anlass, ein »Handbuch für die Praxis« in Angriff zu nehmen, das den Titel *Zugänge zum Heidelberger Katechismus* trägt. Der Band besticht durch das breite Themenspektrum, das eine knappe inhaltliche Zusammenfassung unmöglich macht. Sehr gelungen erscheint der interdisziplinäre Blick auf den Katechismus. Neben drei persönlichen Beiträgen im Stil des Feuilletons sowie sechs historischen und elf theologischen Zugängen werden auch elf praktisch-theologische und pädagogische Fragestellungen erörtert, die im Gespräch mit Zeitgenossen Antworten auf Grundfragen des christlichen Glaubens zu geben versuchen. Einige Beispiele: Sylvia Bukowski, »Von der Lust, an einem Katechismus für heute zu schreiben«; Johannes Ehmann, »Von Breslau in die Pfalz – die Wege des Zacharias Ursinus«; Andreas Mühling, »Die Entstehung des HK«; Magdalene L. Frettlöh, »Leibhaftige Vergewisserung: ›Wahrzeichen und Siegel‹ – Taufe und Abendmahl«; Gerard den Hertog, »›Ein geringer Anfang ... mit fester Absicht‹: Die Zehn Gebote als Regel«; Christian Link, »›Kein Haar von meinem Haupt kann fallen‹: Vorsehung heute«; Georg Plasger, »›Mittler und Erlöser‹ Christus: Die geglaubte Realität der Göttlichen Barmherzigkeit«; Michael Welker, »›Herrschaft‹ Christi als ›Trost‹?«; Uwe Hauser, »Mit Kindern lernen und verstehen«; Okko Herlyn, »›Logische Pointe‹: Beten als gutes Werk«; Walter Herrenbrück, »Der Heidelberger Katechismus in Predigt und Gottesdienst«; Brigitte Schroven, »›In schwersten Anfechtungen gewiss‹: Seelsorge mit dem HK«; Won-Sik Suk, »Reformatorisch und ökumenisch«. Allen Beiträgen gemeinsam ist eine hohe inhaltliche Qualität. Sie bieten Pfarrpersonen und Religionspädagogen ein umfassendes Instrumentarium, um Aspekte und Themen des Katechismus in Gemeinde, Schule und Erwachsenenbildung aufzugreifen. Man kann aber auch allein im Buch herumschweifen und sich Zeit nehmen, immer wieder einmal darin herumzustöbern. Für die Benutzer und Benutzerinnen des Bandes bietet eine mitgelieferte CD-Rom mit Unterrichtsentwürfen und einer Fülle von Materialien, Texten und Bildern eine enorme Hilfe. Wer sich über eine stagnierende Religionspädagogik beschwert, sollte sich durch diesen inhaltsreichen Band eines Besseren belehren lassen.

Eine gute Einführung in den HK legt Georg Plasger in seinem Werk *Glauben heute mit dem Heidelberger Katechismus* vor. Im Gespräch mit den klassischen Aussagen des Katechismus gibt der Autor Anregungen zu einer lebendigen Auseinandersetzung mit den großen Fragen des Glaubens. In vierzehn Kapiteln werden Grundthemen des christlichen Glaubens und Aussagen des Heidelberger Katechismus als Angebot zum Verstehen des Glaubens (manchmal auch kritisch) bedacht. Die Aspekte sind das Gotteserkennen, die Bibel als Heilige Schrift, der Glaube, die Sünde, die Gerechtigkeit, Christus, der gerechte Mensch, Schöpfung, Heiliger Geist, die Kirche, Taufe und Abendmahl, das Gebet, die Dankbarkeit und die Hoffnung. So entsteht ein »modernes Glaubensbuch für Erwachsene«, wie es zu Recht in der Ankündigung heißt. Es sprich für die hohe Fachkompetenz des Verfassers, dass komplexe theologische Fragen mit Tiefenschärfe gestellt und gleichzeitig in allgemeinverständlicher Sprache erörtert werden.

Abschließend soll noch ein kurzer Blick auf die Broschüre *Heidelberg und die Kurpfalz* in der Reihe »Orte der Reformation« geworfen werden. Das reich bebilderte Heft führt auf den Spuren der Reformation durch die historische und gegenwärtige Kurpfalz. Heidelberg mit seiner Universität, seinem Schloss und seinen Kirchen steht zwar im Mittelpunkt, aber auch andere Orte in der Kurpfalz werden beschrieben: Neustadt an der Weinstraße zum Beispiel, wo 1578 Pfalzgraf Johann Casimir eine reformierte Hochschule gründete, oder Bretten, wo Philipp Melanchthon geboren wurde. Auch den Wallonen und Hugenotten in der Kurpfalz ist ein eigenes Kapitel gewidmet, denn bis zum Dreißigjährigen Krieg blieb die Kurpfalz ein »Ketzerasyl« für reformierte Glaubensflüchtlinge.

Schließlich widmet die Zeitschrift *Evangelische Theologie* dem HK ein eigenes Heft unter dem Titel *450 Jahre Heidelberger Katechismus (1563–2013)*, das von Christoph Strohm zusammengestellt wurde und eingeleitet wird. Es enthält gewichtige Beiträge über den Bibelgebrauch des HK (Frank Crüsemann), die Verbreitung des HK in Nordamerika (Jan Stievermann und Daniel Silliman), die Vereinbarkeit von HK und Augsburger Bekenntnis (Johannes Ehmann) und eine Analyse der theologischen Systematik des Katechismus (Christian Link).

Allen besprochenen Veröffentlichungen kommt das Verdienst zu, die Erinnerung an den HK wieder lebendig gemacht zu haben. Gespannt wird man den weiteren noch anstehenden Publikationen und dem großem Heidelberger Symposiumsband entgegensehen dürfen.

Emidio Campi, Zürich

Randolph C. Head, Jenatschs Axt: Soziale Grenzen, Identität und Mythos in der Epoche des Dreissigjährigen Krieges. Aus dem Amerikanischen von Peter Jäger, aktualisiert und autorisiert durch den Verfasser Randolph C. Head, Chur: Desertina, 2012 (Cultura alpina 5), 274 S. – ISBN 978-3-85637-413-6.

Im Jahre 2008 veröffentlichte der amerikanische Historiker Randolph C. Head eine Monographie über Georg Jenatsch, durch Conrad Ferdinand Meyer als Jürg Jenatsch bekannt geworden. Seit der 3. Auflage von Alexander Pfisters umfassender Biographie aus dem Jahre 1984, ergänzt mit einem Zusatzkapitel von Jon Mathieu, in dem die neuen Forschungen seit der ersten Ausgabe von 1951 aufgenommen und ausgewertet wurden, ist keine wesentliche Arbeit zu Jenatsch mehr erschienen. Um so verdienstvoller ist die Arbeit von Head, die hier in einer erweiterten deutschen Übersetzung vorliegt. An Aktualtät mangelt es der Arbeit jedenfalls nicht: So wurden im Jahre 2009 die seit langem verschollenen Ausgrabungsnotizen von Erik Hug (1911–1991) gefunden, die eine neue Beschäftigung mit dem umstrittenen Bündner Nationalhelden hervorriefen. Die erneute Exhumierung des vermuteten Leichnams von Jenatsch sollte den definitiven Beweis der Identität des Leichnams erbringen, doch DNA-Proben brachten nicht die erhoffte Klärung. Derzeit ist die evolutionäre Medizin damit beschäftigt, das Gesicht des Toten zu rekonstruieren und mit zeitgenössischen Bildern von Jenatsch zu vergleichen. Zeitgleich zu diesem Krimi fällt schließlich die Seligsprechung des auf dem Thusner Strafgericht gemarterten Erzpriesters Nicolò Rusca aus Sondrio, für dessen Tod als Folge der Folterqualen Jenatsch nicht ganz unschuldig war. Wie präsent diese Ereignisse noch heute, 400 Jahre später, sind, zeigen die emotionalen, teils konfessionalistischen Debatten im Zusammenhang mit dieser Seligsprechung. Einer emotionalen Beschäftigung mit der Materie sich enthalten zu können, ist mit Sicherheit eines der größten Verdienste der vorliegenden Arbeit. Als Amerikaner mit Schweizer Wurzeln bringt Head die notwendige Distanz zur Thematik mit, was sich mehrfach auszahlt.

Head will mit seiner Biographie über Jenatsch mehr als nur eine chronologische Erzählung des Lebens von Jenatsch leisten. Methodisch folgt er dabei dem Ansatz des Pietismus-Forschers Johannes Wallmann, anhand einer Biographie eine Zeitepoche zu exemplifizieren, im vorliegenden Fall die Zeit der Bündner Wirren beziehungsweise des 30-jährigen Krieges. Heads biographische Darstellung kann tatsächlich als eine »kleine Synthese großer Geschichte« (Olaf Hähner) bezeichnet werden.

Auch in den einzelnen Kapiteln weicht Head von einer traditionellen, chronologisch angeordneten Biographie ab und versucht anhand divergierender Erkenntnisse und aufgrund wechselnder Perspektiven einen andern Zugang zu Jenatsch zu gewinnen und ein ganzheitliches Bild zu zeichnen. Die auffallend vielen »Diskontinuitäten« und »Grenzüberschreitungen« in Jenatschs Biographie führten Head zur Überzeugung, dass Diskontinuitäten und Brüche mehr über Jenatsch aussagen würden als die kohärenten Züge. Diese Methodik basiert auf der seit Michel Foucault in der Geschichtswissenschaft entwickelten Diskursanalyse, die Kontinuität und Homogenität als ein irreales Konstrukt bewertet.

In einem ersten Kapitel werden die großen Linien gezeichnet und Jenatschs Wirken geographisch, religiös, sozial und geschichtlich kontextualisiert. Die folgenden fünf Kapitel widmen sich je einer sozialen Grenze, die Jenatsch zu Lebzeiten überschritt. Das zweite Kapitel handelt von den regionalen und sprachlichen Grenzen, die

Jenatschs junge Jahre prägten und die den Kontext für seinen späteren Aufstieg bildeten. Head stellt dar, wie Jenatsch sich zwischen verschiedenen Kulturen, Sprachgruppen und Bildungsschichten mühelos bewegte. Das dritte Kapitel wendet sich der Religion zu. Es untersucht die Frage, wie der Zelot, der »Eiferer« Jenatsch, der an der Schola Tigurina in Zürich ausgebildet worden war, zum bekehrten Katholiken werden konnte. Head kommt zur Erkenntnis, dass der »Konfessionswandel« Jenatschs mitnichten einfach als politisch motiviert beurteilt werden dürfe. Vielmehr sei diesem Schritt eine lange geistige Entwicklung vorausgegangen.

Im vierten Kapitel wird untersucht, inwiefern Jenatsch in seinen verschiedenen Rollen die Ständeordnung eingehalten, repräsentiert, aber auch gebrochen hat. Jenatsch habe infolge seines Aufstiegs auch Missgunst erregt, so dass verletzter Stolz und gebrochene Standesregeln auch zu seiner späteren Ermordung beigetragen hätten. Daran schließt sich das fünfte Kapitel, das weitere Aspekte von Missgunst aufzeigt: Die teils seit Generationen bestehenden Familienfehden in Bünden, die nicht selten in Blutrache endeten, habe sich Jenatsch zunutze gemacht und großes Geschick bei der Unterscheidung gezeigt, wann Ehre, Stolz und Blutbande beziehungsweise wann Diplomatie notwendig war.

Im abschließenden sechsten Kapitel befasst sich Head mit den verschiedenen Jenatsch-Darstellungen seit 1639. Während in den beiden ersten Jahrhunderten nach seinem Tode zumeist die konfessionellen Grenzen hervorgehoben wurden, rückte in der Romantik die Frage nach der Einheitlichkeit seines Lebens in den Vordergrund (Conrad Ferdinand Meyer). Erst im Übergang zum 20. Jahrhundert wich die Sehnsucht nach Kohärenz der Bemühung, den historischen Jenatsch anhand von Quellen nachzuzeichnen (Ernst Haffter, Alexander Pfister).

Dank der verschiedenen Zugänge zu Jenatsch gelingt es Head tatsächlich ein vielgestaltiges und umfassendes Bild von Jenatsch zu vermitteln. Der narrative Stil der Arbeit lässt allerdings manchmal fragen, ob es sich hierbei eher um »history« oder um »story« handelt. Denn die Arbeit präsentiert wenig neue wissenschaftliche Erkenntnisse und beruft sich öfters einfach auf die quellengestützten Arbeiten von Haffter und Pfister, stellt also keinen eigentlichen Beitrag zur Jenatsch-Forschung dar. Dies hat unter anderem aber auch damit zu tun, dass, abgesehen von den Ausgrabungsnotizen von Erik Hug, seit Pfisters Biographie kaum noch neue Quellen entdeckt worden sind. Bedauernswert ist es um so mehr, dass Head verschiedene wenig bekannte, schwer greifbare Quellen auszuwerten unterlassen hat. Manche derselben hätten seiner Arbeit größeres Gewicht geben können. Aufs Ganze gesehen ist aber Heads »neue« Jenatsch-Biographie eine gelungene Darstellung, die einen alternativen und auffallend neutralen beziehungsweise objektiven Blick auf Jenatschs Leben und Wirken wirft.

Jan-Andrea Bernhard, Castrisch/Zürich

Alfred Ehrensperger, Der Gottesdienst in Stadt und Landschaft Bern im 16. und 17. Jahrhundert, Zürich: Theologischer Verlag Zürich, 2011 (Geschichte des Gottesdienstes in den evangelisch-reformierten Kirchen der Deutschschweiz 2), 356 S. – ISBN 978-3-290-17594-8.

Der zweite Band von Alfred Ehrenspergers Deutschschweizer Gottesdienstgeschichte ist hier anzuzeigen. Das Werk macht glücklich und lässt einen doch etwas unfroh zurück. Einerseits ist diese Geschichte der Genese des reformierten Gottesdienstes in der Tat ein Desiderat. Seit dem späten 19. und dem Anfang des 20. Jahrhunderts sind wenige und verstreute Studien dazu erschienen. Allzu lange wurde Gottesdienst- und Liturgiegeschichte protestantischerseits bestenfalls als historisches Exotentum betrachtet. Insofern ist eine moderne und breit abgestützte, Quellen wie Sekundärliteratur aufarbeitende Reihe dringend nötig. Andererseits zeigen sich auch die Grenzen, wenn das ein einzelner Autor in Angriff nimmt. Denn der so gewählte Ansatz schwankt zwischen Lokalgeschichte im Einzelnen und relativ belangloser Historik im Allgemeinen. Das zeigen die einführenden Bemerkungen des Vf., wenn er auf vier Seiten den (religions-)kulturellen Rahmen des Berner Herrschaftsgebietes über gut 300 Jahre zu skizzieren versucht. Auch ist der vom Autor gewählte historio-geografische Ansatz kontingent. Gewiss legitimiert die örtig verfasste alte Eidgenossenschaft, dies auch zu einem liturgiegeschichtlichen Koordinatensystem zu machen. Zumal gerade die reformierte Reformation sich als städtisch(-zünftische), frühbürgerliche Bewegung der Zuständigkeitsgrenzen jeweiliger Obrigkeiten entlang durchsetzte und sich auch partikulär ausprägte. Doch der Autor setzt mit der Konzeption des siebenbändigen Gesamtwerkes nach geografischen Schwerpunkten ein doch etwas anachronistisches Zeichen innerhalb der Historik. Wo in den letzten Jahren von Kulturräumen über lange Zeitepochen hinweg die Rede war, kann nurmehr schwer ein derart geografisch fokussierter Blick einleuchten. Der Vf. konstatiert denn auch eine kulturelle Pluriformität in seinen Ausführungen über die vorreformatorischen »gottesdienstlichen Aspekte«. Aber auch diese Bemerkungen wie die im übrigen durchaus nützliche Zusammenstellung monastischer Körperschaften in Stadt und Landschaft Bern (S. 21–79) fallen eher summarisch aus und sind aus bestehender Sekundärliteratur wie wenigen Quelleneditionen zusammengetragen. Sie bieten aber insgesamt einen recht anschaulichen Einstieg in die spätmittelalterliche Frömmigkeitswelt (v.a. 80–104).

Ausgewogen scheint dem Vf. anschließend die Tour d'Horizon durch die eigentliche Reformationsjahrzehnte zu gelingen. Auch wenn hierbei wieder größtenteils zusammenfassend formuliert wird, so lässt der Autor doch Quellen sprechen und schafft so einen eigentlichen Studienzugang zur Bernischen Reformation. Originell ist die Auswahl von Niklaus Manuels Satire »Von der Krankheit der Messe« (ca. 1528). Es scheint darin etwas vom Feu sacré auf, das die Gläubigen gegen eine veräußerlichte Kirche aufgebracht hat und sie eine andere Form von Verkündigung hat einfordern lassen. Wichtig ist der Abdruck des Berner Reformationsmandats von 1525. Allerdings ist die Einschätzung durch den Vf. als »ähnlich einer Kirchenordnung« doch arbiträr, ist doch nach frühneuzeitlichem Rechtsverständnis ein Ratsmandat dieser kongruent. Überhaupt ist dann und wann die historiografische Begrifflichkeit leicht schwammig und unpräzis.

Der historische Überblick schließt (143–156) mit einem kurzen Ausblick auf die Konfliktsituation mit den Berner Täufern. Dabei schält der Vf. klug heraus, dass der Berner Reformator Berchtold Haller eine, auch im Vergleich mit den Zürcher Reformatoren, eher tolerante Haltung einnahm und beispielsweise gegen eine allzu harte Bestrafung der Täufer eintrat. Tabellarisch zeigt der Autor sodann auf, worin sich theologisch und »kontroversekklesiologisch«

die grundsätzlichen Differenzen zwischen den Taufgesinnten und den humanistisch-biblisch argumentierenden Reformatoren zeigten. Insbesondere gelingt es dem Vf. auf wenigen Seiten darzulegen, dass die taufgesinnten Gruppen in sich auch theologisch häufig uneinheitlich waren und sich das historische Bild auch unter Beizug der neuesten Quelleneditionen sich sehr viel differenzierter zeigt. Leider sind die Ausführungen insgesamt aber nicht sehr lange und die harten Strafsanktionen der Berner Obrigkeit kommen kaum zur Sprache.

Die zweite Hälfte des Bandes widmet sich sodann der eigentlichen Gottesdienstgeschichte, wobei Kapitel 3 die Entwicklung ab der Berner Disputation von 1528 bis zum Synodus von 1532 beschreibt, die eigentliche reformatorische Prägezeit (157–212). Kapitel 4 sodann zeichnet die Geschichte bis etwa zum Jahr 1700 weiter (213–255), Kapitel 5 listet die im Berner Obrigkeitsbereich erscheinenden historischen Dokumente und Quellen auf (257–304). Hier zeigen sich die unbestrittenen Kenntnisse des Autors, vermag er es doch, auf knapp 50 Seiten das liturgisch-gottesdienstliche Schaffen einer Epoche klar zu umreißen, die Textstücke sorgfältig und in Auszügen zu präsentieren und – so die Annahme des Rezensenten – dies v.a. für Studierende und interessierte Laien aufzuarbeiten. Der Band ist also auch durch diesen Quellenzugang wertvoll in sich und hebt Schätze, die bislang nur Fachexperten mit den nötigen bibliografischen wie bibliotheks- und archivkundlichen Fähigkeiten vorbehalten waren.

Auch das sechste Kapitel vermag in diesem Zusammenhang zu dienen. Hier werden auf knapp 30 Seiten die einzelnen liturgischen Elemente der Gottesdienste beschrieben und in einen knappen historisch-genetischen Rahmen gestellt. Allerdings fällt dieses letzte Kapitel doch etwas knapp aus und hat eher einen lexikografischen Charakter.

Ein Quellen- und Literaturverzeichnis runden das Werk ab, eine etwas gar kurz geratene Übersicht über die im Bernischen Gebiet erschienenen Gesangbücher (erstellt von Andreas Marti) lässt einen unfertigen Eindruck zurück. Gerne hätte man hier über die Gesangbücher als dem genuin protestantischen, ingeniösen Pendant zu den Katechismen mehr erfahren. Dass in einem historischen

Werk falsche und nicht mehr verfügbare Weblinks abgedruckt werden, erhöht kaum die wissenschaftliche Vertrauenswürdigkeit.

Es bleiben noch die übersprungenen zwei historischen Hauptkapitel zu referieren. Im Kapitel drei, das die entscheidenden vier Jahre der Berner Reformation verhandelt, zeigt sich schön, wie das Herz des Vf. für die Reformationsgeschichte schlägt. Es ist nicht eigentlich ein liturgie- oder gottesdiensthistorisches Kapitel, doch dem Autor gelingt es, u.a. unter Beizug bislang ungedruckter Quellen (z.B. der Schrift des ehemaligen Stiftsprobstes und Reformationsgegners Thomas Murner), dem Ringen um Schrift- und Evangeliumsgemäßheit, dem Suchen nach den theologischen Grundpfeilern einer erneuerten Kirche und den zwangsläufigen Fragen wie nach den Bildern, dem richtigen Gebrauch der Sakramente und der Kirchenzucht etc., Farbe und Plastizität zu verleihen. Auch wenn der Vf. nicht wirklich viele neue Dokumente beizieht, das Kapitel ist gut gelungen und offenbar mit Freude geschrieben. Ob das Temperament des Autors nicht etwas gar überschießt, wenn er von einer apostolischen Lehrsukzession der neu ausgebildeten evangelischen Pfarrer spricht und es hier doch theologiegeschichtlich vielleicht subtilere Einschätzungen gäbe, bleibe dahin gestellt.

Das vierte Kapitel hat beim Rezensenten einen zwiespältigen Eindruck hinterlassen. Die Epochen reformatorischer Festigung, Konfessionalisierung wie beginnende Orthodoxie, Pietismus und Frühaufklärung werden in 40 Seiten gestreift. Hier scheint der Autor nicht wirklich heimisch zu sein. Dass in Bern Ende des 17. Jahrhunderts orthodoxe Gegner schriftliche Denunziationen beim Rat einreichten, was den Vf. offenbar irritiert, ist für die Zeit historisches Allgemeinwissen. Die Zusammenfassung der Thesen gegen den Pietismus von 1699 ist zwar illustrativ, in ihrer fehlenden Kommentierung und Einordnung wirkt sie aber arbiträr.

Unter liturgiehistorischen Aspekten und als Nachschlagewerk weist das Buch durchaus nützliche Eigenschaften auf. Studierende und an der lokalen Reformations- wie Gottesdienstgeschichte Interessierte finden Orientierung und ein Basiswissen. Der Band vermag aber ein Fachpublikum nicht wirklich zu begeistern. Gleichwohl gehört das Buch trotz seiner Mängel mit den weiteren Bänden der Reihe in eine gut sortierte Pfarramtsbibliothek.

Michael Baumann, Wiesendangen

Ulrich Pfister, Konfessionskirchen, Glaubenspraxis und Konflikt in Graubünden, 16.–18. Jahrhundert, Würzburg: Ergon, 2012 (Religion und Politik 1), 543 p. – ISBN 978-3-89913-838-2.

Ulrich Pfister's broad new study of confessional institutions, politics and life in Graubünden in the early modern period offers an impressive combination of original research and thoughtful synthesis. *Konfessionskirchen, Glaubenspraxis und Konflikt in Graubünden, 16.–18. Jahrhundert* provides one of the most multi-faceted approaches to the religious history of any single political region in Europe during the confessional era. Pfister's contribution not only represents a new standard work for historians of Graubünden and of religious culture in early modern Switzerland, but will also become an important point of reference for all comparative studies of religious change under various political, economic and social circumstances in this period.

Although Pfister profitably incorporates a wide range of older literature – much of it overtly confessional but valuable for its close engagement with local history – a clear methodological framework unifies his book, namely the confessionalization model that has predominated in post-Reformation scholarship for the last generation (as articulated in the work of Wolfgang Reinhard and especially Heinz Schilling). Pfister carefully incorporates various critiques of Schilling's »strong« confessionalization thesis with its primary focus on state-formation, however, and offers his study of Graubünden – mixed in confession and lacking effective state institutions – as way to reestablish the value of a more nuanced (or »weak«) confessionalization model. Pfister identifies four primary featurs of his approach (19): (1) He redefines confessionalization in terms of the sociology of knowledge (*wissenssoziologisch*), with particular attention to »Veränderungen in der Struktur des Glaubenspraxis«. Pfister argues that verbal discourses gained in importance after 1500 across Europe, transforming religious conflict and emphasizing individual knowledge and discernement among clergy and laity alike. Not surprisingly, therefore, Michel Foucault and especially Norbert Elias appear among his theoretical points of reference. (2) He explains changes in church institutions not primarily in terms of dysfunction or abuses, but rather in terms of these institutions' ability to transmit and construct new religious practices (for both confessions) that had positive social functions, thus attracting individual and community support. (3) He analyzes religious conflict in terms of broader changes in »mentalen Konfliktcodes«. And finally (4), he analyzes an area of mixed rather than unitary confessional adherence, thus including comparison between Catholic and Protestant developments in every aspect of his analysis. As these points show, Pfister remains firmly attached to structural-functional modes of explanation. His book thus represents a nuanced defense of both confessionalization and structural history in general against the hermeneutic and cultural turn of the 1990s (although he readily draws on recent cultural historiography in his analysis.)

One benefit of Pfister's rigorous orientation to the structural background of events and actions is that he is able to provide a remarkably coherent narrative of Graubünden's religious history during the nearly three centuries from the early Reformation to the Enlightenment. Two features of this narrative are noteworthy. First, Pfister reveals that religious change in Graubünden largely conformed to patterns observable across Europe, despite the region's anomalous politics and social organization. Specific developments might have been precocious or modestly delayed, but Graubünden's overall path through the confessional era hewed closely to European norms. Second, within this relatively familiar narrative, Pfister succeeds in explaining the nature and tempo of specific events by connecting them to particular features of Bündner politics and society. The strength of his arguments testifies to the effectiveness of well-executed political sociology based on extensive evidence.

Pfister's exposition of the early Reformation and its aftermath in the Three Leagues generally follows the picture found in the more recent literature. Chapter 1 addresses the region's institutional framework on the threshold of the Reformation, concentrating on a pattern that he calls »pre-confessional reform«. The shift of advowsons (*Kollaturen*) from clerical or noble hands into the control of communes – beginning in the fifteenth century and greatly accelerated by the 1526 Second Ilanz Articles – enabled an anti-clerical movement of church reform to predominate in Graubünden by the 1540s, with only limited references to specifically »evangelical« theological or ecclesiological claims. Building on the fine work of Immacolata Saulle-Hippenmeyer and Oskar Vasella, Pfister confirms that local congregations readily seized control of church endowments and the power to appoint pastors, whether or not they also adopted Protestant teachings. In an appendix, Pfister also provides a comprehensive description of the number and adherence of all Bündner congregations through the eighteenth century – no small feat given Graubünden's tangled ecclesiastical geography.

In chapter 3, Pfister focuses on the emerging Reformed church in Graubünden and its institutions. Although early religious unrest was directed against the Bishop of Chur's jurisdiction, evangelical ideas flourished where a humanistically educated elite cooperated with communalist populism, as in the lower Rhine valley and the Engadine. Both the theological discourses in European circulation and Graubünden's geo-political neighborhood created pressures that eventually welded the early evangelical *Gemeindekirchen* into a theologically orthodox and systematically organized Protestant movement – even though local congregations long showed little interest in such a path. The founding of a Reformed Synod in 1537 was an important step, but Reformed orthodoxy confronted powerful challenges from a homegrown Anabaptist movement and the irenic ideas of the Italian *exuli* who found refuge from persecution in the Republic's Italian-speaking valleys. Not until the 1580s were the Synod's leaders able to examine candidates for the pastorate, finally allowing them to exclude heterodox preachers from parishes. A more uniform clergy enabled the encouragement of new forms of moral and behavioral discipline among the clergy and population. Despite Graubünden's stunningly early adoption of a *cuius regio* approach to religious adherence in 1526, therefore, the formation of a confessional Reformed church took longer than in most of the Empire, and was not fully in place until the early seventeenth century.

Chapter 4 turns to Catholic institutions – above all the see of Chur – which faced enormous challenges during the sixteenth century. The bishops' already modest income was devasted by communal seizure of church resources in the 1520s and 1530s, while the see's awkward division between the Swiss and Habsburg spheres of influence weakened it politically. For most of the sixteenth century, control of the see became a political football among Graubünden's elite clans, culminating in the catastrophic disputed election of 1572. Implementation of Tridentine reforms was entirely beyond the bishops until after 1600; such modest efforts as took place came almost entirely from the sees of Milan and Como, which had claims over some southern valleys. Real reform occurred only after a nuntial visitation in 1598–99 and the election of a strongly pro-Tridentine bishop, Johann V Flugi, in 1601. Tridentine practices spread quickly while the cohesion the Three Leagues was disrupted during the Thirty Years' War: in addition to reorganization of the episcopal curia, the resumption of canon law court jurisdiction and renewed control over parochial appointments, the advent of Capuchin parish clergy in much of the see initiated thoroughgoing Catholic reform among the laity. The outcome followed patterns observable elsewhere in the Holy Roman Empire, including the emergence of a lively Baroque piety among Graubünden's Catholics. A brief review of the literature on the major cloisters, particularly Disentis, ends the chapter.

Chapters 5 and 6 turn from formal institutions to the clerical office as it evolved among Protestants and Catholics, and to the pious practices and cultures that became characteristic for each. Chapter 5 focuses on the professionalization of the clergy of both faiths, and its growing separation (largely imposed from above) from the everyday life of parishioners. The relative poverty of both institutional churches limited such separation, however, since clerics depended on local actors not only for their appointments but also for material support. Graubünden's Catholic church had an easier time, since it drew on outside personnel to staff the parishes with Capuchins, while Feldkirch Jesuits trained secular clergy for the see, along with Colleges in Milan and Rome. Pfister brings both a fresh perspective and fresh evidence to the place of the local clergy in Bündner society and culture, showing how they became a distinct professional group.

Chapter 6 focuses on pious practice and discipline, and rests on extensive original archival research into central and local records. Pfister argues that an increasing orientation to faith through words rather than through collective practice characterized both faiths, though in distinctive ways. For the Reformed, Pfister identifies the regional colloquies as key sites for self-control of the clergy and for shaping the verbally-oriented faith and practices of the laity, until the church's interest in lay discipline faded in the later eighteenth century. Turning to Catholics, Pfister shows that quite different issues connected institutions to clerics to laity. For example, he makes the fascinating observations that cleanliness of liturgical paraments was a prominent concern in Catholic visitations, and that visitors systematically sought to separate sacral from profane space, for example by demanding that a manure pile be moved away from a church's walls. Pfister's discussion of piety and practice ends with concise reviews of vernacular sacred literature as it evolved (notably in Romansh), of schooling, and of the particularly virulent witch crazes that affected Graubünden.

The book's final section, dedicated to confessional conflict, is a masterpiece of systematic and structural analysis that links together the multiple elements that shaped the course of post-confessional struggles in Graubünden from their full onset around 1580 to their ebbing in the mid-eighteenth century. Local cultures of conflict; the spiritual and institutional interests of the two churches; the complex institutional landscape of parishes, neighborhoods, communes and Leagues (not to mention powerful outside instigators or mediators): all played a part in how confessional conflict – in essence a Europe-wide phenomenon – played out in this one bi-confessional corner of the continent. Pfister discusses not only the relatively well-studied conflicts that began in Bergün and the Vier Dörfer in the 1570s and 1580s and continued through the instability of the Thirty Years' War, but also analyzes the much less familiar but equally bitter struggles after 1648 in Samnaun, Poschiavo, Bivio, Sagogn, Ortenstein, and elsewhere. Particularly in the later period, such conflicts could take on two aspects: either confrontations of principle on which no compromise was possible, and which thus threatened to divide not only the communes involved, but the entire Republic; or confrontations over resources that could be solved by agreements about allocation and distribution (often negotiated in part by powerful outsiders). By the eighteenth century, elite actors had developed a repertoire of tactics to avert confrontations over principles, helping to defang the destructive potential of these conflicts.

After a brief overview of the end of the confessional era, connected with new modes of piety among the Reformed (Pietism) and the eventual collapse of the traditional see of Chur for the Catholics, Pfister concludes with an overview of his main contributions. These include the following: (1) a new periodization of confessionalism in Graubünden – one ultimately synchronous with European patterns, but inflected by local conditions; (2) a demonstration that confessionalization in Graubünden took place separately from political consolidation (*Staatsbildung*), thus allowing insights into the non-political dimensions of confessionalization across Europe; (3) a characterization of the new forms of piety that emerged, largely through willing appropriation by the autonomous congregations of Graubünden, that emphasized universalist and verbally-oriented practices – processes that (4) took place in parallel among Catholic and Reformed communities, often generating intense conflict along the way. Pfister thus asserts that his analysis of Graubünden allows (5) a more precise and empirical delineation of the »conceptual, material, and chronological borders of confessionalization« (462). Indeed, *Konfessionskirchen, Glaubenspraxis und Konflikt in Graubünden* not only provides a magisterial analysis of one region's religious and cultural history, but also represents a major empirical contribution – notable for its sociological logic and structural orientation – to our understanding of how the Reformation schism and the subsequent ecclesio-political landscape fundamentally shaped European history. While debate will continue over many of Pfister's specific conclusions as well as over how to balance empiricist and hermeneutic approaches to large-scale phenomena like the »confessional era«, every student of Graubünden and early modern Switzerland, and every theorist of religious conflict and accommodation in Europe, stands to benefit from Pfister's contribution.

Randolph C. Head, University of California, Riverside

Norbert Furrer, Des Burgers Buch: Stadtberner Privatbibliotheken im 18. Jahrhundert, Zürich: Chronos, 2012, 824 S. – ISBN 978-3-0340-1113-6.

Die Privatbibliotheken großer Gelehrter oder wichtiger Persönlichkeiten wie etwa von Martin Luther oder Huldrych Zwingli haben die frühneuzeitliche Forschung bereits vor einem Jahrhundert interessiert, lassen die erhaltenen Exemplare doch interessante Rückschlüsse auf das Geistesleben des Besitzers zu. Noch spannender wird das Studium dieser Sammlungen, wen sich da und dort sogar noch handschriftliche Annotationen finden lassen, die rezeptionsgeschichtlich relevant sind. Die Erforschung der Buch- und Lesekultur von ganzen Personengruppen in frühneuzeitlichen Dörfern und Städten ist aber jüngeren Datums und interessanterweise vor allem in Ostmitteleuropa seit etwa einem halben Jahrhundert gut vertreten. Stellvertretend für die zahlreichen Publikationen aus diesen Ländern sei auf die Arbeiten von Viliam Čičaj und István Monok verwiesen. Mit der äußerst verdienstvollen Arbeit von Norbert Furrer liegt nun erstmals eine entsprechende Studie für eine Schweizer Stadt aus der frühen Neuzeit vor.

Der Autor war im Fall der Stadt Bern in der privilegierten Situation, dass sich dort, etwa im Unterschied zu Zürich, die sogenannten Geldtagsrödel erhalten haben. Es handelt sich dabei um Inventare von Gütern im Hinblick auf Versteigerungen. Da Bücher in der frühen Neuzeit keine Billigware darstellten, wurden auch sie verzeichnet, wobei oft bloß zwei oder drei Titel genannt werden, häufig ein paar Dutzend, seltener aber Hunderte. Die Stadt Bern zählte im 18. Jahrhundert 12000 bis 14000 Einwohner, von denen gemäß der Volkszählung von 1764 schätzungsweise 20% Analphabeten, 69% geschulte Personen, 7,5% Gebildete und 3,5% Gelehrte ausmachten. Furrer gelang es, 145 Kleinstbibliotheken (1–10 Titel), 37 kleine (11–50 Titel) und mittlere Privatsammlungen (51–300 Titel) sowie eine Großbibliothek (571 Titel) zu rekonstruieren. Die umfangreichste Privatbibliothek eines Berners während des Aufklärungsjahrhunderts besaß bekanntlich Albrecht von Haller mit etwa 26000 Titeln, die längst erschlossen und wie auch andere nicht Gegenstand der Geldtagsrödel und somit auch nicht Thema von Furrers Arbeit ist.

Eine der Schlussfolgerungen des Autors lautet (533): »Das bernische 18. Jahrhundert der ›Provinzialität‹ zu bezichtigen, wie dies zeitgenössische Beobachter gern taten, scheint angesichts der breiten Streuung der Verleger und Verfasser, deren Bücher ihren Weg in die privaten Bibliotheken der Stadt Bern fanden, kaum gerechtfertigt. Man darf wohl eher von einem soliden (westeuropäischen) ›Kosmopolitismus‹ sprechen.« Der in mancherlei Hinsicht materialreiche Band, der auf rund 200 Seiten zusätzliche Quellen zum Thema bietet und den der Autor selber als »Handbuch« beziehungsweise als »Materialsammlung« bezeichnet (9), lässt mannigfaltige weitere Aussagen zum bürgerlichen Geistesleben Berns im 18. Jahrhundert zu. Es ist sehr zu wünschen, dass auch für andere Schweizer Städte derartige Untersuchungen angestellt werden.

Urs B. Leu, Zürich

Calvin and His Influence, 1509–2009, ed. Irena Backus and Philip Benedict, Oxford et al.: Oxford University Press, 2011, XVI & 336 p. – ISBN 978-0-19-975185-3.

Only John Calvin's writings themselves say more about the master than the work of the Calvin specialists in this volume. The contemporary research presented here on Calvin and the influence that his work has had in the Western world and beyond for the past 500 years treats us to a wide spectrum of interdisciplinary approaches that provide contrasting, complimentary, and colliding views of Calvin, his world, and the influence he had on our world, religion, politics, and the social developments within culture as we know it. The chapters in this book were presented by plenary speakers at the Geneva Calvin Conference from may 24 to 27, 2009. The celebration was organized and sponsored by the University of Geneva, the Association Calvin 2009, and the Musée Historique de la Réformation et Bibliothéque Calvinienne.

Calvin and His Influence is introduced with an expert essay in its own right. The first thirty-two pages are an overview of the state of Calvin research in 2009, whereby Irena Backus and Philip Benedict lament that intellectual, cultural, and religious dimensions of Calvin's influence have been badly neglected. The volume that is organized in two complimentary sections sets out to bring Calvin research up to date and fill the gaps that have been identified over the years. The first half of the book contains a group of essays that probe Calvin the man and his writings – noteworthy and challenging in these contributions is that each essay defines unique traits of John Calvin's character and accomplishments, indeed each of our experts has a different take on Calvin's predominant traits and a unique interpretation for what the Genevan Reformer did and why he wrote it down. The second half of the book contains abbreviated narratives of Calvin reception in different times and places throughout the history of modernity.

The following are brief impressions of each article for the purpose of denoting the various themes contained in the volume. In chapter 1, Diarmaid MacCulloch asks about »The Fifth Latin Doctor of the Church?« by looking to locate Calvin in relation to Augustine and the Council of Chalcedon. In addition to his ability to delimit 1500 years of tradition by employing his knack for both Scripture and law, the Doctor (Calvin) in this portrait was both visionary and bound to his own era. The Anabaptist themes of discipline and suffering embedded the man in his own culture; however, Calvin remained unique in his understanding of the Eucharist: more than Zwingli's sign, the Lord's Supper is both a sign and reality. Whether or not Calvin was the Fifth Latin Doctor of the church is as relative as the circumstantial nature of his fame. Chapter 2 discusses the evolution of politics in light of Calvin's thought as a sort of *mutatis mutandis*, as Harro M. Höpfl argues in »The Ideal of *Aristocratia Politiae Vicina* in the Calvinist Political Tradition.« The apostolic form of church that Calvin envisioned was an aristocracy of magistrates and ministers melted into constitutionalism by 1580. Calvin attempted to eradicate the abuses of the church, with discipline as an intrinsic part of the new model. »With the things changed that needed to be changed in mind,« Calvin's politics were a series of affirmations, qualifications, and denials, all attributed finally to him or what came to be coined as Calvinism. So was »Calvin the Workaholic« as Max Engammare would claim in chapter 3? The contemporary question placed in hindsight over Calvin's life, has its justification as Engammare knowledgably argues with humorous narratives of Calvin's pacing, his late nights working, constant demands for his preaching and publications, as well as reference to Calvin's weak body. The chapter could bring comic relief to the more serious topics of this book, but for the dead seriousness of Calvin's practice of *recapitulatio* and his eschatological concern that after life he might not be able to complete his work, both of which raise some concerns about Calvin's neurosis and lend insight into the social history of a lesser known Calvin. Chapter 4 by Olivier Millet, provides a linguistic angle in »Calvin's Self-Awareness as Author.« Calvin the humanist author quickly deteriorated or perhaps grew in awareness of his prophetic and apostolic prowess as he worked. Through the lens of a linguist like Millet, Calvin appears to be quite reckless by 1551, pressing on to proclaim the prophetic word rather than limiting himself to the restrictions of literary form. »Calvin's Church in Geneva: Constructed or Gathered? Local or Foreign? French or Swiss?« in chapter 5 by William Naphy investigates the history of Calvin from the perspective of the two tasks that are historically attributed to the Genevan. First, Calvin was to create ecclesial ordinances and then Geneva's post-revolutionary constitutions with a system of checks and balances. Of course, the consistory was created to deal with spiritual affairs. In the end, politics and the church overlapped, which should come to no one anywhere as a surprise. It is hard not to have the image of religion and faith appear to be a deterrence to a sober historical narrative in the legal context portrayed here. Emidio Campi joins the discussion with his chapter 6 and a research up-date that provides an overview of the larger Swiss context and the relationships that influenced Calvin's thought and works. Bern, Basel, and above all, Zurich weathered the Roman Counter-reform, the Radical Reformation, and together they hammered out a form of unity between the Protestant others. Campi knows the players intimately and places them on the game board when he finally asks the questions that continue to weave the threads of the original Calvin conference together: »But what exactly was Calvinism?« and »How much of what has been peddled under the label of ›Calvinism‹ should really be attributed to the thought of Bucer, Zwingli, Oekolampadius, Farel, Viret, Musculus, à Lasco, or Vermigli?« In chapter 7, Herman Selderhuis explores the Christian categories of »Calvin,

1509–2009« from Calvin's own self-identity as a humble servant of God in this world. Calvin and Calvinism are like a father and son, there is something mutual, but actually great differences as well. Selderhuis sums up the perspectives of Calvin the man through a theological lens.

With »Calvin as an Actor in the Early Modern State System around 1600: Struggle for Alliances, Patterns of Eschatological Interpretations, Symbolic Representation,« Heinz Schilling's contribution in chapter 8 forms a bridge between the first section of this book on Calvin the man and the second part on Calvin reception in the last five centuries. How Calvin was received during the so-called era of confessionalization is appraised to determine Calvin's influence from a political perspective. Granted that Calvinism was authoritative in creating the first international state system; yet, Schilling concludes that the balance sheet of Calvinism from a secular perspective remained negative, if military or political success are considered the plum-line to judge this. Richard Muller's addition to the volume aptly follows the era of confessionalization with the era of orthodoxy in the seventeenth century in chapter 9. By this time, Calvinism had morphed into a code-word for Reformed teachings and worship. Following the trail of the historical theological reception of Calvin's works, Muller demonstrates how Calvin became the figurehead representing all of the reformers – even Bullinger's Covenant Theology was attributed to Calvin during this century. In the end, Calvin grew together with the others in the minds of men and became a building block for later thought. In »The Dutch Enlightenment and the Distant Calvin,« chapter 10, by Ernestine van der Wall, a very detailed account of the secularization of the Dutch church during the eighteenth century is spotlighted. The struggle between traditional and liberal Protestantism, the key players, as well as many of the works that evolved eighteenth century thinking in the Netherlands after the Enlightenment provide substantial evidence to the metamorphosis of Calvinism in the Dutch church. André Encrevé, the foremost expert on modern French Protestantism tells of »Lost, Then Found: Calvinism in French Protestantism, 1830–1940,« in chapter 11. The winding path that the French Protestant Church took in which politics and theology were inseparably entwined reminds of the larger European struggle between freedom and monarchy, faith and politics that highlight this second section of the volume. Chapter 12 is written by Friedrich Wilhelm Graf, who presents a social historical analysis of »Calvin in the Plural: The Diversity of Modern Interpretations of Calvinism, Especially in the German and English-Speaking World.« Graf is interested in a contemporary »account of the varied and problematic interpretations of Calvinism.« His essay applies social historical methodology concluding with a confirmation of a »practice of history and memory politics« that plows straight through the garden of Protestant denominations, lending agony to any hope of gaining a concrete definition of Calvinism. Graf concludes that an »inner unity of diverse Calvinisms« is to be defined as »opposition to Rome.« Cornelis van der Kooi returns us to the Netherlands in chapter 13 with a piece on »Calvin, Modern Calvinism, and Civil Society: The Appropriation of a Heritage, with Particular Reference to the Low Countries.« The discussion of neo-Calvinism in the last third of the nineteenth century and Abraham Kuyper integrates the essays relating to the past with the present. Kooi develops the concept of appropriation and the role of »receiving, selecting, and forming an image of the past« now. Notions such as public theology, spirituality interwoven with Reformed theology, and the concept of community in our present pluralism boom forth here for the twenty-first century church to hear. If any culturally interested reader questioned the usefulness of a conference on Calvin and the essays that proceed therefrom, how they are tied together in post-modern vocabulary, theory, and our present context in this essay will convince them of the necessity. David Bebbington's »Calvin and British Evangelicalism in the Nineteenth and Twentieth Centuries« in chapter 14 is the other end of the euphoria. Bebbington describes the power of Calvinism in the British church and politics during the twentieth century. He describes two movements that influenced the church before the Second World War; the first was propelled by none other than Karl Barth and the Oxford Movement, but also the conservative Evangelical Bible Movement. The manner in which Calvin has lost relevance to the English Church and England today appears to be a phenomenon that characterizes international Calvin history. »Calvin(ism) and Apartheid in South Africa in the Twentieth Century:

The Making and Unmaking of a Racial Ideology« by John W. de Gruchy, chapter 15, transfers us from the last 500 years of Western culture to Calvin reception in South Africa. Calvinism and Colonialism arrived hand in hand in South Africa around 1652. Despite Calvin's understanding of unity in the church, in 1857, the Lord's Supper was deemed untenable between black and white people, and this decision of the church gave birth to apartheid. The centuries of struggle in South Africa changed the church, according to De Gruchy. A decline and later revival of Calvin in Kuyper's work, has lead to a hopeful new interpretation of Scripture as Calvin would have it.

Academic Calvin studies have conquered new land in this volume; the work presents plenty of shoulders for junior scholars to stand on in order to continue the historical quest for understanding all of the Reformations. Two achievements deserve particular note here. First, the editor's and author's conscious efforts to make reference to each other's work gives this volume a continuity that is not often found in collections of conference essays. The other highly praiseworthy aspect of this book is well defined in the introductory essay itself, »Curiously, the nonpartisan and nonhostile study of Calvin is a recent development, and the problems of bridging the gap between theologically oriented Calvin specialists on the one hand and political, social, intellectual, legal, and literary historians on the other hand still haunt much of Calvin research nowadays. Why that should be is yet another interesting chapter of the larger story that merits more attention than we have been able to offer here»(2).

I recommend this book to all of those who are interested in understanding Calvin and his influence for the future.

Rebecca Giselbrecht, Zurich

Uwe Wolff, »Das Geheimnis ist mein«: Walter Nigg. Eine Biographie, Zürich: Theologischer Verlag Zürich, 2009, 516 S. – ISBN 978-3-290-17509-2.

Der Leser ist hin und hergerissen. Der Wälzer macht es einem nicht leicht. Vom Stil, der Konzeption und der fehlenden analytischen

Tiefe her ist das Werk gescheitert. Es ist die grenzenlose Bewunderung für den Hagiographen Nigg, welche den Autor leitet. Und das geht natürlich auf Kosten begrifflicher Schärfe, die man sich gerade beim Werk wie bei der Person Walter Niggs gewünscht hätte. Andererseits trägt die bewundernde Haltung auch Früchte. Denn Nigg war ein Grenzgänger und Überschreiter, in manchem progressiv der Zeit voraus, in manchem auch wieder mehr als traditionell, seit seiner tragischen Jugendzeit immer auf der Suche.

Der Vf. beginnt mit den letzten Monaten Niggs um erst dann mehr oder weniger chronologisch seinem Leben zu folgen. Leider bleiben Lücken. Gerade in der Zeit, als Nigg als junger Mann sein Auskommen in der Stadt Zürich suchte, hätte man sich mehr Informationen gewünscht. Offenbar sind die Quellen hierzu nicht eben ausführlich. Der Vf. zeichnet sodann eine eigentliche intellektuelle Biografie. Die schön präsentierten, frühen theologischen Prägungen Niggs durch Hermann Kutter, Karl Barth, Emil Brunner und Eduard Thurneysen sind die große Stärke des Bandes. Auch die baldige Abgrenzung Niggs von seinen Lehrern, in gewisser Weise auch dessen Scheitern, einen Platz in der evangelischen Theologie des 20. Jahrhunderts zu finden, werden klar.

Niggs Thema wurden die Heiligen der christlichen Geschichte. Ein nicht uninteressanter Weg führte ihn zum Versuch einer Synthese zwischen Religionsgeschichte in der Tradition Rudolf Ottos und einem ökumenischen Glauben. Zentrale Begriffe dabei sind die göttliche Liebe und das mystische Suchen nach Gott. Allerdings schwindet dabei schon bei Nigg die definitorische Klarheit. Man kann seinem Werk folgen und in die Lebensbeschreibungen eintauchen, analytisch nachvollziehbar ist manches dabei aber nicht mehr. Nigg bewundert explizit die Heiligenviten, er treibt keine Historie im engeren Sinn, schon gar keine Kritik. Die Heiligenviten stehen als große leuchtende Gegenfolie zur Katastrophe des 20. Jahrhunderts, sie sind das helle Heil im Dunkel der Gegenwart.

Tragischerweise kreist Niggs eigenes Leben um ähnliche Schatten. Der Verlust der Eltern, der Ehepartnerinnen, seine eigene konfessionelle Lebensgeschichte. Hier gelingt dem Vf. doch die Schilderung eines Lebens, das sich manchen Widerwärtigkeiten entgegen gestellt hat und nicht daran zerbrach. Es sind die stärksten Seiten des Buches.

Dann sind da aber auch die langen Abschnitte, die von Bewunderung geradezu triefen. Mystik, Herz und Liebe – es sind diese Worte, die abundant häufig gebraucht werden. In den Titeln, im Lesetext, in den Zitaten, überall. Zudem wähnt man sich zuweilen in einem mystischen Lesezirkel, wo alles und jedes mit allem in Beziehung steht, stehen kann, stehen muss, aber wenig je wirklich begründet wird. Vornamen, Geburtsorte, Daten. Alles verweist in der Lesart des Autors auf anderes, Tiefes, Geheimnisvolles. Das ist wie bei einem Panoptikum faszinierend, mit der Zeit aber einfach nur anstrengend. Der Vf. ist nicht Historiker, sondern eher selbst Hagiograph Niggs. Warum beispielsweise aus dem Geburtstag am Dreikönigstag ein lebenslanges Interesse für die Heiligen folgert, ist dem Rez. bis am Schluss schleierhaft geblieben. Gewisse Urteile des Autors wirken nach der Lektüre späterer Passagen irritierend: Warum schreibt der Vf. beispielsweise, Niggs erste Ehefrau Lily (die tragisch durch Suizid aus der jungen Familie wegstirbt) brauche eine Ehemann, der ihrem Leben eine Ausrichtung gab? Das ist unglücklich.

Im Mittelteil des Buches, wo aus der Fülle von Briefen zu Niggs theologischem und universitären Werdegang zitieren werden kann, schöpft der Autor hingegen aus dem Vollen. Insbesondere die Genese von Niggs Habilitation über Overbeck ist gelungen. Hier wird in Ansätzen wirklich Theologiegeschichte vermittelt, werden Positionen analysiert und der junge Walter Nigg auf seiner Suchbewegung eingeordnet. Leider wird auch da – trotz ganz offensichtlich guter Kenntnis der Schriften Niggs – inhaltlich nicht eben viel diskutiert oder verglichen. Nichtsdestotrotz landet der Vf. gute Treffer: Niggs Urteil beispielsweise, wohl von 1940, über Barths spezifische Form der Aneignung historischer Gestalten und Fakten im Dienst der dialektischen Theologie gehört dazu: »Man darf beinahe gewiss sein, dass wenn Barth eine historische Gestalt erklärt, er immer daneben greift, weil er nicht die Fähigkeit hat, sie in ihrem eigenen Licht zu sehen, sondern sie mit seinen Wünschen vermengt.« Allerdings bleibt der scharfzüngige Dozent dann etwas hinter seinem eigenen Anspruch zurück, wo die zentrale Aufgabe (theologischer) Geschichtswissenschaft gezeichnet werden müsste. Spannend sind auch die Zeilen über den Arzt Jakob Künzler, dem Nigg in seiner ersten Pfarrstelle in Stein (Appenzell Ausserrhoden) begegnet. Selbst Waisenkind wie Nigg, war Künzler nach 1895 freiwillig nach Armenien gereist, um den Verfolgten bis über den ersten Weltkrieg hinaus beizustehen. Auch die späte Begegnung mit dem Schriftsteller José Orabuena, der zeitweise bei Nigg wohnte, ist faszinierend.

Dann zentriert sich der Autor mit Nigg auf dessen zentrales Thema der Heiligen und damit auf eine eigene Form der religiös-mystischen Erwachsenenbildung. Tatsächlich verabschiedet sich Nigg im Prinzip vom akademischen Diskurs, ist eher intellektueller Kulturschaffender als Forscher. Seine publikumswirksamen Bücher wie seine Vorträge stehen in einer guten protestantischen Tradition, weisen ihn als Gelehrten aus, der auch widersprüchliche Traditionen und Kulturen zu verbinden mag. Das kommt im Werk Wolffs klar zum Ausdruck. Gewiss leidet darunter die Schärfe, wird Mystik zum kleinsten gemeinsamen Nenner, wird schon fast inflationär Gottes Liebe in den Lebensentwürfen gesucht. Das ist ambitioniert, zuweilen aber auch vorhersehbar. Klar werden die Grenzen, wo etwa Hans Urs von Balthasar Gotteserfahrungen auch in der Gegenwart erkennen kann, Nigg sich davon aber distanziert. Hier konnte und wollte Nigg nicht mitziehen, seine Mystik erscheint trotz aller Betonung des Hagiographischen seltsam sublimiert und historisiert zu sein. Ja der Begriff Hagiograph selbst, der undiskutiert auf Nigg angewendet wird, wird im ganzen Buch nie deutlich definiert. Was meint damit der Vf., was meinte damit Nigg selbst?

Störend wirken die Autoreninterpretamente und nicht kenntlich gemachte Exzerpte von Niggs Berichten, etwa beim Besuch der Kartause La Valsainte (S. 373 f.): »Verglichen mit ihrer Askese [der Mönche von La Valsainte, Rez.] war jedes Weltkind ein armer Sünder.« Es sind diese Sätze, die einen am Buch aber auch an den theologischen Positionen Niggs stören; weil man weiß, was er meinte und suchte, gleichzeitig aber auch konstatieren muss, dass man es so nicht formulieren kann. Demgegenüber stehen witzige Passagen wie Niggs Zitat: »Mit einem Pfarrer allein konnte ich immer gut reden, aber in einer Pfarrversammlung musste ich stets an Theresia von Avilas humoristisches Wort denken: Hundert Nonnen, das ist die Hölle.«

Anderes ist für moderne Leser anstrengend. Wenn der Vf. den »hohen Ton« Niggs positiv vermerkt, würde es der Rez. eher bourgeois-bigotte Plauderei nennen. Angesichts der schwierigen Momente, etwa während des deutschen Terrors in den späten 1970er Jahren, lässt sich Nigg in der Korrespondenz mit Axel Springer über den Unglauben der Jugend aus. Da spricht dann ein alter Mann, dessen Zeit vorbei war und welcher vielleicht angesichts voller Vortragssäle seine geistige Bedeutung nicht recht einzuschätzen verstand. Ob nicht sein akademisches Scheitern Nigg doch schwerer belastete, als er zeitlebens zugeben wollte?

Fazit: Ein wichtiges Buch über einen wichtigen und nicht unumstrittenen Schweizer Theologen; ein ambitionierter Autor, dessen Begeisterung und Detailkenntnisse überraschen aber auch ermüden; ein kritischeres Lektorat hätte dem Buch gewiss gut getan.

Michel Baumann, Wiesendangen

ISSN 0254-4407 – Zwingliana 40 (2013), 249–251

116. Jahresbericht des Zwinglivereins über das Jahr 2012

Mitgliederversammlung

Die ordentliche Mitgliederversammlung fand unter der Leitung von Vizepräsident Michel Müller am Montag, dem 14. Mai 2012, im Saal der Reformierten Kirche des Kantons Zürich, Hirschengraben 50, Zürich statt.

Der Jahresbericht wurde, ohne Wortmeldung aus dem Plenum, einstimmig angenommen; ebenso die durch Frau Barbara Kobel erläuterte Jahresrechnung 2011 und das Budget 2013.

Der Antrag des Vorstandes, die Höhe der Mitgliederbeiträge beizubehalten (Einzelmitglieder SFr. 60.–, Studierende SFr. 20.– und Kollektivmitglieder SFr. 100.– pro Jahr), fand die einhellige Zustimmung der Versammlung.

Großmünsterpfarrer Pfr. Martin Rüsch wird als neues Vorstandsmitglied vorgeschlagen und diskussionslos und einstimmig gewählt. Die Interimssituation mit Peter Opitz als Geschäftsführer und Michel Müller als Vizepräsident bleibt bestehen.

Im Anschluss an die Versammlung sprach Pfarrer Dr. Frank Jehle zum Thema »Der Kirchenhistoriker Fritz Blanke als Lehrer und Forscher« und daran anschließend wurde das Buch »Fritz Blanke – Querdenker mit Herz« durch den Autor Pfarrer Christoph Möhl präsentiert.

Zwingliana

Der Band des Jahres 2012 konnte wie geplant ausgeliefert werden. Wiederum hat die Schweizerische Akademie der Geistes- und Sozialwissenschaften, vermittelt durch die Schweizerische Theologische Gesellschaft, der Zwingliana einen Druckkostenbeitrag zugesprochen, wofür auch an dieser Stelle herzlich gedankt sei.

Exegetische Schriften Huldrych Zwinglis (Z)

Die Arbeiten konnten im Verlauf der letzten Periode abgeschlossen werden. Die Bände werden im Sommer 2013 dem Druck übergeben werden können.

Heinrich Bullinger, »Tigurinerchronik«

Die Revision des umfangreichen Textes nimmt mehr Zeit in Anspruch als ursprünglich geplant. Sie wird sich ins neue Jahr hineinziehen, so dass erst im Verlaufe des Jahres 2013 mit dem Abschluss gerechnet werden kann.

Dr. h.c. Ruedi Reich

Am 12. August 2012 verstarb Dr. h.c. Ruedi Reich in seinem 67. Lebensjahr. Ruedi Reich war zunächst Gemeindepfarrer, wurde 1973 in die Synode der Zürcher Landeskirche gewählt und war seit 1983 Mitglied des Kirchenrates. Von 1993 bis 2010 amtete er als Zürcher Kirchenratspräsident und war zugleich Vizepräsident des Zwinglivereins. Die Förderung der Edition von Texten der Zürcher Reformation und von deren Erforschung war Ruedi Reich ein großes Anliegen. Lange Jahre setzte er sich mit Erfolg insbesondere für die finanzielle Unterstützung der Bullinger-Briefwechseledition durch die Zürcher Landeskirche ein und nahm selber mit großem Interesse an der wissenschaftlichen Erforschung der Zürcher Reformation Anteil. Die Theologische Fakultät der Universität Zürich verlieh ihm 2005 die Ehrendoktorwürde.

Prof. Dr. Fritz Büsser

Am 7. September 2012 verstarb Prof. Dr. Fritz Büsser in seinem 90. Lebensjahr. Als Ordinarius für Kirchen- und Dogmengeschichte an der Universität Zürich leitete er das Institut für Schweizerische Reformationsgeschichte von 1967 bis zu seiner Emeritierung 1989. In dieser Zeit machte er sich besonders verdient um die Edition der Werke Huldrych Zwinglis und Heinrich Bullingers. In seine Zeit fielen die Großveranstaltungen zum 400. Todesjahr Heinrich Bullingers. Von 1970 bis 1977 war er Präsident des Zwinglivereins.

Prof. Dr. Alfred Schindler

Am 19. November 2012 verstarb Prof. Dr. Alfred Schindler in seinem 78. Lebensjahr. Alfred Schindler war als Ordinarius für Kirchen- und Dogmengeschichte an der Universität Zürich (1990–1998) zugleich Leiter des Instituts für Schweizerische Reformationsgeschichte. Er war ein wichtiger Förderer der Forschung über Zwingli und Bullinger, aber auch der Erforschung des katholischen Widerstands in der Reformation (so etwa initiierte er das Editionsprojekt um die Badener Disputation). Lange Jahre war er Vorstandsmitglied des Zwinglivereins und gestaltete 1997 dessen 100-Jahr-Jubiläum maßgeblich mit. Die Zwingliana, die er in seiner Zeit redaktionell verantwortete, begleitete er noch über seine Amtszeit hinaus als Mitglied der Redaktionskommission.

Mitgliederbestand

Am 31. Dezember 2012 zählte der Verein 245 Einzelmitglieder (2011: 245) und 40 Kollektivmitglieder (2011: 40).

Zürich, im April 2013

Der Geschäftsführer	Der Aktuar
Prof. Dr. Peter Opitz	Dr. Hans Ulrich Bächtold

ISSN 0254-4407 – Zwingliana 40 (2013), 253–256

Personenregister

Das Register erschließt die in den Hauptartikeln genannten Personen.